"Amazingly easy to use. Very portable, very complete."

—*Booklist*

♦

"Complete, concise, and filled with useful information."

—*New York Daily News*

♦

"Hotel information is close to encyclopedic."

—*Des Moines Sunday Register*

♦

"The only mainstream guide to list specific prices. The Walter Cronkite of guidebooks—with all that implies."

—*Travel & Leisure*

Frommer's®

1st Edition

Singapore & Malaysia

by Jennifer Eveland

Macmillan • USA

ABOUT THE AUTHOR

Jennifer Eveland lived in Singapore as a child and has made regular trips back since then. Now a resident of New York City, she works for a nonprofit organization doing international development work in sub-Saharan Africa. Of all the places she's traveled, Singapore is her favorite.

MACMILLAN TRAVEL

A Simon & Schuster Macmillan Company
1633 Broadway
New York, NY 10019

Find us online at **www.frommers.com**

ISBN 0-02-862099-2
ISSN 1093-6971

Editor: Matt Hannafin
Production Editor: Stephanie Mohler
Photo Editor: Richard Fox
Design by Michele Laseau
Digital Cartography by Raffaele DeGennaro

SPECIAL SALES

Bulk purchases (10+ copies) of Frommer's and selected Macmillan travel guides are available to corporations, organizations, mail-order catalogs, institutions, and charities at special discounts, and can be customized to suit individual needs. For more information write to Special Sales, Macmillan General Reference, 1633 Broadway, New York, NY 10019.

Manufactured in the United States of America

Contents

List of Maps

I owe it all to Mom and Dad. Richard Eveland (Dad) brought me to live in Singapore when I was a child and held my little hand on the plane. The following years I spent in Singapore instilled in me a deep appreciation for the people and culture there. Linda Eveland (Mom), was there for me as I wrote this book, holding my big hand through every challenge I encountered. She kept my sense of humor alive and my sanity intact. For her help I am forever indebted.

ACKNOWLEDGMENTS

I wish to thank Pauline Tan, who provided most of the research and wonderful insights for the Malaysia portion of this book.

For cheering me on, I would like to thank Jackie Allen, Joy Cantarella, Regina Caslin, Michelle Cavallaro, David Fix, Michele Hudak, Balkiss and Suliman Hamid, Niamani Mutima, Molly and Tay Chee Beng, and Terence Tay.

For their support, I'd like to thank the good people at the Chinatown Hotel, Tania Goh at the Singapore Tourism Board, Dan Marino at Singapore Airlines, Shu-Hana Shuib at the Malaysia Tourism Board, Bhajan Singh at the Registered Tourist Guides Association of Singapore, and Karen Wos at Spring O'Brien.

Finally, a million thanks to Matt Hannafin for giving me this opportunity.

—Jennifer Eveland

AN INVITATION TO THE READER

In researching this book, we discovered many wonderful places—hotels, restaurants, shops, and more. We're sure you'll find others. Please tell us about them, so we can share the information with your fellow travelers in upcoming editions. If you were disappointed with a recommendation, we'd love to know that, too. Please write to:

Frommer's Singapore & Malaysia, 1st Edition
Macmillan Travel
1633 Broadway
New York, NY 10019

AN ADDITIONAL NOTE

Please be advised that travel information is subject to change at any time—and this is especially true of prices. We therefore suggest that you write or call ahead for confirmation when making your travel plans. The authors, editors, and publisher cannot be held responsible for the experiences of readers while traveling. Your safety is important to us, however, so we encourage you to stay alert and be aware of your surroundings. Keep a close eye on cameras, purses, and wallets, all favorite targets of thieves and pickpockets.

WHAT THE SYMBOLS MEAN

✪ Frommer's Favorites

Our favorite places and experiences—outstanding for quality, value, or both.

The following abbreviations are used for credit cards:

AE	American Express	EURO	Eurocard
CB	Carte Blanche	JCB	Japan Credit Bank
DC	Diners Club	MC	MasterCard
DISC	Discover	V	Visa
ER	enRoute		

Arthur Frommer's Outspoken Encyclopedia of Travel (www.frommers.com) offers more than 6,000 pages of up-to-the-minute travel information—including the latest bargains and candid, personal articles updated daily by Arthur Frommer himself. No other Web site offers such comprehensive and timely coverage of the world of travel.

Report on the Southeast Asian Financial Crisis

In late 1997, the world watched as the much-vaunted East Asian tigers fell into tough financial times. The governments of Thailand, South Korea, Malaysia, Indonesia, the Philippines, and—to a limited extent—Singapore and Hong Kong, saw their currencies drop, banks and businesses flounder, and stock market values plummet. While the world asks, "How could this happen?" you're probably asking, "How will this affect my trip?"

As Southeast Asian governments scramble for answers on how to heal their suffering economies, you can enjoy favorable **exchange rates** for your foreign cash. (Rates given in this book are based on average, pre-crisis values.) Although Singapore is less effected by currency devaluation, reports at this writing say the value is 15% below what it was prior to the crisis. Malaysia, however, has been hit much harder, as the ringgit fell to as low as 40% of it's pre-crisis value. Barring any economic quick-fixes, now might be the time to take advantage of the good rates and do a little extra shopping. If you're really stretching your dollars, you might be able to spend an extra day on holiday for the same money.

Also effected are your costs for **international travel** and **hotel stays.** At press time, airlines were offering discounts of as much as 50% on round-trip airfare to destinations in Southeast Asia. As for hotels, the rates quoted in this book are the standard rack rates for each hotel. With the economic crisis, many Singapore hotels have discounted rooms up to S$50 to S$100 per night. Also common are "throw-ins," as hotels are more likely to give you breakfasts, massage, laundry, or other services free of charge to attract your business. If you take the time to shop around and bargain, you're sure to get incredible deals.

If you're wondering about your **safety,** be comforted. At press time, Singapore and Malaysia had not seen any indications of civil unrest, and Singapore in particular will probably weather the storm quite nicely. However, if you plan a stopover in Indonesia, you may wish to consult your government for travel advisories. Described by *The Economist* as "Asia's economic basket-case," Indonesia has reported shortages of goods and incidents of civil unrest.

Southeast Asia

Getting to Know Singapore

1

Imagine walking down a narrow winding street, warm and steamy from the tropical sun. On either side are tidy rows of houses in vivid blues, greens, pinks—all the colors you can imagine. The houses are connected by shady covered sidewalks tiled in geometric patterns. Wide columns painted with red Chinese characters rise from the sidewalk. Inside dark doorways are medicine halls, tea shops, and tailors. Down a back alley, clothes hang to dry from bamboo poles out a second-story window.

Ahead you see the corner of a temple, its roof a tumble of Hindu gods painted every color of the rainbow. As your eyes follow the tiers of figurines up to the sky, the roof line gives way to a towering skyline of steel and glass skyscrapers beyond. From behind you can hear the Muslim call to evening prayers.

This is the magic of Singapore, where the melding of distinct cultures from China, India, Southeast Asia, and Europe has created a nation that, despite its small size, is richly and startlingly diverse. You'll see these cultural influences on every city block, hear them in every historical account, and taste them in every dish you are served. Each culture in itself is fascinating, but combined they are magical.

For the traveler, this cultural salad provides a distinct advantage: You get Asian and Southeast Asian culture rolled into one small space, and you don't have to go far for cultural changes of scenery, or travel to many different countries to see different sights. Instead, a walk from one ethnic neighborhood to another will bring you a whole new experience.

The diversity of culture also means travelers are rarely "foreigners" here. Singaporeans come in all races and religions and have an extremely cosmopolitan sense of the world. Most everyone speaks English, so exotic cultures become accessible, unfolding through simple inquiries to friendly locals.

In addition, while all of the cultural traditions are preserved, modern Singapore presents travelers with all of the comforts of home. Luxury hotels, an abundance of restaurants serving all manner of international cuisine, and state-of-the-art transportation and telecommunications systems mean you'll never have to rough the wilds—unless you choose to, of course.

However metropolitan downtown Singapore can be, you're always close to nature. Singapore is truly a Garden City. For every skyscraper there's a park; for every highway there's a garden. Not only

Singapore

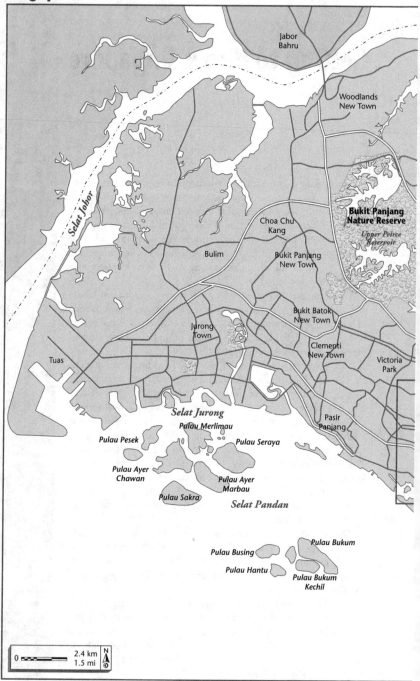

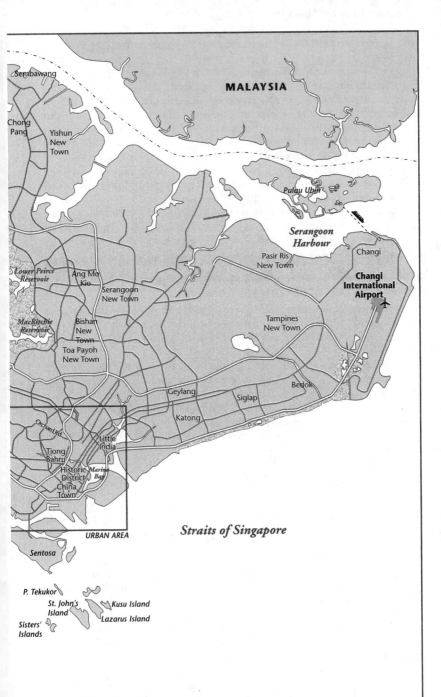

MALAYSIA

Sembawang

Chong
Pang

Yishun
New
Town

Pulau Ubin

Serangoon
Harbour

Lower Peirce
Reservoir

Ang Mo
Kio

Serangoon
New Town

Pasir Ris
New Town

Changi

**Changi
International
Airport**

MacRitchie
Reservoir

Bishan
New
Town

Tampines
New Town

Toa Payoh
New Town

Geylang

Siglap

Bedok

Katong

Orchard Rd

Little
India

Tiong
Bahru

Historic
District

Marina
Bay

China
Town

URBAN AREA

Straits of Singapore

Sentosa

P. Tekukor

St. John's
Island

Kusu Island

Lazarus Island

Sisters'
Islands

are the urban areas green with lush landscaping, but nature reserves located both in and around the city mean you can spend a peaceful vacation enjoying the beauty of the tropical outdoors. Of all the cities in the world, only Singapore and Rio de Janeiro can boast primary tropical rain forest within their limits.

In the last decades, Singapore has positioned itself as the gateway to Southeast Asia; the hub of commerce and trade, politics, the arts, and especially tourism. For that reason, the average visitor stays in Singapore for only 3$^1/_2$ days, either on their way to another destination or on their way home. If you're one of those, you'll want to take in as much of the region's riches as you can before heading to your next destination. I've kept your needs in mind while preparing this guide, and will tip you off to all the best sights and attractions—both the biggies and the lesser-known treasures—and, in chapters 11 through 16, give you suggestions on visiting Malaysia, which is just a day trip away. If you find yourself here for more than 3$^1/_2$ days, though, you'll have no trouble keeping busy, and in fact, you might find yourself falling under the spell of the place and returning again and again—as I have.

1 Frommer's Favorite Singapore Experiences

HAVING CONVERSATIONS WITH THE CABBIES

It's amazing the conversations you have with cabbies in Singapore. I've had Mandarin lessons, heard tales of Chinese superstitions, learned about Malay pop music, and heard the latest political gossip. But best of all was the one about Kuan Yin, the Goddess of Mercy.

At 5:45 in the evening I was lucky to get a cab at all, but I knew I'd really stumbled onto something when I saw the shrine built into the dashboard. Sure, all the cabs have some assortment of lucky tokens dangling from every knob, but this was special. Half the console had been pulled out to make room for a three-dimensional diorama encased in Plexiglas, with a small purple light-up statue, crystal teardrops and faceted balls, plastic lotus flowers, and golden coins in a box lined in yellow and lit with tiny bulbs. It was *amazing*.

The driver was a young guy who spoke English, and after noticing my mesmerized stare he launched into a monologue about Kuan Yin, the Goddess of Mercy, explaining the history behind her dashboard shrine, answering all my questions, and adding all the stories he could pack into the 15-minute cab ride.

These little moments make for some of the best travel memories, and are only a cab fare away—no extra charge for the entertainment.

EATING AT A HAWKER CENTER

Despite all the modernization in Singapore, the hawker centers—jumbles of tiny stalls peddling cheap and fast Chinese, Indian, and local food—are a local tradition that will never die. Singaporeans from all walks of life depend on these places for fast food, and a lot of moms and pops depend on their stalls to support families. As for travelers, it's the best way to experience life as a local and rub elbows with the natives.

Many of these centers are wedged in between city buildings, the small silver food stalls packed tightly together in rows, tables and stools thrown around in the aisles, bright white floodlights glaring from above. The steam and smells wafting throughout will lead you to the perfect meal before the menu boards can give you a clue as to what's cooking. Al fresco is an overstatement in these places, where all you may have to protect you from the elements are some thin pieces of corrugated metal. All in all, it's an adventure that will bring you close to the heart of this place. (See chapter 5 for more info, including a complete rundown on hawker center etiquette.)

WITNESSING BLOODY TRADITIONS

Every so often, a magical Saturday night comes around when you can witness the **Kuda Kepang,** which is not your average traditional dance. It features young men on wooden horses who move like warriors, whirling and spinning and slapping the horses to shake intimidating sounds out of them. Accompanied by rhythmic and repetitive traditional Malay music, the warriors dance in unison, staging battles with each other until, by the end of a long series of dances, the horsemen are in a trance. A pot of burning frankincense is produced, from which they all inhale. After that, all hell breaks loose. The dancers are whipped, fed glass—which they chew and swallow hungrily—walk on glass shards, and shred entire coconuts with their teeth.

While the whipping appears somewhat staged, I assure you the rest is real. It's a traditional dance that's taken very seriously both by the dancers and by the huge and mostly Malay crowds that gather for it. What's more, the next day the dancers don't recall what they did—and they're never injured.

Unfortunately, the dance is not performed on a regular basis. The group works mostly for private ceremonies and gatherings, and appears at **Malay Village** (☎ **65/ 748-4700**) on the off Saturday night when they don't have a gig. Call ahead to find out if they'll be performing. (See chapter 6 for Malay Village write-up.)

If you're not able to catch a performance, but still want a little ceremonial gore, check out the "Calendar of Events" in chapter 2. During the **Thaipusam Festival,** men pierce their bodies with skewers, and during the **Thimithi Festival** they walk on burning coals. To celebrate the **Birthday of the Monkey God,** Chinese priests will slice themselves with sharp implements and write chants and prayers with their own blood. (See chapter 2.)

SIPPING A SINGAPORE SLING AT THE LONG BAR

Ahhhh, the Long Bar. Home of the Singapore Sling. I like to come in the afternoons, before the tourist rush. Sheltered by long timber shutters that close out the tropical sun, the air cooled by lazy *punkahs* (small fans that wave gently back and forth above), you can sit back in old rattan chairs and have your saronged waitress serve you sticky alcoholic creations while you toss back a few dainty crab cakes. Life can be so decadent. OK, so the punkahs are electric, and, come to think of it, the place is air-conditioned (not to mention that it costs a small fortune), but it's fun to imagine the days when Somerset Maugham, Rudyard Kipling, or Charlie Chaplin would be sitting at the bar sipping Slings and spinning exotic tales of their world travels. Drink up, my friend; it's a lovely high. (See chapter 9.)

CHECKING OUT THE ORCHARD ROAD SCENE

You can't find better people-watching than on Orchard Road every Saturday afternoon, when it seems like every Singaporean crawls out of the woodwork to join the parade of shoppers, strollers, hipsters, posers, lovers, geeks, and gabbers. Everybody is here, milling around every mall, clustered around every sidewalk bench, checking everybody out.

At the corner of Scotts Road and Orchard, just under the Marriott, there's an al fresco cafe where you'll find local celebrities hanging out to see and be seen. International celebrities and models have been spotted here on occasion, too. In the mix, you're bound to see most every tourist on the island, coming around to see what all the excitement is about.

On Saturdays, school lets out early, so the malls are filled with mobs of bored teenagers, kicking around, trying to look cool, and watching the music videos in the front window of the new HMV music store in the Heeren. Moms and dads also have half-days at the office, so the strip takes on the feel of an obstacle course, as all the parents race around wielding strollers, trying to run errands while they have the chance. Meanwhile, outside in the shady areas, you can see crowds of *amahs* (housekeepers) and workers relaxing and catching up on the latest news on their free afternoon.

For some, the scene is a madhouse to be avoided; for others, it's a chance to watch life on a typical Saturday afternoon in downtown Singapore. And it is typical, 'cause however huge and delightful the scene is for tourists, it's just part of everyday reality for residents of the Garden City. (See chapter 8 for more info.)

2 The Lay of the Land

On a world map, Singapore is nothing more than a speck nestled in the heart of Southeast Asia, at the tip of the Malaysian Peninsula. In the north, it's linked to Malaysia by a causeway over the Strait of Johor, which is its only physical connection to any other body of land. To the south, the Strait of Singapore separates the island from Indonesia, which you can sometimes see from the tops of high buildings and even from some beaches. Farther north, above Malaysia, are Thailand, Burma, Cambodia, and Vietnam; to the east, East Malaysia, Borneo, and Brunei; to the northeast, the Philippine Islands; and stretching from west to south are the islands of Indonesia.

The country is made up of one main island, Singapore, and around 60 smaller ones, some of which—like Sentosa, Pulau Ubin, Kusu, and St. John's Island—are popular retreats. The main island is shaped like a flat, horizontal diamond, measuring in at just over 42 kilometers (25 miles) from east to west and almost 23 kilometers (14 miles) north to south. With a total land area of only 584.8 square kilometers (351 sq. miles), Singapore is almost shockingly tiny.

Singapore's geographical position, sitting approximately 137 kilometers (82 miles) north of the equator, means that its climate offers uniform temperatures, plentiful rainfall, and high, high humidity.

Don't come expecting a dramatic landscape. Mostly, the profile Singapore presents to the world is undramatic. Small, rolling hills are about the norm, and much of the island is little more than 15 meters (50 ft.) above sea level, with its highest peak, Bukit Timah, rising only 163 meters above sea level. There are a few ridges to the west and southwest. Mount Faber, rising behind the World Trade Centre, is actually a ridge. The coast is almost entirely flat, with maybe a couple of sea cliffs here or there. Actually, the shoreline has changed considerably since the early years of settlement due to major land reclamation projects and swamp drainage. Much of this work was done in colonial times, but here's a figure to play with: From 1964 to 1997, Singapore's Housing Development Board reclaimed over 2,680 hectares (or 6,620 sq. acres) of land. If you play with the numbers (2,680÷33 years) you get about 81 hectares per year. That's a lot of land. Think about it this way: Even if you leave Singapore thinking you've seen it all, there will always be something new to see when you come back.

FLORA & FAUNA

Way back when, before colonialism, dense tropical rain forest stretched from coast to coast across the island of Singapore. Then the British East India Company came to town (more on that in the history section below), and proceeded to clear away the forests for settlement, fell the tropical hardwoods for timber, and carve out plantation areas to grow nutmeg, gambier, clove, pepper, cocoa, and later rubber. Today, primary rain forest covers a minute area of Singapore, mostly a small patch in the **Bukit Timah Nature Reserve.** This forest is characterized by a tier (canopy) of tropical hardwoods that tower up to 40 meters (132 ft.); a lower canopy of lush vegetation that includes ferns, creepers, and flowering plants; and a bed thick with rich, moist peat soil.

Sadly, when the forests were destroyed they took a huge number of local species with them, including some 50 types of orchids that were native to the island and are now gone forever. What rain forest there is now is secondary growth, having sprouted anew and taken back land once cleared and later abandoned. On a curious note, of the plant species used today for landscaping Singapore's parks and gardens, 80% have been imported from as far away as Mexico, South America, and the West Indies. The frangipani? Imported. The bougainvillea? Imported. It always catches me by surprise when I spot popular Western houseplants growing outdoors in gardens here. My houseplants, despite my loving care, look like clumps of crab grass in comparison.

With the clearing of the land and man's expansion into the countryside, plants weren't the only local species to disappear. **Tigers, leopards, and wild boar** were once common on Singapore and the surrounding islands, but while wild boar still live on Pulau Ubin and Pulau Tekong, the country's last tiger was shot in 1932. Of the wildlife that remains, flying lemurs, a couple of squirrel species, the long-tailed macaque, and flying lizards dominate the tree tops. Lower canopy forest life includes shrews, rats, snakes, and tree frogs, and on the ground are more snakes, lizards, frogs, and tortoises. Little mousedeer and anteaters are still around, but you'll be lucky to see any. There are also many varieties of bats, which can still be found in urbanized areas, fluttering in parks and wooded gardens.

Often, the wildlife ventures into the city. Small lizards, called *chichaks,* are a common sight in houses and in parks, and are impossible to catch (I've tried), and I once saw a very panicked iguana at a cafe at the corner of Scotts and Orchard roads. Domestic cats once made up a huge stray population, which the government has done a good job to control.

Bird life is rich on the island, with some 326 species, 215 of which are resident and 52 of which are endangered. With urbanization, common species became more abundant than woodland species. Migrant birds arrive here from as far north as Siberia, and during the winter months (from October to March), bird sanctuaries like Sungei Buloh Nature Park are teeming with life.

Speaking of birds, you'll probably notice that domestic songbirds are a traditional pet in the Chinese community, especially among the elderly, who buy them elaborate cages, take them for walks (swinging the cages and forcing the birds to flutter on their perches, exercising their wings), and enter them in singing competitions. Good places to hear these birds are at Jurong BirdPark's Songbird Terrace, where they have a daily breakfast (see the Jurong BirdPark listing in chapter 7 for more information). More traditional are the early Sunday morning meetings on the corner of Tiong Bahru and Seng Poh roads, where the local old folks (many of whom live in Tiong Bahru) meet by the coffee shop to compare the songs of their beloved pets. These informal songbird competitions are an old Chinese tradition that you'll find all over the mainland.

Factoid

Chinese superstition has it that cats are more perfect creatures than humans. To make them less perfect—and thus to make us look better by comparison—it's common practice to either break their tails to bend them or to remove them completely. So, if you meet any wacky looking cats, don't think you've discovered a new species—just an old superstition.

MARINE LIFE

In the waters offshore, despite heavy shipping traffic, there are living coral reefs with anemones, clownfish, living seashells, sea urchins, and poisonous creatures like scorpion fish and stonefish. Scuba diving will reveal the underwater world somewhat, but most Singaporean divers complain about murky and turbulent waters from traffic and land reclamation. Most divers head for Malaysia or other Southeast Asian destinations for serious underwater adventures. Tioman Island (see chapter 14)—the place where they filmed South Pacific in the fifties—is everything you imagine a South Pacific paradise to be, and the resorts near Kuantan and Cherating (see chapter 14) are also very, very lovely.

Beaches in Singapore are not a main attraction for tourists. Generally, you won't find picturesque blue water with waves tumbling on fine white sand, but rather a yellowish-green translucent sea with little waves. Beach sand is coarse and sometimes streaked with seaweed. The exception is **Sentosa Island,** where the beaches are more picturesque, with lovely palm tree landscaping and wider beaches. The nicest beach by far is at the Shangri-La's Rasa Sentosa Resort (see chapter 5). The shoreline hooks around to create a lagoon, the sand is pretty, and the tropical resort–style landscaping is close to idyllic.

3 Singapore Today

Who would have believed that Singapore would rise to such international fame and become the vaunted "Asian Tiger" it has in recent decades? This small country's political stability and effective government have inspired many other nations to study its methods, and former prime minister **Lee Kuan Yew** is counted among the most renowned political figures in the world. When asked to explain how Singapore's astounding economic, political, and social success was made possible, Lee Kuan Yew always takes the credit—and deservedly so—but in the face of international criticism for dictatorial policies, absolutist law enforcement, and human rights violations, he also stands first in line to receive the blame.

THE GOVERNMENT

In 1954, the pro-Communist People's Action Party (PAP) was formed during a time when the British colonial government was encouraging local political participation. A year later, the young Peranakan-born and Oxford-educated lawyer Lee Kuan Yew was elected as the party's secretary-general. In 1955, Mr. Lee was quoted as saying, "Any man in Singapore who wants to carry the Chinese-speaking people with him cannot afford to be anti-Communist." Master political strategist that he was (and is), Lee used Communism to rally the support of the Chinese population, the largest body of voters in Singapore, though in fact the PAP leaders were moderates. In the election zeal, nobody really noticed. In 1959, the PAP took 43 of the 51 seats in the Legislative Assembly, and Mr. Lee was elected Singapore's first prime minister. Since then, and without debate, it has been his unfailing vision of a First World Singapore that's inspired the policies and plans that created the political and economic miracle we see today. During his tenure he mobilized government, industry, and citizens toward fulfilling his vision, establishing a government almost devoid of corruption, a strong economy built from practically no resources save labor, and a nation of racial and religious harmony from a multi-ethnic melting pot.

Both critics and admirers refer to Lee Kuan Yew as a strict yet generous "father" to the "children" of Singapore, raising them to a high position on the world stage yet dictating policies that have cost citizens many of their personal freedoms. You'll find

The Flor Contemplacion Scandal

On March 17, 1995, Flor Contemplacion, a Filipino maid working in Singapore, was hanged for the double murder of another Filipino maid and the young Chinese boy who was in her care. Ms. Contemplacion had confessed to both crimes during a police interrogation, and was later convicted based upon the evidence presented, but controversy arose after the verdicts as to whether she had been framed. Despite pleas for a stay of execution from the president of the Philippines, Singapore carried out the punishment in a timely fashion according to their laws, refusing to reopen the case.

During the trial, riots had erupted in the Philippines and resident Singaporeans were threatened as Filipinos accused their government of being powerless to help a fellow citizen. The result was a very tense relationship between the two governments as diplomacy and trade came to a bitter standstill. After the execution, Ms. Contemplacion's casket was returned to the Philippines, where she received a martyr's burial.

Eventually, relations were normalized due to political and economic necessity; however, the case brought the Singaporean justice system under the scrutiny of international human rights organizations. Accusations that Ms. Contemplacion only confessed after being subjected to harsh interrogation were not denied by Singaporean authorities, who claimed their methods were quite common for obtaining evidence. Although overwhelming evidence did point to her guilt, the international community had to wonder why Singapore had not tried a little harder to deal sympathetically with the emotions raised by the incident.

---

that the average Singaporean expresses some duality about this: He or she will be outwardly critical of the government's invasion of privacy and disregard for personal freedoms, and of policies that have driven up the cost of housing and health care, but will also recognize all that Lee has done to raise Singaporeans' standard of living, expand their opportunities for the future, and ensure tranquillity at home—achievements that many are willing to sacrifice a certain amount of freedom to enjoy. By and large, they wish to see the current government continue its work.

Lee stepped down from the prime minister's chair in 1990, assuming the position of senior minister. Although the new prime minister, Mr. Goh Chok Tong, has created some policies of his own to promote more openness in the political system, it is understood that Lee still drives the car. To his credit, Goh has been a popular leader. In addition to initiating more citizen participation in the politics of the country, he is supporting local visual and performing arts and encouraging an effort to draw internationally acclaimed theater companies to Singapore, all in an attempt to solve Singapore's current brain drain by encouraging more creative and educated Singaporeans to stay in-country rather than emigrate. Unfortunately, he also has to face suspicion that he's nothing more than a seat-warmer for Lee's son, Lee Hsien Loong, who is currently deputy prime minister.

Whoever the individual officeholders, one constant of Singaporean politics is that the key players are almost exclusively PAP members. Opposition parties have little chance to grab the prize, as the PAP holds all the cards. Elections are said to be influenced by economic threats and repressive laws. In recent years, the PAP has not been winning the overwhelming majority of government seats as it has in the past, but still has enough power to keep its hold.

THE CENSORSHIP QUESTION

One infamous feature of Singapore's government is its control over media, both domestic and international. All national news publications have ties to the government, whose philosophy holds that the role of the media is to promote the government's goals. Articles are censored for any content that might threaten national security, incite riot, or promote disobedience or racism. Offenders face stiff fines. A few days of the *Straits Times* and you'll be sick of cheery reporting that skirts around issues and articles that are grossly transparent in their opinions. The censorship doesn't stop at that old "national security" excuse, either. International publications such as *Time, The Asian Wall Street Journal, Asiaweek,* and *The Economist* have all suffered drastically reduced circulation in Singapore after they published articles the government found insulting. Magazines that are banned completely include *Playboy* and *Cosmopolitan,* for their pornographic content and promotion of harmful Western values.

It doesn't stop at the print media, either. Television is also censored, satellite dishes are banned, and there's only one cable provider, which the government keeps a close eye on for anything resembling pornography.

The Internet provided Singapore with a tough dilemma. By design, the Net promotes freedom of communication, which is taken advantage of by, among others, every political dissident and pornographer who can get his little hands on a 386. This thought so terrified the Singapore government that it debated long and hard about allowing access to its citizens. However, the possibilities for communications and commerce and their implications for the future of Singapore's economy won, and the government paved the way for all Singaporeans to have access by the year 2000— though of course, it goes without saying, that access will be heavily censored. Private and public sector organizations must register with the government, which clears all content, and Internet providers must block questionable sites and monitor hits to Web sites, reporting to the government who's accessing what.

THE ECONOMY

Singapore's economy is a bizarre marriage between free trade and government control. Lee Kuan Yew's vision and resulting policies have created annual national growth rates of 8.9% going on 3 decades now. The biggest money makers are the electronics industry, financial and business services, transportation and communications, petroleum refining and shipping, construction, and tourism. Seventy-six percent of Singapore's exports, exclusive of oil exports, go to the United States, Malaysia, the European Union, Hong Kong, and Japan.

Singaporeans enjoy a high standard of living, with average annual incomes reaching US$23,000. The most commonly heard complaint? The rising cost of real estate.

TOURISM

The Singapore Tourism Board has far-reaching influence that has helped to turn Singapore into a foreign cash–raising machine. Over seven million tourists visit Singapore annually, spending a total of S$11.6 billion during their stays.

Not one to rest on its laurels, Singapore has big plans to dramatically increase these numbers by the year 2000 through implementation of its new Tourism 21 Plan, which will restore landmarks and create Thematic Zones. These are areas within the ethnic neighborhoods where the URA (Urban Redevelopment Authority) plans to restore old buildings and block off vehicular traffic to create pedestrian avenues. If their plans succeed, neighborhoods like Chinatown may become ChinaWorld, as local shops and colorful street life are replaced by tidy restored buildings, glitzy souvenir shops, and ironic little exhibits describing the vibrant community that once thrived in the neighborhood and was run out by high rents.

The first Thematic Zone is currently being constructed in the streets of Chinatown. Additional Tourism 21 actions will include the construction of a new exhibition center at the World Trade Centre, which will begin in mid-1998, and The Esplanade–Theatres on the Bay, a giant concert hall poised at the edge of the marina and modeled after the Sydney Opera House—a project to which very few Singaporeans feel any personal connection.

4 A Look at the Past

Picture a tiny backwater: an overgrown, swampy island approximately 22.4 kilometers (14 miles) wide and 40 kilometers (25 miles) long, about one-third the size of Rhode Island, stuck at the end of a peninsula in the middle of nowhere. Outside the trade routes between Siam (now Thailand) and China, the natives rarely had unexpected company.

A Chinese account from the 3rd century calls the island "Pu-luo-chung." Loosely translated, this means "island at the end of a peninsula," so we know they're talking about our island. Marco Polo stopped by Sumatra during one of his voyages, but there's nothing to support the accounts of those historians who say that Singapore was on his itinerary. By the 1300s, though, we have an authentic, first-hand account. Wang Ta Yuan, a Chinese trader probably blown off course, described the inhabitants as Chinese dressed in native garb. Old Wang went on to describe Singapore's business of the day: piracy. From the highest vantage point on the island, the natives would spy ships heading north to India, do a few quick calculations, and then rush out to sea a couple months later to overtake them, now on their way back to China loaded with goodies. It was a thriving enterprise.

In the *Nagarakretagama,* Java's newspaper of record for 1365, Singapore is referred to as Temasek (or "Sea Town"), as it was by this time a small trading outpost of the Srivijaya empire of Sumatra. By the close of the 14th century, little Temasek was caught in the struggles between Siam and the Majapahit Empire in Java. Around 1390, an ambitious and aggressive young Palembang ruler known as Iskander in Malay histories and Parameswara by the Portuguese renounced his allegiance to the Majapahit. Ensconcing himself on a lion throne, he declared himself a god in a ceremony intended to revive the Srivijaya Empire. You can imagine the Majapahits were none too thrilled with this bratty

Dateline
- 3rd Century Singapore mentioned by Chinese sailors
- 5th Century Tamil (Indian) and Persian traders arrive
- 1295 Marco Polo visits Sumatra, has a swell time
- 1349 Siam (Thailand) attacks Temasek (Singapore)
- 1390 Iskander Shah establishes sultanate on Singapura and ascends the "lion throne," but is eventually ousted
- 1613 Portuguese report having torched a Malay outpost on Singapura
- 1700s Temenggongs rule Singapura
- 1819 Sir Stamford Raffles lands on Singapura, likes what he sees
- 1820s First billiards club, first newspaper, first judicial system, first census (counting 4,727 souls)
- 1824 East India Trading Company buys the island
- 1826 Raffles dies in London
- 1827 Straits Settlements is formed, which includes Malaysia and Singapore; first steamship seen in Singapore
- 1830 The British rule Singapore from India
- 1831 Tiger sighted
- 1833 East India Trading Company loses its foothold in Southeast Asia; population now at 20,978
- 1834 First New Year Regatta

continues

- 1837 First Chamber of Commerce formed
- 1839 Launching of first Singapore vessel
- 1840 First bank opened, Union Bank of Calcutta; population at 33,969
- 1845 First Masonic Lodge; arrival of first P&O mail boat
- 1850 Population at 52,891
- 1854 First Singapore postage stamp printed
- 1860 Telegraph opened between Singapore and Batavia; population at 81,734
- 1864 First use of gas street lighting
- 1867 Singapore is declared a British colony
- 1869 Suez Canal opens; Singapore leaps to prominence
- 1871 Singapore's population reaches 94,816; visit of the King of Siam; telegraph opened between Singapore and Hong Kong
- 1877 Experimental rubber seeds smuggled from Brazil, planted at the Botanic Gardens
- 1877 Chinese Protectorate is formed to curb violence among rival Chinese gangs
- 1879 First telephone; Gen. Ulysses Grant visits Singapore; first official postcards issued
- 1881 Population now at 137,722
- 1886 Steam trams begin operation
- 1887 Statue of Raffles unveiled
- 1888 Rubber trees introduced into Malaysia as a commercial crop
- 1891 Singapore Golf Club formed; population at 181,602; first concert by Philharmonic Society
- 1896 First automobile
- 1901 Population at 226,842
- 1903 Singapore-Kranji Railway opens
- 1904 Motor vehicle registration and drivers' licensing introduced

continues

behavior and drove him out of town. Seeking refuge in Temasek, he quickly overthrew the local chieftains there and announced to all that the Srivijayas were back in business. After 3 years of blood and plunder on the island he was driven away to Malacca, where he set up a successful sultanate that would last several hundred years. This is probably the most credible tale of how Temasek became Singapura, or "Lion City."

A story less believable, though more exciting and colorful, is that of Sri Tri Buana, son of a descendant of Alexander the Great through his marriage to the daughter of the sea god. Buana was ruler of the aforementioned Srivijayas and one fine day decided to check out his empire. As his ship approached Temasek, a monstrous storm forced Buana to take shelter at the mouth of a river, on the island. The tempest abated and Buana spied a magnificent red-headed beast with a black body and a white chest emerging from the jungle. Buana took the beast to be a lion, considered this a good omen, and immediately founded a settlement which he called Singapura or Lion City. The Malay Annals of the 17th century claim this story as the truer version. It must be noted, however, that these Annals had an agenda of their own: Wishing to lay claim to an unbroken descent from Alexander the Great and the Srivijayas, the Malacca rulers used the time-honored trick of rewriting history.

When the Portuguese seized Malacca on the Malay Peninsula in 1511, all the high-class folks fled down the coast to settle on Singapura, relocating the capital to Johor Lama at the tip of the peninsula. The Portuguese destroyed Johor Lama in 1587 and later reported burning down a Malay outpost on Singapura in 1613. During the 1700s, local *temenggongs* (chieftains) set up their feifdoms and, since the island just lay out of the trade winds necessary for the success of a prosperous sea port, had little contact with the outside world. Historically speaking, Singapura ceased to exist.

STAMFORD RAFFLES & THE COLONIAL PERIOD

The year is 1819: Enter Sir Stamford Raffles. An official with the British East India Trading Company, Raffles was not high on anybody's list. He was an ineffectual administrator who espoused the idea that the British Empire, through the powerful East India Trading Company, should transform the Southeast Asian region back to its former glory, abolish slavery and oppression, and revive the region's old cultures. This idea was met with raised eyebrows.

The Dutch, who now had control of Java and Malacca, were snapping up every territory in sight. Raffles was appalled and appealed to his superiors to allow him to establish a trading port in the area to stem the advancement of the Dutch. Not impressed with the plan at first, the East India Trading Company finally relented and told him to go take a look at a couple of islands to the south of the Peninsula—just as long as he didn't do anything to antagonize the Dutch.

And so it was that on January 28, 1819, Sir Raffles and his good friend Col. William Farquhar dropped anchor just off Singapura island. The local chieftain met with Raffles and Farquhar, money found its way into the chieftain's pocket, a treaty was signed, and the East India Trading Company was officially in business. Raffles left the island soon after, leaving Farquhar with orders to get the post up and running. Immigrants, mostly Chinese, began arriving daily looking to cash in on the company's reputation for success.

But Singapura's future was not yet secure. The company belatedly realized that the location of this new post was sure to infuriate the Dutch and they tried to recall Raffles, but it was too late—the treaty was already signed. The Dutch were annoyed, but the British sent an envoy to soothe ruffled feathers and quietly employed 500 Indian troops to defend Singapura . . . just in case. The British foreign minister, recognizing the advantage of having control of a trading port in the region, entered into agreements with the Hague and, for the moment, discussion about the future of Singapura was tabled.

Meanwhile, back on the island, Farquhar was involved in an elaborate plan to get the settlement on its feet as quickly as possible. Not only the Chinese, but Malays, Indians, and Armenians (already settled in Brunei and the Philippines) found their way to Singapura. In 1822, Raffles instituted the Town Plan, which allocated neighborhoods to each of the races who'd come in droves to find work and begin new lives.

Among the eager folk who arrived in Singapore during this period to make their fortunes were the Bugis, a fierce bunch of warrior-traders who, in the preceding years, had become more and more dissatisfied with the control the Dutch were exerting over their trading. Armed clashes ensued, and the Bugis, fearing a retaliation, fled to Singapura—much to the

- 1905 First frozen foods arrive in Singapore; electric trams introduced
- 1907 Singapore Automobile Club founded
- 1911 Population now at 303,321
- 1914 Outbreak of the Great War in Europe
- 1915 Singapore Sling invented at Raffles Hotel (becomes a smashing success)
- 1916 Slavery abolished
- 1919 First airplane arrives in Singapore
- 1921 Britain severs its defense alliance with Japan; population at 418,358
- 1922 Prince of Wales visits
- 1926 First trolley bus service
- 1928 Singapore Flying Club formed
- 1929 Direct Singapore-London telegraph link
- 1931 Population at 570,128
- 1932 Last tiger killed
- 1936 Anti-Japanese riots by Chinese in Singapore; start of wireless broadcasting
- 1937 Sultan Mosque installs loudspeakers for muezzin's call to prayer; Kallang Aerodrome opens; opium sales' proceeds still providing 25% of Straits Settlements' budget
- 1938 First set of synchronized traffic lights installed
- 1939 World War II begins in Europe
- 1942 Japanese invade Singapore from the north
- 1945 Japanese surrender; British rule restored
- 1946 Singapore becomes a Crown Colony
- 1948 Communist Party of Malaya attempts to take control of the Peninsula; emergency powers instituted to discourage such activities
- 1955 Constitution allows a freely elected parliament; People's Action Party (PAP)

continues

is formed; concessions won toward greater political autonomy

- 1958 Singapore granted internal self-government
- 1959 People's Action Party (PAP) wins general election; Lee Kuan Yew becomes first prime minister
- 1961 First oil refinery
- 1963 Singapore is admitted to the Federation of Malaysia; Internal Security Act passed
- 1965 Singapore expelled from Federation and becomes an independent state; Singapore admitted into the United Nations
- 1967 Singapore issues its own currency
- 1981 PAP monopoly ends; Changi International Airport opens, named the best service in Southeast Asia; East Coast Expressway completed; Pan-Island Expressway opens
- 1987 Singapore's policy of limiting families to two children reversed due to declining birth rate; hefty incentives given for third children
- 1988 The Mass Rapid Transit System (MRT), an intra-island subway network built to the tune of S$5 billion, opens
- 1990 Singapore celebrates 25 years of independence; Prime Minister Lee steps down and Goh Chok Tong takes over the reins; Ministry for Information and the Arts formed; Placido Domingo is first opera star to play Singapore
- 1992 Chewing gum banned due to vandals plugging up elevator buttons and subway doors
- 1993 First Christie's auction; Michael Jackson World Tour sellout; *Cats* opens to rave notices and becomes the first

continues

dismay of the island's residents, who were fully aware of the Bugis' rather unsavory (though unwarranted) reputation. If they had arrived with hard eyes and lances drawn this might've been a problem, but the 500 Bugis came with their families, a fact that assured Farquhar of their peaceable intent. The Dutch demanded the Bugis' return, but Farquhar, having already given them asylum and seeing that they were master boatbuilders, told the Dutch to get lost. He was not sending them back.

By 1823, Raffles had left and the Singapore Residency was turned over to Dr. John Crawfurd, a Scotsman familiar with the Malay Peninsula and archipelago. With his austere manner and constant impatience, he was not the most likable fellow, but during his 3-year tenure he managed to increase Singapore's revenues from gambling taxes to such an extent that they exceeded those of Penang.

THE BOOMTOWN YEARS

In 1824, the Dutch finally signed a treaty with Britain acknowledging Singapore as a permanent British possession, and the Sultan Hussein ceded the island to the East India Trading Company in perpetuity. Three years later, Singapore was incorporated, along with Malacca and Penang, to form the Straits Settlements. Penang was acknowledged as the Settlements' seat of government, with direction from the Presidency of Bengal in India. During this period, the first judicial system was established; the first newspaper, the *Singapore Chronicle,* was published; the first census was taken, counting a total of 10,683 people; the island's first sports club, The Billiards Club, opened; and the first official market was opened in Telok Ayer. The busy 1820s drew to a close.

At the onset, Raffles and Farquhar had envisioned Singapore as a center for free trade and promoted a laissez-faire policy between government and local business. Over the years that followed, this philosophy would allow the island to become a booming economic center. Settlement began to push from the island's waterfront into its interior, where ill-planned pepper and gambier plantations operated until a combination of bad farming practices and a plague of tiger attacks sent business into decline. Meanwhile, along the coastline, trade continued to flourish. As with any new settlement, buildings sprang up seemingly overnight. George Drumgold Coleman, one of the first architects in Singapore, strove to set a standard for which Britain could be proud. In addition to many private residences, Coleman built the

Armenian Church and St. Andrew's Cathedral, Singapore's first permanent Roman Catholic church, which were completed in the 1830s and still stand today. His own mansion home later became part of the Parliament Building (see chapter 7).

Meanwhile, more and more immigrants began to arrive, some drawn by the island's prosperity and others dragged there in chains. The same policy that peopled Australia with prisoners of the British Empire brought thousands of Indian prisoners to Singapore, where they were put to work constructing the buildings and clearing the land that the fledgling settlement needed. After they'd worked off their sentences (and in the process learned a trade), many stayed in Singapore instead of returning home, and most became good citizens.

- of several Broadway road shows in Southeast Asia
- 1994 Iztak Perlman plays violin recitals to packed houses
- 1996 Passage of Maintenance of Parents Bill, which mandates that children provide for the care of their older parents

Chinese immigration was heaviest during the 1850s, when many fled the Manchu Empire and its hardships. Landing in Singapore, they quickly joined their own people and became members of clan associations or secret societies. The clan associations were loosely managed organizations that helped immigrants assimilate into society and found them work. The secret societies, however, were more of a threat than a help, and the settlement's lack of law enforcement allowed them to rob and pillage almost at will. In many respects, mid-century Singapore was often as lawless and anarchic as any rough-and-tumble frontier boomtown.

THE LEAP TO PROMINENCE

In 1867, control over Singapore was transferred from Calcutta to London and 2 years later the Suez Canal opened, linking the Mediterranean and the Red Sea and putting Singapore in a prime position on the Europe–East Asia route. In addition, steamship travel made the trip to Singapore less dependent on trade winds. The shorter travel time not only made the trade industry boom but also allowed tourists to consider Singapore an important stop on their itinerary.

Trade during this period centered around tin and rubber. In 1877, Singapore received a shipment of rubber seeds that had been smuggled out of Brazil, and the Botanical Garden's new director, Henry Ridley, thought this was the export that would put the Straits Settlements on the map. He discovered a way to extract the sap without damaging the tree and tried to convince planters to try growing it. For years Ridley pleaded and finally, just after the turn of the century, the first rubber was harvested in Malaysia, and Singapore soon became the world center for rubber export.

WORLD WAR II

Although the British maintained a military base of operations on the island, Singapore was virtually untouched by the First World War. Just before the Great Depression, however, Britain bowed to U.S. pressure and broke off relations with Japan due to that country's increasing military power. Singapore's defense became a primary concern and the British, thinking any invasion would come by sea, installed heavy artillery along the southern coastline, leaving the north of the island virtually unprotected.

The British military leaders were deeply divided over the strategy they assumed the Japanese would employ. They were convinced on the one hand that Japan's main intent was to attack Russia, and on the other that Japan's battles with the Chinese had left them battle weary, and that they had time to prepare. Besides, they thought, nobody in their right mind would mount an invasion during the monsoon season.

In 1941, on the night of December 7, the Japanese attacked Pearl Harbor, invaded the Philippines and Hong Kong, landed in southern Thailand, and dropped the first bombs on Singapore. Still the British clung to their position of maintaining calm among the citizens. No one had any idea of the seriousness of the situation. News censors repeatedly kept insisting there was no alarm and even with the daily air raids, life went on.

Japanese Lieutenant General Yamashita, fresh from battles in Mongolia, saw a definite advantage in Singapore's unprotected northern flank, and stealthily moved three divisions—almost 20,000 troops—down the Malay Peninsula on bicycles. From Johor Bahru, across the Strait of Johor, he had a direct view of Singapore and on the evening of February 8th, the army quietly invaded the island. For days, the British tried to hold off their attackers, but bit by bit they lost ground, and within days, the Japanese were firmly entrenched.

The occupation brought terrible conditions to multi-ethnic Singapore, as the Japanese ruled harshly and punished any word of dissent with prison or worse. Mass executions were commonplace, prisoners of war were tortured and killed, and it was said that the beaches at Changi ran red with blood. The prisoners that survived were sent to Thailand to work on the railway. Conditions were worst for the island's Chinese, many of whom were arrested indiscriminately just because of their ethnicity, rowed out to sea, and dumped overboard. Little information from the outside world reached Singapore's citizens during this time except when the Japanese were victorious.

In a sense, this behavior lost the Japanese one of the best audiences they could have had for their purported ideals of Asian equality and empowerment. During the occupation, they held exciting rallies, regaling the populace with these ideals, but all to naught, as the Japanese strutted boastfully and arrogantly about the city while the populace cowered in terror. In a country of divided ethnic groups, where the majority Chinese and the underdog Malays had lived for years under British colonial rule, these ideals might've fallen on sympathetic ears, but as it happened, the atrocities the Japanese committed against the Singaporeans only gained them the population's enmity.

Mercifully, the Japanese surrender came before Singapore became a battleground once again. On September 5, 1945, British warships arrived and, a week later, the Japanese officially surrendered to Lord Louis Mountbatten, Supreme Allied Commander in Southeast Asia.

THE POST-WAR YEARS

Now back under British rule, Singapore spent the next 10 years revitalizing itself, but efforts to become a fully self-governing country were tantamount. Resentment against the British was still very strong for the way they'd abandoned the island to the Japanese in 1941.

The British Military Administration (BMA), set up to efficiently organize and systematically administrate Singapore's post-occupation reconstruction, was neither efficient nor systematic. Disagreements between the British officials in Singapore and those in the Home Office beleaguered efforts to turn Singapore around. On the streets, conditions were terrible. The city was filthy and overrun with squatters living in ramshackle dwellings, food was scarce and high priced when it was available, hospital facilities were nonexistent, and disease was all around. The BMA eventually got itself under control and proceeded to clean up the port and harbor and return them to civilian control, restore public utilities, and overhaul the distrusted police force. Although food was still scarce, rice was available at a reasonable price.

At the time of the liberation, the Malayan People's Anti-Japanese Army numbered about 4,500, most of them Communists. Sentiment at one time ran high for these heroes among the Singaporeans, but as the reality of the occupation receded, the organization sensed a decline in its popularity and relinquished its hard-line military aims in favor of a political agenda to realize its goal: independence from British rule. One of its prime organizations, the General Labor Union (GLU), had over 60 trade unions under its banner and was able to organize strikes and mass demonstrations that brought Singapore to a standstill. Although concessions were made on both sides, the GLU eventually decided that overt actions weren't going to win any congeniality contests, and so became more involved with quietly reinforcing the trade union movement.

THE RISE OF LEE KUAN YEW & SINGAPOREAN INDEPENDENCE

In 1949, 3 years after the British military regime turned Singapore over to a civil administration as a crown colony once again, six Singaporean students in London formed a discussion group aimed at bringing together Malaysian overseas students. A third-generation Straits-Chinese, Lee Kuan Yew, was a formidable member of the group. Returning to Singapore, his education completed, Lee made a name for himself as an effective courtroom lawyer during the trials of Chinese students arrested during the anti–national service riots of May 1954. Around this time, he had decided that, although he detested their politics, an alliance with the illegal Malayan Communist Party would best serve his aims, and so a new combined party, the People's Action Party (PAP), was inaugurated. In the 1955 elections, the long-shot Labour Front, led by David Marshall, won the majority of seats in the Legislative Assembly, shocking the right-wing parties. Lee Kuan Yew also won a seat in this Assembly.

Marshall's demands that his government become more involved in deciding the best course for Singapore provoked the governor and the Colonial Office. To settle the dispute amicably, the office proposed a seven-member Internal Security Council (ISC) comprised of equal seats for Britain and Singapore with the seventh member chosen from the Malay Federation. Although the Assembly accepted the proposal by a large majority, the plan was not to Marshall's liking, as the Federation was definitely pro-Britain, and he resigned.

By 1957, the Federation of Malaysia had won its independence, and around the same time Britain agreed to allow the establishment of a fully elected, 51-seat Legislative Assembly in Singapore. In the first elections for this body, in 1959, the PAP swept 43 of the seats and Lee Kuan Yew became the country's first prime minister.

Lee's agenda was met with distrust by the Federation of Malaysia. His aim was to have Singapore admitted to the Federation, but the Malaysian government was fearful of a dominant Chinese influence and fought to keep Singapore out. In 1963, however, they broke down and Singapore was admitted as a member. It was a short-lived marriage. When the PAP looked to becoming a national entity rather than a local Singaporean party, an alarmed Federation demanded Singapore be expelled, and so, on August 9, 1965, Singapore found itself a newly independent country. Lee's tearful television broadcast announcing Singapore's expulsion from the Federation and simultaneous gain of independence is one of the most famous in Singapore's history.

In 1971, the last British military forces left the island. The PAP continued to win elections by handsome margins, returning Lee Kuan Yew to power again and again and guiding Singapore to its current status. In 1990, after 3 decades of leadership, Lee Kuan Yew resigned his post and is now senior minister, still a powerful position. Goh Chok Tong is prime minister, continuing the policies of Lee's regime, albeit with a slightly more liberal bent. More than three million people enjoy the highest standard of living in Southeast Asia due in no small part to Lee Kuan Yew. From the aftermath of World War II to the present day, in just 50-odd years, Singapore has gone from reconstruction to being one of Southeast Asia's economic powerhouses and one of the most stable nations in the region, if not the world. It's an accomplishment all Singaporeans can be proud of.

5 The Singaporean People

Many tourists come to Singapore for the shopping or the culture or the sights, but I go for the people, who are some of the most fascinating, open, and friendly folk I've ever met. Most often, when you travel in foreign lands, the people you meet are other international travelers. In Singapore, however, the friends you make will be Singaporeans—I almost guarantee it. And if you're ever lost or need help, there will always be someone with a friendly face who'll volunteer to assist.

The median age of the population is around 32, which means the younger generations, who tend to be on the cosmopolitan and worldly side, rule local trends. I hate to generalize, but the younger set tend to be yuppie in every sense of the word. Most are professionally oriented, and while they work hard, they play hard also, from going out to nightclubs to traveling around the region and the world.

There's an ever-present image consciousness, fueled by heavy consumerism. Fashion, cars, and social scenes are in. Money is in. Success is in. Young Singaporeans strive for what they call the five Cs—Career, Condo, Car, Cash, and Credit cards—and it sometimes seems they'll stop at nothing to achieve them.

Which leads me to the local term *kiasu,* used to describe a person who is afraid to miss out on anything—so afraid, in fact, that he's willing to make a fool of himself trying to grab anything he can. "Mr. Kiasu" is a popular cartoon character who epitomizes the kiasu stereotype. He is a local idiot who piles his plate high at buffets to get every last penny's worth of food, wrestles through crowds at sales to get the bargains, and will go to every extent to outdo his neighbors and peers. Unfortunately, he represents a real phenomenon among the young people, who are aggressively competitive and struggle to keep up with anything new. Stop by a bookstore and pick up one of the Mr. Kiasu cartoon books for a hilarious look at his misadventures and a bit of tongue-in-cheek insight into local culture.

As with any modern society, while the younger generations are busy finding their niche in the world, it is the older generations who keep traditional cultures alive. Singapore's population, now at three million people, is a mix of Chinese (77%), Malays (14.2%), Indians (7.2%), and others, including Eurasians (1.2%). Though the country is overwhelmingly Chinese, the government has embraced all local heritage, recognizing religious holidays and festivals and promoting racial harmony in its policies, all as part of its plan to foster a single national identity, molded from the disparate cultural backgrounds of the Singaporean populace. They've even commissioned the National Association of Registered Tour Guides to take school children to cultural districts and places of historical significance to teach respect for their heritage, and to let them peer through the multicultural prism of what it is to be "Singaporean."

Unfortunately, this government social planning may have contributed to one of the common problems that's plaguing Singapore's younger generations today: a lack of identity. No longer immersed in the traditions of their own ethnic groups; growing up with so many cultural influences, both from inside Singapore and from outside its borders; and with traditional values being rapidly replaced by commercialism and a whole new set of opportunities, it's not surprising to hear so many young people ask, "Who am I?"

THE CHINESE

When Raffles opened Singapore's port for free trade, junk-loads of Chinese immigrated to find their fortunes. Most were poor workers from China's southern regions, who brought with them different cultures and dialects from their respective places of origin. Of the mix, the Hokkiens (from Fujian province) are the largest percentage of Chinese in Singapore at 42%, followed by the Teochews (from Guangdong province), Cantonese (also from Guangdong), Hakkas (from central China), and finally the Hiananese (from Hainan island), at 6%.

Most of the Chinese are Buddhist, a philosophy based on the teachings of ancient Indian philosopher and teacher Gautama Buddha (the Enlightened One) and focused on the Three Jewels that serve as a spiritual guide: They are the Buddha, the Dharma (his teachings), and the Sangha (monastic order). The Chinese in Singapore combine Buddhism with Taoism and Confucianism, which accounts for Buddhist temples that are structurally aligned according to the Taoist practice of *feng shui* (see below), with altars to the Taoist deity Kuan Yin and ancestral tablets that contest to the Confucian values of filial piety.

Feng shui, also called "geomancy," derives from the Taoist belief that people must always live in harmony with their surroundings. More than a simple "Don't litter" kind of message, it's a philosophy that applies to every kind of human environment, from homes to businesses, and says that if you place a home and its furnishing a particular way you can either enhance your luck, health, and wealth or invite doom. The belief is that *chi,* or positive energy, flows through people, buildings, and landscapes; if your home is not properly aligned, this chi can either get trapped and turn into bad stagnant energy, or be chased out of your house altogether. So true to these theories are the Chinese that businesses will pay exorbitant amounts to have feng shui masters come in to consult on their interior decor and even on major construction plans, and will follow their advice to the last detail.

Characteristically, the Chinese are very superstitious, with numbers playing a critical role in everyday decisions, preferring auspicious numbers for automobile license plates, and choosing dates that contain lucky numbers for business openings. Here's another superstition: Don't leave your chopsticks sticking up in your rice bowl. It invites hungry ghosts.

THE MALAYS

When Raffles arrived, Malays had already inhabited the island, fishing the waters and trading with other local seafaring people. Many more were to immigrate in the decades to follow.

Although Singapore's Malay population is very low today, the national language on the street is Malay, some of the best-loved local dishes are Malay, and even the national anthem is sung in Malay. The shame is that, while Malays are recognized as the original inhabitants, they constantly feel the sting of the Chinese domination of Singaporean culture and policy. These people represent an unbalanced percentage of the poor classes, with the lowest levels of education and the highest number of criminal offenders. The government prides itself on policies to promote racial harmony, but it is widely accepted that Malays occupy jobs on the low scale of the economy. Even in the military, while there are many Malays in the enlisted troops, there are almost none in the officers ranks. Some people have explained the economic discrimination as a language barrier: Malays are less likely to learn English, and even less likely to learn Chinese, which is a major strike against them in the job market.

Islam has been by far the most common religion among Malays since it was introduced to the Malaysian Peninsula around the year 1303. The religion's strict moral

Send in the Feng Shui Master

Have you ever noticed how some homes seem to give off terrific vibes the moment you enter the front door while others leave you feeling disturbed and wanting to get out fast? The Chinese believe *feng shui* (pronounced "*fung shway*" and meaning "wind and water") has a lot to do with these positive and negative feelings.

The earliest record of feng shui dates from the Han Dynasty (202 B.C. to A.D. 220) and the practice is still widely followed and highly regarded in Asia today. In essence, the idea of feng shui revolves around the way physical surroundings relate to the invisible flow of *chi* (natural energy), which must move smoothly throughout the home or business in order for life to play itself out beneficially. Walls, doors, windows, or furnishings can throw off this flow through their color, balance, placement, or proportion—even by their points on the compass. Your bed, for example, placed on the wrong wall or facing the wrong way, could encourage chi to rush into a room and out again, taking wealth and health with it. If your bed is situated directly under an exposed beam, you might as well make a standing appointment with the chiropractor, 'cause that's some *baaad* feng shui.

In Singapore, company presidents regularly call upon feng shui masters to rearrange their office furniture, and the master is usually the first person called in on new construction jobs, to assess the building plans for their adherence to good feng shui practices. It's not uncommon to hear stories about buildings being partially torn down late in the construction process, simply because a master hadn't examined the plans earlier and, when finally consulted, had deemed that the structure did not promote good feng shui. The extra cost is considered a valid investment—after all, what's a few dollars saved now if bad feng shui will later cause the business to fail? For the average homeowner who doesn't want to consult a feng shui master (or can't afford to), a plethora of books is available to advise on creating successful living spaces.

For every life situation there's a feng shui solution. And don't worry what people will think when they see those four purple candles in the corner of your living room or the pair of wooden flutes dangling from an exposed beam. Let 'em laugh—you'll be grinning all the way to the bank.

code, based on the Qur'an (or Koran), God's revelation to the Prophet Mohammed, is upheld by the faithful in Singapore, with many Malay women covering their heads and Muslim dietary laws influencing all Malay dishes. The younger generations are not as orthodox, and are seen less and less in the mosques, much to the dismay of their elders.

THE PERANAKANS

Until recently, you didn't hear much about the Peranakans (also called Straits-Chinese), a subculture of the colonial era that grew out of intermarriage between the Chinese and Malays, but recent trends to embrace Singapore's heritage have re-kindled interest in this small yet influential group, who are unique to Singapore and Malaysia.

In the early days of Singapore, immigration of Chinese women was forbidden, so many Chinese men found wives in the native Malay population. The resultant ethnic group, the Peranakans, formed their own culture from a mixing of Chinese and Malay traditions. This mixed heritage allowed them to become strong economic and political players, oftentimes serving as middlemen between Chinese, Europeans, and other locals. Peranakan shophouses combined traditional Chinese and Malay elements, with European influence thrown in. Their pottery used Chinese styles and decorations, but in more flamboyant colors, reflecting Malaysian tastes, and their locally well-known cuisine combined Chinese preparation with locally found ingredients. The clothing worn by Peranakan ladies (or *Nonyas;* Peranakan men were called *Babas*) is also locally famous—the delicately embroidered *kebaya* was worn over a sarong, and the elegant beaded slippers are the most dainty things you've ever seen.

Peranakan literally means "Straits-born," so, technically speaking, all people born in Malaysia can argue they are Peranakan, and in a lot of literature you may see the term used broadly. Today, though, with many Singaporeans able to trace their heritage to this ethnic group, a heritage society has developed to support their interests and keep their culture alive.

THE INDIANS

Many Indians were aboard Raffles' ship when it landed on the banks of the Singapore River, so this group has always been counted as Singapore's first immigrants. In the following decades many more Indians would follow them to find work and wealth, many finding positions in the government as clerks, teachers, and traders.

In 1825, hundreds of Indians who had been in prison in Bencoolen (Sumatra) were transferred to Singapore, where they worked as convict laborers. These Indian convicts built many of the government buildings and cathedrals—for instance St. Andrew's Cathedral, Sri Mariamman Temple, and the Istana—and worked on the heavy-duty municipal projects. Eventually, they served their sentences and assimilated into society, many remaining in Singapore.

Most Indian immigrants were from the southern regions of India, and from such ethnic groups as the Tamils, Malayalis, Punjabis, and Gujratis. So, despite Little India's reputation as an Indian enclave, the Indian population in fact split into groups based on racial divisions and settled in pockets all over the city. The Indians were also divided between religious affiliation. While most were Hindu—which revolves around the Holy Trinity of Shiva, Vishnu, and Brahma, but includes many, many other male and female deities, all of which are considered parts of the same God—Indian religious groups also included Muslims, Christians, Sikhs, and Buddhists.

The Indians tend to be an informal and warm people, adding their own brand of casual ease to Singapore, but any Singaporean will tell you that one of the most precious contributions the Indians made is their cuisine. Indian restaurants are well patronized by all ethnic groups because the southern Indian vegetarian cooking is the only food that can be enjoyed by any Singaporean, no matter what cultural or religious dietary laws they may have.

Recently, Indians have become somewhat discontented with life in Singapore, feeling overwhelmed by a Chinese government they feel promotes Chinese culture. Indians are some of the most open critics of government practices.

6 Singaporean Etiquette & Customs

Here's a delicate one, but there's no way to get around it: Only use your right hand in social interaction. Why? Because in Indian and Muslim society, the left hand is used only for . . . ahem . . . bathroom chores. Not only should you eat with your right hand and give and receive all gifts with your right hand, but you should make sure all gestures, especially pointing (and even *more* especially, pointing in temples and mosques), are made with your right hand. By the way, you should also be sure to point with your knuckle rather than your finger, to be more polite.

The other important etiquette tip is to remember to **remove your shoes** before entering places of worship (except for churches and synagogues) and all private residences. The private residence part is very important. I have yet to meet a local family that does not leave their shoes at the door.

A **traditional Indian greeting** is a slight bow with your palms pressed together in front of your chest. In these modern times, though, a handshake will usually do. When greeting an older man or especially a woman, wait for a gesture, then follow suit.

The **traditional Malay greeting,** called the *salaam,* is still practiced in Malaysia, but is rarely seen in Singapore. In this practice, both parties extend their hands to lightly touch each others', then touch their hearts with their fingertips. This is only done between members of the same sex. While Malay men will offer the more common handshake, always remember that Muslim women are not allowed to touch men to whom they are not related by blood or marriage. A simple smile and nod is fine.

Ladies, if seated on the floor, should never sit with their legs crossed in front of them—instead, always tuck your legs to the side. Both men and women should also be careful not to show the bottoms of their feet. If you cross your legs while on the floor or in a chair, don't point your soles toward other people—it's very rude. Also be careful not to use your foot to point or gesture, as this is also insulting.

Muslims who have traveled to Mecca take the prefix Haji, for males, and Hajjah for females, before their names. Feel free to use these titles if you know the person you're talking with has made the pilgrimage; it's a real mark of pride for them.

As for **Chinese etiquette and customs,** that can be rough. So many elements of Chinese culture make no sense to Westerners that I couldn't possibly cover the whole range. The younger generations are not so strict about these points of cultural etiquette as the older folks, but if you find yourself in a situation, even common sense can't make you a good judge of proper etiquette. You could give a beautiful brush painting to a Chinese as a gift, and the tiniest bird in the background could be a bad omen laying a curse on all of their future generations. Seriously.

If you are invited to a Chinese occasion or need to buy a gift for someone, the best thing you can possibly do is consult a Chinese person for advice. This is where hotel staff come in handy. What color should I wear? What is the proper attire? Will this gift be nice? You'll thank them later.

I can give you some basic rules of thumb that will help:

- **Don't wear all white or all black if you're invited to a festive occasion;** these colors are for mourning. The same is pretty much true for all-blue and all-green outfits. Reds, pinks, oranges, and yellows are great for such gatherings.
- **Gifts should never be knives, clocks, or handkerchiefs,** and don't send *anybody* white flowers. (The sharp blades of knives symbolize the severing of a friendship; in Cantonese, the word for clock sounds the same as the word for funeral; handkerchiefs bring to mind tears and sadness; and white is the color of funeral mourning.)
- **When giving money,** an even amount in a red envelope is presented on auspicious occasions, and an odd number in a white envelope is presented at funerals. There's no correct amount, but if there's a meal involved, the amount should at least cover the cost. By the way, the Chinese do not open gifts in public.
- The main rules regarding **table manners** revolve around the use of chopsticks. Don't stick them upright in any dish, don't gesture with them, and don't suck on them. Dropped chopsticks are also considered bad luck.

As **for greetings,** Chinese men and women are all pretty well accustomed to the standard handshake.

If you're conducting business in Singapore, you'll most likely be exchanging **business cards.** All Singaporeans present and receive business cards using both hands, as if giving or accepting a gift. If a card is given to you, hang on to it a bit before putting it away—to stow it immediately is a sign of disrespect.

7 Recommended Books

Singapore publishes quite a few good reads about itself—its history, culture, and people. English bookstores are all over the city. The biggest is **MPH** (corner of Stamford Road and Armenian Street in the Historic District; ☎ **65/336-3633**). **Times The Bookshop** has many outlets. The biggest one is in Centrepoint (#04-08/16; ☎ **65/734-9022**).

ARCHITECTURE

Gretchen Liu's *In Granite and Chunam* (Landmark Books) discusses Singaporean architecture, its history, and the origins of its unique character; and Robert Powell's *Living Legacy* (Singapore Heritage Society) is a neat little peek inside restored residential shophouses and bungalows.

THE ARTS

The Arts in Singapore: Directory and Guide (edited by Dora Tay and published by Accent Communications and the National Arts Council) has a great overview of the major influences of Singapore's arts scene, and lists local theater groups, art galleries, dance troupes, and much more. *Singapore: Global City for the Arts* (Singapore Tourism Board and the Ministry of Information and the Arts) provides an overview of Singapore's creative side.

GOVERNMENT PUBLICATIONS

Singapore Facts and Pictures (Ministry of Information and the Arts) is updated annually and packed with recent statistics and facts about the nation, including trade figures, population estimates, and even unusual and little-known facts. *Singapore 1998* (Ministry of Information and the Arts) is updated annually. It reads like a textbook and will tell you anything you want to know about Singapore's government, economy, and society.

HISTORY

A History of Singapore (edited by Ernest C. T. Chew and Edwin Lee, Oxford University Press) is a collection of scholarly accounts of the history of Singapore, with chapters on national identity, Singapore's relationship with ASEAN (Association of Southeast Asian Nations) neighbors, and more. C. M. Turnbull's *A History of Singapore, 1819–1988* (Oxford University Press) tells the story of Singapore from precolonial days to the political and social developments in the 1980s.

LOCAL CUISINE

Wendy Hutton's *Singapore Food* (Times Books International) is an anecdotal description of the history and traditions behind the ingredients and preparation involved in Singaporean cuisine, with recipes. *Singapore's Best Restaurants 1998* (Illustrated Magazine Publishing) is a list of the top 100 restaurants as judged by *The Singapore Tattler,* a local high-profile society gossip magazine. Djoko Wibisono and David Wong's

The Food of Singapore (Periplus Editions) is about the origins and influences of the various cuisines that make up Singapore's favorite dishes, with recipes.

LOCAL CULTURE

David Brazil's *Street Smart Singapore* (Times Books International) is a book of vignettes telling the tales that surround the places and people of Singapore, and Pugalenthi Sr's *Myths and Legends of Singapore* (VJ Times) tells the Chinese, Indian, and Malay legends of Singapore. *Portraits of Places: History, Community and Identity in Singapore* (edited by Brenda S. A. Yeoh and Lily Kong, Times Editions) is a fascinating collection of scholarly writings examining the driving social and psychological forces behind the identity of Singaporeans.

If you're interested in brushing up on your manners before diving into multicultural Singapore, there are a number of books that will help. Elizabeth Devine and Nancy L. Braganti's *The Travelers' Guide to Asian Customs and Manners* (St. Martin's Press) tells you everything you need to know about the customs of Asia. Raelene Tan's *Chinese Etiquette: A Matter of Course* (Landmark Books) gives concise tips on Chinese etiquette practices, and *Indian & Malay Etiquette: A Matter of Course,* by the same author and publisher, spells out the basic rules of Indian and Malay etiquette.

For a look at Chinese festivals, check out Tan Huay Peng's *Fun with Chinese Festivals* (Federal Publications), which explains the origins of the customs associated with them. Goh Pei Ki's *Origins of Chinese Festivals* (Asiapac) is a cartoon history of China's major festivals and the traditions that make them unique.

If you want to learn about feng shui, there are scads of books you can peruse. Kristen M. Newleaf's *Feng Shui: Arrange Your Home to Change Your Life* (Lagatree) is a short read of basic feng shui principles you can apply in your own home, while Sarah Rossbach's *Feng Shui: The Chinese Art of Placement* (Rider) is a deep study and detailed explanation of the principles of feng shui. Derek Walters' *The Feng Shui Handbook: A Practical Guide to Chinese Geomancy* (Thorsen's) is yet another explanation of the Chinese art of geomancy.

TRAVEL

For a look at what travel to Singapore was like in the old days, check out *Travelers' Singapore, An Anthology* (edited by John Bastin, Oxford University Press), which presents excerpts from old travelogues, with views of Singapore between 1819 and 1942 through the eyes of tourists. Similarly, *Travelers' Tales of Old Singapore* (edited by Michael Wise, In Print) shares the experiences of early travelers.

JUST FOR FUN

Jim Aitchinson and Theseus Chan's *The Official Guide to the Sarong Party Girl* (Angsana Books) is a bawdy humor book that pokes fun at Singaporean women who chase Western men. Of a more general nature, Catherine Lim's *O Singapore! Stories in Celebration* (Times Books International) tells witty stories, each designed to make fun of stereotypical Singaporean behavior.

Don't leave without grabbing at least one of the Mr. Kiasu books—*Everything I Also Want, Everything Also Must Grab, Everything Also Number One,* and *Everything Also Want Extra* (Comix Factory Pte. Ltd.). These are hilarious comic books starring local comic hero (and alter ego of young Singaporeans), Mr. Kiasu.

2

Planning a Trip to Singapore

raveling to Singapore is a piece of cake. Why? First, because it's a hub for Southeast Asian business and travel, so there's a booming hotel and tourism industry that's just crawling all over itself to win your business. Second, because modern communications and a high proportion of English-speaking Singaporeans mean that it's easy to make your own arrangements via telephone, fax, or the Internet. Finally, the Singapore Tourism Board (STB) is a wealthy and well-oiled machine that has anticipated the needs of travelers and filled in all the gaps.

The STB is perhaps one of the most visible government agencies in Singapore, and it's impossible for any tourist to get out of the country without encountering at least one of their many publications or postings or coming face-to-face with one of their innumerable representatives. If you have access to one of their offices prior to your trip, they are a great source of information. (STB's international offices are listed under "Visitor Information," below.)

In this chapter, I'll run through the nuts and bolts of travel to Singapore, letting you in on everything from how much your money will buy, to the best time of year to travel and what to wear, to what sea creatures to watch out for if you go swimming.

1 Visitor Information & Entry Requirements

VISITOR INFORMATION

The long arm of the Singapore Tourism Board (STB)—which until recently was known as the Singapore Tourist Promotion Board (STPB)— reaches many overseas audiences through its branch offices, which will gladly provide brochures and booklets to help you plan your trip, and through their Web site, at **www.newasia-singapore.com**.

IN THE U.S.

- **New York:** 590 Fifth Ave., 12th Floor, New York, NY 10036 (☎ **212/302-4861;** fax 212/302-4801)
- **Chicago:** Two Prudential Plaza, 180N Stetson Ave., Suite 1450, Chicago, IL 60601 (☎ **312/938-1888;** fax 312/938-0086)
- **Beverly Hills:** 8484 Wilshire Blvd., Suite 510, Beverly Hills, CA (☎ **213/852-1901;** fax 213/852-0129)

IN CANADA
- **Toronto:** The Standard Life Centre, 121 King St. West, Suite 1000, Toronto, Ontario, Canada M5H 3T9 (☎ 416/363-8898; fax 416/363-5752)

IN AUSTRALIA & NEW ZEALAND
- **Sydney:** Level 11, AWA Building, 47 York St., Sydney NSW 2000, Australia (☎ 2/241-3771 or 2/241-3772; fax 2/252-3586)

IN THE U.K.
- **London:** 1st Floor, Carrington House, 126–130 Regent St., London W1R 5FE, United Kingdom (☎ 71/4370033; fax 71/7342191)

ENTRY REQUIREMENTS

To enter Singapore, you must have a valid passport. Visas are not necessary for passport holders from the United States, Canada, the U.K., Australia, and New Zealand for a stay of up to 30 days if your travel is by plane, or up to 14 days if your travel is by ship or overland from Malaysia.

If you do plan a longer stay, direct your visa inquiries to Singapore representative offices in your home country.

In Singapore, there's a 24-hour automated inquiry system for questions about visa requirements at the Singapore Immigration Department (☎ 800/538-5400). During office hours, you can reach their help lines at ☎ 65/530-1813 and 65/530-1817 (Monday through Friday from 8am to 5pm, Saturday from 1am to 1pm, Singapore time).

If you need to extend your visa, apply at the Ministry of Home Affairs Immigration Department, located at 10 Kallang Rd., just above the Lavender MRT Station (☎ 65/532-2877). They hold standard business hours and are open in the mornings on Saturdays. The lines are long, but the system is efficient and if you show up early in the morning, you'll be out in an hour or 2.

If you overstay your visa, report immediately to the Immigration Department. Even the most conscientious travelers can overstay their visas—even me, your trusty travel guide advisor. At immigration, you'll be asked to hand over your passport, departure record, possibly your airline ticket to prove your return flight, and a letter to explain why you did not depart on time. They'll ask you to return the next day to retrieve your documents. In certain cases they may even require that you undergo an interview with an immigration official. If this happens, I strongly recommend that you act very humble, grovel, and beg forgiveness, as some people get off with no penalty charge at all while others have been known to be fined a couple hundred dollars. As in most countries, a little respect to the civil service goes a long way.

While in Singapore, **if you need to replace travel documents** or have other problems, the foreign mission contacts are: **United States**, 30 Hill St. (☎ 65/338-0251); **Canada,** 80 Anson Rd., #14/15-00 IBM Towers (☎ 65/225-6363); **Australia,** 25 Napier Rd. (☎ 65/737-9311); **New Zealand,** 13 Nassim Rd. (☎ 65/235-9966); **United Kingdom,** Tanglin Road (☎ 65/473-9333).

IN THE U.S.
- **Washington, D.C.:** The Singapore Embassy, 3501 International Place NW, Washington, DC 20008 (☎ 202/537-3100; fax 202/537-0876)
- **California:** Singapore Consulate-General, 2424 SE Bristol #320, Newport Beach, CA 92660 (☎ 714/476-2330; fax 714/476-8301); or the Singapore

CyberDeals for Net Surfers

It's possible to get some great deals on airfare, hotels, and car rentals via the Internet. So go grab your mouse and start surfing—you could save a bundle on your trip. The Web sites I've highlighted below are worth checking out, especially since all services are free.

Microsoft Expedia (www.expedia.com)   The best part of this multipurpose travel site is the "Fare Tracker": You fill out a form on the screen indicating that you're interested in cheap flights to Singapore from your hometown, and, once a week, they'll e-mail you the best airfare deals. The site's "Travel Agent" will steer you to bargains on hotels and car rentals, and you can book everything, including flights, right on-line. This site is even useful once you're booked: Before you go, log onto Expedia for oodles of up-to-date travel information, including weather reports and foreign exchange rates.

Preview Travel (www.reservations.com and www.vacations.com)   Another useful travel site, "Reservations.com" has a "Best Fare Finder," which will search the Apollo computer reservations system for the three lowest fares for any route on any days of the year. Say you want to go from Chicago to Singapore and back between December 6th and 13th: Just fill out the form on the screen with times, dates, and destinations, and within minutes, Preview will show you the best deals. If you find an airfare you like, you can book your ticket right on-line—you can even reserve hotels and car rentals on this site. If you're in the pre-planning stage, head to Preview's "Vacations.com" site, where you can check out the latest package deals for Singapore and other destinations around the world by clicking on "Hot Deals."

Travelocity (www.travelocity.com)   This is one of the best travel sites out there. In addition to its "Personal Fare Watcher," which notifies you via e-mail of the lowest airfares for up to five different destinations, Travelocity will track the three lowest fares for any routes on any dates in minutes. You can book a flight right then and there, and if you need a rental car or hotel, Travelocity will find you the best deal via the SABRE computer reservations system (a huge database used by travel agents worldwide). Click on "Last Minute Deals" for the latest travel bargains.

Trip.Com (www.thetrip.com)   This site is really geared toward the business traveler, but vacationers-to-be can also use Trip.Com's valuable fare-finding engine, which will e-mail you every week with the best city-to-city airfare deals on your selected route or routes.

Discount Tickets (www.discount-tickets.com)   Operated by the ETN (European Travel Network), this site offers discounts on airfares, accommodations, car rentals, and tours.

—Jeanette Foster

Consulate, 1670 Pine St., San Francisco, CA 94109 (☎ **415/673-8573;** fax 415/673-0883)

- **Minneapolis:** Singapore Consulate-General, c/o Personnel Decisions Inc., 2000 Plaza VII, 45 S. Seventh St., Minneapolis, MN 55402 (☎ **612/ 337-3643;** fax 612/337-3640)

- **New York:** Singapore Mission to the United Nations, 231 E. 51st St., New York, NY 10022 (☎ **212/826-0840;** fax 212/826-2964)

IN CANADA

• **Vancouver:** Singapore High Consulate-General, Suite 1305, 999 W. Hastings St., Vancouver, British Columbia, V6C 2W2 Canada (☎ **604/669-5115;** fax 604/669-5153)

IN AUSTRALIA

• **Canberra:** Singapore High Commission, 17 Forster Crescent, Yarralumla ACT 2600, Canberra, Australia (☎ **6/273-3944;** fax 6/273-3260)

IN NEW ZEALAND

• **Wellington:** Singapore High Commissioner, 17 Kabul St., Khandallah, P.O. Box 13-140, Wellington, New Zealand (☎ **4/479-2076;** fax 4/479-2315)

IN THE U.K.

• **London:** Singapore High Commission, 9 Wilton Crescent, London, SW 1X 8SA, United Kingdom (☎ **71/235-8315;** fax 71/245-6583)

CUSTOMS REGULATIONS

There's no restriction on the amount of currency you can bring into Singapore. For those above 18 years of age who have arrived from countries other than Malaysia and have spent more than 48 hours outside Singapore, allowable duty-free concessions are 1 liter of spirits; 1 liter of wine; and 1 liter of either port, sherry, or beer, all of which must be intended for personal consumption only. There are no duty-free concessions on cigarettes or other tobacco items. If you exceed the duty-free limitations, you can bring them in upon payment of goods and services tax (GST) and customs duty.

The following items are not allowed through customs unless you have authorization or an import permit: animals; birds and their by-products; plants; endangered species or items made from these species; arms and explosives; bulletproof clothing; toy guns of any type; weapons, including decorative swords and knives; cigarette lighters in the shape of pistols; toy coins; pornographic pre-recorded video tapes and cassettes, books, or magazines; controlled substances; poisons; materials that may be considered treasonable (plutonium, military maps—that kind of thing). For all pharmaceutical drugs, especially sleeping pills, depressants, or stimulants, you must provide a prescription from your physician authorizing personal use for your well-being. All inquiries can be directed to the **Customs Office** at Changi International Airport (☎ 65/542-7058) or the **Customs and Excise Department** (☎ 65/543-0755).

Other tips: Make sure you declare all prohibited or controlled items, as failure to do so is punishable. You are required to unpack your bags to reveal the contents inside if asked by customs. On a nice note, the officers are required to help you repack if they're not busy.

With all of the publicity surrounding the issue, Singapore's strict **drug policy** shouldn't need recapitulation, but here it is. Importing, selling, or using illegal narcotics is absolutely forbidden. Punishments are severe, up to and including the death penalty (automatic for morphine quantities exceeding 30 grams, heroin exceeding 15 grams, cocaine 30 grams, marijuana 500 grams, hashish 200 grams, and opium 1.2 grams). If you're crazy enough to try and you are caught, no measure of appeal to your home consulate will grant you any special attention.

It should be noted that even with these drug laws, narcotics abuse still continues in Singapore. Despite aggressive government campaigns to stop drug abuse, marijuana consumption is very quiet and underground, there are rumors of some heroin abuse,

---

Whatever You Do, Don't Drop Your Chewing Gum

Though as a visitor it's perfectly legal for you to bring chewing gum into Singapore for your own personal consumption, and you can chew it on the streets or anywhere else, it's completely illegal to sell or buy chewing gum within Singapore itself. Why? This is the story I heard.

After Singapore built the MRT subway system, truly a remarkable feat of engineering and efficiency, the government brought visiting international dignitaries into the system to show off their pride and joy. When the train pulled into the station, the doors jammed, and complete and irremediable embarrassment ensued. When the authorities demanded an investigation into the problem, it was found that someone had jammed chewing gum into the door mechanism. As a result, the government banned chewing gum, citing that Singaporeans were unable to responsibly dispose of the stuff.

---

and lately there have been problems with younger generations consuming the most recent fashionable drug, Ecstasy. Do yourself a favor: If you're in an area where you know illegal drug consumption is taking place, get the hell away from there as fast as you can. If narcotics are an important part of your vacation enjoyment, reconsider Singapore. Frommer's has a wonderful travel guide available for Amsterdam, which I'd recommend you take a peek at.

If you do try to bring in any of the above articles, they will be confiscated and you will need to defend yourself to the relevant authorities. Pornographic materials will be confiscated, and upon occasion, videotapes will be returned with questionable scenes erased.

Upon departure, you'll be required to pay a **departure tax** of S$15 (US$9.45). Coupons for the amount can be purchased at most hotels, travel agencies, and airline offices.

THE TOURIST REFUND SCHEME

Singapore has a great incentive for travelers to drop big bucks: the Tourist Refund Scheme. If you purchase goods at a value of S$350 (US$220) or more at a shop that displays the Tax Refund logo, customs will reimburse the 3% GST (goods and services tax) you paid for the purchase. Here's how it works: When you purchase the item(s), apply with the retailer for a GST Claim Form. Then, when you're leaving Singapore, present your claim form, your receipts, and the items purchased at the Tax Refund Counters located in the Departure Hall at Changi Airport's terminals 1 or 2. Within 12 weeks, you'll receive a check for the GST refund—or, if you used a credit card for the purchase, your bill can be credited. Choose the method of reimbursement when you prepare your claim form. Some shops may include a fee for the service. For more information, contact the **Singapore Tourism Board** at ☎ 800/738-3778 or 800/738-3779.

2 Money

The local currency unit is the **Singapore dollar.** It's commonly referred to as the "Sing dollar," and retail prices are often marked as S$ (a designation I've used throughout this book). Notes are issued in denominations of S$1, $2, $5, $10, $20, $50, $100, $500, and $1,000. Notes vary in size and color from denomination to denomination. Coins are issued in denominations of S1¢, 5¢, 10¢, 20¢, 50¢, and the

Singapore Dollar Conversion Chart

S$	U.S.$	Can$	Aust$	NZ$	U.K.£
.10	.06	.08	.09	.10	.04
.20	.13	.16	.18	.20	.10
.50	.32	.45	.45	.51	.19
1.00	.63	.90	.90	1.02	.38
2.00	1.26	1.79	1.81	2.04	.76
5.00	3.17	4.48	4.52	5.11	1.89
10.00	6.34	8.95	9.04	10.21	3.78
20.00	12.68	17.90	18.07	20.42	7.56
50.00	31.71	44.76	45.18	51.05	18.90
100.00	63.41	89.52	90.36	102.10	37.79
500.00	317.05	447.60	451.80	510.50	188.95
1000.00	624.10	895.20	903.60	1021.00	377.90

fat, gold-colored $1. Singapore has an interchangeability agreement with Brunei, so the Brunei dollar is accepted as equal to the Singapore dollar.

At the time of this writing, exchange rates on the Singapore dollar were as follows: US$1 = S$1.57, Canadian $1 = S$1.12, British Pound £1 = S$2.64, Australian $1 = S$1.10, New Zealand $1 = S98¢. These are the exchange rates used throughout this book, but before you begin budgeting your trip, I suggest you obtain the latest conversions so you don't suffer any shocks at the last minute. A neat and easy money conversion program can be found on the Internet through CNN's Web site at **www.cnn.com/TRAVEL/CURRENCY**.

EXCHANGING MONEY

While hotels and banks will perform currency exchanges, you'll get a better rate at any one of the many money changers that can be found in all the shopping malls and major shopping districts (look for the certificate of government authorization). Many shops are also authorized to change money, and will display signs to that effect. Money changers usually give you the official going rate for the day, and sometimes the difference in rate between hotels and money changers can be as much as US8¢ to the dollar. Lastly, while some hotels and shops may accept your foreign currency, they will always calculate the exchange rate in their favor.

GETTING CASH ON THE SPOT

Singapore has thousands of conveniently located 24-hour **automated teller machines** (ATMs). With debit cards on the MasterCard/Cirrus or Visa/PLUS systems, you can withdraw Singapore currency from any of these machines, and your bank will deduct the amount from your account at the going exchange rate. This is a very good way to access cash for the most favorable currency rate, but make sure you check with your bank before you leave home, to find out what your daily withdrawal limits are. If you're unsure where the nearest ATM is, ATM locator services are available through MasterCard/Cirrus and Visa/PLUS. Dial the operator, request an international collect call, and then dial ☎ **314/275-6690** for MasterCard/Cirrus or ☎ **410/581-7931** for Visa/PLUS dial. They'll be glad to help you find one.

What Things Cost in Singapore

Taxi from the airport to city center	S$22–S$25 (US$14–US$16)
MRT from Orchard to Jurong West stations	S$1.30 (US80¢)
Local telephone call	S30¢ (US20¢)
Double room at an expensive hotel	S$450 (US$283)
Double room at a moderate hotel	S$250 (US$157)
Double room at an inexpensive hotel	S$150 (US$94.35)
Dinner for one at an expensive restaurant	S$100 (US$62.90)
Dinner for one at a moderate restaurant	S$40 (US$25.15)
Dinner for one at an inexpensive restaurant	S$15 (US$9.45)
Glass of beer	S$10.00 (US$6.30)
Coca-Cola	S90¢ (US60¢)
Cup of coffee at common coffee shop	S70¢ (US 45¢)
Cup of coffee at Starbucks, Coffee Club etc.	S$4 (US$2.50)
Roll of 36-exposure color film	S$4 (US$2.50)
Admission to the National History Museum	S$15.00 (US$9.40)
Movie ticket	S$7 (US$4.40)

TRAVELER'S CHECKS

The two most easily recognizable traveler's checks in Singapore are from **American Express** and **Thomas Cook.** They can be cashed at banks and hotels, but money changers will cash them at the day's official exchange rate (as opposed to charging a fee or giving their own rate). Upon occasion they may try to charge a fee, but if you indicate you'll take your business elsewhere they may change their minds. To cash a traveler's check you will need to show your passport. Occasionally, an international driver's license or your driver's license from home will suffice.

CREDIT CARDS

American Express (AE) is accepted widely, as are Diners Club (DC), MasterCard (MC), EuroCard (EC), Japan Credit Bureau (JCB), and Visa (V), though you'll find that some budget hotels, smaller shops, and restaurants will accept no credit cards at all. Purchases made with credit cards will appear on your bill at the exchange rate on the day your charge is posted, *not* what the rate was on the day the purchase was made. It's also worth noting that if your signature is slightly different on the slip than it is on your card, shop owners will make you re-do the slip. They're real sticklers for signature details, so don't leave out a middle initial or forget to cross a T.

Because of the number of travel services it offers, **American Express** is a recommended asset for all travelers. Their Charge Card Guarantee Service, for instance, allows you to cash personal checks up to US$1,000 every 21 calendar days while you travel. (Note that if the checks are not honored by your financial institution, American Express will charge it to your bill and will freeze your account until the entire amount is recovered.) Also available is their Sign and Travel Service. Sign up prior to your trip, and if you qualify, purchases of US$350 and over that are made toward air travel, hotel accommodations, cruises, and tour packages can be paid off in installments in a revolving credit account. Similarly, the Special Purchases Account lets you opt to make payments on retail purchases of US$350 or more. Also neat if you plan to be away for a long period is their World Travel Service, which allows you to temporarily forward your mail (letters only) to American Express offices anywhere in the world, where it will be held until you pick it up. And finally, their Global Assist program will help you recover lost or stolen bags, offer medical referrals in the event of emergencies, or even help you find legal council should you be unfortunate enough to require it. For more information, check AmEx's Web site at **www. americanexpress.com**.

In Singapore, the American Express office is located at #01-04/05 Winslan House, Killiney Road (a short walk from Orchard Road). The direct line for travel services is ☎ **65/235-5788.** The 24-hour membership services hot line is ☎ 1800/ 732-2244. The 24-hour traveler's check refund hot line is ☎ 1800/738-3383.

MasterCard has toll-free access to report lost or stolen cards. Dial the operator and request an international collect call. The number is ☎ **314/275-6690.** MasterCard will notify your issuing institution and get an emergency card to you or help you access emergency cash. MasterCard's local Singapore number is ☎ **65/533-2888,** and their Web site is **www.mastercard.com**.

Visa's toll-free access is also through an international collect call to ☎ **410/ 581-7931.** Visa will also notify your issuing institution, get you an emergency card, and help you access emergency cash. Visa's local number is ☎ **65/224-9033,** and their Web site is at **www.visa.com**.

For both MasterCard and Visa, there are other services available, but it depends on the type of card you hold and the institution that issued it. Contact your issuing institution prior to your trip to find out what travel benefits you're eligible to receive.

WIRING FUNDS

Although other travel books report the contrary, Western Union does not operate in Singapore. However, there are alternatives. **Thomas Cook Overseas Ltd.** can wire funds to and from other international Thomas Cook locations or can wire money from any Thomas Cook to your bank account. The transfer service costs US$35 plus 1% of the amount. Also through the Thomas Cook office, you can send and receive MoneyGram transfers. Fees are based on a percent scale and range from about US$12 for a US$100 transfer to US$50 for a US$1,000 transfer. Either wire transfer option takes only 10 to 15 minutes to send or receive money. Thomas Cook will also draft cashier's checks in foreign currencies. Should you need this service, it costs US$10. The Singaporean Thomas Cook office is located at 79 Anson Rd. #22-03, beside the Harbour View Hotel (☎ 65/222-9928).

3 When to Go

CLIMATE

At approximately 137 kilometers (82 miles) north of the equator, with exposure to the sea on three sides, you can make a sure bet that Singapore will be hot and humid year-round. Temperatures remain uniform, with a daily average of 80.6°F (26.7°C), afternoon temperatures reaching as high as 87.44°F (30.8°C), and an average sunrise temperature as low as 75.03°F (23.9°C). Relative humidity often exceeds 90% at night and in the early morning. Even on a "dry" afternoon, don't expect it to drop much below 60%. The daily average is 84.4% relative humidity. Rain falls year-round, much of it coming down in sudden downpours that end abruptly and are followed immediately by the sun. Don't expect it to cool off any after a shower, though. On the contrary, downpours leave the air thick and heavy as water quickly evaporates from pavement and hot surfaces. The annual rainfall is 94.08 inches (2,352mm).

The Northeast Monsoon occurs between December and March, when temperatures are slightly cooler, relatively speaking, than other times of the year. Even in December, though, one of the "cooler" months, you can still break a sweat past midnight. The heaviest rainfall occurs between November and January. The Southwest Monsoon falls between June and September. Temperatures are higher and July reports the lowest recorded average rainfall. In between monsoons, thunderstorms are frequent. Also interesting, the number of daylight hours and number of nighttime hours remains almost constant year-round. February is the sunniest month, while December is generally more overcast.

While these seasons are called monsoons, they are not necessarily of the "bend the palms and blow your beach shack down" variety. While the Northeast Monsoon month of January brings the heaviest rainfall, for the most part the rain comes down in short heavy gusts and goes quickly away. Wind speeds are rarely anything more than light. As for the Southwest Monsoon, it is during this time of year when Singapore gets the *least* rain. The monsoons therefore are merely to keep track of the wind directions, which at one time were important for sea merchants, but nowadays are only a distinction between what small seasonal changes Singapore has.

CLOTHING CONSIDERATIONS

Common sense will tell you that the ideal clothes to pack are lightweight, loose fitting, and of natural fibers. To ward off the tropical heat, many public places are air-conditioned to Arctic-freeze temperatures, so it's a good idea to bring a light sweater or jacket so you'll have something warm if you're stuck in the theater, in a restaurant, or on a tour bus for hours—it's also helpful if you plan on going in and out of air-conditioning frequently throughout the day. These types of sudden temperature changes have been known to ruin many vacations with summer colds.

Another good consideration is to bring shoes that fit you very loosely. If you come from colder climates, your feet will swell from the heat, as well as from being on them all day while you're taking in the sights. Don't even trust your favorite pair. If they're a snug fit, they'll turn into your worst enemies before long, and nothing feels worse than having to pinch your feet into tight and uncomfortable shoes when you want to have fun.

For sightseeing, shorts and T-shirts are probably the most comfortable attire, but keep in mind if you plan to visit a mosque that neither men nor women are permitted to wear shorts, and women are not permitted to wear miniskirts or sleeveless, backless, or low-cut tops. As for footwear, if you can find slip-on shoes that are comfortable for walking, they'd be the most convenient, as all mosques, temples, and private residences will require you to remove your shoes at the door.

Most restaurants and nightclubs will request attire that is **dress casual,** meaning a shirt and slacks for men and a dress or skirt/slacks and top for women. Because of the heat, many places are forgiving when it comes to dress codes—you can't be expected to be a fashion plate all the time—however, when formal attire is required, you should take it seriously. Men will be expected to appear in a jacket and tie and women in dress slacks or a formal dress. This will only be the case at very expensive restaurants or high-toned events.

CALENDAR OF PUBLIC HOLIDAYS & EVENTS

There are eleven official public holidays: New Year's Day, Lunar New Year or Chinese New Year (2 days), Hari Raya Puasa, Good Friday, Labour Day, Hari Raya Haji,

Vesak Day, National Day, Deepavali, and Christmas Day. On these days, expect government offices, banks, and some shops to be closed.

Holidays and festivals are well publicized by the **Singapore Tourism Board (STB),** which loves to introduce the world to the joys of all Singapore's cultures. A stop by an STB office either prior to your trip or when you arrive will let you know the what, where, and when of what's happening.

The headquarters for STB in Singapore is at Tourism Court, 1 Orchard Spring Lane, across the street from Traders Hotel (☎ **65/736-6622;** fax 65/736-9423). Their toll-free number in Singapore is ☎ **1800/738-3778** or 1800/738-3779.

In the U.S.: In New York STB is located at 590 Fifth Ave., 12th Floor, New York, NY 10036 (☎ **212/302-4861;** fax 212/302-4801); in Chicago, Two Prudential Plaza, 180N Stetson Ave., Suite 1450, Chicago, IL 60601 (☎ **312/938-1888;** fax 312/938-0086); and in California, 8484 Wilshire Blvd., Suite 510, Beverly Hills, CA (☎ **213/852-1901;** fax 213/852-0129). **In Canada:** Look for STB at The Standard Life Centre, 121 King St. West, Suite 1000, Toronto, Ontario, Canada M5H 3T9 (☎ **416/363-8898;** fax 416/363-5752). **In the U.K.:** 1st Floor, Carrington House, 126–130 Regent St., London W1R 5FEm, United Kingdom (☎ **71/437-0033;** fax 71/734-2191). STB has a regional office for **Australia and New Zealand** at Level 11, AWA Building, 47 York St., Sydney NSW 2000, Australia (☎ **2/241-3771** or 2/241-3772; fax 2/252-3586).

January/February

- **New Year's Day.** The first day of the calendar year is celebrated in Singapore by all races and religions. New Year's Eve in Singapore is always cause for parties and celebrations similar to those in the West. January 1.

- ☼ **Lunar New Year or Chinese New Year.** If you want to catch the biggest event in the Chinese calendar and pretty much the biggest in Singapore, come during the Chinese New Year celebrations, which include parades and festivals. Two days, late January / early February. For details, see the box in this chapter.

- ☼ **Thaipusam Festival.** If you're lucky enough to be in Singapore during this event, you're in for a bizarre cultural treat. This annual festival is celebrated by Hindus to give thanks to Lord Subramaniam, the child god who represents virtue, youth, beauty, and valor. During Thaipusam, male Hindus who have made prayers to Subramaniam for special wishes must carry *kavadis* in gratitude. These huge steel racks are decorated with flowers and fruits and are held onto the men's bodies by skewers and hooks that pierce the skin. Carrying the *kavadis,* the devotees parade from Sri Perumal Temple in Little India to Chettiar's Temple on Tank Road, where family members remove the heavy structures. For an additional spectacle, they will pierce their tongues and cheeks with skewers and hang fruits from hooks in their flesh. The devotees have all undergone strict diet and prayer before the festival, and it is reported that, afterward, no scars remain. Late January / early February.

- **Hari Raya Puasa.** Hari Raya Puasa marks the end of Ramadan, the Muslim month of fasting during daylight hours. During Ramadan, food stalls line up around the Sultan Mosque in Kampong Glam, ready to sell Malay and Indian food at sundown. It's a 3-day celebration (though only the first day is a public holiday) of thanksgiving dinners, and non-Muslims are often invited to these feasts, as the holiday symbolizes an openness of heart and mind and a renewed sense of community. During the course of the 3 evenings, Geylang, the area around Geylang Road, is decorated with lights and banners and the whole area is open for a giant *pasar malam,* or night market. Late January / early February.

Ringing in the New Year, Chinese-Style

Chinese New Year, a 15-day celebration of the new year according to the Lunar Calendar, is the most important festival of the Chinese culture and a huge occasion in Singapore. It was originally called *Chun Jie* or Spring Festival, to celebrate the passing of winter and spring's promise of a fertile and prosperous growing season. In modern times, it is still seen as a chance to put the past behind and start afresh, with new hopes for prosperity, health, and luck. During the celebration, homes and businesses display large red banners with the characters *Gong Xi Fa Cai,* which mean "Wishing you great prosperity." Stores generally mark up prices dramatically just before the New Year to cash in on the opportunity. Outside of homes, the Chinese hang the character Fu, which means "luck." The fu is usually hung upside down because in Chinese the words for "luck upside down" sound similar to the words for "luck arrives." Red, symbolizing luck and prosperity, is predominant in banners and is the color of the *hong bao,* packets of money given to children and single young adults by parents and married friends. Money is given in even dollar amounts (as even numbers are considered auspicious) and should be opened in private. Oranges and tangerines are given as gifts (also in even numbers), symbolizing gold and luck, both in their colors and in Chinese puns. Also important are noisy firecrackers, which are believed to ward off evil spirits and also serve (through their noise) as a sign of life. Unfortunately, firecrackers are banned in Singapore, so you won't find much of that going on.

New Year's Day, the first day of celebration, generally falls somewhere between January 21 and February 19. In preparation for New Year's Day, the Chinese pay off old debts, since debt is believed to lead to bad luck in the coming year if not taken care of, and clean their homes from tip to toe, sweeping the floors in a symbolic clearing away of old misfortunes. All cleaning is done before New Year's Eve, because New Year's Day is auspicious, and to sweep on this day would be to sweep away good luck. (So hide your broom.) New Year's Eve is the night of the reunion feast, where family members gather and invite the spirits of deceased ancestors to gather for a meal, the centerpiece of which is a large fish to symbolize unity.

New Year's is a time for rejoicing with family and friends, praying to ancestors, and going to the Chingay parade, a brilliant procession of dragon dances, stiltwalkers, and floats, that heads down Orchard Road. All meals taken are vegetarian, so as not to kill living creatures and invite bad vibes. While the first and second days are spent visiting friends and family, the third is considered unlucky for visiting, and most people return to work.

The final day of the celebration, the 15th day, is the Lantern Festival, which coincides with the first full moon of the new year. Paper lanterns are hung in doorways, which to Westerners is a romantic backdrop for this day, which the Chinese consider auspicious for lovers.

March/April

- **Good Friday.** Churches and cathedrals hold special services on this Christian holiday to commemorate the death of Christ. St. Joseph's on Victoria Street holds an annual candlelight procession. Late March / early April.
- **Qing Ming (All Souls' Day).** Qing Ming, or All Souls' Day, was originally a celebration of spring. On this day, Chinese families have picnics at ancestral graves, cleaning the graves and pulling weeds, lighting red candles, burning joss sticks and "Hell Money" (paper money whose smoke rises to the afterworld to be used by the

ancestors) and bringing rice, wine, and flowers for the deceased in a show of ancestral piety. Early April.

- **The Singapore International Film Festival.** This event showcases critically acclaimed works, including international films and Singaporean short productions. It has become a renowned showcase for Asian films, which constitute 40% of films featured. The festival includes competitions, workshops, and tributes to filmmakers. Information can be obtained from the **Festival Secretariat** at ☎ **65/ 738-7567.** You can get tickets by calling the **TicketCharge Hotline** at ☎ **65/ 296-2929.** April.

- **Hari Raya Haji.** One of the five pillars of Islam involves making a pilgrimage to Mecca at least once during your lifetime, and Hari Raya Haji is celebrated the day after pilgrims make this annual voyage to fulfill their spiritual promise. Muslims who have made the journey adopt the title of Haji (for men) and Hajjah (for women). After morning prayers, sheep and goats are sacrificed and their meat is distributed to poor families. Late April / early May.

May

- **Vesak Day.** Buddhist shrines and temples are adorned with banners, lights, and flowers and worshippers gather to pray and chant in observance of the birth, enlightenment, and Nirvana of the Buddha. Good places to watch the festivities, unless you're afraid of crowds, are the Temple of a Thousand Lights in Little India or Thian Hock Keng Temple in Chinatown. On this day, Buddhists will refrain from eating meat, donate food to the poor, and set animals (especially birds) free to show kindness and generosity. It falls on the full moon of the fifth month of the lunar calendar—which means somewhere around mid-May.

June

- ✪ **Festival of Asian Performing Arts.** During this month-long festival, first-class local, regional, and international music and dance performances are staged in a number of venues. The cultural performances, some modern and some traditional, are always excellent and are highly recommended. Contact the Singapore Tourism Board (STB) for a full program with details of each event. Information can be obtained from the **National Arts Council** at ☎ **65/270-0722.** June.

July

- **The Singapore Food Festival.** Local chefs compete for honors in this month-long exhibition of international culinary delights. It's a good time to be eating in Singapore, as restaurants feature the brand-new creations they have entered in the events. Contact the **STB** for details. July.

- **The Great Singapore Sale.** This is a month-long promotion to increase retail sales, and most shops will advertise huge savings for the entire month. It's well publicized with red banners all over Orchard Road. July.

- **Singapore World Invitational Dragon Boat Races.** The annual dragon boat races are held to remember the fate of Qu Yuan, a patriot and poet during the Warring States period in Chinese history, who threw himself into a river to end the suffering of watching his state fall into ruin under the hands of corrupt leadership. The people searched for him in boats shaped like dragons, beating gongs and throwing rice dumplings into the water to distract the River Dragon. Today, the dragon boat races are an international event, with rowing teams from 20 countries coming together to compete. Drums are still beaten, and rice dumplings are still a traditional favorite. Contact the **STB** for information. Late June / early July.

- **Maulidin Nabi.** Muslims celebrate the birth of the Prophet Mohammed on this day. Sultan Mosque is the center of the action for Muslims who come to chant in praise. July 17.

August

✪ **National Day.** On August 9, 1965, Singapore separated from the Federation of Malaysia, becoming an independent republic. Singaporeans celebrate this as a sort of independence day, with a grand parade with spectacular floats and marching bands. They also stage a fireworks display in the evening. August 9.

• **Festival of the Hungry Ghosts.** The Chinese believe that once a year the gates of purgatory are opened and all the souls inside are let loose to wander among the living. These are the poor souls who either died violent deaths or whose families failed to pay them respects after they died—fates that cause them to menace people as much as they can. To appease the spirits and prevent evil from falling upon themselves, the Chinese burn joss, Hell money, and paper replicas of luxury items, the latter two meant to appear in the afterworld for greedy ghosts to use. The main celebration is on the 15th day of the 7th month of the lunar calendar, and is celebrated with huge feasts to settle hungry ghosts. At markets, altars are placed under tents. Chinese operas are performed throughout the month to entertain the spirits and make them more docile. For information on these performances, try calling the **Singapore Amateur Players,** Telok Ayer Street (☎ **65/221-5684**), or the **Chinese Opera Institute,** 111 Middle Rd. (☎ **65/339-1292**). During the festival, Chinese opera is everywhere, though the performances are usually unannounced—the troupes just throw up tents in the street. Begins in August and lasts for 1 month.

September

• **The Mooncake and Lantern Festivals.** Traditionally called the mid-autumn festival, it was celebrated to give thanks for a plentiful harvest. The origins date back to the Sung Dynasty, when Chinese officials would exchange round mirrors as gifts to represent the moon and symbolize good health and success. Today, the holiday is celebrated by eating mooncakes, which are sort of like little round hockey pucks filled with lotus seeds or red bean paste and a salted duck egg yolk. Children light colorful plastic or paper lanterns shaped like fish, birds, butterflies, and more recently, cartoon characters. There's an annual lantern display and competition out at the Chinese Garden, with acrobatic performances, lion dances and night bazaars. Late September / early October.

October/November

• **Navarathiri Festival.** During this 9-day festival, Hindus make offerings to the wives of Shiva, Vishnu, and Brahma. The center point in the evenings is Chettiar's Temple (at 15 Tank Rd.), where dances and musical performances are staged. Performances begin around 7:30pm. Contact the **STB** for information. Late October / early November.

• **Deepavali.** Hindus and Sikhs celebrate Deepavali as the first day of their calendar. The new year is ushered in with new clothing, social feasts, and gatherings. It's a beautiful holiday, with Hindu temples aglow from the tiny earthen candles placed in cutouts up the sides of the buildings. Hindus believe that the souls of the deceased come to earth during this time, and the candles help to light their way back to heaven. During the celebration, **Serangoon Road** in Little India is a crazy display of colored lights and decorative arches. Children love this holiday, as it is customary to hand out sweets, especially to the little ones, and many businessmen choose this time to close their books from the year's accounts and start afresh. Late October / early November.

✪ **Thimithi Festival.** Thimithi begins at the Sri Perumal Temple in Little India and makes its way in parade fashion to the Sri Mariamman Temple in Chinatown. Outside the temple, a bed of hot coals is prepared and a priest will lead the way, walking first over the coals, to be followed one at a time by devotees. Crowds gather to watch the spectacle, which begins around 5pm. Make sure you're early so you can find a good spot. Contact the **STB** for information. Late October / early November.

- **Birthday of the Monkey God.** In the Chinese temples ceremonies are performed by mediums who pierce their faces and tongues and write prayers with the blood. In the temple courtyards you can see Chinese operas and puppet shows. The **Tan Si Chong Su Temple** on Magazine Road, upriver from Boat Quay, is a good bet for seeing the ceremonies. Contact the **STB** for information. Late September / early October.

- **Festival of the Nine-Emperor God.** Celebrated on the first 9 days of the 9th month of the lunar calendar (to the Chinese, the double nines are particularly auspicious), the temples are packed with worshippers and hawkers sell religious items outside. Chinese operas are performed for the Nine-Emperor God, who is made of nine former emperors who control the prosperity and health of worshippers. At the height of the festival, priests write prayers with their own blood. On the 9th day, the festival closes as the Nine-Emperor God's spirit, contained in an urn, is sent to sea on a small decorated boat. Contact the **STB** for information. Late October.

- **Pilgrimage to Kusu Island.** During this month-long period, plan your trips to Kusu Island wisely, as the place becomes a mob scene. Throughout the month (the lunar month, that is), Chinese travel to this small island to visit the temple there and pray for another year of health and wealth. October/November.

December

- **Christmas Light-Up.** Orchard Road is brilliant in bright and colorful streams of Christmas lights and garlands. All of the hotels and shopping malls participate, dressed in the usual Christmas regalia of nativity scenes and Santa Clauses. November 15 through January 2.

- **Christmas Day.** On this day, Christian Singaporeans celebrate the birth of Christ. December 25.

4 Health & Insurance

BEATING THE HEAT & HUMIDITY   As Singapore's climate guarantees heat and humidity year-round, you should remember to take precautions. Make sure you give yourself plenty of time to relax and regroup on arrival to adjust your body to the new climate (and to the new time, if there is a time difference for you). Also, *drink plenty of water.* This may seem obvious, but remember that tea, coffee, colas, and alcohol dehydrate the body and should never be substituted for water if you're thirsty. Singapore's tap water is absolutely potable, so you don't have to worry about any wee beasties floating around in your glass.

Avoid overexposure to the sun. The tropical sun will burn you like thin toast in no time at all. You may also feel more lethargic than usual. This is typical in the heat, so take things easy and you'll be fine. Be careful of the air-conditioning, though. It's nice and cooling, but if you're prone to catching a chill, or find yourself moving in and out of air-conditioned buildings a lot, you can wind up with a horrible summer cold.

DIETARY PRECAUTIONS   Generally speaking, you'll have no more problems with the food in Singapore than you will in your home town, barring any digestive bugaboos you may experience simply because you're not used to the ingredients. All the same sanitary rules apply, too—for instance, as at home, you should thoroughly wash any fruits or vegetables you buy, to rinse away any bacteria.

Chinese restaurants in Singapore still use monosodium glutamate (MSG), the flavor enhancer that was blamed for everything from fluid retention to migraine headaches, and has been squeezed out of most Chinese restaurant cuisine in the West. The MSG connection has just started to catch on here, but not in full force. Most places are slow to alter recipes, but it's sure to happen in the coming years. If you know you're particularly sensitive to the stuff, you may want to dine elsewhere.

VACCINATIONS   Singapore doesn't require that you have any vaccinations to enter the country, but strongly recommends immunization against diphtheria, tetanus, hepatitis A and B, and typhoid. If you're particularly worried, follow their advice; if you're the intrepid type, ignore it.

TROPICAL DISEASES   While there's no risk of contracting malaria (the country's been declared malaria-free for decades by the World Health Organization), there is a similar deadly virus—**dengue fever**—that's carried by mosquitoes and has no immunization. Dengue fever is a problem in the tropics around the world; however, Singapore has an aggressive campaign to prevent the responsible mosquitoes from breeding, spraying dark corners with insecticide and enforcing laws so people mop up pools of stagnant water. Symptoms of dengue fever, also just called dengue, include sudden fever and tiny red spotty rashes on the body. If you suspect you've contracted dengue, seek medical attention immediately (see the listing of hospitals under "Fast Facts" in chapter 3). If gone untreated, this disease can cause internal hemorrhaging and even death. Your best protection is to wear insect repellent, especially if you are heading out to the zoo, bird park, or any of the gardens or nature preserves.

OCEAN SAFETY   The worst thing that can happen to you in the ocean is injury caused by sea creatures. Sea urchins crawl along the ocean bed, and stonefish, sting rays, and cone shells will sting if provoked. Even if you're staying in by the shore, at certain times of the year jellyfish get washed in pretty close. The best protection is to wear hard rubber tennis shoes or fins at all times while in the water—and don't taunt any strange fish.

If you're unfortunate enough to get a sea urchin splinter, you can neutralize the poison by soaking the wound in hot water for 30 minutes to an hour. The spines can't be removed like splinters, but if they're small, your body can dissolve them. If they're large, seek medical attention.

Stings from creatures like stonefish, sting rays, and cone shells can be very painful and can even lead to respiratory paralysis. If you are stung, remain calm and, if possible, try to keep the wound well below the level of your heart. You can put hot water on the wound and use a tourniquet (not on a joint), but be sure to seek medical attention for all such injuries.

For jellyfish stings, first douse the wound with a disinfectant and put on meat tenderizer. (Which I'm sure you'll just happen to have in your beach kit!) Don't rub the area; instead, sprinkle talcum powder on it, which causes the stings to stick together, and scrape them off.

DANGEROUS ANIMALS & PLANTS   Singapore has a whole slew of **snakes,** and they're not only in the deepest, darkest parts of the island—sometimes, they're forced from their homes by construction and left to look for trouble in more populated areas. The venomous kinds are cobras, kraits, coral snakes, pit vipers, and sea snakes. If you encounter a sea snake, don't splash around, as this will just encourage an attack.

If you're bitten by a snake, keep yourself calm, try to position the wounded area below the level of your heart, and wrap a tourniquet loosely above the wound (but not on a joint). Don't take any aspirin or other medications unless it's an over-the-counter pain reliever that doesn't contain aspirin. There are only two facilities in Singapore with snake antivenin; these are **Singapore General Hospital** (☎ 65/321-4103) and **National University Hospital** (☎ 65/772-5000).

Dangerous insects are scorpions, spiders, centipedes, bees, and wasps. If stung, wash the area with disinfectant and apply ice to reduce the pain and prevent the venom from being absorbed further. If you have an allergic reaction, seek medical help.

There are a lot of **plants** in Singapore that have poisonous parts. Some of the more common ones are common bamboo, arcea palm, frangipani, mango tree, papaya, and tapioca. Only parts of these plants are poisonous. If you're unsure, just don't nibble on anything strange. For more information, contact the **Poison Information Centre** (☎ 65/225-5333).

INSURANCE

Before you travel, check to see what kind of theft, medical, and emergency coverage you have on your present insurance policies, whether automobile, medical, or homeowner's—some have coverage for travel emergencies. Also, some credit cards offer assistance or coverage in many travel-related emergencies, including, sometimes, flight cancellation coverage. Many tour operators offer standard coverage or coverage for a small fee. If you decide you'd like more complete coverage, there are companies that offer emergency insurance on a short-term basis specifically for travel abroad. These include **Access America**, 6600 W. Broad St., Richmond, VA 23230 (☎ 800/284-8300); **Insure America / Travel Guard International**, 1145 Clark St., Stevens Point, WI 54481 (☎ 800/826-1300); **Tele-Trip Company,** Mutual of Omaha Plaza, Omaha, NE 68175 (☎ 800/228-9792); and **Travel Insurance International**, Travelers Insurance Co., P.O. Box 280568, Hartford, CT 06128-0568 (☎ 800/243-3174).

5 Tips for Travelers with Special Needs

TRAVELERS WITH DISABILITIES   There's a handy free guide called *Access Singapore,* put together by the Singapore Council of Social Services, which lists information on places that are accessible for everyone. To get one, contact either the **National Council of Social Services** at ☎ 65/336-1544 or the **Singapore Tourism Board (STB)** at ☎ 65/738-3778. (See "Visitors Information" earlier in this chapter for international STB offices.)

SENIORS   Most attractions and museums have discounted admission for people over 60 years of age. Hotels, airlines, and tour operators will also quote you discounted packages if you request senior rates.

The **STB** will also help plan your trip, and can offer their own advice for senior travelers. Regarding this service, here's my advice: If you work out your itinerary with the help of STB, make sure you're firm about time constraints. Many of the tours and daily itineraries are rushed, with little time for a rest here and there. A common complaint is exhaustion by the end of just 1 day. In the heat, this is not only uncomfortable, but dangerous as well.

GAY & LESBIAN TRAVELERS   Naturally, the conservative government frowns on alternative lifestyles, but even though it's illegal to practice homosexual acts, gay and lesbian culture is alive and well in Singapore. What you'll find is that older gays and lesbians are paranoid and therefore less open to discussion, while the younger generations have very few qualms about describing the local scene and their personal experiences as a gay or lesbian in Singapore.

There are tons of Web sites on the Internet for gays and lesbians in Singapore. Start at **www2.best.com/~utopia/tipssing.htm** for travel advice and links to other sites with personal opinion and commentary by locals.

Chapter 9 lists some gay and lesbian clubs and karaoke lounges that are all nice places with friendly folks.

FAMILIES   Because of their focus on business travelers, hotels in Singapore are not especially geared toward children. You can get extra beds in hotel rooms (this can cost anywhere from S$15 to S$50/US$9.50 to US$31.50 each), and most hotels will arrange a baby-sitter for you on request, though most ask for at least 24 hours notice. While almost all hotels have pools to keep the kiddies cool and happy, only two, the **YMCA International House** and **Metro YMCA,** have lifeguards on duty, and only one—**Shangri-La's Rasa Sentosa Resort**—has activity programs specifically for children. See chapter 4 for more information on these hotels.

Children have their own special rates of admission for just about every attraction and museum. The cutoff age for children is usually 12 years of age, but if your kids are older, be sure to ask if they have a student rate for teens. If the kids get edgy during the "boring" parts of the trip, plan a morning trip to the **Singapore Zoological Gardens** or out to Sentosa Island's **Fantasy Island water park.** These are the two places where I can almost guarantee they (and you) will have a great time.

In Singapore, childhood innocence is revered, so you will rarely find crimes being committed against them. You can rest assured that if your child is missing, he or she is probably just around the corner looking for you—maybe even with the help of a concerned Singaporean.

Given the strictures of Muslim culture, women who are **breast-feeding** should strictly limit the activity to private places. In the West it may be a statement, but here it'll just freak people out.

BUSINESS TRAVELERS   Businesspeople, Singapore is your town. Every hotel has special accommodations for business travelers, which can include nicer rooms; higher floors; free extras such as newspapers, shoe shines, and suit pressings; and club lounges where you can have a free breakfast and evening cocktails while you watch CNN or work on one of the hotel's PCs.

Most multinational corporations have accounts with major hotel chains, so your firm may tell you where to stay. If you make your arrangements on your own, though, remember that every hotel has a corporate rate, which is sometimes up to 40% off the going room rate.

Refer to the "Singaporean Etiquette & Customs" section of chapter 1 before your first meeting, so you know how to greet people and trade business cards in the appropriate style.

6 Getting There

BY PLANE

If you're hunting for the best airfare, there are a few things you can do. First, plan your trip for the low-volume season, which runs from September 1 to November 30. Between January 1 and May 31, you'll pay the highest fares. Plan your travel on weekdays only, and, if you can, plan to stay for at least 1 week. Book your reservations in advance—waiting until the last minute can mean you'll pay sky-high rates. Also, if you have access to the Internet, there are a number of great sites that'll search out super fares for you. See the **"CyberDeals for Net Surfers"** feature earlier in this chapter.

FROM THE U.S.

Singapore Airlines (☎ 800/742-3333; www.singaporeair.com) has a daily flight from New York, two daily flights from Los Angeles, and two daily flights from San Francisco (only one on Sunday).

United Airlines (☎ 800/241-6522; www.ual.com) has daily flights from both Los Angeles and San Francisco.

In partnership with Singapore Airlines, **Delta Airlines** (☎ 800/221-1212; www.delta-air.com) offers a daily flight from New York aboard the Singapore Airlines flight. You can use or accumulate Delta frequent-flyer miles for the trip.

Northwest Airlines (☎ 800/447-4747; www.nwa.com) has a daily afternoon flight from Minneapolis via Tokyo, with daily departures from Detroit, Los Angeles, New York, San Francisco, and Seattle connecting to Singapore through either Tokyo/Narita or Hong Kong.

FROM CANADA

Singapore Airlines (☎ 800/742-3333; www.singaporeair.com) has morning flights on Monday and Saturday and an afternoon flight on Thursday, all from Vancouver.

FROM AUSTRALIA

Singapore Airlines (☎ 131011 for all Australia; www.singaporeair.com) has daily flights from Melbourne; twice-daily flights from Sydney and Perth; flights from Adelaide on Tuesday, Thursday, and Saturday; from Brisbane on Monday, Tuesday, Thursday, and Saturday; from Cairns on Monday, Tuesday, and Saturday; and from Darwin on Tuesday.

Quantas Airways Ltd. (☎ 131211; www.quantas.com) has daily flights from Cairns and Darwin, at least two flights daily from Sydney and Perth, and four flights weekly from Adelaide, Brisbane, and Melbourne.

British Airways (☎ 322/223-3123 in Brisbane or 425-7711 in Perth; www.british-airways.com) has daily flights from Perth and flights from Brisbane each day but Thursday and Friday.

Royal Dutch Airlines (KLM) (☎ 1800/505747; www.klm.nl) has flights from Sydney.

Gulf Air, Egypt Air, and **Emirates** also fly routes from Australia to Singapore.

FROM NEW ZEALAND

Singapore Airlines (☎ 3032129 in Auckland or 3668003 in Christchurch; www.singaporeair.com) has daily flights from Auckland and Christchurch.

Air New Zealand (☎ 0800/737000; www.airnewzealand.co.nz) has daily flights from Christchurch and a daily Singapore Airlines flight from Auckland (so you can use or accumulate frequent-flyer miles).

FROM THE U.K.

Singapore Airlines (☎ 7470007 in London or 4895768 in Manchester; www.singaporeair.com) has two daily flights departing from London's Heathrow Airport and flights four times a week departing from Manchester.

British Airways (☎ 0345/222111 local call from anywhere within the U.K.; www.british-airways.com) has daily flights from London.

Quantas Airways Ltd. (☎ 0345/747767; www.quantas.com) has daily flights on weekdays and flights twice daily on weekends from London.

Royal Brunei Airlines also runs service from London.

GETTING INTO TOWN FROM THE AIRPORT

Most visitors to Singapore will land at **Changi International Airport,** which is located toward the far eastern corner of the island. The airport's two terminals are very modern and clean, with in-transit accommodations, restaurants, duty-free shops, money changers, ATMs, car rental desks, accommodation assistance, and tourist information.

The city is easily accessible by public transportation. **A taxi trip** to the city center will cost around S$22 to S$25 (US$14 to US$15) and take around 20 minutes. You'll traverse the wide Airport Boulevard to the Pan-Island Expressway (PIE), past public housing estates and other residential neighborhoods in the eastern part of the island, over causeways, and into the city center.

A number of **buses** run from the airport into the city as well. Bus nos. 16 and 16E, whose stops are located in the basement level, will take you on a route to Orchard Road and Raffles City (in the Historic District). Bus nos. 24 and 34 will take you to Tanah Merah MRT (subway) station, from which you can access most major areas.

For **arrival and departure information,** you can call Changi International Airport toll-free at ☎ **1800/542-4422.**

BY TRAIN

The Keretapi Tanah Melayu Berhad railroad company runs express and local trains from **Thailand to Singapore** four times daily. There's a line up the west coast making stops in Johor Bahru, Malacca, Kuala Lumpur, and almost every other town in between. Another line branches off this line halfway to Kuala Lumpur and heads northeast to Kota Bahru.

In Kuala Lumpur, you can pick up the train at the Central Railway Station on Jalan Hishamuddin (☎ 274-7435). The trip to Singapore costs between RM17 (US$3.75) for third-class passage and RM55 (US$12.20) for first-class air-conditioned passage, and takes around 6 hours to complete. There is a daily mail train from Kuala Lumpur that'll cost about half as much, but takes 10 hours. In **Johor Bahru,** the train station is on Jalan Campbell (☎ 6-07/223-3040). The trip costs between RM4 and RM10 (US88¢ and US$2.20), takes between 30 and 40 minutes, and departs four times daily. All trains let you off at the Singapore Railway Station (☎ 65/222-5165). The station, on Keppel Road, is in Tanjong Pagar, not far from city center. Many buses run along this route, but a taxi into town should not be too expensive from here.

The Eastern & Orient Express (E&O) operates a route between Bangkok, Kuala Lumpur, and Singapore. Traveling in the luxury style of the Orient Express, the entire journey takes about 42 hours from its start to its finish at the Singapore Railway Station. Contact **E&O Services,** Carlton Building, 90 Cecil St. #05-01 (☎ 65/323-4390).

BY BUS

All buses into Singapore from Malaysia will let you off at the **Ban Sen Terminal,** which is nothing more than a dirt lot at the corner of Queen Street and Arab Street in Kampong Glam. To get to public transportation or to find a taxi, take Arab Street down to Beach Road.

The **Singapore–Johor Bahru Express** (☎ 65/292-8149) takes less than an hour and departs at 10- to 15-minute intervals from 6:30am to midnight.

The **Kuala Lumpur–Singapore Express** (☎ 65/292-8254) departs Kuala Lumpur three times daily and takes just under 6 hours.

The **Malacca-Singapore Express** departs eight times daily and takes 4^1/2 hours to complete.

BY FERRY

From **Tanjung Belungkor** on the east coast of Malaysia (ferry terminal ☎ **07/ 251-7404,** 07/251-7407, or 07/251-7408; fax 07/251-7414) you can catch a FerryLink ferry and be in Singapore in 45 minutes. The boat leaves four times daily, at 9:45am, 12:45pm, 3:45pm, and 6:45pm. Check-in time is 1 hour before sailing. The one-way fare for adults is RM15 (US$3.33), for children 12 to 18 is RM13 (US$2.90), and for children under 12 is RM9 (US$2). Round-trip is RM27 (US$6) for adults, RM24 (US$5.35) for students, and RM16 (US$3.55) for children. The ferry lets you off at Changi Ferry Terminal on the east coast of Singapore. Take SBS (Singapore Bus Service) bus no. 2 to the MRT, and you're home free.

From **Tioman Island** you can catch an Auto Batam Ferries and Tours ferry to Singapore at the Berjaya Jetty every day except Wednesday. The ferry leaves at 2:30pm, but check-in time is 1 hour before departure. The trip takes about 3^1/2 hours and lets you off in Singapore at the Tanah Merah Ferry Terminal. Take SBS bus no. 35 to the MRT to get into town. This service does not operate from mid-October to early March, due to the monsoon season.

PACKAGE TOURS

Group package tours are convenient because you don't have to plan the details of your own trip. They can also be less expensive than making arrangements on your own, because packagers can arrange special discounts on everything from airfare to hotel rooms to meals. On the downside, you have less freedom to decide when you go, and the group's schedule may not allow you to see places that may be meaningful to you.

A tremendous number of tour operators offer package tours that include Singapore, but I've just listed some of the ones available from the major groups, to give you an idea of what's available. These and other packages can be booked through your friendly neighborhood travel agent.

Jetset (Malaysia Airlines) has packages to Singapore and Malaysia. Different packages offer visits to a combination of cities like Kuala Lumpur, Malacca, Langkawi, Penang, Kuching (Sarawak), Kota Kinabalu, Kuantan, Tioman, and then of course, Singapore. **Passport Travel Management Group** advertises budget tours and minipackages to Singapore and many Malaysian destinations. **World Travel Consultants, Inc.** has a 15-day Hong Kong, Singapore, Malaysia, and Thailand trip; a 13-day Malaysia, Thailand, and Singapore trip; a 12-day Malaysia and Singapore trip; and a 13-day Singapore and Indonesia trip. **Asian Affair Holidays** (Singapore Airlines) has tours for Singapore and Malaysia. **Isram World of Travel** offers 15-day packages to Bangkok, Bali, Singapore, and Hong Kong; a 17-day package to Bangkok, Kuala Lumpur, Kuching, Kota Kinabalu, Sedakan, and Singapore; and many other smaller packages. **G.W.T. Inc.** has 12-day Singapore and Bali trips and a 14-day Asian Odyssey that includes Java as well. **Visits Plus, Inc.** has a few different options for tours that cover Singapore, Kuala Lumpur, Bangkok, Bali, and Hong Kong. **United Vacations** (United Airlines) has excursions to Singapore and Malaysia, and also combines Singapore in mainland China tour packages. **Pacific Holidays** has many different Southeast Asian packages and also a 21-day China and the Orient package that includes Singapore. **Pacific Delight Tours** (Cathay Pacific) has over seven different excursions in Southeast Asia that run between 9 and 16 days. **Tauck Tours** has a 20-day excursion that includes Hong Kong, Beijing, Xian, Guilin, Bangkok, Singapore, and Bali.

Learning Your Way Around Singapore

3

Although Sir Stamford Raffles, when planning the layout of Singapore, tried very hard to keep to a tidy urban grid, the terrain didn't always permit straight paths through jungles and over streams. Try as you may, it can still be a pain finding your way around Singapore. When I was younger, I'd get on a bus and ride it to the end of the line just to see where it went and to find my way around. Still to this day I pass familiar landmarks and think, "That's where this is?!" So don't feel bad if you haven't mastered the streets by the end of your stay. Few do.

This chapter will give you some sense of where you're going. There's information about the major neighborhoods in the city and suburbs, as well as information on how to get around.

1 Visitor Information

The main office for the **Singapore Tourism Board** is at Tourism Court, 1 Orchard Spring Lane, across the street, or Traders Hotel (☎ **65/736-6622,** or 1800/738-3778 or 1800/738-3779 toll-free within Singapore; fax 65/736-9423).

When you get to Singapore, stop by the STB and inquire about a Singapore Plus card, which entitles tourists to discounts at restaurants, shops, tours, and attractions. They instituted the card in 1997 and continued it into the beginning of 1998 because it was so popular, so they may have extended it further. Ask, just to be on the safe side.

2 The View from the Ground— Singapore's Neighborhoods

Singapore is a city-state, which basically means that the city *is* the country. That doesn't necessarily mean that the entire country is urban, but that the whole of the country and the city is "Singapore," without provincial divisions.

Now, you do have an urban center and smaller suburban neighborhoods: The urban area centers around the Singapore River at the southern point of the island. Within the urban center are neighborhood divisions, which are handy to know as a tourist. They are the **Historic District** (also referred to as the city center or cultural district), **Chinatown, Tanjong Pagar** (which is oftentimes lumped together with Chinatown due to its close proximity), the **Orchard**

Urban Singapore Neighborhoods

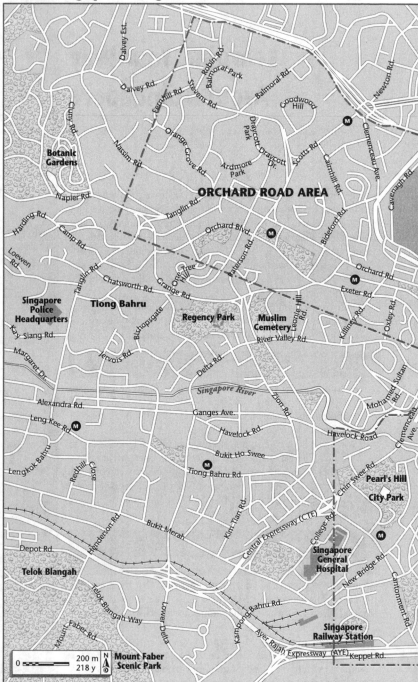

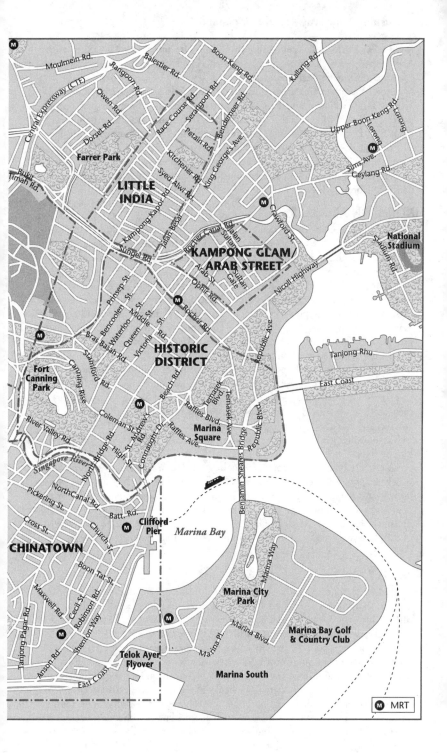

Road area, Little India, and **Kampong Glam** (also mistakenly referred to as the Arab District—mistakenly because the district is more Muslim than Arabic, although there are some major Arabic influences).

Beyond the urban area are suburban neighborhoods. Some suburbs are old, like **Katong** and **Geylang,** dating back to the turn of the century. Some are new, and are therefore referred to as "HDB New Towns." (HDB stands for "Housing Development Board," the government agency responsible for public housing.) HDB New Towns such as **Ang Mo Kio** or **Toa Payoh** are clusters of public housing units that have sprung up around the island. Each new town has its own network of supporting businesses: provision shops, restaurants, health-care facilities, and sometimes department stores.

FINDING AN ADDRESS

Unless you're familiar with a particular street, it is unfortunately difficult to distinguish what neighborhood a place is located in simply from the written address. Most addresses are simply a number and a street name. Postal codes won't give you much of a clue either.

One exception is addresses in the New Towns, when you'll see the name of the neighborhood in the body of the address. These neighborhoods are blocks of buildings, each with a corresponding block number that will appear in the address—for example, "Lorong Toa Payoh, Blk #14." These buildings are mostly private apartment blocks. It may help to know that in Malay, *lorong* is lane, *jalan* is street, and *bukit* is hill. These are used quite frequently in Singapore.

One clue for locating shops in shopping malls and offices or apartments in large buildings: Numbers for these addresses are written as, for example, #03-15. Where you see this, the first set of digits represents the level (in this case the third floor) of the place, and the second set represents the location on the floor numerically. Where you see, say, #03-15/16/17, the place occupies three storefront or office units. Generally, you won't get lost in malls or offices. Almost all places have directories on the ground floor.

Almost all cabbies have a copy of a book called *The Singapore Street Directory,* which includes very detailed road maps for the whole island. You can look places up with just the name of the road, and know where you need to go. Get a copy for yourself and you'll never be lost for long. It's particularly helpful when you find one of the few cabbies with poor English, a new guy, or a guy who has never heard of the place you need to go. If you can find it for him on the map, he can take you there.

THE CITY

The urban center of Singapore spans quite far from edge to edge, so walking from one end to the other—say, from Tanjong Pagar to Kampong Glam—might be a bit much. However, once you become handy with local maps, you'll be constantly surprised at how close the individual districts are to one another.

The main focal point of the city is the **Singapore River,** which on a map is located at the southern point of the island, flowing west to east into the Marina. It's here that Sir Stamford Raffles landed and built his settlement for the East India Trading Company. As trade prospered, the banks of the river were expanded to handle commerce, behind which neighborhoods and administrative offices took root. In 1822, Raffles developed a Town Plan, which allocated neighborhoods to each of the races who'd come in droves to find work and begin lives. The lines drawn then still remain today, shaping the major ethnic enclaves held within the city limits.

On the south bank of the river, go-downs, or warehouses, lined the waterside. Behind the buildings, offices and residences sprang up for the Chinese community of merchants and "coolie" laborers who worked the river- and sea-trade. Raffles named this section **Chinatown,** a name that stands today.

Neighboring Chinatown to the southwest is **Tanjong Pagar,** a small district where wealthy Chinese and Eurasians built plantations and manors. With the development of the steamship, Keppel Harbour, a deep natural harbor just off the shore of Tanjong Pagar, was built up to receive the larger vessels. Tanjong Pagar quickly developed into a commercial and residential area filled with workers who flocked there to support the industry.

In these early days, both Chinatown and Tanjong Pagar were amazing sites of city activity. Row houses lined the streets, with shops on the bottom floors and homes on the second and third. Chinese coolie laborers commonly lived sixteen to a room, and the area flourished with gambling casinos, clubs, and opium dens for them to spend their spare time and money. Indians also thronged to the area to work on the docks, a small reminder that although races had their own areas, they were never exclusive communities.

As recently as the seventies, a walk down the streets in this area was an adventure: The shops housed Chinese craftsmen and artists; on the streets, hawkers peddled food and other merchandise. Calligrapher scribes set up shop on sidewalks to write letters for a fee. Housewives would bustle, running their daily errands; children would dash out of every corner; and bamboo poles hung laundry from upper stories.

Today, both of these districts are sleepy in comparison. Modern HDB (Housing Development Board) apartment buildings have siphoned residents off to the suburbs, and though the Urban Redevelopment Authority has renovated many of the old shophouses in an attempt to preserve history, they're now tenanted by law offices and architectural, public relations, and advertising firms. About the only time you'll see this place hustle anymore is during weekday lunchtime, when all the professionals dash out for a bite.

The **north bank** was originally reserved for colonial administrative buildings, and is today commonly referred to as the **Historic District.** The center point was The Padang, the field on which the Europeans would play sports and hold outdoor ceremonies. Around the field, the Parliament Building, Supreme Court, City Hall, and other municipal buildings sprang up in grand style, and behind these buildings, Government Hill—the present day **Fort Canning Park**—was the home of the governors. The Esplanade along the waterfront was a center for European social activities and music gatherings, when colonists would don their finest Western styles and walk the park under parasols or cruise in horse-drawn carriages. These days, the Historic District is still the center of most of the government's operations, and close by high-rise hotels and shopping malls have been built. The area on the bank of the river is celebrated as Raffles' landing site.

To the northwest of the Historic District, in the areas along **Orchard Road and Tanglin,** a residential area was created for Europeans and Eurasians. Homes and plantations were eventually replaced by apartment buildings and shops, and in the early 1970s, luxury hotels ushered tourism into the area in full force. In the 1980s, huge shopping malls sprang up along the sides of Orchard Road, turning the Orchardscape into the shopping hub it continues to be. The Tanglin area is home to most of the foreign embassies in Singapore.

The natural landscape of **Little India** made it a natural location for an Indian settlement. Indians were the original cattle hands and traders in Singapore, and this area's natural grasses and springs provided their cattle with food and water, while

---

Factoid

It's estimated that up to 50,000 expatriates live in Singapore. Japanese make up the greatest percentage of these, followed by Americans, British, Germans, Swiss, Canadians, French, and Dutch. The high concentration of Western residents is evident in the density of expatriate schools in the Holland Village area.

---

bamboo groves supplied necessary lumber for their pens. Later, with the establishment of brick kilns, Indian construction laborers flocked to the area to find work. Today, many elements of Indian culture persist, although Indians make up a small percentage of the current population. Shops, restaurants, and temples still serve the community, and on Sundays, Little India is a true mob scene, when all the workers have their day off and come to the streets here to socialize and relax.

Like Little India, the area around **Bugis Street** is adjacent to the Historic District. This neighborhood was originally allocated for the Bugis settlers who came from the island of Celebes, part of Indonesia. The Bugis were welcomed in Singapore, and because they originated from a society based on seafaring and trading, they became master shipbuilders. Today, regrettably, nothing remains of Bugis culture outside of the national museums. In fact, for most locals, Bugis Street is better remembered as a 1970s den of iniquity where transvestites, transsexuals, and other sex performers would stage seedy Bangkok-style shows and beauty contests. The government "cleaned up" Bugis Street in the 1980s, so that all that remains is a huge shopping mall and a sanitized night market.

Kampong Glam, the neighborhood beyond Bugis Street, was given to Sultan Hussein and his family as part of his agreement to turn control of Singapore over to Raffles. Here he built his *istana* (palace) and the Sultan Mosque, and the area subsequently filled with Malay and Arab Muslims, who imparted a distinct Islamic flavor to the neighborhood. The area is still a focal point of Singapore Muslim society, thanks to Sultan Mosque, but the istana has fallen into disrepair, and serves as a sad reminder of the economic condition into which Singapore's Malay community has fallen. Arab Street is perhaps the most popular attraction for tourists and locals, who come to find deals on fabrics and regional crafts.

Two areas of the city center are relatively new, having been built atop huge parcels of reclaimed land. Where the eastern edges of Chinatown and Tanjong Pagar once touched the water's edge, land reclamation created the present-day downtown business district, which is named after its central thoroughfare, **Shenton Way.** This Wall Street–like district is home to the magnificent skyscrapers that grace Singapore's skyline and to the banks and businesses that have made the place an international financial capital. During weekday business hours (9am to 5pm), Shenton Way is packed with scurrying businesspeople. After hours and on weekends, it's nothing more than a quiet forest of concrete, metal, and glass.

The other area is **Marina Bay,** on the other side of the river, just east of the Historic District. **Suntec City,** Southeast Asia's largest convention and exhibition center, is located here, and has become the linchpin of a thriving hotel, shopping mall, and amusement zone.

SUBURBAN SINGAPORE

With rapid urbanization in the 20th century, plantations and farms turned into suburban residential areas, many with their own ethnic roots.

To the east of the city is **Katong,** a famous residential district inhabited primarily by Peranakan (Straits-Chinese) and Eurasian families. Its streets were, and still are, lined with Peranakan-style terrace houses, a residential variation of the shophouse found in commercial districts. The Peranakans and Eurasians were tolerant groups, a result of interracial marriages and multicultural family life, who created a close-knit community with a laid-back feeling that's carried over to the present day. Main streets are still lined with Peranakan restaurants and there are many Catholic churches and schools that served the Eurasians.

As public transportation opened up the eastern sections of the island, neighborhoods extended farther out. **Geylang,** the neighborhood just beyond Katong, was and still is primarily a Malay district. Joo Chiat and Geylang roads were once lined with antique shops and restaurants where *halal* foods—corresponding to Islamic dietary laws—were served. Today, a lot of the shophouses are being renovated, but it's still a good area to find housewares, fabrics, and modern furniture shops. **Joo Chiat Complex** (601 Joo Chiat Rd., at the corner of Geylang Road and across the street from Malay Village) has shops with Muslim religious artifacts, fabrics, and Indo-Malay pop and traditional recordings. At night, parts of Geylang are notorious for partially regulated prostitution.

Also to the east is **Changi Village,** at the far eastern tip. It was built as the residential area of a British military post, but the Brits are gone now and Changi is pretty quiet, with not much to see other than a few antique shops, a large hawker center with some great seafood, and a public beach from which you can see Singapore's northern islands, Malaysia, and Indonesia. The one really notable aspect of the place is that it's where you pick up **ferries** to Pulau Ubin and Malaysia.

To the west is an old neighborhood, **Tiong Bahru.** Its original inhabitants were Chinese from the Chinatown and Tanjong Pagar districts, and the neighborhood remains largely Chinese today. In the 1960s, the Housing Development Board (HDB) replaced small homes and makeshift housing with high-rise public apartment housing. The younger generations have moved on to bigger housing in the new estates, leaving the place mostly populated by the elderly.

Located to the west of the city, **Holland Village** is another famous neighborhood that's become a tourist attraction in its own right. Its nucleus of shops carries merchandise catering to the wants and needs of Westerners, many of whom reside in the vicinity. Despite the Western customers, these aren't necessarily Western goods, but rather the kind of rattan furnishing, baskets, pottery, and other regional goods that you find adding "color" to otherwise Western-style homes.

THE "NEW TOWNS"

In the 1960s, to deal with the growing Singapore population, the HDB created a scheme to build residential areas along an imaginary circle around the Central Water Catchment Reserve in the center of the island. These "New Towns" would consist of blocks of high-rise public apartments around which shops, markets, and restaurants could settle to support the residents. Kampungs, villages, farms, and orchards were leveled, swamps were drained, and local streams were turned into concrete channels to make way for New Towns such as Bedok, Tampines, Pasir Ris, Toa Payoh, Bishan, Ang Mo Kio, Yishun, Woodlands, and Clementi, which sprang up in all parts of the island. One trip on a subway and all these names become familiar, as the Mass Rapid Transit System (MRT) was brought into the scheme to provide affordable transportation to all the towns.

Since 1960, over 766,570 government apartments have been built. That's a lot of Singaporeans living in public housing. But however appealing this scheme to provide everyone with modern housing sounded at first, residents in New Towns have their complaints. The apartments have become extremely expensive, and long waiting lists are filled with couples who wish to buy their first homes and families who need to

Kampung Life

When modern, hectic, businesslike society gets them down, many modern Singaporeans look back with longing to the days when life was simple, and when they do, the kampung villages always come to mind.

Kampung (sometimes "Kampong") is Malay for "village," and once upon a time, many of Singapore's rural laborers and fishermen—mostly Malays but also Chinese and Indians—lived in these villages, small clusters of houses that were built from wood and *attap* (thatch) and raised on stilts, irrespective of whether they rested on swampland or dry earth. Built along the shores of the island and close to jungles, the buildings were nestled in backdrops of idyllic greenery, surrounded by banana and coconut groves and marshes. Homes had land for chicken coops and kitchen gardens, and backyards in which children could play; villages had central wells, provision shops, and sometimes a mosque. Despite their poverty, the kampung villages represented community.

The 1950s and 1960s were the heydays of kampung life. Later, the houses were "improved" with corrugated metal, concrete, and wallboard, all of which rusted and rotted over time, making the kampungs look more like slums than the homely villages they once were. Inside, modernization brought government-mandated running water and plumbing, and even electrical appliances like TVs, refrigerators, and telephones, but all in all, life was hardly opulent.

Today, this entire way of life is just a memory. Every last kampung has been razed, the inhabitants relocated by the government to public housing estates. Many former kampung inhabitants have had a difficult time adjusting to life in concrete highrises, with no front porch or backyard, and neighbors who are too busy to remember their names. Despite the truth—that kampung life reflected poverty and struggle—their memory remains a link to older days that, however irrelevant to the modern world and however romanticized, still warms the hearts of many Singaporeans.

upgrade to larger digs. Beyond questions of expense, though, there's the fact that the New Towns are singularly *depressing,* with block after block of similarly characterless high-rises looming overhead and compartmentalized living creating an urban anonymity between the many inhabitants. Certain towns are said to have their own identities, stemming from larger populations of one ethnic group or another or from a particular majority age group, but even this modest differentiation is under attack by various government initiatives aimed at interspersing the races and encouraging a "Singaporean" national homogeneity.

3 Getting Around

The many inexpensive mass transit options make getting around Singapore pretty easy. Of course, taxis always simplify the ground transportation dilemma. They're also very affordable, and, by and large, drivers are helpful and honest if not downright personable. The **Mass Rapid Transit (MRT)** subway service has four lines that run over two main routes (roughly east-west and north-south) and are very easy to figure out. **Buses** present more of a challenge because there are so many routes snaking all over the island, but they're a great way to see the country while getting where you want to go. In the bus section, below, I've thrown in some tips that will hopefully demystify the bus experience for you.

MRT Transit Map

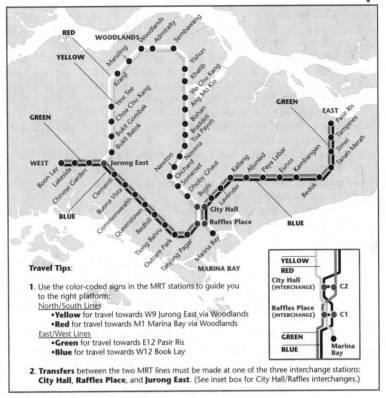

Travel Tips:

1. Use the color-coded signs in the MRT stations to guide you to the right platform:
   North/South Lines
   - **Yellow** for travel towards W9 Jurong East via Woodlands
   - **Red** for travel towards M1 Marina Bay via Woodlands
   East/West Lines
   - **Green** for travel towards E12 Pasir Ris
   - **Blue** for travel towards W12 Book Lay

2. **Transfers** between the two MRT lines must be made at one of the three interchange stations: **City Hall**, **Raffles Place**, and **Jurong East**. (See inset box for City Hall/Raffles interchanges.)

Of course, if you're just strolling around the urban limits, many of the sights within the various neighborhoods are within walking distance, and indeed, some of the neighborhoods are only short walks from each other—getting from Chinatown to the Historic District is only a cross over the Singapore River, and from Little India to Kampong Glam is not far at all. However, I advise against trying to get from, say, Chinatown (in the west) to Kampong Glam (in the east). The distance can be somewhat prohibitive, especially in the heat.

BY PUBLIC TRANSPORTATION

Stored-fare **TransitLink fare cards** can be used on both the subway and the buses, and can be purchased at TransitLink offices in the MRT stations. These save you the bother of trying to dig up exact change for bus meters; plus, if you transfer from a bus to the MRT, or between buses, you'll save S25¢. At the end of your stay, you can cash in your card for the remaining value, and still get one extra trip for about S10¢.

BY MASS RAPID TRANSIT (MRT)

The MRT is Singapore's subway system. It's cool, clean, safe, and reliable, providing service from the far west reaches of the island to the far east parts on the east-west line and running in a loop around the north part of the island on the north-south line. The lines are color coded to make it easy to find the train you're looking for (see the MRT map in this chapter for specifics). The two lines intersect at the Raffles Place

Interchange in Chinatown / Shenton Way, at City Hall in the Historic District, and in the western part of the island at the Jurong East Interchange. (By the way, don't let the "East" fool you—Jurong East is actually in the western part of the island.) MRT operating hours vary between lines and stops, with the earliest train beginning service daily at 5:15am and the last train ending at 12:47am.

Fares range from S60¢ to S$1.50 (US40¢ to US95¢), depending on which stations you travel between. System charts are prominently displayed in all MRT stations to help you find your appropriate fare, which is paid using a TransitLink fare card. Single fare cards can be purchased at vending machines at MRT stations. See above for information on stored-fare cards.

TransitLink also has an **MRT Tourist Souvenir Ticket** for S$6 (US$3.80). It's good for 120 days for trips up to S$5.50 (the extra S50¢ is the deposit). If you travel over your limit, you pay the difference at the end of your trip at station control. No refunds are made on the value remaining.

For more information, call **Mass Rapid Transit** toll-free at ☎ **1800/336-8900** (except Sunday and public holidays).

BY BUS

Singapore's bus system comprises an extensive web of routes that reach virtually everywhere on the island. It can be intimidating for newcomers, but once you get your feet wet, you'll feel right at home. There are two main bus services, SBS (Singapore Bus Service) and TIBS (Trans-Island Bus Service). Most buses are clean, but not all are air-conditioned.

Start off first by purchasing a **TransitLink Guide** for S$1.40 (US90¢) at the TransitLink office in any MRT station, at a bus interchange, or at selected bookstores around the city. This tiny book is a very handy guide that details each route and stop, indicating connections with MRT stations and fares for each trip. Next to the guide, the best thing to do is simply ask people for help. At any crowded bus stop there will always be somebody who speaks English and is willing to help out a lost stranger. You can also ask the bus driver where you need to go, and he'll tell you the fare, how to get there, and even when to get off.

All buses have a machine just to the right as you board. Tell the driver your fare and feed the machine either your TransitLink card or exact change, then push the button with the corresponding fare (it's pretty much an honor system to make sure you pay the correct rate). You'll get a receipt back with your fare stamped on it. Sometimes the authorities come around and check to see that people are paying the correct fare, and if you've made a mistake, this is a good time to play up the ignorant tourist routine—otherwise you could be charged the highest fare as punishment.

The **Singapore Explorer** is a special deal for tourists. The 1-day pass is S$5 (US$3.15) and the 3-day pass is just S$12 (US$7.55), and both are good for unlimited trips around the island on either SBS or TIBS buses. Using one of these will save you having to worry about calculating the correct fare or coming up with exact change. You can pick one up at any TransitLink office and at hotels, money changers, provisioners shops, or travel agents. Unfortunately, there's no handy-dandy sign identifying which shops sell them, so you'll have to ask.

For more information, contact either of the two operating bus lines: **Singapore Bus Service** (SBS) (☎ **1800/287-2727**) or the **Trans-Island Bus Service** (TIBS) (☎ **1800/482-5433**).

BY TAXI

Taxis are a very convenient and affordable way to get around Singapore, and there's every chance you'll get a good conversation with the driver in the bargain (see

"Frommer's Favorite Singapore Experiences" in chapter 1). Despite this, I advise against relying completely on taxicabs, since Singapore's excellent public transportation system will take you practically anywhere you need to go for a fraction of the price. Even in the middle of nowhere there's always a bus route to take you to familiar territory—just remember to keep your TransitLink Guide (see above) handy, so you'll know where the bus you're about to hop is headed.

In town, all of the shopping malls, hotels, and major buildings have taxi queues, which you're expected to use. During lunch hours and the evening rush, the queues can be very long, but the turnover is often quick and the lines move fast. Most destinations in the main parts of the island can be reached fairly inexpensively, while trips to the outlying attractions can cost between S$10 and S$15 (US$6.30 and US$9.45) one way. If you're at an attraction or restaurant outside of the central part of the city where it is more difficult to hail a cab on the street, you can ask the cashier or service counter attendant to call a taxi for you. The extra charge for pickup is around $3.20 (US$2), and the most popular taxicab companies are **CityCab** (☎ 65/553-3880), **Comfort** (☎ 65/552-1111), and **TIBS** (☎ 65/481-1211).

All taxis charge the metered fare, which is S$2.40 (US$1.50) for the first kilometer and S10¢ for each additional 240 meters or 30 seconds of waiting. Extra fares are levied on top of the metered fare depending on where you're going and when you go. Peak-period surcharges of S50¢ (US30¢) apply for trips outside the Central Business District (see below) Monday to Friday 7:30am to 6:30pm and Saturday and the eve of public holidays 7:30am to 2pm. Also, for rides between midnight and 6am, you'll be charged an extra 50% of your fare.

A couple of warnings: Between 5pm and 6pm each day, the cabbies change shifts, and it can be really frustrating if you're in the middle of nowhere and find taxi after taxi passing you by because they're all on their way to the depot and don't want any new fares.

Warning #2: The heart of the city—encompassing the areas around Orchard Road, Chinatown, Shenton Way, and the Historic District—is the **Central Business District (CBD),** a special high-traffic area that the government has marked off to target traffic reduction. All vehicles entering the CBD are required to display daily access badges between the hours of 7:30 and 9:30am weekdays and Saturday, on weekdays from 4:30 to 7pm, and again on Saturdays from 11:30am to 2pm. Huge overhead signs flash when the CBD restrictions are in effect. Taxis traveling into the CBD will charge an extra S$1.50 (US95¢) for the trip. Also, cabbies are required to purchase a S$3 (US$1.90) CBD badge for the day upon first entry in the morning. If you're the first CBD-bound passenger, you foot the bill for it.

Most cabbies are honest about charging the correct fare, but from time to time you may find someone trying to charge you the CBD surcharge, claiming your destination is in the CBD when it's not. There's not enough room in this guide to go through the CBD boundaries, so the best way to go about avoiding this inconvenience is to inquire with your hotel concierge to find out if the places you want to visit are in the zone—or, for that matter, if your hotel is in it.

BY CAR

Singapore's public transportation systems are so extensive, efficient, and inexpensive that you shouldn't need a car to enjoy your stay. In fact, I don't advise it. While most hotels and restaurants and many attractions do have parking facilities, parking in lots can be expensive, and on-street parking is by pre-purchased, color-coded parking tickets that are confusing for even Singaporeans to use. In addition, if you're not accustomed to driving on the left side of the road, you'll need to take the time to pick up a new skill.

There is also the business of the Central Business District (CBD), which I talked about in the taxi section, above. For private vehicles to enter the Restricted Zone (RZ) within the CBD, you must purchase a S$2 (US$1.25) half-day or S$3 (US$1.90) whole-day permit, which must be displayed on your windshield. Within the CBD, the RZ is marked off by huge overhead signs that light up during the hours that rules are in effect (Monday through Friday 7am to 6:30pm, and Saturday and the eve of public holidays from 7:30am to 2pm). Enforcement officers stand guard at all entrances to make sure drivers comply.

RENTING A CAR

There are two main impediments to renting a car in Singapore, but if you're really determined, you can overcome them.

The first problem involves **licensing:** You'll be required to produce an international driver's license, which you should obtain in your home country before your trip. You can get one in Singapore, but first you must get a Singapore driver's license, which you then convert to an international one—kinda impractical if you're on a holiday or just in town quickly for business. It's a mess of red tape, but if you want to try, you can start by calling the Driving License Section of the **Traffic Police Department** at ☎ **65/221-0000.**

The second problem involves **cost:** Because of heavy government taxes aimed at reducing traffic congestion and air pollution, everything to do with cars in Singapore is outlandishly expensive—the going price for a simple Toyota Corolla, for instance, can be as high as S$125,000 (US$78,750). This attempt to reduce automobile traffic is also extended to you, the traveler, through rental charges up to S$1,000 (US$630) plus taxes for 1 week's rental of the smallest car on the lot.

One good reason to rent a car is if you plan to **drive into Malaysia.** Back in the 70s, driving in Malaysia was risky because of highway bandits. These days, though, it's relatively safe traveling, and thanks to the new toll road—the North-South Highway from Singapore all the way up to the Thai border—it's pretty convenient (see chapter 13 for more on this subject). But, again, renting a car is not cheap. Two good places to seek out a rental car are:

- **Avis:** Changi Airport Terminal 1 (☎ **65/543-2331**); Changi Airport Terminal 2 (☎ **65/542-8855**), Boulevard Hotel (☎ **65/737-1668**); or Suntec City (☎ **65/334-8835**). Their toll-free number in Singapore is ☎ **1800/737-9477,** and in Malaysia it's ☎ **800/1053.** You must be at least 23 years old to rent, and the minimum rental period is 24 hours. Rates in Singapore are S$145 to S$265 (US$91.35 to US$167) daily and S$870 to S$1,590 (US$548 to US$1,001.70) weekly. For travel to Malaysia, the rates are S$170 to S$305 (US$107 to US$192.15) daily or S$1,045 to S$1,870 (US$658.35 to US$1,178) weekly. One-way rentals are available, with varying drop-off fees for Malacca, Kuala Lumpur, Kuantan, Terengganu, Kota Bahru, Alor Setar, Ipoh, and Penang. All major credit cards are accepted.
- **Hertz:** Changi Airport Terminal 2, Arrival Meeting Hall South (☎ **65/542-5300**) or 125 Tanglin Rd., Tudor Court Shopping Gallery (☎ **65/734-4646**). You must be at least 21 years of age to rent and the minimum rental period is 24 hours. Rates for rental within Singapore are S$149 to S$489 (US$93.85 to US$308) daily and S$894 to S$2,934 (US$563.20 to US$1,848.40) weekly. The high-end rates are for rental of either a BMW or Mercedes Benz. For driving to Malaysia, Hertz tacks on additional charges from between S$25 and S$80 (US$15.75 and US$50.40) per day. For one-way trips

to Malaysia there are varying drop-off charges for Johor Bahru, Kuala Lumpur, Kuantan, and Penang. Hertz accepts all major credit cards.

In addition, both rental agencies offer **hourly rentals** of chauffeur-driven vehicles. There is usually a minimum of 3 hours for the rental, which can range from around S$45 (US$28.35) per hour for a smaller Mazda sort of vehicle up to around S$55 (US$34.65) per hour for a Mercedes Benz.

4 Suggested Itineraries

Probably because most people see Singapore as a jumping-off point for other Southeast Asian destinations, the average visitor spends only 3 1/2 days here. A jumping-off point it certainly is, but I assure you, you'll have no problem filling your days if you stay for a week or more.

Following are suggested itineraries for a trip lasting the standard 3 1/2 days, but if you're staying for at least a week, take a look at the really great itinerary I've included for you. It's made up of theme days that will walk you through the major cultures and influences in Singapore, from the colonial period all the way up to Singapore today. The itinerary is very relaxed, and includes sights, attractions, shopping, and recommended eating experiences that, at the end, will have given you a well-rounded view of what this small but wonderful country is all about.

If You Have 3¹/₂ Days

Day 1   Take a walking tour of the **Historic District** (see chapter 7), then visit the **National Museum** and the **Asian Civilisations Museum** (see chapter 6). If you have time, try to catch the **Singapore Art Museum** (see chapter 6). Spend your evening at one of the 100+ bars and restaurants on **Boat Quay** and **Clarke Quay** (see chapters 5, 6, and 9).

Day 2   Take the Little India walking tour followed by the Arab Street / Kampong Glam tour (see chapter 7). Feel free to take your time and shop along the way. Try a Malay dinner at Aziza's (see chapter 5).

Day 3   Take the Chinatown walking tour (see chapter 7) in the morning and spend the afternoon at Orchard Road, shopping and people-watching (see chapter 8). Have a seafood dinner out at Long Beach Seafood Restaurant (see chapter 5).

Day 4   Only a half-day to work with here, so spend the morning at the Singapore Botanic Gardens (see chapter 6).

If You Have a Week

Day 1: Chinese Day   This will be an easy day, since it's your first day in Singapore and I don't want to exhaust you. Begin with a **walking tour of Chinatown** in the morning, past the temples and little shops selling Chinese herbs and bric-a-brac (see chapter 7). Spend a little time in the **Chinaman Scholar's Gallery** on Trengganu Street (see chapter 6), then head over to **Chinatown Complex** to check out the cheap souvenirs, cheongsams, and leather bags. Across New Bridge Road / Eu Tong Sen Street is the **People's Park Complex** shopping mall, and farther down the road is **Yue Hua,** a Chinese goods emporium (see chapter 8). Break up your day with a nice lunch at **Chen Fu Ji Fried Rice** on Erskine Road (see chapter 5). In the afternoon, head for **The Tea Village** on Erskine Road for a traditional Chinese tea ceremony (see chapter 5) and a little rest. If you still have some time, take the MRT or a bus out to Toa Payoh to see the **Siong Lim Temple** (see chapter 6). The recommended Chinese dinner experience is at **Imperial Herbal** at the Metropole

Hotel (see chapter 5). If you can find a *wayang* (Chinese opera) being performed, that would be the best way to close out the evening with entertainment (see chapter 9). For night owls, check out the **Next Page Pub** on Mohamed Sultan Lane (see chapter 9). Let the giant portrait of a smiling Mao Zedong fill your dreams at the end of Chinese Day.

Day 2: Malay Day   Start off with the **walking tour of Kampong Glam,** filled with Malay and Muslim heritage, and **Arab Street,** for great shopping (see chapter 7). A great lunch suggestion is to have *murtabak,* a Muslim specialty, at **Zam Zam's** on North Bridge Road, just behind Sultan's Mosque. In the afternoon, take the MRT out for a little shopping at **Joo Chiat Centre** (see chapter 8) in Geylang and try to catch the late-afternoon cultural performances at **Malay Village** (see chapter 6). If you're hearty, take a walk down Joo Chiat Road to East Coast Road. Hang a left and across the street and down a ways you'll find the **Katong Antique House,** filled with Peranakan antiques that will bring Straits-Chinese heritage to life (see chapter 8). The perfect dinner for the day is at **Aziza's,** for traditional Malay cuisine (see chapter 5). If you're lucky, they may be staging more cultural music and dance there during dinner hours. For the evening's entertainment, contact one of the local Malay theater or dance troupes to see what performances they're staging (see chapter 9).

Day 3: Indian Day   Naturally, Indian Day starts with the morning **walking tour of Little India** (see chapter 7). Have lunch at either **Muthu's Curry** on Race Course Road (see chapter 5) or at my favorite, **Komala Vilas** on Buffalo Road (see chapter 5). Don't forget to check out the bargains on Indian silk and gold jewelry at **Mustapha's** (see chapter 8). In the afternoon, head over to **Chettiar's Temple** on Tank Road (see chapter 6). Have dinner accompanied by live Indian music at the **Tandoor** in the Parkview Holiday Inn (see chapter 5). Contact one of the local Indian theater or dance troupes to see what performances they have scheduled for the evening's entertainment (see chapter 9).

Day 4: Colonial Day   Take the **Historic District walking tour** (see chapter 7), and while you're at the **Raffles Hotel,** stop in for lunch at the **Tiffin Room,** just like the colonists used to do (see chapter 5). There's some great shopping at the **Raffles Hotel Arcade** and in **Raffles City Shopping Centre** for modern Western fashions (see chapter 8). After you've spent your savings, spend the rest of the afternoon with a cool **Singapore Sling at the Long Bar** in Raffles Hotel (see chapter 9). If you want the true decadent dining experience, go back to your hotel, scrub up, and head to the **Raffles Grill** (see chapter 5). See what's playing at the **Singapore Symphony Orchestra** or the ballet, or check to see if there's a touring production of a West End show (see chapter 9)—or maybe take a **trishaw ride** around the Colonial District.

Day 5: Nature Day   Have a glorious breakfast at the Songbird Terrace at the **Jurong BirdPark** (see chapter 6). Later, head over to the **Singapore Botanic Gardens** (see chapter 6), and take a lovely walk through the place after catching a quick lunch at the **hawker center** by the front gate. (Make sure you try the Roti John—it's the best here!) After a delightful stroll through the gardens and the **National Orchid Garden,** head up to the **Singapore Zoological Gardens** (see chapter 6) for a fantastic afternoon with the animals.

If you like your nature just a tad wilder, visit **Sungei Buloh Nature Park** in the morning (see chapter 10) to watch the birds, and then head to **Bukit Timah Nature Reserve** (see chapter 10) for a stroll through primary rain forest.

You can have a nice local dinner at the Singapore Zoological Gardens' **Night Safari,** and stick around for a wonderful adventure into the lives of some nocturnal creatures, or catch a cab to either **Long Beach Seafood** or **UDMC** (see chapter 5) to taste some of the local sea creature varieties. For true animal nightlife, go to

Useful Malay Phrases

Bahasa Malaysia, the Malay language, is spoken commonly in Singapore. In addition to Malays, many Indians and Chinese talk the talk, which is a common language in markets and shops. Knowing a few phrases can sometimes get you better deals if the shop owner thinks you are an expatriate and not a tourist. Written Malay uses the same alphabet as English, so it's easy to read. Sounding out the syllables phonetically is fairly simple. One note on pronunciation: Where a *k* appears at the end of a word, "swallow" the sound, or just don't pronounce the *k* in a hard fashion.

Greetings

Good morning	Selamat pagi (sell-*ah*-mat *pah*-gee)
Good night	Selamat malam (sell-*ah*-mat *mah*-lahm)
How are you?	Apa khabar? (*ah*-pah *kah*-bar)
I'm fine	Khabar baik (*kah*-bar *bah*-ee)

Common Phrases

Thank you	Terimah kasih (ter-*ee*-mah *kah*-see)
You're welcome	Sama-sama (*sah*-mah *sah*-mah)
What does this mean?	Apa makna ini? (*ah*-pah *mahk*-nah *ee*-nee)
What time is it?	Pukul berapa? (*poo*-kool ber-*ah*-pah)
Is this seat taken?	Ada orang duduk di sini?
	(*ah*-dah *ohr*-ahng *doo*-doo dee *see*-nee)

Handy Phrases

Where is. . .	Di mana (dee *mah*-nah). . .
the toilet?	tandas? (*tan*-dahs)
a coin phone?	pondok telefon? (*pohn*-doh *teh*-leh-fohn)
a taxi stand?	perhentian teksi? (pehr-*hen*-tyohn *tek*-see)

Taxi Talk

How far is it?	Berapa juah? (behr-*ah*-pah *joo*-ah)
Stop here please	Tolong berhenti di sini
	(*toh*-long behr-*hen*-tee dee *see*-nee)

Shopping Talk

I'm just looking around	Saya hanya melihat-lihat saja
	(*sah*-yah *hahn*-yah meh-*lee*-haht *lee*-haht *sah*-jah)
What is the price?	Berapa harganya? (behr-*ah*-pah hahr-*gahn*-yah)
This is too expensive	Ini terlalu mahal (*ee*-nee tehr-*lah*-loo mah-*hahl*)
Is that your lowest price?	Adakah ini harga yang paling rendah? (*ah*-dah-kah *ee*-nee *hahr*-gah yahng *pah*-ling *ren*-dah)
Do you accept credit cards?	Adakah kamu menerima kad kredit? (*ah*-dah-kah *kah*-moo mehn-eh-*ree*-mah kahd *krehd*-eet)

In Case You Need a Doctor

I need a doctor	Saya hendak berjumpa doktor
	(*sah*-yah *hen*-dah behr-*joom*-pah *dohk*-tohr)
I am allergic to antibiotics	Saya alergik kepada antibiotik (*sah*-yah ah-*ler*-jihk keh-*pah*-dah ahn-tee-bee-*oh*-tee)
I am seeing double	Penglihatan saya berlapis (*pehng*-lee-hah-tahn *sah*-yah behr-*lah*-pees)
I am seeing double	Penglihatan. saya berlapis (*pehng*-lee-hah-tahn *sah*-yah behr-*lah*-pees)

Brannigan's (see chapter 9)—the nocturnal creatures there will put the animals at the Night Safari to shame. Or, walk down **Boat Quay** (see chapter 9), select your favorite bar, and take your drink by the side of the river.

Day 6: Singapore Heritage Day   Soak up the culture at the **National Museum** (see chapter 6) then head over to the **Asian Civilisations Museum** (see chapter 6) for a glimpse of Singapore in the context of its Asian neighbors. For the shoppers among you, nothing is more perfect than a day at **Tanglin Shopping Centre** or out at **Dempsey Road** browsing through all the antique shops, which display Chinese, Peranakan, Malay, and Indonesian treasures (see chapter 8). Have dinner at **Newton hawker center** (see chapter 5) where you can try out all the local specialties. Then head down to **Peranakan Place** in the evening for a stroll down Emerald Hill Road to take a peek at some of the exquisite private residences in the old renovated shophouses. **No. 5 Emerald Hill** is a great little bar in an old shophouse, or try **Que Pasa,** a great little wine bar in the shophouse just next door. Call some of the local theater groups or dance troupes to see if you can catch a cultural performance (see chapter 9).

Day 7: Modern Singapore Day   Take a morning **bumboat ride** up and down the Singapore River and out into the harbor (see chapter 7) to fill yourself up with the beautiful panorama of the cityscape. Then cruise the shopping malls of the **Orchard Road** tourist shopping mecca (see chapter 8). When you can't take any more, have a quiet time at the **Singapore Art Museum,** taking in all the local, regional, and international artwork in splendid display (see chapter 6). From there, it's a short walk to **Doc Cheng's,** modern Singapore's tongue-in-cheek answer to Chinese heritage (see chapter 5). Tonight is the night to check out a modern Singapore **theater performance** or see if any local films are running to wrap up all of your experiences and learn how modern-day Singaporeans enfold their culture and history into the contemporary context (see chapter 9). For the nightclubbers, go to **Zouk** or **Velvet Underground** out at Jiak Kim Street or to **Neo Pharaohs** on Cairnhill Road, all very good examples of how cosmopolitan Singapore can be (see chapter 9). Now, run down to **Johnny Two Thumb Tattoo Studio** at 14 Scotts Rd. #04-15 (☎ **65/737-4861**) for a souvenir that will last forever. (*Just kidding*—and don't blame me if you do it.) Stay out all night, then run to catch your plane!

FAST FACTS: Singapore

American Express   The American Express office is located at #01-04/05 Winslan House, Killiney Road (a short walk from Orchard Road). The direct line for travel services is ☎ **65/235-5788.** The 24-hour membership services hot line is ☎ **1800/732-2244.** The 24-hour traveler's check refund hot line is ☎ **1800/738-3383.** See the "Money" section of chapter 2 for more details on member privileges.

Baby-Sitters   Most hotels will arrange for a reliable baby-sitter with at least 24 hours advance notice.

Business Hours   Shopping centers are open Monday through Saturday from 10am to 8pm, and stay open until 10pm on some public holidays. **Banks** are open from 9:30am to 3pm Monday through Friday, and from 9am to 11am on Saturdays. **Restaurants** open at lunchtime from around 11am to 2:30pm and for dinner they re-open at around 6pm and take last order sometime around 10pm. **Nightclubs** stay open until midnight on weekdays and until 2am on Fridays and Saturdays. **Government offices** are open from 9am to 5pm Monday through

Friday and from 9am to 3pm on Saturdays. **Post offices** conduct business from 8:30am to 5pm on weekdays and from 8:30am to 1pm on Saturdays.

Cameras & Film   There are many camera equipment shops in the malls on **Orchard Road,** and some will take repairs. Avoid the shops in Far East Plaza and Lucky Plaza, as these are not as reputable. Film is readily available everywhere at prices comparable to the West. Many of the major shopping centers have fast and inexpensive film-developing services, and developing quality is generally excellent.

Climate   See "When to Go" in chapter 2.

Credit Cards   To report lost or stolen credit cards, the number to call for **American Express** is ☎ **1800/732-2244.** For **MasterCard,** the international collect call number is ☎ **314/275-6690** (dial the international operator and request a collect or reverse-charges call). The same applies for **Visa,** at ☎ **410/581-7931.** If your **Diners Club** card is lost or stolen, call locally ☎ **65/294-4222.**

Crime   Because of harsh laws, strict enforcement, and traditional cultural beliefs, there is not a lot of crime in Singapore. Murder and rape are almost nonexistent. A few pickpockets do creep around tourist-populated areas, though, so take care. All hotels have either a safe deposit box in the room or a safe behind the front counter. The only other thieves you need to be aware of are shop owners who may overcharge you for purchases, all in the sport of savvy salesmanship. To defend yourself, see chapter 8 for tips on how to bargain effectively, and have a ball negotiating your way to some great prices.

   Also, you probably don't want to become a criminal yourself. Violations that bring on large fines include littering, jaywalking, smoking in prohibited areas, and failing to obey taxi queues (meaning that if there's a taxi queue nearby, it's against the law to hail a cab out of the queue).

   The number to call for a **police emergency** is ☎ **999.**

Currency   See "Money" in chapter 2.

Customs   See "Customs Regulations" in chapter 2.

Dentists   Dental care in Singapore is excellent, and most procedures will cost less than they would at home. Some hospitals offer emergency dental care at affordable rates, should your teeth be unfortunate enough to require attention during your trip.

Doctors   Most hotels have in-house doctors on call 24 hours a day. A visit to a private physician can cost anywhere between S$25 and S$100 (US$15.75 and US$63). In the event of a medical emergency call ☎ **995** for an ambulance.

Driving Rules   See "Getting Around" earlier in this chapter.

Drug Laws   If you are caught in possession of morphine quantities exceeding 30 grams, heroin exceeding 15 grams, cocaine 30 grams, marijuana 500 grams, hashish 200 grams, or opium 1.2 grams, the Singapore government will consider you to be a drug trafficker and you will receive the death penalty—no questions asked. See the "Customs Regulations" section in chapter 2 for more details.

Electricity   Standard electrical current is 220 volts. Consult your concierge to see if your hotel has converters and plug adapters in-house for you to use. If you are using sensitive equipment, do not trust the cheap voltage transformers. Nowadays, a lot of electrical equipment—including portable radios and laptop computers—has built-in converters, so you can follow the manufacturer's directions for changing them over. FYI, videocassettes taped on different voltage currents are recorded on machines with different record and playback cycles. Prerecorded videotapes are not interchangeable between currents unless you have special equipment that can play either kind.

Embassies & Consulates   See "Visitor Information & Entry Requirements" in chapter 2.

Emergencies   For police dial ☎ **999.** For medical or fire emergencies call ☎ **995.**

Etiquette   See "Singaporean Etiquette & Customs" in chapter 1.

Hairdressers/Barbers   Most major hotels have unisex salons, and you can find them in many shopping malls as well. For the gentleman who wants a special shave 'n' a haircut, you can always try the back alley behind the Allsagoff School off Sultan Road in Kampong Glam. They don't make places like these anymore . . .

Hitchhiking   Definitely not recommended in Singapore. Heaven knows what fines you'll invite.

Holidays   See the "Calendar of Public Holidays & Events" in chapter 2.

Hospitals   If you need to seek emergency medical attention, go to either of the following centrally located private hospitals: **Mount Elizabeth Hospital Ltd.,** 3 Mount Elizabeth Rd., near Orchard Road (☎ **65/737-2666**) or **Singapore General Hospital,** Outram Road, in Chinatown (☎ **65/222-3322**). Medical care in Singapore is of superior quality. In fact, throngs of ASEAN neighbors make annual trips to Singapore for their physical examinations and other medical treatments. You can be assured of excellent care, should you need it.

Language   The official languages are Malay, Chinese (Mandarin), Tamil, and English. Malay is the national language while English is the language for government operations, law, and major financial transactions. Most Singaporeans are at least bilingual, with many speaking one or more dialects of Chinese, English, and some Malay.

Laundry   Almost all Singaporeans have washing machines in their homes, so the concept of self-service laundry is not terribly common here. There are some laundries listed in the Singapore Yellow Pages directory, but most of them are out in the Housing Board developments, so it may be a trek. A few hotels offer self-service launderettes, and most of them have a laundry service, but you'll pay inflated prices for clean clothes. (I've noted which hotels provide these facilities/services in chapter 4.)

Liquor Laws   The legal age for alcohol purchase and consumption is 18 years. Some of the smaller clubs rarely check identification, but the larger ones will, and sometimes require patrons to be 21 years to enter, just to weed out younger crowds. Public drunk-and-disorderly behavior is against the law, and may snag you for up to S$1,000 (US$624) in fines for the first offense, or even imprisonment—which is unlikely, but still a great way to ruin a vacation. There are strict drinking and driving laws, and road blocks are set up on weekends to catch party people on their way home to the housing developments.

Mail   Most hotels have post services at the front counter. **Singapore Post** has centrally located offices at #04-15 Takashimaya Shopping Centre (☎ **65/738-6899**); Tang's department store at 320 Orchard Rd. #03-00 (☎ **65/738-5899**); World Trade Centre, 1 Maritime Sq. #01-41 (☎ **65/270-6899**); Chinatown Point, 133 New Bridge Rd. #02-42/43/44 (☎ **65/538-7899**); and at Change Alley, 16 Collyer Quay #02-02 (☎ **65/538-6899**). Plus there are five branches at Changi

International Airport. The going rate for international airmail letters to North America and Europe is S$1 (US63¢) for 20 grams plus S35¢ for each additional 10 grams. For international airmail service to Australia and New Zealand, the rate is S70¢ for 20 grams plus S30¢ for each additional 10 grams. Postcards and aerograms to all destinations are S50¢.

Your hotel will accept mail sent for you at their address. For other mail services, refer to the section on American Express under "Money" in chapter 2—AmEx has a special mail delivery and holding deal for cardmembers.

Maps   The *Singapore Street Directory,* a book detailing every section of the island, is carried by most taxi drivers, and can be very helpful if you're trying to get some-place and he either doesn't know where it is or can't understand you. The street listing in the front will direct you to the corresponding map. A good cabbie can take it from there.

Newspapers & Magazines   Local English newspapers available are the *International Herald Tribune, The Business Times, The Straits Times,* and *USA Today International.* Following an article criticizing the Singapore government, the *Asian Wall Street Journal* was banned from wide distribution in Singapore. Most of the major hotels are allowed to carry it, though, so ask around and you can find one. *The New Paper* is an "alternative publication" that may be a useful source for find-ing out what's happening around town. Major hotels, bookstores, and magazine shops sell a wide variety of international magazines.

Pets   Singapore has strict quarantine regulations, and I'll be shocked if you can find a hotel that will take pets. Keep poochie at home.

Pharmacies/Chemists   **Guardian Pharmacies** is a very reliable pharmacy chain. Convenient locations include #B1-05 Centrepoint Shopping Centre (☎ **65/737-4835**); Changi International Airport Terminal 2 (☎ **65/545-4233**); #02-139 Marina Sq. (☎ **65/338-9253**); and #03-09 Raffles Place MRT Station (☎ **65/535-2762**).

Police   Given the strict law enforcement reputation in Singapore, you can bet the officers here don't have the greatest senses of humor. If you find yourself being ques-tioned about anything, big or small, be dead serious and most respectful. For emer-gencies, call ☎ **999.** If you need to call the police headquarters, dial ☎ **65/ 235-9111.**

If you are arrested, you have the right to legal council, but only when the police decide you can exercise that right. You get no call unless they give you permission. Bottom line: Don't get arrested.

Radio/TV   There are five channels in Singapore, four of which are mostly English-language programming. These days, more shows are being produced locally, but there's still a heavy rotation of the latest hits from the United States, the U.K., and Australia. At the time of writing, the hottest import was *The X-Files.* The larger hotels all have HBO and some have CNN, as well as other satellite programming.

There are five FM radio stations, which broadcast in all of the national languages.

Rest Room / Toilets   Rest rooms are easy to find in Singapore and most of the time they are clean. Note that the authorities levy fines for not flushing, though I've never seen anyone actually come in and check. The more modern facilities will have toilet bowls, but you won't get out of Singapore alive without encountering a "squatter"— a small porcelain bowl in the floor over which you are expected to hover. Be pre-pared. If you head out to beach areas or to surrounding islands, bring spare tissue.

Safety   Singapore is a pretty safe place by any standards. There's very little violent crime, even late at night. If you stay out, there's very little worry about making it home safe. If your children are missing, they probably aren't kidnapped, but are being consoled by a friendly passerby while they search for you. This may sound naive, but the Chinese are culturally a very family-oriented people, and most would never dream of harming a child.

In recent years, some pickpocketing has been reported. Hotel safe deposit boxes are the best way to secure valuables, and traveler's checks solve theft problems in a jiff.

Smoking   It's against the law to smoke in public buses, elevators, theaters, cinemas, air-conditioned restaurants, shopping centers, government offices, and taxi queues.

Taxes   Many hotels and restaurants will advertise rates followed by "+++." The first + is the goods and services tax (GST), which is levied at 3% of the purchase. The second + is 1% cess (a 1% tax levied by the STB on all tourism-related activities). The third is a 10% gratuity. See the "Customs Regulations" section in chapter 2 for information on the GST Tourist Refund Scheme, which lets you recover the GST for purchases of goods over S$350 in value.

Taxis   See "Getting Around" earlier in this chapter.

Telegrams & Wiring Money   See "Money" in chapter 2 for information on wiring money. To send a telegram, consult your hotel. Many of them offer this service for a fee.

Telephones & Faxes   Almost all hotels will send faxes locally and internationally for you and add the charge to your bill.

Public phones are abundant and can be operated by coins or by phone cards, which can be purchased in increments of S$2, S$5, and S$10 (US$1.25, US$3.15, and US$6.30) values at post offices, provisioners shops, and some money changers. The charge for a local call is S10¢ for 3 minutes. A tone will interrupt your call when your time is up to remind you to add another coin. Calls to numbers beginning with 1800 are toll-free.

International Direct Dialing (IDD) is the long-distance service used by most hotels, businesses, and private residences in Singapore, with direct dialing to 218 countries. Depending on where you are calling, there is rarely a delay or echo on the line, and reception is incredibly clear.

Before you leave your home country, contact your long-distance provider to see if they offer a **long-distance calling card,** which will allow you to access their international operators and have your calls charged to your home phone bill at their rates. Singapore has some of the lowest international call rates in the world, but unfortunately, hotels charge a whopping surcharge for these calls.

- **To place a call from your home country to Singapore,** dial the international access code (011 in the U.S., 0011 in Australia, 0170 in New Zealand, or 00 in the U.K.), plus the country code (65), plus the seven-digit phone number (for example, 011 + 65 + 000-0000). Note that many hotels have toll-free numbers for calling from all these countries; where this is the case, I've listed them in the individual hotel reviews.
- **To place a call within Singapore,** just dial the seven-digit number. The "65" prefix need not be used. Toll-free numbers in Singapore use the standard "1800" prefix.

- **To place a direct international call from Singapore,** dial the international access code (005) plus the country code, the area or city code, and the number (for example, 005 + 01 + 212/000-0000).
- **To reach the international operator,** dial ☎ 104.
- **To call Malaysia from Singapore** via an operator, dial ☎ 109; to call direct, dial the international access code (005) plus Malaysia's country code (60) plus the city code and the number (for example, 005 + 60 + 000-0000).
- **To call AT&T direct,** call ☎ 800/011-1111; for MCI, call ☎ 800/011-2112; and for Sprint, call ☎ 800/017-7177.

In case you forget, **international country codes** are as follows: for the U.S. and Canada 01, for Australia 61, for New Zealand 62, and for the U.K. 44. Singapore's is 65.

Other useful numbers are for the **time** (☎ 1711), and for the **weather** (☎ 65/542-7788). For **telephone directory assistance,** dial ☎ 100.

Time   Singapore Standard Time is 8 hours ahead of Greenwich mean time (GMT). International time differences will change during daylight saving or summer time. Basic time differences are: New York – 13, Los Angeles – 16, Montreal – 13, Vancouver – 16, London – 8, Brisbane + 3, Darwin + 1, Melbourne + 2, Sydney + 3, and Auckland + 4. For the current time within Singapore, call ☎ 1711.

Tipping   Tipping is discouraged at hotels, bars, and in taxis. Basically, the deal here is not to tip. A gratuity is automatically added into guest checks, and there's no need to slip anyone an extra buck for carrying bags or such. It's not expected.

Tourist Offices   See "Visitor Information & Entry Requirements" in chapter 2.

Water   Tap water in Singapore passes World Health Organization standards and is potable.

Yellow Pages   The Singapore Yellow Pages is the place to start for any need that may come up. They are standard in most hotel rooms. They're rarely found at public phones, but shopkeepers may let you take a peek at theirs if you ask nicely.

4 Accommodations

At last count, the number of official (gazetted) hotels in Singapore was approaching 90, and the number of hotel rooms was somewhere over 30,000. Now here's another fact to chew over: On any given night, up to 80% of these rooms are occupied by business travelers. International business is the Singaporean hotel industry's bread and butter, and so competition between hotels is fierce, causing them to invest in the most high-priced renovations of the most deluxe-super-royal-regal executive facilities, all in an attempt to lure business folks and—eventually, hopefully—land lucrative corporate accounts.

Of course, this all means that budget accommodations are not a high priority on the island. Between the business community's demand for luxury on the one hand and the inflated Singaporean real estate market on the other, room prices tend to be high. What this means for leisure travelers is that you may end up paying for a business center you'll never use or a 24-hour stress-reliever masseuse you'll never call—and all this without the benefit of a corporate discount rate.

Don't fret, though: I'm here to tell you that there's a range of accommodations out there—you just have to know where to find 'em. In this chapter, I'll help you pick the right accommodations for you, based on your vacation goals and your travel budget, so you can make the most of your stay.

CHOOSING YOUR NEIGHBORHOOD

In considering where you'll stay, think about what you'll be doing in Singapore—that way, you can choose a hotel that's close to the particular action that suits you. (On the other hand, since Singapore is a small city and public transportation is excellent, nothing's really ever too far away.)

Orchard Road has the largest cluster of hotels in the city, and is right in the heart of Singaporean shopping-mania—the malls and wide sidewalks where locals and tourists stroll to see and be seen. The **Historic District** has hotels that are near museums and sights, while those in **Marina Bay** center more around the business professionals who come to Singapore for Suntec City, the giant convention and exhibition center located there. **Chinatown** and **Tanjong Pagar** have some lovely boutique hotels in quaint back streets, and **Shenton Way** has a couple of high-rise places for the convenience of people doing business in the downtown business district. Many hotels have free morning and evening shuttle buses to Orchard Road, Suntec City, and Shenton Way. I've also listed two hotels on **Sentosa,** an island to the south that's a popular day or weekend trip for many Singaporeans. (It's connected to Singapore by a causeway.)

CHOOSING YOUR HOME AWAY FROM HOME

What appeals to you? A big, flashy, internationalist palace or a smaller, homier place? Hyatt, Sheraton, Hilton, and Hotel Intercontinental are just a few of the international chain hotels you will find in Singapore. Many hotels, such the Mandarin; The Marco Polo, Singapore; the Shangri-La; and the Hilton, were built in the seventies, during Singapore's economic boom, and while they've seen many major renovations over the years, they're not as flashy as the newer properties. One benefit, however, is these older hotels sometimes have larger rooms and more landscaped ground space. For the most part, the modern hotels are nondescript towers—though the Westin has the distinction of being the tallest hotel in the world.

The newest trend is the **boutique hotel.** Conceived as part of the Urban Restoration Authority's renewal plans, rows of old shophouses and buildings in ethnic areas like Chinatown and Tanjong Pagar have been restored and transformed into small, lovely hotels. Places like Albert Court Hotel, the Duxton, and the Royal Peacock are beautiful examples of local flavor turned into elegant accommodations. While these places can put you closer to the heart of Singapore, they do have their drawbacks: Both the hotels and their rooms are small, for one, and, due to lack of space and building codes, they're unable to provide facilities like swimming pools, Jacuzzis, or fitness centers.

While **budget hotels** have very limited facilities and interior stylings that never made it much past 1979, you can always expect a clean room. What's more, service can sometimes be more personal in smaller hotels, where front desk staff have fewer faces to recognize and are accustomed to helping guests with the sorts of things a business center or concierge would handle in a larger hotel. Par for the course, many of the guests in these places are backpackers, and mostly Western backpackers at that. However, you will see some ASEAN people staying in these places. *One note:* The budget accommodations listed here are places decent enough for any standards. While cheaper digs are available, the rooms can be dreary and depressing, musty, and old, or downright sleazy.

Unless you choose one of the extreme budget hotels, there are some standard features you can expect to find everywhere. While no hotels offer a courtesy car or limousine, many have **courtesy shuttles** to popular parts of town. Security key cards are catching on, as are in-room safes (yes, even in safe and secure Singapore). You'll also see in-house movies and sometimes CNN on your TV, as well as a nifty interactive service that lets you check on your hotel bill, order room service, and get general information on Singapore with the touch of a button. Voice mail is gaining popularity, and fax services can always be provided upon request. You'll find most places have adequate fitness center facilities, almost all of which offer a range of massage treatments. Pools tend to be on the small side, and Jacuzzis are often placed in men's and women's locker rooms, making it impossible for couples to use them together. While tour desks are in some lobbies, car rental desks are rare.

Many of the finest **restaurants** in Singapore are located in hotels, whether they operated by the hotel directly or just inhabiting rented space. Some hotels can have up to five or six restaurants, each serving a different cuisine. Generally, you can expect these restaurants to be more expensive than places not located in hotels. In each hotel review, the distinguished restaurants have been noted; these restaurants are also fully reviewed in chapter 5.

Urban Singapore Accommodations

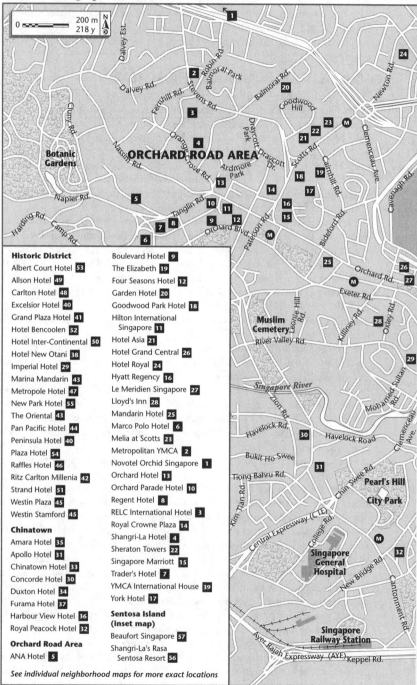

0 ▬▬ 200 m
218 y

N

Botanic Gardens

ORCHARD ROAD AREA

Balmoral Park

Goodwood Hill

Ardmore Park

Draycott Park

Muslim Cemetery

Singapore River

Pearl's Hill City Park

Singapore General Hospital

Singapore Railway Station

Historic District
Albert Court Hotel **53**
Allson Hotel **49**
Carlton Hotel **48**
Excelsior Hotel **40**
Grand Plaza Hotel **41**
Hotel Bencoolen **52**
Hotel Inter-Continental **50**
Hotel New Otani **38**
Imperial Hotel **29**
Marina Mandarin **43**
Metropole Hotel **47**
New Park Hotel **55**
The Oriental **43**
Pan Pacific Hotel **44**
Peninsula Hotel **40**
Plaza Hotel **54**
Raffles Hotel **46**
Ritz Carlton Millenia **42**
Strand Hotel **51**
Westin Plaza **45**
Westin Stamford **45**

Chinatown
Amara Hotel **35**
Apollo Hotel **31**
Chinatown Hotel **33**
Concorde Hotel **30**
Duxton Hotel **34**
Furama Hotel **37**
Harbour View Hotel **36**
Royal Peacock Hotel **32**

Orchard Road Area
ANA Hotel **5**

Boulevard Hotel **9**
The Elizabeth **19**
Four Seasons Hotel **12**
Garden Hotel **20**
Goodwood Park Hotel **18**
Hilton International Singapore **11**
Hotel Asia **21**
Hotel Grand Central **26**
Hotel Royal **24**
Hyatt Regency **16**
Le Meridien Singapore **27**
Lloyd's Inn **28**
Mandarin Hotel **25**
Marco Polo Hotel **6**
Melia at Scotts **23**
Metropolitan YMCA **2**
Novotel Orchid Singapore **1**
Orchard Hotel **13**
Orchard Parade Hotel **10**
Regent Hotel **8**
RELC International Hotel **3**
Royal Crowne Plaza **14**
Shangri-La Hotel **4**
Sheraton Towers **22**
Singapore Marriott **15**
Trader's Hotel **7**
YMCA International House **39**
York Hotel **17**

Sentosa Island (inset map)
Beaufort Singapore **57**
Shangri-La's Rasa Sentosa Resort **56**

See individual neighborhood maps for more exact locations

68

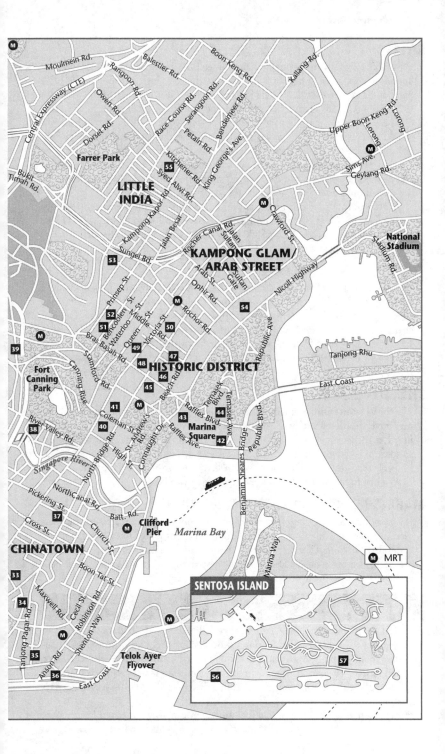

RATES

Let's talk money. Rates for double rooms range from as low as S$80 (US$50) at the Strand on Bencoolen (a famous backpacker's strip) to as high as S$650 (US$411) a night at the exclusive Raffles Hotel. Average rooms are usually in the S$200 to S$300 (US$126 to US$189) range, but keep in mind that although all prices listed in this book are the going rates, they rarely represent what you'll actually pay. In fact, you should *never* have to pay the advertised rate in a Singapore hotel, as many offer special rates just after a renovation, or for reservations made through the Internet or through a travel agent, or for visitors booking long-term stays or stays that begin and end on weekdays. When you call for your reservation, always ask what special rates they are running and how you can get the lowest price for your room.

For the purposes of this guide, we've divided hotels into the categories **Very Expensive,** S$400 (US$252) and up; **Expensive,** S$300 to S$400 (US$189 to US$252); **Moderate,** S$200 to S$300 (US$126 to US$189); and **Inexpensive,** under S$200 (US$126).

TAXES & SERVICE CHARGES

All rates listed are in Singapore dollars, with U.S. dollar equivalents provided as well (remember to check the exchange rates when you're planning, though, as they will almost certainly be different). Most rates do not include the so-called "+++" taxes and charges: the 10% service charge, 3% goods and services tax (GST), and 1% cess (a 1% tax levied by the STB on all tourism-related activities). Keep these in mind when figuring your budget. Some budget hotels will quote discount rates inclusive of all taxes.

THE BUSY SEASON

The busy season is from January to around June. In the late summer months, business travel dies down and hotels try to make up for drooping occupancy rates by going after the leisure market. In fall, even tourism drops off somewhat, making the season ripe for budget-minded visitors. These may be the best times to get a deal. Probably the worst time to negotiate will be between Christmas and the Chinese New Year, when folks travel on holiday and to see their families.

MAKING RESERVATIONS ON THE GROUND

If you are not able to make a reservation prior to your trip, there is a **reservation service** available at Changi International Airport. The Singapore Hotel Association operates desks in both Terminals 1 and 2, with reservation services based upon room availability for many hotels. Discounts for these arrangements are sometimes as high as 30%. The desks are open daily from 7:30am to 11:30pm.

1 Best Bets

- **Best Feng Shui:** No doubt about it, for a little extra good vibes, stay at the **Hyatt Regency.** This hotel suffered from low occupancy rates until it consulted a Chinese monk to put the structure in harmony with its surrounding elements, seen and unseen. The day after the recommended adjustments were completed (at quite some cost), the hotel reopened and immediately ran at full capacity for 3 days straight.
- **Best Romantic Hideaway:** The **Beaufort Sentosa, Singapore** is a favorite spot for honeymooners. Request dinner anywhere (even in the woods or by the sea) and they will make your dreams come true.

- **Best Hotels for the Suit and Tie Set:** While all of the international hotels have good executive club facilities, the **Hyatt Regency** and the **Royal Crowne Plaza** have the most exciting rooms. Very powerful. Go get 'em.
- **Best Hotel for History Nuts:** **Raffles Hotel** and the **Goodwood Park Hotel** are both historical landmarks. Go to town.
- **Best Local-Flavor Accommodations:** The **Albert Court Hotel** and the **Hotel Inter-Continental's** Shophouse Rooms have captured a truly lovely local feel and combined it with the comfort of a modern facility. You can experience Singapore culture without leaving your room.
- **Best View:** From the upper floors of the **Westin Stamford Hotel** you can see all the way across the water to Indonesia. The **Marina Mandarin** has gorgeous views of the marina on one side of the hotel, while the **Ritz-Carlton** has spectacular views on both sides. **Shangri-La's Rasa Sentosa Resort** on Sentosa has to be given a special award for the breathtaking view of the beach and surrounding seas. At night, the lights from docked ships twinkle on the horizon. It's simply gorgeous.
- **Best View from a Tub:** You have to see it to believe it, but every huge bathtub in the **Ritz-Carlton** sits just beneath an octagonal picture window with views of the harbor and marina. You can sightsee while you have a soak!
- **Best Pool:** The **Beaufort Sentosa, Singapore** has a large outdoor pool tiled in midnight blue specked with mica. During the day it glistens almost black; at night it shimmers emerald green. **Shangri-La's Rasa Sentosa Resort's** pool is a mass of curvy spaces with lots of fun pool equipment to play around with. The kiddie pool has rock slides that will make you wish you were 9 again.
- **Most High-Profile Address:** If you live to impress, **Raffles Hotel** is where you will stay. It was the first choice of Michael Jackson and every other famous figure to pass through Singapore since God knows when.
- **Best Hotels for Shopaholics:** Anywhere on Orchard Road.
- **Best Hotels for Tourists Who Don't Want to Miss Anything:** The **Marco Polo, Singapore; Traders Hotel;** and the **Regent** are all located right across the street from the headquarters of the Singapore Tourism Board (STB).
- **Best Hotels for Penny-Pinchers:** I challenge you to find better value for money than at **RELC International Hotel.**
- **Best Hotel for Backpackers:** The **Strand** is the freshest in its class. And while hostels are not common here, the **YMCA International** is a clean and safe alternative.
- **Best Hotel for Tree Huggers:** The **Shangri-La** and the **Beaufort Sentosa, Singapore** boast extensive gardens and live up to expectations.
- **Best Spa:** The **Grand Plaza Hotel,** the **Plaza,** and the **Four Seasons.** See the feature "Meet Me at the Spa, Dahling . . ." later in this chapter to find out why.
- **Best Butt Kissing:** The **Four Seasons** will pamper you like a VIP, with style and grace.

2 The Historic District

VERY EXPENSIVE

✪ **Raffles Hotel.** 1 Beach Rd., Singapore 189673. ☎ **800/525-4800** from the U.S. and Canada, 008/251-958 from Australia, 0800/441098 from New Zealand, 0800/964470 from the U.K., or 65/337-1886. Fax 65/339-7650. www.slh.com/slh/. 104 suites. A/C MINIBAR TV TEL. S$650–S$6000 (US$409–US$3,780) suite. AE, DC, JCB, MC, V. Near City Hall MRT.

Raffles Hotel has been legendary since its establishment in 1887. Named after Singapore's first British colonial administrator, Sir Stamford Raffles, it was founded by the Armenian Sarkies brothers. Originally, it was a bungalow, but by the 1920s and 1930s it had expanded to become a mecca for celebrities like Charlie Chaplin and Douglas Fairbanks, for writers like Somerset Maugham and Noel Coward, and for various and sundry kings, sultans, and politicians. Always at the center of Singapore's colonial high life, it's hosted balls, tea dances, and jazz functions, and during World War II was the last rallying point for the British in the face of Japanese occupation and the first place for refugee prisoners of war released from concentration camps. In 1987, Raffles Hotel was declared a landmark and restored to its early-20th-century splendor, with 14-foot molded and be-fanned ceilings, grand arches, tiled teak and marble floors, oriental carpets, and period furnishings. Outside, the facade of the main building was similarly restored, complete with the elegant cast-iron portico and the verandahs that encircle the upper stories.

Because it is a national landmark, thousands of people pass through the open lobby each day, so in addition there's a private inner lobby marked off for "residents" only. Nothing feels better than walking along the dark teak floors of the verandahs, past little rattan-furnished relaxation areas overlooking the green tropical courtyards. Each suite entrance is like a private apartment door: Enter past the living and dining area dressed in oriental carpets and reproduction furniture, then pass through louvered doors into the bedroom with its four-poster bed and beautiful armoire, ceiling fan twirling high above. Now imagine you're a colonial traveler, fresh in town from a long ocean voyage. Raffles is the only hotel in Singapore where you can still fully play out this fantasy, and it can be a lot of fun.

Hotel services include an airport limousine and 24-hour room valet and concierge. Facilities include in-room VCRs with video rental, small outdoor pool (open 24 hours), 24-hour business center, and 24-hour fitness center with Jacuzzi, sauna, steam, and massage.

Accommodations aside, the hotel's restaurants and nightlife also draw the crowds, who come to eat at the Tiffin Room, Raffles Grill, and Doc Cheng's (all reviewed in chapter 5) and to lounge in the Bar and Billiards Room and Long Bar. The Raffles Hotel arcade was designed in architectural harmony with the original design and houses a theater playhouse, Raffles Culinary Academy, the Raffles Hotel Museum, and 65 exclusive boutiques.

✪ **The Ritz-Carlton Millenia Singapore.** 7 Raffles Ave., Singapore 039799. ☎ **800/ 241-3333** from the U.S. and Canada, or 65/337-8888. Fax 65/338-0001. www.ritzcarlton.com. 610 units. A/C MINIBAR TV TEL. S$430 (US$271) double; S$1350 (US$850) suite. AE, DC, JCB, MC, V. 10-minute walk to City Hall MRT.

Touted as the ultimate in Singapore luxury hotels, the Ritz-Carlton Millenia is just that, but you have to love ultra-modern design. The space-age lobby is like a science museum, and off to the right is a giant open space with elegant contemporary seating areas under a greenhouse skylight. The sculptures and artworks displayed throughout this place are very daring and innovative, but, luckily for guests, the guest rooms don't try too hard at innovation: They just stick to being warm and friendly. All rooms have views of either Kallang Bay or the more majestic Marina Bay. Even the bathrooms have views, as the huge tubs are placed under octagonal picture windows so you can gaze as you bathe. Oh, the decadence. Guest rooms here are about 25% larger than most five-star rooms elsewhere. There's room for lovely seating areas, big two-poster beds, and full walk-in closets.

Twenty-four-hour maid service is available, and facilities include voice mail; a health club with aerobics, massage, sauna, steam, hot and cold plunge pools, and spa cuisine; an outdoor tennis court; a beauty salon; and a gift shop. The hotel pool is a gorgeous 25-meter Greco-Roman monster done in streaks of shimmering blue tile.

Historic District Accommodations

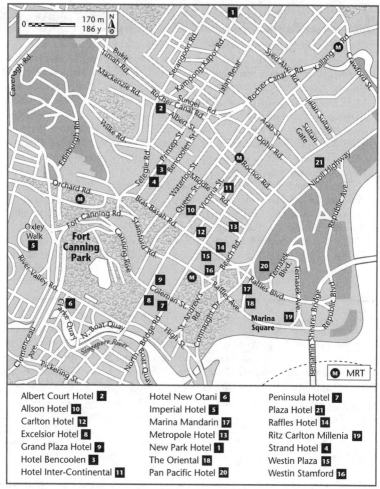

Albert Court Hotel **2**	Hotel New Otani **6**	Peninsula Hotel **7**
Allson Hotel **10**	Imperial Hotel **5**	Plaza Hotel **21**
Carlton Hotel **12**	Marina Mandarin **17**	Raffles Hotel **14**
Excelsior Hotel **8**	Metropole Hotel **13**	Ritz Carlton Millenia **19**
Grand Plaza Hotel **9**	New Park Hotel **1**	Strand Hotel **4**
Hotel Bencoolen **3**	The Oriental **18**	Westin Plaza **15**
Hotel Inter-Continental **11**	Pan Pacific Hotel **20**	Westin Stamford **16**

At the far end is a Jacuzzi tucked beneath a cascading waterfall. The elegant poolside cafe serves meals while you laze about.

EXPENSIVE

Carlton Hotel Singapore. 76 Bras Basah Rd., Singapore 189558. ☎ **65/338-8333.** Fax 65/339-6866. www.carlton.com.sg. E-mail: RoomReservations@Carlton.com.sg. 477 units. A/C MINIBAR TV TEL. S$320 (US$202) double; S$450 (US$283) suite. AE, DC, JCB, MC, V. 5-minute walk to City Hall MRT.

The most appealing features of the Carlton are its location, in the heart of the Historic District, and the view from its front rooms—of the harbor, river, and financial district plus an aerial view of the entire Chijmes block, just across the street. Make sure you specify rooms with the views, as the back view (or "city view") is not nearly as spectacular. The lobby is a dimly lit space distinguished by garden plantings and lots of marble and oak, creating an atmosphere that's much more inviting than the austere and cold grandeur of a lot of its competitors. (*Note:* The coin fountain in the lobby collects money for the Kidney Dialysis Foundation—toss a couple coins in.)

🏨 Family-Friendly Hotels

Unfortunately, Singapore's hotels are geared so heavily to the business traveler that very few have good facilities for families. For every rule there's an exception, of course, and in Singapore that exception is the truly phenomenal **Shangri-La's Rasa Sentosa Resort** (see page 96). For the younger kids, there's a day-care center with activities, lunches, and nap time. A video arcade and table tennis games keep older kids occupied, and the kiddie pool has rock-formation slides that are a childhood dream come true. For teens, the Rasa Sentosa offers nature walks, rock climbing, beach volleyball, and windsurfing, and has in-line skates for rent. Basically, they offer all you could ever want to make your kids' vacation as good as yours, and even have a little quiet time to yourself.

The inexpensive **YMCA International House** (see page 95) is a good deal for traveling families. The rooms are big enough for extra beds, the pool has a full-time lifeguard on duty, and the McDonald's in the lobby means the kids won't go hungry if they turn up their noses at the local fare.

The **Novotel Orchid Singapore** (see page 92) is out of the way, but the rooms are big and each one has a sofa bed. Games by the pool keep the kids busy when you're too pooped to care, and a self-service launderette helps cut laundry costs.

The rooms have large sunny windows and a nice, casual ambiance, but aren't much by way of counter and closet space. The small bathrooms have very good showers. Facilities include Jacuzzi, sauna, a tour desk, and a beauty salon. Unfortunately, for a hotel in this price range, the fitness center facilities, pool area, and business center are not as modern, well equipped, or attractive as the competition.

The Grand Plaza Hotel. 10 Coleman St., Singapore 179809. ☎ **800/44-UTELL** from the U.S. and Canada, or 65/336-3456. Fax 65/339-9311. E-mail: gph@pacific.net.sg. 338 units. A/C MINIBAR TV TEL. S$300–S$320 (US$189–US$201) double; S$360–S$380 (US$227–US$239) club; S$600–S$1,200 (US$378–US$756) suite. AE, DC, JCB, MC, V. 5-minute walk to City Hall MRT.

The Grand Plaza was built on top of (and incorporating) 2 blocks of prewar shophouses, and you can see hints of shophouse detail throughout the lobby, which is otherwise like any other hotel's. The old alleyway that ran between the shophouse blocks has been transformed into a courtyard where dinner is served alfresco.

The Grand Plaza's guest rooms are of average size, have considerable closet space, and sport sharp Italian contemporary furniture in natural tones, with homey touches like snugly comforters on all the beds. Facilities include a small outdoor pool from which you can see the steeple of the Armenian Church across the street; a modern fitness center with hot and cold Jacuzzis, sauna, and steam; a beauty salon; and a small shopping arcade.

The hotel's Saint Gregory Marine Spa is Singapore's largest and most exclusive spa. There are 20 private treatment rooms where you can enjoy hydrotherapy baths, jet showers, Jacuzzis, steam baths, facial and body treatments, and massage therapies. Tell them about your aches and pains, even jet lag, and they'll have an amazing treatment to help you out.

The hotel is located at the corner of Coleman and Hill streets, just across from the Armenian Church, the Asian Civilisations Museum, the Singapore Arts Museum, and Fort Canning Park. A shuttle will take you to Orchard Road.

✪ Hotel Inter-Continental Singapore. 80 Middle Rd., Singapore 188966 (near Bugis Junction). ☎ **65/338-7600.** Fax 65/338-7366. 406 units. A/C MINIBAR TV TEL. S$375 (US$236) double; S$850 (US$535) suite. AE, DC, JCB, MC, V. Bugis MRT.

The government let Inter-Continental build a hotel in this spot with one ironclad stipulation: The hotel chain had to retain the original shophouses on the block and incorporate them into the hotel design. No preservation, no hotel. Reinforcing the foundation, Hotel Inter-Continental built up from there, giving touches of old architectural style to the lobby, lounge, and other public areas on the bottom floors while imbuing it with the feel of a modern hotel. Features like beamed ceilings and wooden staircases are warmly accentuated with Chinese and European antique reproductions, Oriental carpets, and local artworks. The second and third floors have "Shophouse Rooms" styled with such Peranakan trappings as carved hardwood furnishings and floral linens, and with homey touches like potted plants and carpets over wooden floors. These rooms are very unique, presenting a surprising element of local flair that you don't often find in large chain hotels. Guest rooms on higher levels are large, with formal European styling and large luxurious bathrooms. Although the pool area has a terrible view, the space is beautifully landscaped, with a wooden deck and comfortable lounge chairs. The hotel also has a rooftop garden. Facilities include a 24-hour health club, outdoor Jacuzzi, sauna, a car rental desk, and a tour desk.

Imperial Hotel Singapore. 1 Jalan Rumbia, Singapore 239616. ☎ **65/737-1666.** Fax 65/737-4761. 644 units. A/C MINIBAR TV TEL. S$300 (US$189) double; S$500 (US$315) suite. AE, DC, JCB, MC, V. 10-minute walk to Dhoby Ghaut MRT.

The Imperial Hotel is in the middle of a floor-by-floor renovation, and one look at the older sections and you'll know why: The wallpaper is peeling off in the dark, musty hallways, the rooms have wood paneling straight from the seventies that's so awful it doesn't even count towards retro chic, and the bathrooms have horrible showers with hard-to-maneuver heads you clip to the wall. By contrast, the newer Emerald Rooms and suites on the fourth through eighth floors are fresh and airy, though naturally they're more expensive. Most of the guests here are from the Asia Pacific region (particularly India), which has an exotic effect on the atmosphere and decor choices. By 1999, all the rooms may have been refurbished, but just make sure in the meantime that you don't get stuck with an oldie.

Facilities include a fitness center, a beauty salon, and a souvenir shop, and there's an excellent Indian restaurant, Rang Mahal, on the premises (see chapter 5 for a review). Surrounding construction has destroyed the view from the pool area, which might otherwise be nice given the large, open sundeck and wall of cascading water. The location, just behind Chettiar's Temple, is relatively quiet and is within walking distance of Fort Canning Park.

✪ Marina Mandarin Singapore. 6 Raffles Blvd., Marina Sq., Singapore 039594. ☎ **65/338-3388.** Fax 65/339-4977. www.marina-mandarin.com.sg. 575 units. S$320–S$360 (US$202–US$227) double; S$600–S$3,500 (US$378–US$2,205) suite. AE, DC, JCB, MC, V. 10-minute walk to City Hall MRT.

There are a few hotels in the Marina Bay area built around the atrium concept, and of them, this one is the loveliest. The atrium lobby opens up to ceiling skylights 21 stories above, guest corridor balconies lined with hanging plants line the sides, and in the center hangs a glistening metal mobile sculpture in red and gold. One of the most surprising details is the melodic chirping of caged songbirds, which fills the open space every morning. In the evening, live classical music from the lobby bar drifts upwards.

The rooms are equally impressive: large and cool, with two desk spaces and standard balconies. Try to get the Marina view—you won't be sorry. The bathrooms have double sinks, a separate shower and tub, and a bidet. Hotel facilities include a large outdoor pool; a fitness center with aerobics and massage, Jacuzzi, sauna, and steam room; a 24-hour business center; a squash court; two outside tennis courts; a putting green; a beauty salon; and a number of boutiques.

The Oriental, Singapore. 5 Raffles Ave., Marina Sq., Singapore 039797. ☎ **800/ 526-6566** from the U.S. and Canada, 1800/653328 from Australia, 0800/962667 from the U.K., or 65/338-0066. Fax 65/339-9537. 522 units. A/C MINIBAR TV TEL. S$360 (US$227) double; S$420 (US$265) suite. AE, DC, JCB, MC, V. 10-minute walk to City Hall MRT.

Another atrium-concept hotel, the Oriental is not as spectacular as the Marina Mandarin or the Pan Pacific. The atrium here is dark and quiet and the glass elevators look like strange little lighted barrels. Rooms are large and modern, but the bathrooms are not as luxurious as you might hope for in this price range. For an additional S$20, you can have the harbor view, which on the higher floors is worth the money. Tennis is available through courts shared with the Marina Mandarin, and other facilities include a Jacuzzi, sauna, a steam room, a beauty salon, and a number of boutiques. The hotel pool has underwater music and a nice, relaxed garden atmosphere. Next to the pool, the new fitness center is at press time being carved from the old squash courts. Once it's done, it'll be large and sport all new equipment.

The Pan Pacific Hotel Singapore. 7 Raffles Blvd., Marina Sq., Singapore 039595 (near Suntec City). ☎ **65/336-8111.** Fax 65/339-1861. 784 units. A/C MINIBAR TV TEL. S$300 (US$189) double; S$540 (US$340) suite. AE, DC, JCB, MC, V. 10-minute walk to City Hall MRT.

Because of its location and design, the Pan Pacific Hotel competes heavily with the Marina Mandarin and the Oriental, and though of the three I prefer the Marina Mandarin, this is a very nice hotel as well. And as nice as it is, it'll be even more attractive next year, when the lobby area is completely redecorated. Guest rooms are nice-size and comfortable, and are equipped with PCs that have an interactive system that allows you to access hotel information and other info on Singapore. The hotel facilities are even better: The pool is large and has an underwater sound system; the fitness center is huge and state-of-the-art, with aerobics classes, massage, and a very large indoor Jacuzzi; and there are boutiques, two outdoor tennis courts, a beauty salon, squash courts, a mini putting green, and a driving range. For children, there's a sandy playground by the pool, right next to which is an herb garden planted by the chef from the hotel's Tuscany restaurant.

MODERATE

✪ **Albert Court Hotel.** 180 Albert St., Singapore 189971. ☎ **65/339-3939.** Fax 65/ 339-3252. www.fareast.com.sg/hotels. 136 units. S$200–S$220 (US$126–US$139) double; S$280 (US$176) suite. AE, DC, JCB, MC, V. 5-minute walk to Bugis MRT.

The Albert Court was first conceived as part of the Urban Redevelopment Authority's master plan to revitalize this block, which involved the restoration of two rows of pre-war shophouses. The eight-story boutique hotel that emerged once the dust settled has all the Western comforts but has retained the charm of its shophouse roots. Decorators placed local Peranakan touches everywhere from the carved teak panels in traditional floral design to the antique china cups used for tea service in the rooms. (Guaranteed: The sight of them brings misty-eyed nostalgia to the hearts of Singaporeans.)

The rooms are small—though the ones at the ends of the corridors are slightly larger—and traffic noises sometimes waft up from the street below, a problem the hotel is in the process of fixing with soundproofing around the windows. Details like the teak molding, floral batik bedspreads, bathroom tiles in bright Peranakan colors, and old-time brass electrical switches give this place true local charm and distinction. Secretarial services are available.

Allson Hotel Singapore. 101 Victoria St., Singapore 188018. ☎ **65/336-0811.** Fax 65/339-7019. 450 units. A/C MINIBAR TV TEL. S$240–S$250 (US$151–US$157) double; S$450 (US$283) service apt; S$650–S$750 (US$409–US$472) suite. AE, DC, JCB, MC, V. 5-minute walk from Bugis Junction MRT.

The Allson Hotel has a great location right on Victoria Street: You walk one way and you're having fun at Bugis Junction; walk the other, you're in the heart of the city center. Sporting a large, open lobby and spacious public areas, they've reserved most of the nicest details for the guest floors. You enter into the guest rooms through beautiful carved rosewood doors, and even the less expensive rooms have Ming-style beds, tables, cabinets, and armchairs, plus colorful floral fabrics that are a welcome change from the usual any-city/anywhere room decor you generally see. The bathrooms are not as elaborate as some, and are small, but a recent overhaul of the plumbing has corrected a persnickety lack of hot water that plagued the hotel for years. Hotel facilities include a small outdoor pool; a fitness center with massage, Jacuzzi, sauna, and steam; a beauty salon; and a number of boutiques. The warm and inviting Liu Hsiang Lou Sichuan restaurant in located off the main lobby on the second floor. (See chapter 5 for a review.)

Excelsior Hotel. 5 Coleman St., Singapore 179805. ☎ **65/338-7733.** Fax 65/339-3847. 271 units. A/C MINIBAR TV TEL. S$250–S$290 (US$157–US$183) double; S$420–S$1,400 (US$265–US$882) suite. AE, DC, JCB, MC, V. 5-minute walk to City Hall MRT.

The Excelsior is not the most stylish place, but it—and its sister hotel the Peninsula—always run at high occupancy rates due to its low room rates and good arrangements with travel agents and tour group organizers. The majority of guests are tour groups and independent leisure travelers, and they have a very large regular clientele of Australians. Rooms, both deluxe and superior, are exactly the same aside from altitude: The former are on higher floors and have a few more amenities (such as slightly nicer toiletries). Headboards on the beds are a very bizarre peacock design, and sofa seating areas are tucked into small window bays. Check out the very unusual and oh-so-tacky two-story bird sculpture in the fifth-floor stairwell. Gracious.

There's no business center, but secretarial services are available. Hotel facilities include a small outdoor pool and use of the fitness center at the Peninsula Hotel, next door. One plus: The hotel is very accommodating about flight departure schedules and will let you stay and even use the shower while waiting for an evening flight.

Hotel New Otani Singapore. 177A River Valley Rd., Singapore 179031. ☎ **800/421-8795** from the U.S. and Canada, 800/273-2294 from California, or 65/338-3333. Fax 65/339-2854. www.newotani.co.jp/index-e.htm. 408 units. A/C MINIBAR TV TEL. S$280 (US$176) double; S$600 (US$378) suite. AE, DC, JCB, MC, V. Far from MRT stations.

The Hotel New Otani sits along the Singapore River just next to Clarke Quay (a popular spot for nightlife, dining, and shopping) and a stroll away from the Historic District. At night, you have access to nearby Boat Quay bars and restaurants to one side, and to the unique clubs of Mohamed Sultan Road on the other. The hotel was renovated in 1993, and recent additions (to all rooms) include multimedia PCs with Microsoft Office and tourist information. Internet access and computer games are also available for an extra charge. All rooms have small balconies letting on to unique views of the river, the financial district, Fort Canning Park, and Chinatown, and the standard rooms have large luxurious bathrooms like those you typically see in more deluxe accommodations. Facilities include a large outdoor pool; a fitness center with aerobics, a Jacuzzi, sauna, facials, and massage (you can even get a massage poolside). The hotel runs daily shuttle service to Orchard Road, Shenton Way, and Marina Square, and each guest receives free Singapore Trolley passes and a free river cruise.

New Park Hotel. 181 Kitchener Rd., Singapore 208533. ☎ **800/221176** from Australia, 0800/656666 from New Zealand, or 65/291-5533. Fax 65/297-2827. 531 units. A/C MINIBAR TV TEL. S$220–S$240 (US$139–US$151) double; S$300 (US$189) penthouse rm; S$350 (US$220) family rm; S$700 (US$441) suite. AE, DC, JCB, MC, V. 15-minute walk to Lavender MRT.

Located in Little India, this hotel is close to some of the best mosques and temples in Singapore, but far from just about everything else (including the MRT station, which is a confusing 15-minute walk, cutting through apartment blocks). Nevertheless, the staff is courteous and the guest rooms have been recently renovated with new, tasteful furnishings. The high-ceilinged guest rooms are very comfortable, have excellent storage space for luggage and clothing, and offer unique views across the rooftops of the busy shophouse neighborhood surrounding the hotel. Though the tiled bathrooms are spotless, they could use refurbishing, as the tiles appear shabby in comparison to the marble stylings of newer hotel bathrooms. The fitness center is practical, with few luxuries, but at least they have piped-in music for workout motivation. The pool is equally utilitarian, and there are plastic chairs on the sparse sundeck. There's a self-service launderette and a shopping arcade on the premises.

Peninsula Hotel. 3 Coleman St., Singapore 179804. ☎ **800/223-0888** from the U.S. and Canada, 0800/252840 from the U.K., or 65/337-2200. Fax 65/339-3580. 307 units. A/C MINIBAR TV TEL. S$240–S$260 (US$151–US$164) double; S$360–S$700 (US$227–US$441) suite. AE, DC, JCB, MC, V. 5-minute walk to City Hall MRT.

Not extraordinary but not a bad place at all, the Peninsula caters mostly to tourist markets, and busloads of people can sometimes be found milling about the lobby. Security is tight, with card-key access to guest floors. Rooms are large, but furnishings are not overly inviting. Some rooms have a harbor view, and it's worth asking for. *Be warned if you are tall:* Bathroom shower nozzles are positioned very low. Hotel facilities include a small outdoor pool and a small fitness center. The Peninsula is the sister hotel to the Excelsior (see above), and in the coming years both hotels will be combined to share a single lobby and mutual guest facilities. No word on when construction will begin, so make sure you ask when you inquire about reservations.

The Plaza Hotel. 7500 Beach Rd., Singapore 199591. ☎ **65/298-0011.** Fax 65/297-3600. 350 units. A/C MINIBAR TV TEL. S$250–S$340 (US$157–US$214) double; S$370–S$550 (US$233–US$346) suite. AE, DC, JCB, MC, V. 10-minute walk to Bugis MRT.

You're a little off the beaten track at the Plaza Hotel, situated just across a busy street from typical local shophouse businesses but somewhat far from the city center. The hotel has guest rooms, facilities, and services which are perfectly in keeping with its price category. Rooms, while average size, are comfortable and airy.

What deserves special mention here are the gorgeous and luxurious recreation and relaxation facilities. The pool is a half-size Olympic with a diving board (a rarity in Singapore); its sundeck, decorated in a lazy-days Balinese-style tropical motif, is a dream; and its poolside cafe, cooled by ceiling fans, continues the Bali theme. Two gyms to the side have plenty of space and new equipment, but the most exquisite facility of all is the spa. Designed in conjunction with Susan-Jane Beers, an expert on Indonesian herbs, the spa has body scrubs, healing massages, and beauty treatments that incorporate wet and dry applications of Indonesian herbs, some of which are grown fresh on the hotel's rooftop. Other hotel facilities include outdoor and indoor Jacuzzis, sauna, and steam room.

✪ The Westin Stamford & Westin Plaza. 2 Stamford Rd., Singapore 178882. ☎ **800/ 228-3000** from the U.S. and Canada, 008/803849 from Australia (Sydney 2/2903664), 0800/ 441737 from New Zealand , 0800/282565 from the U.K., or 65/338-8585. Fax 65/338-2862. www.asia-online.com/westin. E-mail: westin1@singnet.com.sg. 2,062 units. A/C MINIBAR TV TEL. Westin Stamford: S$305–S$335 (US$192–US$211) double; S$500–S$680 (US$315– US$428) suite. Westin Plaza: S$320–S$350 (US$202–US$220) double; S$365–S$380 (US$230– US$239) club; S$550 (US$346) suite. AE, DC, JCB, MC, V. City Centre MRT.

The combined Westin Stamford and Westin Plaza hotels are a giant complex comprising 2,062 combined guest rooms, the Raffles City Convention Centre, and 14 food and beverage outlets, all sitting directly atop the Raffles City Shopping Complex and City Hall MRT station. Both hotels opened in 1986, and ever since, the Westin Stamford has been in the Guinness Book of World Records as the tallest hotel in the world. Its 70 floors measure in at 226.13 meters (735 ft.).

Guest rooms have balconies, and as you'd guess, some pretty spectacular views are to be had from the Stamford. The rooms themselves are slightly larger than average. If you will be conducting business, Westin offers Guest Offices at an additional S$30 over your room rate. Westin also has weekend promotional rates. Oddly, though the Westin Plaza only has a mere 26 stories (and thus lacks the Stamford's views), its rooms cost slightly more.

Facilities include a large outdoor pool with lifeguard; 24-hour fitness center with aerobics, Jacuzzi, sauna, and steam room; six outdoor tennis courts; two squash courts; and table tennis. The excellent Compass Rose restaurant is perched right at the top of the hotel, offering stunning views in addition to some mighty scrumptious meals. (See chapter 5 for a full review.)

INEXPENSIVE

Hotel Bencoolen. 47 Bencoolen St., Singapore 189626. ☎ **65/336-0822.** Fax 65/336-2250. 89 units. A/C TV TEL. S$83 (US$52) double, S$88 (US$55) executive double. MC, V. 10-minute walk to City Hall MRT.

Bencoolen is the signature backpacker hotel on the block, and it is definitely budget minded through and through: To get into the place you have to enter through the ground-level car park; the rooms are on the small side, and filled with old and oddly matched furnishings; and the double beds are two twins pushed together. Even the walls are strange combinations of painted concrete, tiles, and padded paneling. The showers here are a nightmare, with handheld shower nozzles and no clips on the walls to hang them. Executive rooms are slightly nicer—the same size, but with bigger closets, a small desk area, and a TV set, hair dryer, and fridge in each. For only five dollars more a night, I'd say go for it. The hotel has a rooftop restaurant, and parking is available.

Metropole Hotel. 41 Seah St., Singapore 188396. ☎ **65/336-3611.** Fax 65/339-3610. 54 units. A/C TV TEL. S$124–S$156 (US$78–US$98) standard to studio deluxe. Rates include continental breakfast. AE, DC, JCB, MC, V. 5-minute walk to City Hall MRT.

Located at the corner of Beach Road and Seah Street, the Metropole Hotel is right next to the Raffles Hotel, which means you'll either enjoy the proximity or feel like a passenger in steerage staring up at first class. The lobby is nothing to speak of, and the rooms are sparsely furnished and on the musty side, with desks, a stock-it-yourself fridge, radios, small windows, small closets, and no views. Baby-sitting and fax services are available. Sure, the rates include breakfast, but you could do better at the Strand (see below) for less money.

A coffeehouse and the Imperial Herbal restaurant (reviewed in chapter 5 and a good place for the cure to what ails you) are on the premises.

✪ Strand Hotel. 25 Bencoolen St., Singapore 189619. ☎ **65/338-1866.** Fax 65/338-1330. 130 units. A/C TV TEL. S$95–S$130 (US$60–US$82) double. No credit cards. 10-minute walk to City Hall MRT.

The Strand is by far the best of the backpacker places in Singapore. The lobby is far nicer than you'd expect, and your S$95 a night gets you a clean and neat room. Although there are some hints that you really are staying in a budget hotel—older decor and uncoordinated furniture sets, for instance—they provide some little niceties, like hotel stationery. The no-frills bathroom is clean and adequate. There are no coffee- and tea-making facilities, but there is 24-hour room service and a cafe on the premises. Free parking is available.

3 Chinatown

EXPENSIVE

The Duxton. 83 Duxton Rd., Singapore 089540. ☎ **800/882-3383** from the U.S. and Canada, 800/251664 from Australia, 800/446110 from New Zealand, or 65/227-7678. Fax 65/227-1232. www.integra.fr/relaischateaux/duxton. E-mail: duxton@singnet.com.sg. 49 units. A/C MINIBAR TV TEL. S$310 (US$195) double; S$450 (US$283) suite. Rates include full English breakfast. AE, DC, JCB, MC, V. 5-minute walk to Tanjong Pagar MRT.

The Duxton was one of the first Singaporean accommodations to experiment with the boutique hotel concept, transforming their shophouse structure into a small hotel and doing it with an elegance that's earned them a place in the worldwide Relais & Chateau luxury hotel group. From the outside, the place has old-world charm equal to any lamplit European cobblestone street, but step inside and there are very few details to remind you that you are in a quaint old shophouse—or in the historic Chinese district, for that matter. It's a sophisticated and romantic little place, done entirely in turn-of-the-century styling that includes reproduction Chippendale furniture and pen-and-ink Audubon-style drawings. Each room is different (to fit the structure of the building), but even with the limited spaces they have to work with, they've succeeded in creating rooms that feel airy and open. Of course, regulations do not allow for pools and space does not allow for fitness centers, but you do get complimentary chocolates, fruit basket, mineral water, and shoe-shine services, and a free shuttle to Shenton Way and Orchard Road. Secretarial services are also available.

MODERATE

Amara Singapore. 165 Tanjong Pagar Rd., Singapore 088539. ☎ **65/224-4488.** Fax 65/224-3910. 338 units. A/C MINIBAR TV TEL. S$250 (US$157) double; S$550 (US$346) suite. AE, DC, JCB, MC, V. 5-minute walk to Tanjong Pagar MRT.

Amara is located in the Shenton Way financial district, which makes it attractive to business travelers—so attractive that, at press time, construction had recently begun to add another tower to the hotel, to be completed sometime in 1999. In the present tower, four floors are reserved for leisure travelers (the 7th through the 10th), while the eight upper floors are reserved for the business and executive clubs and for the "Japanese Floor," with Japanese decor. Rooms on the Leisure Floors have an unappealing combination of green and white painted furniture, and the rooms have very little to offer in terms of views. The hotel does have other convenience facilities like a self-service launderette and ice machines and shoe polishers on each floor, plus the usual: a large outdoor pool, a fitness center, Jacuzzi, sauna, two outdoor tennis courts, a jogging track, and a shopping arcade. One of the planned renovations will convert the squash courts into a larger fitness center.

Chinatown Accommodations

Amara Hotel **7**   Duxton Hotel **6**
Apollo Hotel **2**   Furama Hotel **3**
Chinatown Hotel **5**   Harbour View Hotel **8**
Concorde Hotel **1**   Royal Peacock Hotel **4**

Apollo Hotel. 405 Havelock Rd., Singapore 169633. ☎ **65/733-2081.** Fax 65/733-1588. E-mail: aposin@mbox2.singnet.com.sg. 368 units. A/C MINIBAR TV TEL. S$210 (US$132) double; S$380 (US$239) suite. AE, DC, JCB, MC, V. 15-minute walk to Outram MRT.

Reviewing this place is a study in juggling the present situation and the future's prospects. For instance, as it stands, the hotel's location can be a bit daunting, as it's not really within walking distance to anything. Chinatown will take maybe 15 or 20 minutes to get to. However, plans are underway for the city to build a bridge across the Singapore River close to the hotel. When this happens, it will be easier to get around from this presently secluded site. (Either way, they do offer a complimentary shuttle to Orchard Road, Suntec City, Chinatown, and Shenton Way.) Then there are the rooms and facilities. The present rooms are smaller than most, with small closets and no writing desks, and tiled bathrooms that have none of the lovely marble work you see in many other hotels—however, around mid-1998, the Apollo should be finishing up a major 2-year renovation that will add 135 presumably more appealing rooms as well as a larger lobby, a pool, Jacuzzi, outdoor tennis courts, a ballroom, and a lobby bar. Until then, facilities include a self-service launderette, an outdoor pool, fitness center, Jacuzzi, one outdoor tennis court, a beauty salon, and shops. It's a bit noisy from traffic.

Concorde Hotel Singapore. 317 Outram Rd., Singapore 169075. ☎ **65/733-0188.** Fax 65/733-0989. 515 units. A/C MINIBAR TV TEL. S$210 (US$132) double; S$400 (US$252) suite. AE, DC, JCB, MC, V. 15-minute walk to Outram MRT.

This place originally opened as the Glass Hotel, a name it's found difficult to shake, since its curving facades are covered to the seams with smoky windows. That famous facade is undergoing a face-life at press time, as part of renovations that will also spruce up the large circular atrium and guest rooms. All renovations should be completed by the time you read this. The newly refurbished rooms that I've seen (and, presumably, all the ones they've yet to finish) are airy and spacious, with new furniture in simple contemporary style. The bathrooms, while not as opulent as some, are as comfortable as home. Hotel facilities include a fitness center, one outdoor tennis court, a beauty salon, and a number of shops. There are three pools: one small private pool for the Presidential Suite; the sixth-floor guest pool, which is very basic but new; and the rooftop pool, for club floor guests. None of the pools is particularly attractive, and there are no Jacuzzis or saunas, but the view from the rooftop pool has been used by many filmmakers over the years. The Xin Cuisine restaurant is on the premises (and is reviewed in chapter 5). The Concorde's location is not central, but if the government builds another bridge across the Singapore River—as it may, if the major condominium complex that's being proposed nearby actually happens—access to Orchard Road, Clarke Quay, and the Historic District will be much easier.

Furama Hotel Singapore. 60 Eu Tong Sen St., Singapore 059804. ☎ **65/533-3888.** Fax 65/534-1489. E-mail: fhsg@furama-hotels.com. 355 units. A/C MINIBAR TV TEL. S$220 (US$139) double; S$350 (US$220) suite. AE, DC, JCB, MC, V. 10-minute walk to Outram MRT.

Located smack-dab between the heart of Chinatown and the Boat Quay and Clarke Quay areas, the Furama is a good moderately priced choice if you want to be near shopping and nightlife. The first high-rise hotel built in Chinatown, it has a funky, arching multilevel rooftop that always attracts attention. Guest rooms are good-size and as cozy as home, and the bathrooms are large, leaving you plenty of space to spread out. One small bugaboo is the lack of any foyer or entranceway between the corridors and the rooms themselves—the doors just open right in. Hotel facilities include a small outdoor pool, a small fitness center with Jacuzzi, and a shopping arcade.

Harbour View Hotel. 81 Anson Rd., Singapore 079908. ☎ **65/224-1133.** Fax 65/222-0749. www.harbourview.com.sg. 416 units. A/C MINIBAR TV TEL. S$260 (US$164) double; S$420 (US$265) suite. AE, DC, JCB, MC, V. 5-minute walk to Tanjong Pagar MRT.

Because of its proximity to Shenton Way, Harbour View has a very high proportion of business guests, which explains the lobby TV monitors that display Changi International Airport arrival and departure schedules and international weather forecasts, and the 24-hour, fully serviced offices that can be booked by hotel guests. Despite these niceties, the accommodations are not as good as those at other hotels in this price range. The rooms are sparse, the TVs are relics, and if you're tall, the shower will spray no higher than your chest. Also, the business center does not have Internet access. A small outdoor pool and a sauna are available for guests' use.

INEXPENSIVE

✪ **Chinatown Hotel.** 12–16 Teck Lim Rd., Singapore 088388. ☎ **65/326-6766.** Fax 65/367-8695. 42 units. A/C TV TEL. S$155–S$180 (US$98–US$113) double. AE, DC, MC, V. 5-minute walk to Outram MRT.

Chinatown Hotel definitely has its pros and cons, but for clean rooms, friendly service, and a good rate, it's one of my favorites. *Be prepared:* Because this is a boutique hotel with limited space, the rooms, though modern and well maintained, are tiny, and the bathrooms *are* the shower—just a showerhead coming out of the wall as you stand in front of the sink. Some rooms have no windows, so specify when you make reservations if you're fond of natural light. The hotel has one movie channel on the TVs and no facilities to speak of, not even coffee and tea service in the rooms, but there's free coffee, tea, and soup in the lobby. Larger hotels will charge higher rates so you can enjoy the luxury of a pool, fitness center, and multiple food and beverage outlets, but if you're in town to get out and see Singapore, it's nice to know you won't pay for things you'll never use. Besides, the folks at the front counter will always remember your name and are very professional without being impersonal.

The Royal Peacock. 55 Keong Saik Rd., Singapore 089158. ☎ **65/223-3522.** Fax 65/221-1770. www.sunflower.singnet.com.sg/~ariane/hotels/royalpeacock/page1.html. 79 units. A/C MINIBAR TV TEL. S$145 (US$91) double with no window; S$180–S$215 (US$113–US$135) double with window; S$235 (US$148) junior suite. AE, DC, MC, V. 5-minute walk to Outram MRT.

In the center of Chinatown's historic red-light district is one of Singapore' smallest boutique hotels, the Royal Peacock. Occupying 10 restored prewar shophouses, the place is tiny but colorful inside and out. As with other hotels of this type, the existing shophouse structure and strict restoration regulations make very small rooms de rigueur, but you've got to wonder about the hotel's decision to decorate them in the darkest colors they could find: Each room has one wall painted deep red, and purple carpet is used throughout. It's visually exciting, sure, but it makes you (or me, at least) feel claustrophobic. Adding to the problem is the fact that the less expensive rooms have no windows, and, where there are windows, they're just small squares. Yikes. All told, though, and even taking these criticisms into account, the rooms have flair. All rooms have pretty wooden sleigh beds, and the bathrooms (which, due to restoration regulations, don't have tubs) are separated from the rooms with louvered shutters and are done in terra-cotta tiles. Rumor has it they're rethinking the entire design scheme. Room service is available for lunch and dinner till 10:30pm, and secretarial services are available as well.

4 Orchard Road Area

VERY EXPENSIVE

✪ **Four Seasons Hotel Singapore.** 190 Orchard Rd., Singapore 248646. ☎ **800/332-3442** from the U.S. and Canada, or 65/734-1110. Fax 65/733-0682. www.fshr.com. 154 units. A/C MINIBAR TV TEL. S$435–S$490 (US$282.75–US$318.50) double; S$570–S$620 (US$359–US$403) club; S$750–S$4,400 (US$487.50–US$2,772) suite. AE, DC, JCB, MC, V. 5-minute walk to Orchard MRT.

A lot of upmarket hotels will try to convince you that staying with them is like visiting a wealthy friend. Four Seasons actually delivers. The guest rooms are very spacious and inviting, and even the standard rooms have creature comforts you'd expect from a suite, such as complimentary fruit, terry bathrobes and slippers, CD and laser disc players, and an extensive complimentary laser disc and CD library that the concierge is just waiting to deliver to your room. Each room has two-line speaker phones with voice mail and an additional data port. The Italian marble bathrooms have double vanities, deep tubs, bidets, and surround speakers from the TV and stereo. Did I mention remote control drapes? Everything here is comfort and elegance done to perfection. In the waiting area off the lobby you can sink into the sofas and appreciate the antiques and artworks selected from the owner's private collection and not care if your appointments are late. Consider a standard room here before a suite in a less expensive hotel. You won't regret it.

The fitness center has a state-of-the-art gymnasium with TV monitors, videos, tape players and CD/LD players, a Virtual Reality Bike, aerobics, sauna, steam rooms, massage, facials, body wraps and aromatherapy treatments, and a staff of fitness professionals. Want more? How about a flotation tank and a Mind Gear Syncro-Energiser (a brain relaxer that uses pulsing lights), a billiards room, and an OptiGolf Indoor Pro-Golf System. Two indoor, air-conditioned tennis courts and two outdoor courts are staffed with a resident professional tennis coach to provide instruction or play a game. There are two pools: a 20-meter lap pool and a rooftop sundeck pool, both with adjacent Jacuzzis.

In addition to business packages, Four Seasons also offers special shopping, spa, and tennis packages.

Goodwood Park Hotel. 22 Scotts Rd., Singapore 228221. ☎ **65/737-7411.** Fax 65/732-8558. 235 units. A/C MINIBAR TV TEL. S$425–S$465 (US$276–US$293) double; S$615–S$650 (US$387–US$409) poolside suite, S$888–S$3,000 (US$559–US$1,890) suite. AE, DC, JCB, MC, V. 5-minute walk to Orchard MRT.

The Goodwood Park Hotel is a national landmark. Built in 1900 and designed in the manner of castles along the Rhine, it served as the Teutonia Club, a social club for the German community, before becoming the Goodwood Park Hotel in 1929. During World War II, high-ranking Japanese military used it as a residence, and 3 years later it served as a British War Crimes Court before reverting back to a hotel. Over the years the hotel has expanded from 60 rooms to 235, and has hosted a long list of international celebrities and dignitaries.

For the money, there are more luxurious facilities, but while most hotels have bigger and better business and fitness centers (Goodwood has *the* smallest fitness center), only Raffles Hotel can rival Goodwood Park's historic significance. The poolside suites off the Mayfair Pool are the best rooms in the house, offering direct access to the small Mayfair Pool with its lush Balinese-style landscaping. There are also suites off the main pool, which is much larger but offers little privacy from the lobby and surrounding restaurants. The original building has large and airy guest rooms, but beware of the showers, which have handheld showerheads that clip to the wall, making it difficult to aim and impossible to keep the water from splashing out all over the bathroom floor. The staff is attentive; look for the bellhop who's been with the hotel *forever.*

Restaurants on the premises include the Bice Ristorante Italiano, Chang Jiang, Gordon Grill, and Shima (all reviewed in the next chapter).

✪ Hyatt Regency Singapore. 10–12 Scotts Rd., Singapore 228211. ☎ **800/228-9000** from the U.S., or 65/738-1234. Fax 65/732-1696. www.hyatt.com. 693 units. S$350–S$460 (US$220–US$290) double; S$500–S$2,500 (US$315–US$1,575) suite. Near Orchard MRT.

Rumor has it that, despite its fantastic location, this hotel was doing pretty poorly until they had a feng shui master come in and evaluate it for redecorating. According to the Chinese monk, because the lobby entrance was a wall of flat glass doors that ran parallel to the long reception desk in front, all the hotel's money was flowing from the desk right out the doors and into the street. To correct the problem, the doors are now set at right angles to each other, a fountain was built in the rear, and the reception was moved around a corner to the right of the lobby. Since then, the hotel has enjoyed some of the highest occupancy rates in town. Feng shui or not, the new decor is modern, sleek, and sophisticated, an elegant combination of polished

Orchard Road Accommodations

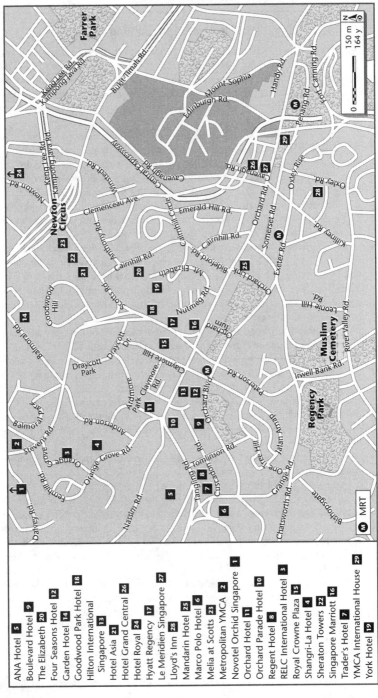

ANA Hotel **5**
Boulevard Hotel **9**
The Elizabeth **20**
Four Seasons Hotel **12**
Garden Hotel **14**
Goodwood Park Hotel **18**
Hilton International Singapore **13**
Hotel Asia **21**
Hotel Grand Central **26**
Hotel Royal **24**
Hyatt Regency **17**
Le Meridien Singapore **27**
Lloyd's Inn **28**
Mandarin Hotel **25**
Marco Polo Hotel **6**
Melia at Scotts **23**
Metropolitan YMCA **2**
Novotel Orchid Singapore **1**
Orchard Hotel **11**
Orchard Parade Hotel **10**
Regent Hotel **8**
RELC International Hotel **3**
Royal Crowne Plaza **15**
Shangri-La Hotel **4**
Sheraton Towers **22**
Singapore Marriott **16**
Trader's Hotel **7**
YMCA International House **29**
York Hotel **19**

Meet Me at the Spa, Dahling . . .

After a long day on your feet sightseeing in the hot sun, I'll bet I know what you want: a massage, a soak in a hydrotherapy tub, or a nice herbal or floral wrap. (This all before a relaxing and romantic dinner, of course.) Most of the major hotels have massage rooms in their fitness centers, but a few offer luxurious facilities that go above and beyond the call of relaxation and hedonistic beauty pleasures. Here's the best:

At the Grand Plaza Hotel's **Saint Gregory Marine Spa,** 10 Coleman St. #01-23 (☎ 65/432-5588), even nonguests can make advanced appointments to enjoy services in quiet and peaceful surroundings. The spa treatments center around water. Pools are snuggled amidst lush green plants, with soothing sounds of waves lilting through the air. The focal treatments are the hydrotherapy baths, but you can also get jet showers, steam baths, facials and body treatments, and hand, foot, and body massage. The 20-room center has separate facilities for men and women, but couples can enjoy VIP suites for treatments for two.

The gorgeous, Bali-style spa at the Plaza Hotel's **Plaza Fitness Club,** 7500 Beach Rd., Level Three (☎ 65/298-0011), has exotic details right down to the floors, which are bejeweled with tiny seashells. Treatments have been developed by Susan-Jane Beers, a local authority on Indonesian herbal health and beauty treatments. Enjoy aromatherapy, wet or dry herbal and floral wraps, body and facial massage, and foot reflexology.

If exercise and relaxation are high on your list of vacation priorities, consider staying at the **Four Seasons Hotel Singapore,** 190 Orchard Rd. (☎ 65/734-1110). Their fitness center is perhaps the best at any hotel on the island, covering two floors and with state-of-the-art exercise facilities as well as personal trainers and nutrition guides. Massages are given utilizing both Asian and European techniques, and facials, body wraps, and aromatherapy treatments are also available. If you're into this sort of thing, there's even a flotation tank—a la Michael Jackson—and something called a Mind Gear Syncro-Energiser, which relaxes the brain with pulsing light.

Many shopping arcades have outlets advertising **foot reflexology,** a technique whose popularity is just booming these days. Foot reflexology uses pressure techniques to massage the feet in spots that correspond to various parts of your body, relaxing the whole body while only touching the feet. A lot of these places aren't worth the money or time, as the certificate requirements for practitioners aren't exactly demanding. I do recommend one place, though: **Vincien Foot Reflexology** in the Tanglin Shopping Centre at 19 Tanglin Rd. #03-44 (☎ 65/739-9639). Call ahead for an appointment and request Bernard, a retired businessman whose lifetime hobbies have included Chi Gong (Chinese energy transfer), Reiki (Japanese energy transfer), foot reflexology, and Swedish massage, to name only a few. He comes into the shop by appointment only, and because his heart and soul are in his work, he is worth every penny you pay him. Forty-minute foot reflexology treatments start at an affordable S$30 (US$19). A full hour is only S$40 (US$25). Full body treatments are S$80 (US$50.40) for 1 hour.

black marble and deep wood. Quiet corridors with great artwork lead to bright guest rooms distinguished by small glass-enclosed alcoves looking over the hotel gardens. Bathrooms are large, with lots of marble counter space. All rooms have voice mail and data ports.

Two lush tropical gardens decorate the hotel, with rock formations, flowers, and a total of 16 waterfalls. Tucked inside the gardens is the swimming pool. There's also a children's slide pool, two floodlit tennis courts, and an air-conditioned badminton court. The fitness center has modern equipment, TV monitors, landscaped Jacuzzi, sauna and steam room areas, aerobics classes, and massage and beauty treatments.

EXPENSIVE

ANA Hotel Singapore. 16 Nassim Hill, Singapore 258467. ☎ **800/ANA-HOTELS** from the U.S. and Canada, or 65/732-1222. Fax 65/235-1516. www.ana-hotels.com/ana. E-mail: anahotel@singnet.com.sg. 456 units. A/C MINIBAR TV TEL. S$300–S$360 (US$189–US$227) double; S$360 (US$227) cabana double or club; S$400–S$2,000 (US$252–US$1,260) suite. AE, DC, JCB, MC, V. 10-minute walk to Orchard MRT.

ANA is located in the embassy area and a 10-minute walk from the Botanic Gardens, which is a great place for joggers. From the outside, the building is not much to see, and on the inside, everything is turn-of-the-century, European-style decor—no hints of Asia at all. The rooms are a good size and sport the latest interactive system for hotel service, shopping, and video-on-demand directly through your TV. The bathrooms have clip-on showerheads, which can be inconvenient. Cabana rooms with poolside patios are available.

Facilities include the Wellness Centre, which, in addition to a gym, has aerobics, massage, sauna, and steam facilities, and diet and stress-relief consultations.

Hilton International Singapore. 581 Orchard Rd., Singapore 238883. ☎ **800/445-8667** from the U.S., or 65/737-2233. Fax 65/732-2917. www.travelweb.com/thisco/hiltnint/common/search/html. E-mail: hiltopia@hiltonint.com. 423 units. S$350–S$370 (US$220–US$233) double; S$440 (US$277) club; S$500–S$2,000 (US$315–US$1,260) suite. AE, DC, EU, MC, V. Near Orchard MRT.

There may be newer hotels along Orchard Road, but if you count the luxury cars that drive up to the valet at the Hilton, you'll know this is still a good address to have while staying in Singapore. Probably the most famous feature of the Hilton is its shopping arcade, where you can find your Donna Karan and blah, blah, blah. Ask the concierge for a pager, and they'll beep you for important calls while you window-shop or try some of the 45 fragrant vodkas at the lobby bar. Security is guaranteed through key-activated elevators to the guest floors. With all this, the guest rooms should be pretty sumptuous, no? Well, no. The rooms are simpler than you'd expect, with nothing flashy or overdone. There are floor-to-ceiling windows in each, and while views in the front of the hotel are of Orchard Road and the Thai Embassy property, views in the back are not so hot. Data ports and voice mail are standard in every room. Hotel facilities include a 24-hour business center, a small outdoor pool, and a modern fitness center with sauna and steam. The hotel's award-winning Harbour Grill restaurant is reviewed in chapter 5.

Le Meridien Singapore. 100 Orchard Rd., Singapore 238840. ☎ **800/543-4300** from the U.S. and Canada, 800/622240 from Australia, 0800/454040 from New Zealand, 0800/404040 from the U.K., or 65/733-8855. Fax 65/732-7886. 407 units. A/C MINIBAR TV TEL. S$330–S$370 (US$208–US$233) double; S$390 (US$246) club; S$1,400–S$1,800 (US$882–US$1,134) suite. AE, DC, MC, V. Dhoby Ghaut/Somerset MRT.

Atrium lobbies are big in Singapore, and I think Le Meridien's is the oldest. Long, straight corridors look out into the huge, open, skylighted space and down to the colorful lobby lounge decorated with plants and fresh flowers. The lobby is one of the brightest atrium lobbies around, but in order to get to it on foot from the street you have to walk along ramps to parking garage access, which is a bit annoying.

Standard rooms are fresh with simple Chinese decor, and bathrooms are state-of-the-art. The Jade and Opal suites are the best spaces, but the club facilities are not as attractive as other hotels in this category. Hotel facilities include VCRs in all rooms, a small outdoor pool, and a large fitness center with aerobics, Jacuzzi, and sauna. The shopping arcade has some great antique furniture places.

Mandarin Singapore. 333 Orchard Rd., Singapore 238867. ☎ **800/380-9957** from the U.S. and Canada, or 65/737-4411. Fax 65/235-6688. www.commerceasia.com/mandarin. 1,235 units. A/C MINIBAR TV TEL S$360 (US$227) South Wing double, S$380 (US$239) Main Wing double; S$460 (US$290) club; S$500–S$2,500 (US$315–US$1,575) suite. AE, DC, JCB, MC, V and Air Plus. Near Orchard MRT.

Smack in the center of Orchard Road is the Mandarin Hotel, a two-tower complex with Singapore's most famous revolving restaurant topping it off like a little hat. The 39-story Main Tower opened in 1973, and with the opening of the South Wing 10 years later the number of rooms expanded to 1,200. Massive renovations of both wings and most of the facilities were completed in 1995. True to its name, the hotel is decorated in Chinese style, from the huge lobby mural of the "87 Taoist Immortals" to the black-and-red Ming-design carpet murals and black lacquer-style guest room entrances. The South Wing is predominantly for leisure travelers, who have access to the tower from the side of the hotel off Orchard Road. The guest rooms here are slightly smaller and furnished with Chinese-style dark wood modular units. The guest rooms in the Main Tower are brighter and larger. All bathrooms have bidets and scales. Hotel facilities include one outdoor tennis court, one squash court, a midsize outdoor pool, a shopping arcade, and a large fitness center with aerobics, Jacuzzi, sauna, and steam.

The revolving restaurant, the Top of the M, serves continental cuisine while you gaze on a 360-degree view of the city. The Chatterbox is a good place to try local favorites, including their award-winning Hainanese Chicken Rice. (I've reviewed Chatterbox in chapter 5.)

The Marco Polo, Singapore. 247 Tanglin Rd., Singapore 247935. ☎ **65/474-7141.** Fax 65/471-0521. 660 units. A/C MINIBAR TV TEL. S$300 (US$189) double, S$400–S$430 (US$252–US$271) business double; S$700 (US$441) suite. AE, DC, JCB, MC, V. 10-minute walk to Orchard MRT.

The Marco Polo's Tanglin Wing was built in 1968, before real estate prices skyrocketed, so this hotel can boast a rare 1.6 hectares (4 acres) of lush landscaped grounds that welcome you with green trees and fountains as you pull up the circular drive to the entrance—a nice change from most of the hotel properties in this area, which are generally crowded between shopping malls and skyscrapers. And the "green" theme doesn't end at the entrance: The hotel's "green rooms" supply biodegradable amenities and tips for environmentally conscious guests. The less expensive rooms are more Chinese in decor, while the more upmarket rooms are continental; poolside rooms with patios are also available. The hotel has a 24-hour business center; a fitness center with aerobics, Jacuzzi, and sauna; and a swimming pool that's larger than most, with a swim-up bar if you want to *really* relax. While there may be more conveniently located hotels, after a day in the rush of Orchard Road, you may welcome the 10-minute walk to a more relaxed environment. Plus, you're only a 10-minute walk from the Botanic Gardens, which has one of the best jogging tracks in the city.

Orchard Hotel Singapore. 442 Orchard Rd., Singapore 238879. ☎ **800/465-6486** from the U.S. and Canada, 800/655147 from Australia (Sydney 02/92237422), 0800/442519 from New Zealand, 0800/252854 from the U.K., or 65/733-5482. E-mail: orcharde@singnet.com.sg. 680 units. A/C MINIBAR TV TEL. S$320–S$390 (US$202–US$246) double; S$430 (US$271) club; S$650–S$1,800 (US$409–US$1,134) suite. AE, DC, JCB, MC, V. 5-minute walk to Orchard MRT.

Just this past year, the Orchard completed a major renovation of its guest rooms, lobby, and facilities, and the new touches add a lot of comfort and style. While their Harvest Rooms (at the high end of the price range) are done in tasteful and attractive florals, the less expensive doubles sport the kind of unassuming pastels you'd expect to see in just about any hotel room. The rooms are just slightly smaller than most, and have an interactive TV system for guest room services. Facilities include a midsize outdoor pool, a fitness center with sauna, a shopping mall, and state-of-the-art function rooms.

The Regent Singapore. 1 Cuscaden Rd., Singapore 249715. ☎ **800/332-3442** from the U.S. and Canada, or 65/733-8888. Fax 65/732-8838. www.fshr.com. 441 units. A/C MINIBAR TV TEL. S$350–S$370 (US$220–US$233) double; S$525–S$1,300 (US$331–US$819) suite. 10-minute walk to Orchard MRT.

Check out the lobby in this place! It's a huge, three-level atrium affair with windows on three sides, a skylight, fountains, plenty of small, private meeting nooks, and Jetsons-style raised walkways. The generous-size rooms have high ceilings and are decorated with Southeast Asian–style fabrics, but the bathrooms are smaller than at most other comparable hotels. You have to request coffee- and tea-making facilities in your room; otherwise the service is free in the tea lounge, which also serves a high tea the old-fashioned way—on silver tray service, not buffet. Hotel facilities include a business center with private office space rental and secretarial support; a small outdoor pool; and a midsize, modern fitness center with Jacuzzi, steam, massage, and beauty treatments.

The Regent is tucked between Cuscaden and Tanglin roads, right across the street from the Singapore Tourism Board office.

Royal Crowne Plaza Singapore. 25 Scotts Rd., Singapore 228220. ☎ **800/465-4329** from the U.S. and Canada, 800/221066 from Australia, 0800/442222 from New Zealand, 0800/987121 from the U.K., or 65/737-7966. Fax 65/737-6096. www.crowneplaza.com. E-mail: royal@crowneplaza.com.sg. 495 units. A/C MINIBAR TV TEL. S$350–S$370 (US$220–US$233) double; S$390–S$410 (US$246–US$258) club; S$540–S$1,700 (US$340–US$1,071) suite. AE, DISC, DC, MC, V. Orchard MRT.

This hotel's poor lobby has fallen victim to "confused interior decorator disease." First you get a huge and palatial white marble entranceway with marble staircases arching up either side to the mezzanine, then three tiffany glass domes up above, murals of tropical foliage and birds, and gold baroque-o-rococo touches all over, each added during separate renovations, and, it appears, at huge cost. To top it all, there's no greeting area save the coffee shop off the side of the entrance. Welcome to Royal Crowne Plaza; wanna cuppa joe?

Royal Crowne is the upmarket branch of Holiday Inn, so you can be pretty sure you'll get a good, solid room for your money, but this hotel definitely caters to the business traveler more than the holiday visitor. Deluxe rooms and rooms on the club floors are beautiful, with a contemporary, masculine room design that's a gorgeous mix of black and wood tones—no elegant detail is spared. The standard rooms, on the other hand, are average and serviceable—usual hotel style. All rooms have interactive TV service linking them to video-on-demand and hotel services. The fitness center is huge, with modern equipment, aerobics, and a sauna. The newly renovated pool is landscaped Balinese style, with an arbor cafe. Water-sports equipment can be arranged, and there are two badminton courts, a squash court, and a billiards room for guest use.

✪ Shangri-La Hotel. 22 Orange Grove Rd., Singapore 258350. ☎ **800/942-5050** from the U.S. and Canada, 800/222448 from Australia, 0800/442179 from New Zealand, or 65/

737-3644. Fax 65/733-7220. www.shangri-la.com. 879 units. A/C MINIBAR TV TEL. S$375 (US$236) Tower double, S$520 (US$328) Garden double; S$490 (US$309) Garden deluxe; S$425 (US$268) Horizon Club; S$555 (US$350) Valley double; S$495 (US$312) Valley deluxe; S$1,000–S$2,200 (US$624–US$1,386) suite. All published rates include free round-trip limo service to airport, breakfast, laundry, and dry cleaning. AE, DC, JCB, MC, V. 10-minute walk to Orchard MRT.

It may not be as centrally located as other hotels in the area, but the Shangri-La is a lovely place, with strolling gardens, a putting course, and an outdoor pool paradise that are great diversions from the hustle and bustle all around. Maybe that's why visiting VIPs like George Bush, Benazir Bhutto, and Nelson Mandela have all stayed here.

The hotel has three wings: The Tower Wing is the oldest and houses the lobby and most of the guest rooms, which were recently renovated. The Garden Wing has bougainvillea-laden balconies, half of which overlook the tropical atrium with its cascading waterfall and exotic plants. These rooms feel the most like resort rooms. The exclusive Valley Wing has a private entrance and very spacious rooms, and is linked to the main tower by a sky bridge that looks out over the hotel's 6 hectares (15 acres) of landscaped lawns, fruit trees, and flowers. Rooms in all wings have interactive TV, and fax machines are available on request. Facilities include two pools (one large outdoor and one small heated indoor); four tennis courts; two squash courts; and a fitness center with hot and cold Jacuzzis, steam, sauna, and massage. Sports equipment rentals are available. Xanadu, a disco, is located in the basement, and there's a fine restaurant, Latour, located in the rear of the lobby (see chapter 5 for a full review).

Sheraton Towers Singapore. 39 Scotts Rd., Singapore 228230. ☎ **800/325-3535** from the U.S. and Canada, 800/073535 from Australia, 0800/443535 from New Zealand, 0800/353535 from the U.K., or 65/737-6888. Fax 65/737-1072. www.sheraton.com. 410 units. S$370–S$430 (US$233–US$271) double; S$475 (US$299) cabana rm; S$700–S$2,200 (US$441–US$1,386) suite. AE, DC, ER, JCB, MC, V and Access. 5-minute walk to Newton MRT.

One of the first things you see when you walk into the lobby of the Sheraton Towers is the service awards the place has won; check in, and you'll begin to see why they won 'em. With the Deluxe (standard) room they'll give you a suit pressing on arrival, daily newspaper delivery, shoe-shine service, and complimentary movies. Upgrade to a Tower room and you get a personal butler, complimentary nightly cocktails and morning breakfast, free laundry, free local calls, your own pants press, and free use of the personal trainer in the fitness center. The Cabana rooms, off the pool area, have all the services of the Tower Wing in a very private resort room. Get a suite here only if you are very fond of the color peach.

Hotel facilities include a pool with a nice view of the surrounding trees and a small fitness center with a sauna but, curiously, no windows. The lobby cafe features waterfalls and huge glass atrium walls that look out on yet more waterfalls.

Singapore Marriott Hotel. 320 Orchard Rd., Singapore 238865. ☎ **800/228-9290** from the U.S. and Canada, 800/251259 from Australia (Sydney 02/92991614), 0800/221222 from the U.K., or 65/735-5800. Fax 65/735-9800. www.marriott.com. 390 units. A/C MINIBAR TV TEL. S$380 (US$239) double; S$420 (US$265) club; S$650–S$1,880 (US$409–US$1,184) suite. AE, DC, JCB, MC, V. Orchard MRT.

You can't get a better location than at the corner of Orchard and Scotts roads. The hotel's giant green-roofed pagoda is a classic landmark that is easily recognizable, but guest rooms here are small because they're squeezed into the octagonal structure, and their dark color scheme makes them feel even more cramped. Additionally, not all rooms have good views. The lobby makes up for all the limitations the octagonal structure places on the facilities, though: You enter through sheets of water flowing over black marble, feng shui–style, into a seating area nestled between nine towering preserved palm trees. The sidewalk cafe off the lobby is a favorite place for international and Singaporean celebrities who like to be seen.

Marriott, who bought this property in 1995, caters to the business traveler, so the rooms on the club floors get most of the hotel's attention. The club lounge, for instance, has a great view and there's not a tacky detail in the comfortable seating and dining areas. Data ports, three phones, and voice mail are standard in all the hotel's rooms, as are an iron and ironing board.

Facilities include a 24-hour business center, two outdoor tennis courts, a squash court, and a very deep, midsize outdoor pool with a nice view and great inexpensive snack bar. The fitness center has aerobics, Jacuzzi, sauna, and steam room. Tang's, Singapore's largest indigenous department store, is located just beneath the hotel.

MODERATE

Boulevard Hotel. 200 Orchard Blvd., Singapore 248647. ☎ **800/635-0980** from the U.S., 0800/899515 from the U.K., or 65/737-2911. Fax 65/737-8449. 521 units. A/C MINIBAR TV TEL. S$280–S$400 (US$176–US$252) double; S$450–S$1,200 (US$283–US$756) suite. AE, DC, JCB, MC, V. 15-minute walk to Orchard MRT.

Orchard Boulevard runs parallel to Orchard Road, the main hub of it all, and yet Orchard Boulevard's got trees and chirping birds, which makes the Boulevard Hotel close to the action, but more relaxing. Unlike most hotels in Singapore, this place caters less to business guests and more to the leisure set, as evidenced by the lobby, which is still bustling at 10am with excited travelers from all over the world (at this point in the morning, most other hotels have shipped their guests off to work).

This is yet another hotel built around an atrium concept, only Boulevard's atrium is not as open and airy as most. A giant metallic monument to prosperity towers up the shaft of the atrium. It's rather plain by day, but dramatic when it's lit at night. Guest rooms in the Cuscaden Wing—the oldest part of the hotel, built in 1976—are good sized, decorated in darker hues, and are less expensive than the guest rooms in the newer Orchard Wing, built in 1984. Hotel facilities include a fitness center with sauna, two midsize outdoor pools, and shops. Boulevard's pastry shop, next to the coffee shop, is famous for its chicken pies—a tasty and inexpensive treat.

The Elizabeth Singapore. 24 Mount Elizabeth, Singapore 228518. ☎ **65/738-1188.** Fax 65/732-3866. 246 units. A/C MINIBAR TV TEL. S$300–S$340 (US$189–US$214) double; S$650–S$950 (US$409–US$598) suite. AE, DC, JCB, MC, V. 10-minute walk to Orchard MRT.

This small, quaint hotel has cozy rooms and the most friendly and accommodating staff around. Done in dark, cool European styling throughout, from the lobby to the guest rooms, this modern hotel's most dramatic feature is the lobby area's fantastic cascading waterfalls, which drop over a vertical tropical rock-and-plant garden nestled behind three-story-high glass panels. Both the business center and fitness center are small, but the pool is in a pretty, columned courtyard—and they pipe in underwater music. Other facilities include a gift shop, and, for those of you in the mood for cuddly, a specialty teddy bear shop.

Meliá at Scotts. 45 Scotts Rd., Singapore 228232. ☎ **800/336-3542** from the U.S. and Canada, 0800/282720 from the U.K., or 65/732-5885. Fax 65/732-1332. www.solmelia.com. E-mail: meliasct@pacific.net.sg. 245 units. A/C MINIBAR TV TEL. S$295–S$335 (US$186–US$211) double; S$350 (US$220) club; S$530 (US$334) suite. AE, DC, JCB, MC, V. 10-minute walk to Newton MRT.

Despite this property's odd-shaped pyramid design, huge awkward entrance awning, and not-exactly-grand lobby entrance, inside you'll find stately corridors leading to rooms with great interior decor that masks the hotel's age. Hotel facilities include a small outdoor pool, a small fitness center with sauna, and a boutique. Soft pop drifts from the sunken lobby bar and there's live entertainment in the evenings 6 nights a week.

Meliá at Scotts is on Scotts Road, but is closer to Bukit Timah Road—technically in the Orchard Road area, but not as close to the action as other hotels, so you may find yourself relying slightly more on taxis. It is, however not too far from the Newton MRT station and to Newton Circus, Singapore's most famous hawker center.

Novotel Orchid Singapore. 214 Dunearn Rd., Singapore 299526. ☎ **800/221-4542** from the U.S. and Canada, 800/642244 from Australia, 0800/444422 from New Zealand, 800/616-1367 within Singapore, or 65/250-3322. Fax 65/250-9292. E-mail: novosing@mbox2.singnet.com.sg. 437 units. A/C MINIBAR TV TEL. S$240–S$260 (US$151–US$164) double, S$260 (US$164) garden (poolside) deluxe double; S$320 (US$202) family; S$320–S$370 (US$202–US$233) suite. AE, DC, MC, V. Far from MRT stations.

In 1997, Novotel finished a huge lobby renovation, redesigning the space in a very open and contemporary style, with straight lines and light wood paneling a la IKEA. Of course, the renovations were not without the addition of a lucky koi pond, full of golden fish to bring you luck and fortune, and nestled in an adorable, brightly painted courtyard that can be viewed from the lobby bar. The pond runs from the courtyard under the floor of the bar to a pool and fountain inside. The newness of this part of the hotel adds contrast to the older sections—as you walk down the covered but otherwise open-air corridors, you can see signs of age. Nevertheless, guest rooms here are big and not unpleasant, with tall stucco walls and high ceilings. The rooms in the Plymouth Wing in the back of the complex have a sofa bed in addition to the regular beds, and offer plenty of desk and counter space.

Novotel has installed the interactive GuestServe TV and also has a self-service launderette; shopping; a health center with massage, sauna, and steam room; and a free shuttle to Orchard Road for the convenience of guests. The hotel's worst feature is probably its pool, which has pretty landscaping but is on the ground level, separated from a noisy main street by only a vine-covered fence. There's a game area with a billiards table to the side.

Orchard Parade Hotel. 1 Tanglin Rd., Singapore 247905. ☎ **65/737-1133.** Fax 65/733-0242. www.farest.com.sg/hotels. 387 units. A/C MINIBAR TV TEL. S$270–S$300 (US$170–US$189) double; S$400 (US$252) club; S$320–S$350 (US$202–US$220) family studio; S$330 (US$208) junior suite, S$420–S$1,200 (US$265–US$756) suite. AE, DC, JCB, MC, V. Orchard MRT.

In a mad dash to compete, every hotel in Singapore is either planning a renovation, currently renovating, or just finishing one up. Orchard Parade is no exception. Their renovation is a 2-year S$40 million renovation of the swimming pool, guest rooms, lobby, driveway, front entrance, and food and beverage outlets, and will culminate with a new facade at about the time this book comes to print. Decorated in a Mediterranean theme integrating marble mosaics, plaster walls, beamed ceilings, and wrought-iron railings, the hotel will expand from its original 324 rooms to 387. The large pool on the sixth floor roof will get a face-lift with tiles and draping arbors, as will the new fitness center. If it's important to you, you may need to specify a room with a view here, as I suspect some rooms may end up with worse views than others. What's the good thing about renovations? Introductory room rates, which will come into effect when they launch the new design in May 1998.

Modestos, a popular dance club for the younger set, is located on the ground level. There's a shopping arcade on the premises.

✪ Traders Hotel Singapore. 1A Cuscaden Rd., Singapore 249716. ☎ **800/942-5050** from the U.S. and Canada, 800/222448 from Australia, 0800/442179 from New Zealand, or 65/

738-2222. Fax 65/831-4314. www.shangri-la.com. 543 units. A/C TV TEL. S$265–S$310 (US$167–US$195) double; S$345 (US$217) club; S$540 (US$340) studio apt, S$725 (US$457) 2-bedrm family apt; S$540–S$1,000 (US$340–US$624) suite. AE, DC, JCB, MC, V. 10-minute walk to Orchard MRT.

A fantastic bargain for leisure travelers in Singapore, Traders advertises itself as a "value-for-money" hotel. A spin-off of Shangri-La (see above), this hotel anticipates the special needs of travelers and tries on all levels to accommodate them. Rooms have an empty fridge that can be stocked from the supermarket next door (show your room card key at nearby Tanglin Mall for discounts from many of the shops); there are spanking clean self-service launderette facilities with ironing boards on six floors; and there are vending machines and ice machines. They even provide a hospitality lounge for guests to use after check-out, with seating areas, work spaces with data ports, card phones, safe-deposit boxes, vending machines, and a shower.

Guest rooms are smaller than average, but feature child-size sofa beds and large drawers for storage. The large, landscaped pool area has a great poolside al fresco cafe, Ah Hoi's Kitchen, serving up tasty Chinese dishes at reasonable prices. Hotel facilities include a data port in each room and a fitness center with outdoor Jacuzzi, sauna, steam, massage and facial services. Services include voice mail, free shuttle service to Orchard Road, Shangri-La Hotel, Shangri-La Rasa Sentosa Resort, Suntec City, and Shenton Way business district. (Taking advantage of the Rasa Sentosa Shuttle may save you admission to Sentosa Island.) Be sure to ask about promotion rates when you book your room. If you're planning to stay longer than 2 weeks they have a long-stay program that offers discount meals, laundry and business center services, and half-price launderette tokens.

York Hotel Singapore. 21 Mount Elizabeth, Singapore 228516. ☎ **800/221023** from Australia, 0800/899517 from the U.K., or 65/737-0511. Fax 65/732-1217. 406 units. A/C MINIBAR TV TEL. S$265–S$285 (US$167–US$180) double; S$285 (US$180) cabana; S$400 (US$252) split-level cabana; S$430–S$910 (US$271–US$573) suite. AE, DC, JCB, MC, V. 10-minute walk to Orchard MRT.

A little off the beaten track, this small hotel can boast a very professional and courteous staff (and spiffy "Have a Nice Day" carpets in the elevators!), but it doesn't offer all the facilities of the higher-profile hotels in this category. The hotel attracts a lot of tour groups, mostly Japanese, which probably accounts for the constant cigarette smoke drifting through the lobby from people standing around waiting for buses. The rooms are a bland decor of older-style, white-painted furniture, but the deluxe rooms are very spacious and some of the views of surrounding trees are quite nice. Bathrooms throughout are downright huge. Cabana rooms look out to a pool and sundeck decorated with giant palms. Despite surrounding buildings, it doesn't feel claustrophobic, as do some of the more centrally situated hotels. There's a Jacuzzi, but the business center is tiny and there's no fitness center at all. Guests in single-occupancy rooms are often upgraded to doubles.

INEXPENSIVE

Garden Hotel Singapore. 14 Balmoral Rd., Singapore 259800. ☎ **65/235-3344.** Fax 65/235-9730. E-mail: garden@pacific.net.sg. 216 units. A/C TV TEL. S$210 (US$132) double; S$220 (US$139) cabana; S$260 (US$164) family; S$300 (US$189) suite. AE, DC, EU, JCB, MC, V, Barclays. 15-minute walk to Newton MRT.

This five-story hotel is in a discreet building in a quiet residential neighborhood north of the Orchard Road area—and that's its main downfall: It's pretty far out from where all the action is. (The hotel compensates with a free shuttle to Orchard Road.) Other than location, this isn't a bad place to stay. It serves a mostly Western market of leisure travelers and families, discouraging tour groups to avoid noisy throngs loitering around the lobby area and crashing the food and beverage outlets at feeding times. The good news is that 75% of the guest rooms have balconies. The bad news is, some of them are *indoors,* with a view of the atrium coffee shop. The rooms here are average size and bright, if only slightly musty. There's no minibar, but each room has an empty fridge you can stock yourself. There are two pools, a rooftop pool that gets good sun and a small ground-level landscaped pool in a courtyard surrounded by cabana rooms. Inexpensive baby-sitting services are available, and hotel facilities include gift shops and a midsize fitness center with sauna.

Hotel Asia Singapore. 37 Scotts Rd., Singapore 228229. ☎ **65/737-8388.** Fax 65/733-3563. www.hotelasia.com.sg. E-mail: hotasia@singnet.com.sg. 146 units. A/C MINIBAR TV TEL. S$220 (US$139) double; S$300 (US$189) suite. AE, DC, MC, V. 5-minute walk to Newton MRT.

This place is as no-frills as it gets, which is surprising for its price category. It's a plain older building with nondescript public areas, no pool, no health club, and no business center. Wide corridors lead to medium-size guest rooms that are adequate at best—just slightly more comfortable than at this hotel's main competitor, the Grand Central Hotel. Concierge and secretarial services are available, and there's valet parking and a tour desk. What justifies the high rates? Their location, only a 10-minute walk to Orchard Road.

Hotel Grand Central, Singapore. 22 Cavenagh Rd./Orchard Rd., Singapore 229617. ☎ **800/331006** from Australia, or 65/733-3922. Fax 65/733-6022. 390 units. A/C MINIBAR TV TEL. S$210–S$230 (US$132–US$145) double; S$300 (US$189) suite. AE, DC, MC, V. Somerset MRT.

Most of the hotels in this price category are at least a 10-minute walk outside the main drag, but Hotel Grand Central is right on it, with an exclusive Orchard Road address. The hotel always runs at high occupancy, its lobby a hustle and bustle of mostly ASEAN (Association of Southeast Asian Nations) vacation travelers who, truth to tell, seem to have worn dull the front counter staff's service edge. The building was originally eight floors, but recent renovations added an extra floor to the top, which houses executive club rooms. The corridors are on the dreary side and the guest rooms and bathrooms are a little run-down. Windows are positioned high, so there's not much in the way of views—although rooms in the center of the building offer views of rooms on the opposite side, if that's your idea of fun. Facilities include a small fitness center with Jacuzzi and sauna, a beauty salon, and a shopping arcade, and the hotel offers a full range of services (excluding concierge). To the side of the rooftop pool is a special corner reserved for dead hotel houseplants—a tip-off that maybe this isn't the most luxurious place on Orchard Road.

Hotel Royal. 36 Newton Rd., Singapore 307964. ☎ **65/253-4411.** Fax 65/253-8668. www.hotelroyal.com/hotelroyal. E-mail: royal@hotelroyal.com.sg. 355 units. A/C MINIBAR TV TEL. S$170–S$230 (US$107–US$145) double; S$260 (US$164) king leisure or family; S$300–S$700 (US$189–US$441) suite. AE, DC, JCB, MC, V. 10-minute walk to Newton MRT.

Hotel Royal is typical of most of the other hotels in this area and price category: It's close enough to Orchard Road that it can charge high rates for facilities that simply aren't worth the money. Most of the business here is tour groups, the rooms are average, and the bathrooms could use some upgrading. As for facilities, there's a beauty salon and gift and sundry shops, but it might be more instructive to tell you what the place *doesn't* have: The pool is small, has no snack bar, and can only be accessed by passing through a back stairwell; the health center has sauna and massage, but no workout equipment; there's no business center; and they don't offer a shuttle to bring you closer to the action. The most interesting features of the hotel are the huge, weird sandstone plaques placed above the awning. They've made the building a visual landmark, but nobody seems to know anything about where they came from. In a word? You may want to stay away.

Lloyd's Inn. 2 Lloyd Rd., Singapore 239091. ☎ **65/737-7309.** Fax 65/737-7847. 34 units. A/C TV TEL. S$95 (US$60) double. MC, V. 10-minute walk to Somerset MRT.

Lloyd's is a budget motel in every sense. It's a two-story building on a relatively quiet, low-traffic street. The corridors are open-air and the rooms are small, with a definite budget feeling, though all have air-conditioning and phones. Each room has its own bathroom, though they tend to be mildewy. The published rates include the "+++" taxes (see "Taxes & Service Charges," above), there's no discount offered for long-term stays, you must pay for your room when you check in, and if you use a credit card, it'll cost you an extra 2%. As for the parking, this place is squeezed into its lot like a snail in its shell, so there's room for about two cars—and that's it. No pool, no fitness center, no nothing—you got your room; that's what you got.

Metropolitan YMCA Singapore. 60 Stevens Rd., Singapore 257854. ☎ **65/737-7755.** Fax 65/235-5528. www.singnet.com.sg/~mymca/. E-mail: info@mymca.org.sg. 94 units. A/C TV TEL. S$70–S$110 (US$44–US$69) double; S$90–S$140 (US$57–US$88) family; S$145 (US$91) suite. AE, DC, JCB, MC, V. 15-minute walk to Newton MRT.

This place is a little out of the way and the rooms are looking a little on the older side, but they're clean and efficient. One oddity here: The least expensive rooms have no windows; for sunlight, you'll have to pay a little extra. There are nine family rooms outfitted with either three twin beds or a double and a twin. The family rooms are the same size as the other rooms, but the bathrooms are bigger and there's a lot more closet space. In early 1998, they opened a new multipurpose fitness center here, installed all new equipment, and hired a trainer. The pool is a nice size, as is the kiddie pool, and they have a lifeguard on duty from 9am to 9pm daily. No dorm rooms are available, but concierge, dry cleaning, laundry, and secretarial services are. Plus, there's a self-service launderette, a coffee shop, a tour desk, and a gift shop on the premises.

✪ **RELC International Hotel.** RELC Building, 30 Orange Grove Rd., Singapore 258352. ☎ **65/737-9044.** Fax 65/733-9976. www.hotel-web.com. E-mail: relcih@singnet.com.sg. 128 units. A/C TV TEL. S$112 (US$71) double; S$165 (US$104) suite. Rates include American breakfast for 2. DC, JCB, MC, V. 10-minute walk to Orchard MRT.

My money is on the RELC because, for the rate, they give you more added value than just prime location. Close to the Shangri-La (see above), its only a 10-minute walk to Orchard Road, and its facilities are generally more comfortable and useful than hotels that charge up to S$100 more for their rooms. There are four types of rooms here—superior twin, executive twin, Hollywood queen, and alcove suite—but no matter what the size, none ever feels cluttered, close, or cramped. Rooms have balconies, TVs with two movie channels, and a fridge with free juice boxes and snacks. Bathrooms are large, with full-length tub shower and hair dryers standard. Between the higher range rooms, I'd choose the Hollywood queen over the alcove suite—its decor is better and it can sleep a family very comfortably. The "superior" rooms don't have coffee- and tea-making facilities, but all rates include daily American breakfast for two. A self-service launderette is available.

✪ **YMCA International House.** 1 Orchard Rd., Singapore 238824. ☎ **65/336-6000.** Fax 65/337-3140. 109 units. A/C TV TEL. S$90 (US$56.70) single; S$100 (US$63) double; S$120 (US$76) family rm, S$130 (US$82) superior rm; S$28 (US$18) dormitory. Non-YMCA members must pay S$5 (US$3.15) temporary membership fee at check in. AE, DC, JCB, MC, V. Near Dhoby Ghaut MRT.

Of the two YMCAs in Singapore, this one has the better location. At the lower end of Orchard Road, it's only a short walk to the Dhoby Ghaut MRT station, making it very convenient for getting around via mass transit. The guest rooms have just been renovated and have private bathrooms that are better than I've seen at some much pricier hotels. All rooms have air-conditioning, a telephone (with free local calls), color television, and a stock-it-yourself refrigerator. The dormitories are small, dark, and quiet, with two bunk beds per room. Across the hall are men's and women's locker rooms for showering. Most of the public areas have no air-conditioning, including the old fitness facility, billiards center, and squash courts— *be warned:* These can become unbearably hot. The rooftop pool is nothing to write home about, but there is a full-time lifeguard on duty. There's a coffee shop and a McDonald's in the lobby. The hotel staff is amazingly friendly.

5 Sentosa Island

There are only two hotel properties on Sentosa Island, the Shangri-La Rasa Sentosa, located right on the water and designed for families and fun, and the Beaufort, located close to the water and even closer to golfing, and designed for secluded, romantic getaways.

✪ **The Beaufort Sentosa, Singapore.** 2 Bukit Manis Rd., Sentosa, Singapore 099891. ☎ **800/637-7200** from the U.S. and Canada, 800/655147 from Australia, 0800/962115 from the U.K., or 65/275-0331. Fax 65/275-0228. E-mail: beaufort@singnet.com.sg. 214 units. A/C MINIBAR TV TEL. S$380 (US$239) double; S$450 (US$283) suite; S$1,500 (US$945) villa. AE, DC, JCB, MC, V. See "Sentosa Island" in chapter 6 for public transportation.

Designed with romance in mind, the Beaufort's small resort-style buildings, designed after the famous resorts of Phuket, Thailand, are connected with covered walkways encircling lily ponds and courtyard gardens. Lazy terraces and cozy alcoves are tucked into quiet spots all over the grounds, and guests can request a full candlelight dinner anywhere they like.

The standard guest rooms in the four-story hotel building are small but stunning, and feature Taiwanese camphor burl wood doors and accents, Thai silk screens in dreamy blues and greens, and deep tubs and separate showers in the bathrooms, surrounded by thick celadon green tiling and sleek black granite details. Ask for views of the golf course, which are much prettier than the views of the hotel courtyards and buildings. If you want a little additional privacy, the Beaufort's Garden Villas are the ultimate—little houses with individual pools. Twenty-four-hour butler service is standard in all rooms.

Hotel facilities include VCR and video rentals for suites. The pool is done in midnight blue tiles, which look black and sexy by day and like shimmering emeralds by night, and the tree-lined sundeck looks out to ships in the harbor. A large health club is located in a separate restored colonial building and features a gym, Jacuzzi, and sauna. Three floodlit tennis courts (with coach), two squash courts, a 20-meter lap pool, and an archery range are available for guest use. Mountain bikes can be rented for tooling around the island. The Beaufort has special packages for honeymoon and golf excursions.

In a tree just behind the open-air lobby, look for Tommy the monkey, who sometimes hangs out with one or two of his wives or kids. You have to love any resort that has a resident monkey family.

MODERATE

Shangri-La's Rasa Sentosa Resort. 101 Siloso Rd., Sentosa, Singapore 098970. ☎ **800/942-5050** from the U.S. and Canada, 800/222448 from Australia, 0800/442179 from New Zealand, or 65/275-0100. Fax 65/275-0355. 459 units. A/C MINIBAR TV TEL. Weekdays S$260 (US$164) hill-view double, S$320 (US$202) cabana double or pool double, S$350 (US$220) deluxe sea-facing double; from S$550 (US$346) terrace rm or suite. Weekend S$310 (US$195.30) hill-view double, S$370 (US$233) cabana double or pool double, S$400 (US$252) deluxe sea-facing double. AE, DC, JCB, MC, V. See "Sentosa Island" in chapter 6 for public transportation.

Set on an immaculate white sandy beach fringed with coconut palms, Shangri-La's Rasa Sentosa Resort is Singapore's first and only beachfront hotel. It's frequented by Singaporeans looking to get away from it all, but for a tourist to Singapore, it might not be the most appropriate choice—after all, you'll probably want to be thrown *into* all the stuff they're trying to get *away* from. Also, access to the island is by ferry, cable car, bus, or expensive taxi, so getting in and out for your sightseeing, shopping, and eating adventures can be a chore.

What are the pluses? Great outdoor activities is the big one. The resort has extensive recreational facilities, including a sea sports center offering windsurfing, sailing, and paddle skiing. Other facilities include a large outdoor free-form swimming pool; a fully equipped spa with gym, sauna, body, and facial treatments, hydromassage, and massage therapies; a jogging track; canoe and paddleboat rentals; and outdoor Jacuzzi. The hotel also organizes nature walks, cycling tours, aerobics, and beach volleyball. For children, they have a childrens' pool with water slides (no lifeguard, though), a playground, a nursery, and a video arcade. There are five food and beverage outlets, and a complimentary shuttle service to town that helps beat the cost of the commute.

As for the rooms, the decision between whether to take the hill-view room or the slightly more expensive sea-facing room is a no-brainer: The view of the sea is King, and if you don't go for it, you'll miss out on glorious mornings, throwing back the curtains and taking in the view from the balcony.

5 | Dining

Take three million people, put 'em on a tiny island for their whole lives, and what have you got? Three million very bored people. Sure, the sights and attractions can keep visitors occupied for weeks, but how many times can you go to Sentosa before is becomes the same old same old? The locals have seen and done it all.

So what do Singaporeans do for boredom relief? They eat. Dining out in Singapore is the central focus of family quality time, the best excuse for getting together with friends, and the proper way to close that business deal. That's why you find such a huge selection of local, regional, and international cuisine here, served in settings that range from bustling hawker centers to grand and glamourous palaces of gastronomy. But to simply say "If You Like Food You'll Love Singapore!" doesn't do justice to the modern concept of eating in this place. The various ethnic restaurants, with their traditional decor and serving styles, hold their own special sense of theater for foreigners, but Singaporeans don't stop there, dreaming up new concepts in cuisine and ambiance to add fresh dimensions to the fine art of dining. For a twist, new variations on traditions pop up, like the Chinese cuisine served French-style at Chang Jiang or the East-meets-West New Asia cuisine dished up at Doc Cheng's. Theme restaurants turn regular meals into attractions. Take, for example, Imperial Herbal's intriguing predinner medical examination or The Drake's "nothing but duck" humor (see reviews for more info).

Recent figures say Singapore has over 2,000 eating establishments, so you'll never be at a loss for a place to go. In this chapter, I'll begin by providing an overview of the main types of traditional cuisine to help you decide, and also list those signature dishes that each style has contributed to the "local cuisine," dishes that have crossed cultures to become time-honored favorites—the Singaporean equivalent to bangers and mash or burgers and fries. These suggestions are especially helpful when navigating the endless choices at hawker centers.

The restaurants I've chosen for review in this chapter offer a crosscut of cuisine and price ranges, and were selected for superb quality or authenticity of dishes. Some were selected for the sheer experience, whether it's a stunning view or just plain old fun. Beyond this list, you're sure to discover favorites of your own without having to look too far.

A good place to start is right in your hotel. Many of Singapore's best restaurants are in its hotels, whether they're run by the hotel itself or operated by outfits just renting the space. Hotels generally offer wide varieties of cuisine, and coffee shops almost always have Western selections. Shopping malls have everything from food courts with local fast food to midpriced and upmarket establishments. Western fast-food outlets are always easy to find—McDonald's burgers, Dunkin' Donuts, or Starbucks coffee—but if you want something a little more local, you'll find coffee shops and small home-cookin' mom-and-pop joints down every back street. Then there are hawker centers, where, under one roof, the meal choices go on and on.

1 One Little Island, Lots & Lots of Choices

CHINESE CUISINE

The large Chinese population in Singapore make this obviously the most common type of food you'll find, and by rights, any good description of Singaporean food should begin with the most prevalent Chinese regional styles. Many Chinese restaurants in the West are lumped into one category—Chinese—with only mild acknowledgment of Sichuan and dim sum. But China's a big place, and its size is reflected in its many different tastes, ingredients, and preparation styles.

CANTONESE CUISINE   Cantonese-style food is what you usually find in the West. Your stir-fries, wontons, and sweet-and-sour sauces all come from this southern region of China. Cantonese cooks emphasize freshness of ingredients, which explains why some Cantonese homemakers will shop up to three times a day for the freshest picks. Typical preparation involves quick stir-frying in light oil, or steaming for tender meats and crisp, flavorful vegetables. These are topped off with light sauces that are sometimes sweet. Cantonese-style food also includes roasted meats like suckling pig and the red-roasted pork that's ever present in Chinese dishes you find in the West. Compared to northern styles of Chinese cuisine, Cantonese food can be bland, especially when sauces and broths are overthickened and slimy. Singaporean palates demand the standard dish of chili condiment at the table, which sometimes helps the flavor. One hearty Cantonese dish that has made it to local cuisine fame is **clay pot rice,** which is rice cooked with chicken, Chinese sausage, and mushrooms, prepared in—you guessed it—a clay pot.

The Cantonese are also responsible for **dim sum** (or tim sum, as you'll sometimes see it written around Singapore). Meaning "little hearts," dim sum is a variety of deep-fried or steamed buns, spring rolls, dumplings, meatballs, spare ribs, and a host of other tasty treats. It's a favorite in Singapore, especially for lunch. At a dim sum buffet they wheel trolleys of dishes from table to table and you simply point to what looks nice. Food is served in small portions, sometimes still in the steamer. Take only one item on your plate at a time, and stack the empty plates as you finish each one. Traditionally, you'd be charged by the plate, but sometimes you can find great all-you-can-eat buffets for a good price.

BEIJING CUISINE   In contrast to Cantonese is Beijing-style food, which comes to us from the north of China. Northern cuisine is the food of the emperors, and its rich garlic and bean-paste flavoring has just a touch of chili. Another difference is that you'll find mutton on a northern Chinese menu, but certainly not on any southern menu. The most famous Beijing-style dish is **Beijing duck** (also known as Peking duck). The crispy skin is pulled away and cut into pieces, which you then wrap in thin pancakes with spring onion and a touch of sweet plum sauce. The meat is served later in a dish that's equally scrumptious.

SHANGHAI CUISINE   Shanghai-style cuisine is similar to Beijing-style but tends to be more oily. Because of its proximity to the sea, Shanghai recipes also include more fish. The exotic **drunken prawns** and the popular **drunken chicken** are both from this regional style, as is the mysterious **bird's nest soup,** made from swift's nests.

SICHUAN CUISINE   Sichuan-style cuisine, second only to Cantonese in the West, also relies on the rich flavors of garlic, sesame oil, and bean paste, but is heavier on the chilies—*much* heavier on the chilies. Sugar is also sometimes added to create tangy sauces. Some dishes can really pack a punch, but there are many Sichuan dishes that are not spicy. Popular are **chicken with dried chilies** and **hot-and-sour soup.** Another regional variation, **Hunan-style food,** is also renowned for its fiery spice, and can be distinguished from Sichuan-style by its darker sauces.

TEOCHEW CUISINE   Teochew-style cuisine uses fish as its main ingredient, and is also known for its light soups. Many dishes are steamed, and in fact **steamboat,** which is a popular poolside menu item in hotels, gets its origins from this style. For Steamboat, boiling broth is brought to the table, and you dunk pieces of fish, meat, and vegetables into it, a la fondue. Other Teochew contributions to local cuisine are the **Teochew fishball,** a springy ball made from pounded fish with salt and water served in a noodle soup, and the traditional Singaporean breakfast dish **congee** (or moi), which is rice porridge served with fried fish, salted vegetables, and sometimes boiled egg. Also, if you see **braised goose** on the menu, you're definitely in a Teochew restaurant.

HOKKIEN CUISINE   Although the Hokkiens are the most prevalent dialect group in Singapore, their style of cuisine rarely makes it to restaurant tables, basically because it's simple and homely. Two dishes that have made it as local cuisine favorites are the **oyster omelet,** flavored with garlic and soya, and **Hokkien mee,** which is thick wheat noodles with seafood, meat, and vegetables in a heavy sauce.

HAKKA CUISINE   If Hokkien food is simple and homely, Hakka food is the homeliest of the homely. Flavored with glutinous rice wine, many dishes feature tofu and minced seafood and meats. Hakkas are also known for not wasting an animal body part—not exactly requisite for haute cuisine. Good dishes to try are **salt-baked chicken** and **minced seafood** wrapped in a fried tofu cake.

NOTES ON THE CHINESE PALATE

A very touchy topic for many Westerners: Chinese cuisine employs many a strange ingredient that sometimes makes queasy the unaccustomed stomach. A saying from way back in my family goes, "The Chinese will eat anything that doesn't eat them first," and it's almost true. Turtle, sea urchin, and sea cucumber are all popular Singaporean dishes, though their meats are unpleasantly mushy to those accustomed to more Western tastes. Many Singaporeans devour these creatures for their taste and some for their health and restorative powers. In fact, some Chinese restaurants are creating dishes using unusual ingredients, which they claim balance the body's energy (its yin and yang) to promote health, beauty, and longevity. Indeed, frog's glands are pretty tasty in scrambled egg, and the next day your skin will glow like never before!

On the more appealing side are other Chinese-inspired local favorites like carrot cake—white radishes that are steamed and pounded until soft, then fried in egg, garlic, and chili; Hokkien bak ku teh—boiled pork ribs in a seasoned soup; Teochew kway teow—stir-fried rice noodles with egg, prawns, and fish; and the number-one favorite for foreigners, Hainanese chicken rice—boiled sliced chicken breast served over rice cooked in chicken stock.

New Asia cuisine has been hitting the market hard as globalization takes control of Singaporean palates. Also called "Fusion Food," this cuisine combines Eastern and Western ingredients and cooking styles for a whole new eating experience. Some of it works, some of it doesn't, but true gourmet connoisseurs consider it all a culinary atrocity.

MALAY CUISINE

Malay cuisine combines Indonesian and Thai flavors, blending ginger, turmeric, chilies, lemongrass, and dried shrimp paste to make unique curries. Heavy on coconut milk and peanuts, Malay food can at times be on the sweet side. The most popular Malay curries are **rendang,** a dry, dark, and heavy coconut-based curry served over meat; **sambal,** a red and spicy chili sauce; and **sambal belacan,** a condiment of fresh chilies, dried shrimp paste, and lime juice.

The ultimate Malay dish in Singapore is **satay,** sweet barbecued meat kebabs dipped in chili peanut sauce. Another popular dish is **roti john,** which is minced mutton and onion in French bread that's dipped in egg and fried. **Nasi lemak**—coconut rice surrounded by an assortment of fried anchovies, peanuts, prawns, egg, and sambal—is primarily a breakfast dish, but can be eaten anytime.

PERANAKAN CUISINE

Peranakan cuisine came out of the Straits-born Chinese community and combines such mainland Chinese ingredients as noodles and oyster sauces with local Malay flavors of coconut milk and peanuts. **Laksa lemak** is a great example of the combination, mixing Chinese rice flour noodles into a soup of Malay-style spicy coconut cream with chunks of seafood and tofu. And **otak otak** is all the rage. It's toasted mashed fish with coconut milk and chili, wrapped in a banana leaf and grilled over flames.

INDIAN CUISINE

SOUTHERN INDIAN CUISINE   Southern Indian food is a superhot blend of spices in a coconut milk base. Rice is the staple, along with thin breads such as *prata* and *dosai,* which are good for curling into shovels to scoop up drippy curries. Vegetarian dishes are abundant, a result of Hindu-mandated vegetarianism, and use lots of chickpeas and lentils in curry and chili gravies. **Vindaloo,** meat or poultry in a tangy and spicy sauce, is also well known.

Banana leaf restaurants, surely the most interesting way to experience southern Indian food in Singapore, serve up meals on banana leaves cut like place mats. It's very informal. Spoons and forks are provided, but if you want to act local and use your hands, remember to use your right hand only (see "Singaporean Etiquette & Customs" in chapter 1), and don't forget to wash up before and after at the tap.

One tip for eating very spicy foods is to mix a larger proportion of rice to gravy. Don't drink in between bites, but eat through the burn. Your brow may sweat but your mouth will build a tolerance as you eat, and the flavors will come through more fully.

NORTHERN INDIAN CUISINE   Northern Indian food combines yogurts and creams with a milder, more delicate blend of herbs and chilies than is found in its southern neighbor. It's served most often with breads like fluffy naans and flat *chepatis.* Marinated meats like chicken or fish, cooked in the tandoor clay oven, is always the highlight of a northern Indian meal.

Northern Indian restaurants are more upmarket and expensive than the southern ones, but while they offer more of the comforts associated with dining out, the southern banana leaf experience is more truly an adventure.

Some Singaporean variations on Indian cuisine are **mee goreng,** fried noodles with chili and curry gravy, and **fish head curry,** a giant fish head simmered in a broth of coconut curry, chilies, and fragrant seasonings.

Muslim influences on Indian food have produced the **murtabak,** a fried prata filled with minced meat, onion, and egg. Between the Muslims' dietary laws (*halal*) forbidding pork and the Hindus' regard for the sacred cow, Indian food is the one cuisine that can be eaten by every kind of Singaporean.

SEAFOOD

One cannot describe Singaporean food without mentioning the abundance of fresh seafood. But, most importantly, is the uniquely Singaporean **chili crab,** chopped and smothered in a thick tangy chili sauce. Restaurants hold competitions to judge who has the best, and everyone has their favorite—one local tried to send me all the way out to Pongol—all the way on the north coast—to find his pick of "The Best Chili Crab." **Pepper crabs** and **black pepper crayfish** are also a thrill. Instead of chili sauce, these shellfish are served in a thick black-pepper-and-soya sauce.

FRUITS

A walk through a wet market at any time of year will show you just what wonders the tropics can produce. Varieties of banana, fresh coconut, papaya, mango, and pineapple are just a few of the fresh and juicy fruits available year-round, but Southeast Asia has an amazing selection of exotic and almost unimaginable fruits. From the light and juicy **star fruit** to the red and hairy **rambutan,** they are all worthy of a try, either whole or juiced.

Dare it if you will, the fruit to sample—the veritable King of Fruits—is the **durian,** a large, green, spiky fruit which, when cut open, smells worse than old tennis shoes. The "best" ones are in season every June, when Singaporeans go wild over them. In case you're curious, the fruit has a creamy texture and tastes lightly sweet and deeply musky.

One interesting note on fruits: The Chinese believe that foods contain either yin or yang qualities with corresponding "heaty" and "cooling" effects. Fried foods and hot soups are "heaty" and therefore should be kept to a minimum in the tropics, and the same is true for some fruits. Whereas watermelon, star fruit, and oranges are cooling, mangoes, lychees, and especially durians are heaty. Too many heaty foods are believed to result in a sore throat, for which the best remedy is Chinese tea.

2 Tips on Dining

Of course, in any foreign land, the exotic cuisine isn't the only thing that keeps you guessing. Lucky for you, the following tips will make dining no problem.

HOURS   Most restaurants are open for lunch as early as 11am, but close around 2:30pm or 3pm to give them a chance to set up for dinner. You're better off not taking meals between 3pm and 6pm. Where closing times are listed, that is the time when the last order is taken.

TIPPING   Don't tip. Restaurants always add a gratuity to the bill, and to give extra cash can be embarrassing for the wait staff.

RESERVATIONS   Some restaurants, especially the more fashionable or upscale ones, may require that reservations be made up to a couple days in advance.

Reservations are always recommended for Saturday and Sunday lunch and dinner, as eating is a favorite national pastime, and a lot of families take meals out for weekend quality time.

ATTIRE   Because Singapore is so hot, "dress casual" (meaning a shirt and slacks for men and a dress or skirt/slacks and top for women) is always a safe bet in moderate to expensive restaurants. For the very expensive restaurants, formal is required. For the cheap places, come as you are, as long as you're decent.

ORDERING WINE WITH DINNER   Singaporeans have become more wine savvy in recent years, and have begun importing estate-bottled wines from California, Australia, New Zealand, France, and Germany. However, these bottles are heavily taxed. A bottle of wine with dinner starts at around S$50 (US$31.50), and a single glass runs between S$10 and S$25 (US$6.30 and US$15.75), depending on the wine and the restaurant. Chinese restaurants usually don't charge corkage fees for bringing your own.

ORGANIZATION OF RESTAURANT LISTINGS   I've organized the restaurants in this chapter in a few different ways. First, I've grouped them in a simple list by style of cuisine, so if you decide you want a nice Peranakan dinner, for instance, you can scope out your choices all together before referring to the individual restaurant reviews. Secondly, I've arranged the reviews into four basic neighborhoods: the Orchard Road area, the Historic District, Chinatown, and Little India. Within these divisions, I've arranged them by price. Keep in mind that the divisions by neighborhood are almost as arbitrary as they were when Stamford Raffles created them in 1822. Everything in the city is relatively close and easily accessible, so don't think you should plan your meals by the neighborhood your hotel sits in when a short taxi ride will take you where you *really* want to go.

The restaurants listed here have been selected because they have some of the best food and most memorable atmospheres, but there are hundreds of other restaurants serving any kind of food in a variety of price ranges. Many magazines on dining in Singapore are available at newsstands and can help you find favorite restaurants of your own. (And if you find any that are really super, drop a line to let me know about 'em—the address is in the front of the book.)

LUNCH COSTS   Lunch at a hawker center can be as cheap as S$3.50 (US$2.10), truly a bargain. Many places have set-price buffet lunches, but these can be as high as S$45 (US$28.35). Indian restaurants are great deals for inexpensive buffet lunches and can be found as reasonably as S$10 (US$6.30) per person for all you can eat.

DINNER COSTS   In this chapter, prices for Western restaurants list the range for standard entrees and prices for Chinese restaurants list the range for small dishes intended for two. As a guideline, here are the relative costs for dinner in each category of restaurant, without wine, beer, cocktails, or coffee, ordered either a la carte or from a set-price menu:

- **Very Expensive:** At a very expensive restaurant, you can expect to pay as much as S$145 (US$91.35) per person. The more expensive cuisines are Western and Japanese, but a full-course Cantonese dinner, especially if you throw in shark's fin, can be up to S$125 to S$150 (US$78.75 to US$94.50) per person.
- **Expensive:** At an expensive restaurant, dinner can be between S$50 and S$80 (US$31.50 and US$50.40) per person.
- **Moderate:** At a moderate restaurant, dinner for one can be as low as S$25 (US$15.75) and as high as S$50 (US$31.50).
- **Inexpensive:** Some inexpensive dinners can be under S$5 (US$3.15) at hawker stalls, and up to around S$15 (US$9.45) for one if you eat at local restaurants.

Urban Singapore Dining

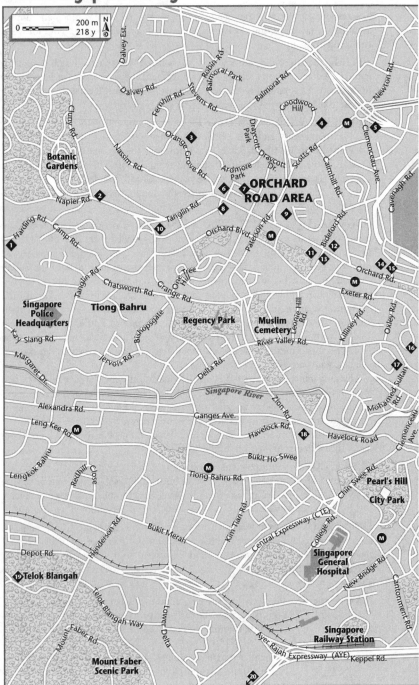

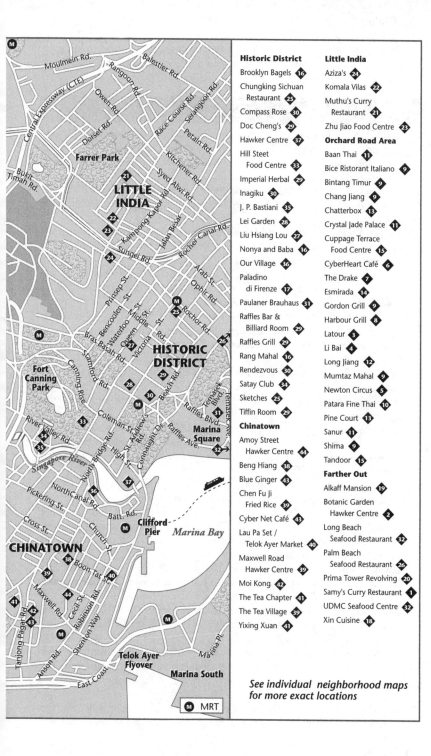

Historic District

Brooklyn Bagels 16
Chungking Sichuan
  Restaurant 25
Compass Rose 30
Doc Cheng's 29
Hawker Centre 37
Hill Steet
  Food Centre 33
Imperial Herbal 29
Inagiku 30
J. P. Bastiani 35
Lei Garden 28
Liu Hsiang Lou 27
Nonya and Baba 16
Our Village 36
Paladino
  di Firenze 17
Paulaner Brauhaus 31
Raffles Bar &
  Billiard Room 29
Raffles Grill 29
Rang Mahal 16
Rendezvous 30
Satay Club 34
Sketches 25
Tiffin Room 29

Chinatown

Amoy Street
  Hawker Centre 44
Beng Hiang 38
Blue Ginger 43
Chen Fu Ji
  Fried Rice 39
Cyber Net Café 43
Lau Pa Set /
  Telok Ayer Market 40
Maxwell Road
  Hawker Centre 39
Moi Kong 42
The Tea Chapter 41
The Tea Village 39
Yixing Xuan 41

Little India

Aziza's 24
Komala Vilas 22
Muthu's Curry
  Restaurant 21
Zhu Jiao Food Centre 23

Orchard Road Area

Baan Thai 11
Bice Ristorant Italiano 9
Bintang Timur 9
Chang Jiang 9
Chatterbox 13
Crystal Jade Palace 11
Cuppage Terrace
  Food Centre 15
CyberHeart Café 6
The Drake 7
Esmirada 14
Gordon Grill 9
Harbour Grill 8
Latour 3
Li Bai 4
Long Jiang 12
Mumtaz Mahal 9
Newton Circus 5
Patara Fine Thai 10
Pine Court 13
Sanur 11
Shima 9
Tandoor 15

Farther Out

Alkaff Mansion 19
Botanic Garden
  Hawker Centre 2
Long Beach
  Seafood Restaurant 32
Palm Beach
  Seafood Restaurant 26
Prima Tower Revolving 20
Samy's Curry Restaurant 1
UDMC Seafood Centre 32
Xin Cuisine 18

*See individual neighborhood maps
for more exact locations*

M MRT

105

Fortunately, Singapore is not only a haven for cultural gastric diversity, but it's also possible to eat exotic foods here to your heart's content, all while maintaining a shoestring budget.

3 Best Bets

- **Best View:** Perched atop the Westin Stamford, the **Compass Rose** offers views of Singapore, Malaysia, and Indonesia that are as glorious as the food.
- **Most Romantic:** Take a lesson from the Italians. **Paladino di Firenze** is intimate and charming and the food is very sensual.
- **The Most Delectable Chinese Food You've Ever Eaten: Li Bai** has an ever-changing menu of traditional recipes and new creations that will melt in your mouth.
- **Tastiest Scorpion:** At **Imperial Herbal** it's the macho dish to order, and after the house physician gives you a checkup, he'll have the kitchen add specific herbs to your dish that will cure your ailments.
- **Best Aquarium Display:** No respectable Chinese restaurant is without the obligatory live seafood display in full view of the clientele. My favorite is the Wall-o'-Aquariums at **Long Beach Seafood Restaurant.**
- **Best Wait Staff:** The folks at **Esmirada** are under strict house orders to have as much fun as the patrons. Breaking bread hasn't been this joyous in a long time.
- **Best Year-Round Christmas Decorations:** They're subtle, but they're there. And they're not the only sense of humor at **Doc Cheng's,** a restaurant risen from the legend of a famous Chinese drunkard who wrote strange prescriptions for health and happiness.
- **Best Wine List:** The wine steward at **Raffles Grill** will suggest the perfect wine for each course.
- **Best Chili and Pepper Crabs:** Every Singaporean has an opinion about where the best chili and pepper crabs are. At **UDMC,** there are eight restaurants to choose from, each one excellent and inexpensive. You're bound to find a good one here.
- **Best Performance by a Leading Man with a Ginsu Knife:** Gather round the grill at **Shima** for some good traditional Japanese showmanship.
- **Best Vegetarian Feast:** Lucky for vegetarians, Hindus don't eat meat, and since there are lots of Hindus in Singapore, there's also lots of vegetarian restaurants. **Komala Vilas** has the best Indian vegetarian dishes, and you can confirm this with any local. Order the dosai.
- **Hottest Indian Food You'll Ever Eat:** The sweat will drip from your brow, your nose will run, and your eyes will tear when you eat at **Samy's Curry Restaurant.** You have my promise.
- **Best Local Tradition:** Everybody loves satay, and in Singapore they've devoted a whole club—the **Satay Club**—to the little Malay shish kebabs. It's touristy, but still, it's a tradition.
- **Best Place to Experiment with Local Cuisine:** Of course the hawker centers are the best place, but if you prefer a more modern atmosphere, try **Chatterbox.** The staff is very helpful, and the selection is very complete. It may not be exactly authentic, but it's pretty close.
- **Best Caesar Salad:** At the **Harbour Grill,** it's better than making your own. The ingredients are brought out on a trolley, and you direct the chef for your own blend of dressing.

4 Restaurants by Cuisine

CHINESE

Beijing

The Drake (Hotel Negara, off Orchard Road, *I*)

Prima Tower Revolving (Keppel Road, Shenton Way Business District, see section 9, *M*)

Cantonese

Chungking Sichuan Restaurant (Parco Bugis Junction, Historic District, *M*)

Crystal Jade Palace (Takashimaya Shopping Centre, Orchard Road, *M*)

Lei Garden (Chijmes, Historic District, *E*)

Li Bai (Sheraton Towers, near Newton MRT, Orchard Road, *E*)

Pine Court (Mandarin Hotel, Orchard Road, *M*)

Xin Cuisine (also Herbal cuisine, Concorde Hotel, Chinatown, see section 9, *M*)

Hakka

Moi Kong (Murray Street, Chinatown, *I*)

Herbal

Imperial Herbal (Metropole Hotel, near Raffles Hotel, Historic District, *M*)

Xin Cuisine (also Cantonese, Concorde Hotel, Chinatown, see section 9, *M*)

Hokkien

Beng Hiang (Amoy Street, Chinatown, *I*)

New Asia

Doc Cheng's (Raffles Hotel Arcade, Historic District, *M*)

Shanghainese

Chang Jiang (Goodwood Park Hotel, off Orchard Road, *E*)

Sichuan/Hunan

Chungking Sichuan Restaurant (Parco Bugis Junction, Historic District, *M*)

Liu Hsiang Lou (Allson Hotel, Historic District, near Bugis Junction, *M*)

Long Jiang (Crown Prince Hotel, Orchard Road, *M*)

CONTINENTAL

Compass Rose (The Westin Stamford, Historic District, *E*)

Gordon Grill (Goodwood Park Hotel, off Orchard Road, *E*)

Harbour Grill (Hilton International Singapore, Orchard Road, *E*)

FRENCH

Latour (Shangri-La Hotel, off Orchard Road, *E*)

Raffles Grill (Raffles Hotel, Historic District, *VE*)

GERMAN

Paulaner Brauhaus (Marina Walk, Raffles Boulevard, Historic District, *I*)

INDIAN (NORTHERN)

Mumtaz Mahal (Far East Plaza, off Orchard Road, *I*)

Our Village (Boat Quay, Historic District, *I*)

Rang Mahal (Imperial Hotel, Historic District, *M*)

Tandoor (Holiday Inn Parkview, off Orchard Road, *M*)

INDIAN (SOUTHERN)

Komala Vilas (Serangoon Road, Little India, *I*)

Muthu's Curry Restaurant (Race Course Road, Little India, *I*)

Samy's Curry Restaurant (Dempsey Road, western Singapore, *I*)

Tiffin Room (Raffles Hotel, Historic District, *E*)

Key to Abbreviations: *E*=Expensive; *I*=Inexpensive; *M*=Moderate; *VE*=Very Expensive

ITALIAN

Bice Ristorante Italiano (Goodwood Park Hotel, off Orchard Road, *E*)

Paladino di Firenze (Mohamed Sultan Road, Historic District, *E*)

Sketches (Parco Bugis Junction, Historic District, *I*)

JAPANESE

Inagiku (The Westin Plaza, Historic District, *VE*)

Shima (Goodwood Park Hotel, off Orchard Road, *E*)

LOCAL FAVORITES

Chatterbox (Mandarin Hotel, Orchard Road, *I*)

Chen Fu Ji Fried Rice (Chinatown, *I*)

Rendezvous (Raffles City Shopping Centre, Historic District, *I*)

Satay Club (Clarke Quay Festival Village, Hawker Center, Colonial District / City Centre, *I*)

MALAY/INDONESIAN

Alkaff Mansion (Telok Blangah Hill Park, near Mount Faber, see section 9, *E*)

Aziza's (Albert Court, near Bugis Junction, Little India, *M*)

Bintang Timor (Far East Plaza, off Orchard Road, *I*)

Sanur (Ngee Ann City, Orchard Road, *I*)

MEDITERRANEAN

Esmirada (Orchard Road at Peranakan Place, *E*)

J.P. Bastiani (Clarke Quay, Historic District, *E*)

PERANAKAN

Blue Ginger (Tanjong Pagar Road, Tanjong Pagar / Chinatown, *I*)

Nonya and Baba (River Valley Road, Historic District, *I*) .

SEAFOOD

Long Beach Seafood Restaurant (East Coast Parkway, see section 9, *M*)

Palm Beach Seafood Restaurant (Stadium Walk, Kallang Park, see section 9, *M*)

UDMC Seafood Centre (East Coast Parkway, *I*)

THAI

Baan Thai (Ngee Ann City, Orchard Road, *M*)

Patara Fine Thai (Tanglin Mall, off Orchard Road, *M*)

5 Historic District

VERY EXPENSIVE

Inagiku. The Westin Plaza, 2 Stamford Rd. ☎ 65/431-5305. Reservations recommended. Set lunch starts at S$30 (US$18.90), but can go up to S$100 (US$63) per person for sushi and sashimi. AE, DC, JCB, MC, V. Daily noon–2:30pm and 6:30–10:30pm. JAPANESE.

At Inagiku, not only will you have excellent Japanese food that gets top marks for ingredients, preparation, and presentation, but you'll get service that's second to none. In delicately lighted and subtle decor, you can enjoy house favorites like sashimi, tempura, and teppanyaki. The tokusen sashimi morikimi is masterful in its presentation: An assortment of raw fish—including salmon, prawns, and clams—is laid out in an ice-filled shell inside of which nestles the skeleton of a whole fish. It's odd and delightful at the same time. The restaurant will recommend the tempura moriawase, a combination of seafood and vegetables that's very lightly deep fried. Also highly recommended is the teppanyaki: kobe beef with a peanut sauce. In addition to sake, they also have a good selection of wines.

✪ **Raffles Grill.** Raffles Hotel, 1 Beach Rd. ☎ 65/337-1886. Reservations required. Entrees S$42–S$52 (US$26.45–US$32.75); set dinner S$130, S$140, S$150 (US$82, US$88.20, US$94.50) per person. AE, DC, JCB, MC, V. Mon–Fri noon–2pm and 7–10pm; Sat–Sun 7–10pm. FRENCH.

Historic District Dining

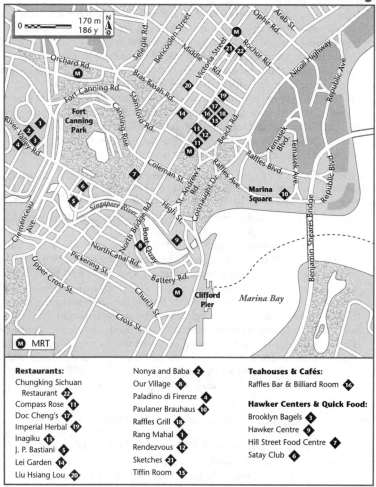

Restaurants:
Chungking Sichuan Restaurant ㉒
Compass Rose ⑪
Doc Cheng's ⑰
Imperial Herbal ⑲
Inagiku ⑬
J. P. Bastiani ⑤
Lei Garden ⑭
Liu Hsiang Lou ⑳

Nonya and Baba ②
Our Village ⑧
Paladino di Firenze ④
Paulaner Brauhaus ⑩
Raffles Grill ⑱
Rang Mahal ①
Rendezvous ⑫
Sketches ㉑
Tiffin Room ⑮

Teahouses & Cafés:
Raffles Bar & Billiard Room ⑯

Hawker Centers & Quick Food:
Brooklyn Bagels ③
Hawker Centre ⑨
Hill Street Food Centre ⑦
Satay Club ⑥

Dining in the Old Dame of Singapore achieves a level of sophistication unmatched by any other five-star restaurant. The architectural charm and historic significance of the old hotel will transform dinner into a cultural event, and the food is outstanding as well. Three set dinners allow you to select from the a la carte menu dishes like grilled tenderloin of U.S. beef and smoked salmon steak with Iranian caviar cream. The most requested dish since the restaurant's opening has been the Raffles mixed grill of lamb, veal, and beef. The 400-label wine list (going back to 1890 vintages) could be a history lesson, and for S$55 (US$34.65) extra the Cellarmaster will select a wine to match each course. The fabulously attentive service from the wait staff will make you feel like you own the place, and they're very patient if you get tipsy and pretend you're a colonist. This is the pinnacle of dining experiences in Singapore.

EXPENSIVE

✪ **Compass Rose.** The Westin Stamford, 2 Stamford Rd., Level 70. ☎ **65/338-8585.** Reservations required. Buffet lunch S$22 (US$13.85); dinner entrees S$40.50–S$45 (US$25.50–US$28.35). AE, DC, JCB, MC, V. Daily noon–2:30pm and 7–10:30pm. CONTINENTAL.

What a view. From the top of the Westin Stamford, the tallest hotel in the world, you can see out past the marina to Malaysia and Indonesia—and the restaurant's three-tier design means every table has a view. It's decorated with contemporary-styled Roman arches, pediments, and columns, and when the sun sets, the whole place turns the many colors of the sky. Lunch is an extensive display of seafood served in a host of international recipes, with chefs searing scallops to order. Don't even talk about the dessert buffet—it's so tantalizing, you'll think the altitude has gotten to your head. Dinner is a la carte, with dishes inspired by lighter tastes and low-fat recipes. Try the peppered lobster tail and sea scallops with hot garlic sauce. The Dutch veal tenderloin and grilled goose liver is served with a pumpkin rosette, carrot, and tarragon cream sauce. For dessert, order the sample plate.

J.P. Bastiani. 3A River Valley Rd., Clarke Quay Merchant's Court #01-12. ☎ **65/433-0156.** Reservations recommended. Entrees S$28–S$45 (US$17.65–US$28.35). AE, DC, JCB, MC, V. Mon–Fri 11:30am–3pm and 6:30–10:30pm; Sat–Sun 6:30–11:30pm. MEDITERRANEAN.

The real-life J. P. Bastiani was a trader who owned a pineapple cannery at Clarke Quay, and the restaurant named after him has a homey Mediterranean feel, with a walled courtyard patio in the back for cocktails, a wine cellar with a huge international collection on the first floor, and a gorgeous dining room upstairs that's just dripping with romantic Mediterranean elegance. One of the best dishes they serve is the ginger-and-peppercorn-crusted salmon with celery root puree and cabernet butter sauce, with rich and buttery flavors that are not too heavy. You can also try the excellent traditional paella; the lightly sweet baked chicken breast filled with wild mushrooms, red-skinned potato puree, and caramelized shallots; or the grilled filet mignon wrapped with bacon and served with sweet potato, spinach gratin, and black peppercorn sauce. The dishes, though truly rich, are all prepared and presented in a light nouvelle cuisine style, which is perfect if you are on vacation and want to enjoy delectable food, but don't want to slow yourself down digesting heavy main courses.

✪ **Lei Garden.** Victoria St., Chijmes #01-24. ☎ **65/339-3822.** Reservations required. Small dishes S$28–S$45 (US$17.65–US$28.35). AE, DC, JCB, MC, V. Daily 11:30am–3pm and 6–11pm. Second branch at Boulevard Hotel, 200 Orchard Blvd. (☎ 65/235-8122). CANTONESE.

There are two Lei Gardens, one here in Chijmes and the other located at the Boulevard Hotel on Orchard Boulevard. Some say that while the restaurant in Chijmes is more elegant in decor, the Orchard Boulevard branch serves the better food. In truth, the food is excellent at both restaurants, though I agree that the Chijmes branch is much prettier: a large, airy room set with tables a good distance from each other. The elegance created from the light tones is enhanced by the view of the Chijmes courtyard, which can be seen through the picture windows lining the restaurant's side. Highly recommended dishes are the "Buddha jumps over the wall," a very popular Chinese soup made from abalone, fish maw (stomach), shark's fin, and Chinese ham. It's generally served on special occasions. To make the beggar's chicken, they take a whole stuffed chicken and wrap and bake it in a lotus leaf covered in yam, which makes the chicken moist with a delicate flavor you'll never forget. For either of these dishes, you must place your order at least 24 hours in advance when you make your dinner reservation. Also try the barbecued Peking duck, which is exquisite. A small selection of French and Chinese wines is available.

✪ **Paladino di Firenze.** 7 Mohamed Sultan Rd. (off River Valley Rd.). ☎ **65/738-0917.** Reservations required. Entrees S$38–S$48 (US$23.95–US$30.25). AE, DC, JCB, MC, V. Daily noon–3pm and 7–11pm. NORTHERN ITALIAN.

This has to be one of the most romantic and cozy restaurants in Singapore. There's not a lot of space in this old restored shophouse, but they don't overcrowd the tables, separating little areas with plantings and crazy little metal trees. Whitewashed exposed brick walls and oriental carpets on the floor create a homey feeling, while copper- and gold-colored tablecloths add shimmer in the candlelight. The northern Italian cuisine here is excellent. The Crespelle alla Paladino are Tuscan-inspired homemade crepes filled with beef, fresh mushrooms, and Parmesan, and the rack of lamb is smothered in Parmesan and fresh thyme. Items recommended by the chef are indicated on the menu with asterisks. They have a large selection of wines to choose from. Make your reservations early because this place is small and very popular. After dinner, stroll the clubs along Mohamed Sultan Road.

Tiffin Room. Raffles Hotel, 1 Beach Rd. ☎ **65/337-1886.** Reservations recommended. All meals served buffet style. Breakfast S$30 (US$18.90); lunch S$35 (US$22); high tea S$25 (US$15.75); dinner S$45 (US$28.35). AE, DC, JCB, MC, V. Daily 7:30–10am, noon–2pm, 3:30pm–5pm (high tea), and 7–10pm. SOUTHERN INDIAN / TIFFIN CURRY.

Tiffin curry came from India and is named after the three-tiered container that Indian workers would use to carry their lunch. The tiffin box idea was stolen by the British colonists, who changed around the recipes a bit so they weren't as spicy. The cuisine that evolved is pretty much what you'll find served at Raffles' Tiffin Room, where a buffet spread lets you select from a variety of curries, chutneys, rice, and Indian breads. The restaurant is just inside the lobby entrance of Raffles Hotel and carries the trademark Raffles elegance throughout its decor.

MODERATE

Chungking Sichuan Restaurant. 200 Victoria St., Parco Bugis Junction #02-53/54. ☎ **65/337-9915** or 65/337-9920. Reservations recommended. Small dishes from S$18 (US$11.35). AE, DC, JCB, MC, V. Mon–Fri 11:15am–2:30pm and 6:15–10:30pm; Sat–Sun and public holidays 11:15am–4:30pm and 6:15–10:30pm. SICHUAN/CANTONESE.

In typical Chinese dining-hall style, Chungking is brightly lit with rows of tables, some small and some big and round, but with an unexpected touch of elegance. Located on the second floor of Parco Bugis Junction shopping mall, its large windows open up the room and provide views of the streets below, which are flanked with shophouses. The menu features dishes that blend two styles: Cantonese and spicy Sichuan. The Sichuan smoked duck is a favorite, either a half or full bird, smoked with Chinese tea leaves and herbs in a sweet black sauce. For a lighter dish, try the steamed fillet of codfish deep fried in a soya-bean crust topped with a light soya sauce. Deep-fried live prawns with special peppercorn Sichuan sauce leave a tingle in the mouth, but never fear, the staff is very flexible about spice. Chungking also serves the standard dim sum lunch. The owner is a wine connoisseur, and has stocked some lovely wines, but they'll never charge corkage if you bring your own.

✪ **Doc Cheng's.** Raffles Hotel Arcade #02-20, Level 2. ☎ **65/331-1612.** Reservations recommended. Entrees S$21.50–S$28.50 (US$13.50–US$18). AE, DC, JCB, MC, V. Mon–Fri noon–2pm and 7–10pm; Sat–Sun 7–10pm. NEW ASIA.

They call themselves "The Restaurant for Restorative Foods," but you won't find any ancient Chinese secrets here. Doc Cheng, the hero of the joint, was part man and part mythological colonial figure. Educated in Western medicine in England, he was a sought-after physician who became a local celebrity and notorious drunk. His concept of restorative foods is therefore rather skewed, but the restaurant banks on the decadence of the attraction and serves up "trans-ethnic" dishes smothered in tongue-in-cheek humor. Guest chefs make the menu ever changing, but you can always get lemongrass chicken cooked in a tandoor oven, peppered venison, or Hawaiian-style steamed whole snapper for two. The house wine is a Riesling (sweet wines are more popular with Singaporean palates) from Raffles' own vineyard. Three separate dining areas allow you to dine under the verandah, on the patio, or in cozy booths inside. Black-and-white check floor tiles play off black and white rattan furnishings. If you look closely, you'll see Christmas decorations all times of the year, just like Mom used to leave up!

✪ **Imperial Herbal.** Metropole Hotel, 3rd Floor, 41 Seah St. (near Raffles Hotel). ☎ **65/ 337-0491** or 65/331-5112. Reservations recommended. Small dishes S$14–S$24 (US$8.80– US$15.10). AE, DC, JCB, MC, V. Daily 11:30am–2:30pm and 6:30–10:30pm. HERBAL.

People come again and again for the healing powers of the food served here, enriched with herbs and other secret ingredients prescribed by a resident Chinese herbalist. Upon entering, go to the right, where you'll find the herb counter. The herbalist, who is also trained in Western medicine, will ask for the symptoms of what ails you and take your pulse. While you sit and order, he'll prepare a packet of ingredients and ship them off to the kitchen, where they'll be added to the food in preparation. Surprisingly, dishes turn out tasty, without the anticipated medicinal aftertaste. If all this isn't wild enough for you, order the scorpion.

The herbalist is in-house every day but Sunday. It's always good to call ahead, though, as he's the main attraction. When you leave, present him with a small *ang pau*—maybe S$5 or S$7.

Liu Hsiang Lou. Allson Hotel, 101 Victoria St. ☎ **65/336-0811.** Reservations recommended but not necessary. Small dishes S$12–S$30 (US$7.55–US$18.90); set dinner for 2 S$98 (US$61.75). AE, DC, JCB, MC, V. Daily noon–2:30pm and 6:30–10pm. SICHUAN.

As you enter there's a veritable zoo of tanks filled with lobsters, long neck clams, and frogs to let you buddy up to your dinner while you wait for your table. In addition to seafood, Liu Hsiang Lou also specializes in amazingly tender venison, which can be prepared sautéed with black pepper, dried red chili, garlic, or chives. Camphor- and tea-smoked duck is a fragrant and delicious Sichuan specialty, and they prepare it marinated in authentic style and bring it out in thin slices for you to wrap in pancakes with plum sauce. Soon hock is fish steamed with a tasty mix of tofu, mushrooms, vegetables, and chili. The most popular dishes are the sautéed diced chicken with dried red chili and the sour and spicy soup with shredded meat and fish maw (stomach). In addition, they have lunch hour dim sum. Carved rosewood chairs and landscape paintings make for a warm atmosphere.

Rang Mahal. Imperial Hotel, 11 Jalan Rumbia. ☎ **65/737-1666.** Reservations recommended. Entrees S$10–S$40 (US$6.30–US$25.20); lunch buffet S$25 (US$15.75). AE, DC, JCB, MC, V. Daily noon–2:30pm and 7–11pm. NORTHERN INDIAN.

Live music drifts through this richly decorated space, which was the first nonpareil Indian restaurant in Singapore. The buffet is never ending, with salads; soups; and a host of excellent meat, seafood, and vegetarian dishes. You can't possibly try them all. For a dreamy entree, the murgh mumtaz is tandoori chicken in a very rich buttery tomato sauce. Also good is the mutton rogan josh, a Kashmir specialty of goat cooked in a deep spicy gravy. Vegetarian dishes are abundant, and the service is very pleasant.

INEXPENSIVE

Nonya and Baba. 262 River Valley Rd. (close to the Imperial Hotel). ☎ **65/734-1382** or 65/ 734-1386. Reservations recommended. Small dishes S$6–S$8 (US$3.80–US$5). AE, DC, MC, V. Daily 11am–3pm and 6–10:30pm. PERANAKAN.

Like a little Peranakan diner, Nonya and Baba serves a menu of traditional standards from time-honored recipes. It's frequented often by locals, many of whom come to eat Straits-Chinese comfort food like Mom used to make. The menu has about 16 dishes, with photos and very detailed descriptions of the preparations and ingredients of each, and the staff is willing and able to help you decide, and will turn down the spice upon request. Sambal udang, a dry sambal over prawns and tomatoes, seems to be the favorite for Westerners. The same goes for the satay ayam (chicken satay). Otak otak, fish cake with chili and shrimp paste wrapped in banana leaf and grilled, makes a great snack. However, a most special dish is the Ayam Buah Keluak, whose preparation time includes 3 days to soak-crack the hard Indonesian nuts to get to the black paste inside, which is then mixed with shrimp and pork, restuffed, then fried. The ambiance here is very local, with coffee shop–style marble-top tables and chairs a la Peranakan. The walls are decorated with framed kebayas (formal Nonya embroidered blouses), some batiks, and photos of the house specialties.

✪ **Our Village.** 46 Boat Quay (take elevator to 5th floor). ☎ **65/538-3058.** Reservations recommended on weekends. Entrees S$9–S$13 (US$5.65–US$8.20). AE, DC, MC, V. Mon–Fri 11:30am–2pm and 6:30–10:30pm; Sat–Sun 6:30–10:30pm. NORTHERN INDIAN.

With its antique white walls stuccoed in delicate and exotic patterns and glistening with tiny silver mirrors, you'll feel like you're in an Indian fairyland here. Even the ceiling twinkles with silver stars, and hanging lanterns provide a subtle glow for the heavenly atmosphere—it's a perfect setting for a delicate dinner. Everything here is handmade from hand-selected imported ingredients, some of them coming from secret sources. In fact, the staff is so protective of their recipes, you'd almost think their secret ingredient was opium—you'll be floating so high after tasting the food that it might as well be. There are vegetarian selections as well as meats (no beef or pork) prepared in luscious gravies or in the tandoor oven. The dishes are light and healthy, with all natural ingredients and not too much salt.

Paulaner Brauhaus. No. 9 Raffles Blvd., Marina Walk #01-01/#02-01/#03-01. ☎ **65/337-7130.** Reservations recommended. Entrees S$15–S$20 (US$9.45–US$12.60). AE, DC, JCB, MC, V. Daily 11:30am–2:30pm and 6–10pm. GERMAN.

People rarely come to Singapore to try the local kielbasa and sauerkraut, but this place goes to show you that you can pretty much get anything you want here. A German chef packs his own sausage—about six different kinds—and cooks up feasts of German specialties like pork knuckles and roast pork, and less traditional dishes like grilled spring chicken. The restaurant is on the second level, with a balcony loft. It's a huge space with German-theme decor that has everything except a polka night. Try not to come late, as this upper level turns into a disco after 10:30 or so, complete with dance floor and light show. The first level is a microbrewery where a brewmaster, also a German, concocts two house beers, one dark and one light, in two giant copper kettles above the bar.

Rendezvous. #02-19 Raffles City Shopping Centre, 525 North Bridge Rd. ☎ **65/339-7508.** Reservations not accepted. Meat dishes sold per piece S$3.30–S$7 (US$2.10–US$4.40). AE, MC, V. Daily 11am–9pm. LOCAL CUISINE.

Recommended for a quick lunch on the run, Rendezvous is a cafeteria. It's nothing fancy, but you'll get good and inexpensive local food served in a clean, air-conditioned restaurant. Serving up a rotating list that includes nasi padang, curry chicken, beef rendang, mutton curry, fish curry, and prawn sambal, you grab a tray, get in line, eyeball the dishes, and tell them which ones you'd like. It's a popular place for working folks grabbing a quick meal, and is conveniently located in Raffles City Shopping Centre. Definitely recommended for a bite in between sights.

Sketches. 200 Victoria St., #01-85/86/87 Parco Bugis Junction. ☎ **65/339-8386.** S$9.90 (US$6.30) hungry; S$13.90 (US$8.80) starving. AE, DC, JCB, MC, V. Daily noon–3pm and 6–10pm. ITALIAN.

Pasta is always an easy and agreeable choice, and sometimes when you're traveling, familiar tastes can be welcome from time to time. Not only is this place fast, inexpensive, and good, it's also pretty unique. The concept is "Design-a-Pasta," where they give you a menu on which is a series of boxes you check off: one set for pasta type; one set for sauce type; another for add-ins like meats, mushrooms, and garlic; and boxes for chili, Parmesan, and pine nuts. The kitchen is in the center of the restaurant, with bar seating all around. This is the best place to be if you want to watch those cooks hustle through menu card after menu card—it's a great show. You can also sit at one of the tables in the restaurant or out on the patio inside the shopping mall, but then you'd miss the fun of eating here.

6 Chinatown

Beng Hiang. 112–116 Amoy St. ☎ **65/221-6695.** Reservations recommended on weekends. Small dishes S$6–S$20 (US$3.80–US$12.60) (most between S$8–S$12/US$5.05–US$7.55). AE, MC, V. Daily 11:30am–2:30pm and 6–9:30pm. HOKKIEN.

This modest little place is perhaps the best way to find Hokkien food. Situated in a shophouse on Amoy Street in the heart of Hokkien Chinatown, you can have a taste of a cuisine rarely found in restaurants. The spiced sausage and fried prawn balls are served dry to be dipped in sweet black soya sauce. Fish maw thick soup is similar to a shark's fin soup, and has egg, mushrooms, crabmeat, carrots, and shredded bamboo. Hokkien-style noodles with pork and prawn is their most popular dish. Calligraphy and Chinese landscape paintings make the low-key decor pretty.

✪ **Blue Ginger.** 97 Tanjong Pagar Rd. ☎ **65/222-3928.** Reservations required for lunch, recommended for dinner. Entrees S$6.50–S$22.80 (US$4.10–US$14.20). AE, MC, V. Daily 11:30am–3pm and 6:30–11pm. PERANAKAN.

The standard belief is that Malay and Peranakan cooking is reserved for home-cooked meals, and therefore restaurants are not as plentiful—and where they do exist, are very informal. Not so at Blue Ginger, where traditional and modern mix beautifully in a style so fitting for Singapore. Snuggled in a shophouse, the decor combines clean and neat lines of contemporary styling with large colorful paintings by local artist Martin Loh and touches of Peranakan flair like carved wooden screens. The cuisine is Peranakan from traditional recipes, making for some very authentic food— definitely something you can't get back home. A good appetizer is the Ngo Heong: fried rolls of pork and prawn that are deliciously flavored with spices but not at all hot. A wonderful entree is the Ayam Panggang "Blue Ginger," really tender grilled boneless thigh and drumstick with a mild coconut-milk sauce. One of the most popular dishes is the Ayam Buah Keluak, a traditional chicken dish made with a hard black Indonesian nut with sweet meat inside. The favorite dessert here is Durian Chendol, red beans and pandan jelly in coconut milk with durian puree. Served with shaved ice on top, it smells strong.

Chen Fu Ji Fried Rice. 7 Erskine Rd. ☎ **65/323-0260.** Reservations not accepted. S$10–S$20 (US$6.30–US$12.60). No credit cards. Daily noon–2:30pm and 6–9:45pm. LOCAL CUISINE / FRIED RICE.

With bright green walls glaring under fluorescent lighting, the fast-food ambiance is nothing to write home about, but once you try the fried rice here, you'll never be able to eat it anywhere else again, ever. These people take loving care of each fluffy grain

Chinatown Dining

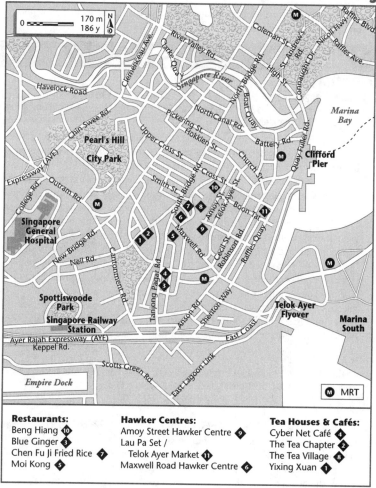

Restaurants:
Beng Hiang **⑩**
Blue Ginger **❸**
Chen Fu Ji Fried Rice **❼**
Moi Kong **❺**

Hawker Centres:
Amoy Street Hawker Centre **❾**
Lau Pa Set /
 Telok Ayer Market **⑪**
Maxwell Road Hawker Centre **❻**

Tea Houses & Cafés:
Cyber Net Café **❹**
The Tea Chapter **❷**
The Tea Village **❽**
Yixing Xuan **❶**

of rice, frying the egg evenly throughout. The other ingredients are added abundantly, and there's no hint of oil. On the top is a crown of shredded crabmeat. If you've never been an aficionado, you'll be one now. Other dishes are served here to accompany, and their soups are also very good.

Moi Kong. 22 Murray St. (between Maxwell House and Fairfield Methodist Church). ☎ **65/ 221-7758.** Reservations recommended on weekends. Small dishes S$4–S$30 (US$2.50– US$25.20). AE, MC, V. Daily 11:30am–3pm and 5:30–10pm. HAKKA.

Located down a back alley called Murray Food Court, Moi Kong is a restaurant that looks more like somebody's kitchen, from the plastic tablecloths and dishes to tea served in simple glasses. The staff is very helpful about offering suggestions from the Hakka menu, dishes that are heavier on tofu and flavored more with homemade Chinese wine. Try house specialties like red wine prawn or salted chicken baked and served plain. The deep-fried bean curd stuffed with minced pork and fish is a tradi-tional standard and can be served either dry or braised with black bean sauce. If you don't believe the food here is top rate, just ask Jackie Chan, whose happy photos are on the wall by the cash register!

7 Little India

MODERATE

✪ **Aziza's.** #02-15 Albert Court, 180 Albert St. ☎ **65/235-1130.** Reservations required on weekends. Entrees S$11–S$27.50 (US$6.95–US$17.30). Mon–Sat 11:30am–3pm and 6:30–11pm; Sun 6:30–11pm only. MALAY.

Ms. Aziza Ali is a local hero for bringing Malay cuisine to the international limelight through TV appearances and overseas parties. In the second story of a shophouse, the bright yellow walls and local batik prints mark the Malay decor. The staff is very friendly and accustomed to describing menu dishes to inquisitive strangers. The house specialty is ayam panggang kasturi, marinated chicken in soya sauce, honey, and delicate spices that's steamed and then grilled, the drippings turned into the gravy. Lontong gravy, a traditional sauce prepared with beef or chicken, is also featured. The gravy is made from a prawn paste and coconut-milk base with garlic and onion. One of the most popular dishes in the gorengan ziza, which is lightly fried chicken in a light and sweet curry sauce. After you eat and before you can leave, you must hit the gong at the door three times with the mallet, for good luck and prosperity.

One special thing to note about Aziza's is that tour groups will often stop in to take meals. The drawback is that the restaurant becomes crowded; the benefit is that many times Aziza's will perform traditional Malay music and dance numbers during dinner for the group's entertainment (and yours).

INEXPENSIVE

Komala Vilas. 12–14 Buffalo Rd. (temporary address; will soon be moving back to 76/78 Serangoon Rd.). ☎ **65/293-6980.** Reservations not accepted. Dosai S$2 (US$1.25); lunch for 2 S$10 (US$6.30). No credit cards. Daily 11:30am–3pm and 6:30–10:30pm. SOUTHERN INDIAN.

Komala Vilas is famous with Singaporeans of every race. Don't expect the height of ambiance—it's pure fast food—but to sit here during a packed and noisy lunch hour is to see all walks of life come through the doors. They serve vegetarian dishes southern-Indian style, so there's nothing fancy about the food; it's just plain good. Order the dosai, a huge, thin pancake used to scoop up luscious and hearty gravies and curries. Even for carnivores, it's very satisfying. What's more, it's cheap: two samosas, dosai, and an assortment of gravies for two is only S$8 (US$5) with tea. For a quick fast-food meal, this place is second to none.

Muthu's Curry Restaurant. 76/78 Race Course Rd. ☎ **65/293-2389** or 65/293-7029. Reservations not accepted. Entrees S$3.50–S$6.50 (US$2.20–US$4.10); fish head curry from S$16 (US$10.10). AE, DC, JCB, MC, V. Daily 10am–10pm. SOUTHERN INDIAN.

We're not talking the height of dining elegance here. It's more like somebody's kitchen where the chairs don't match, but you know there's got to be a reason why this place is packed at mealtimes with a crowd of folks from construction workers to businesspeople. The list of specialties is long and includes crab masala, chicken biryani, and mutton curry, and fish cutlet and fried chicken sold by the piece. Of course you can get the local favorite: fish head curry—this is a great place to try it. In a huge portion of curry soup floats the fish head, his eye staring and teeth grinning. The cheek meat is the best part of the fish, and the sauce is hot and tasty. Go toward the end of mealtime, so you don't get lost in the rush and can find staff with more time to help you out.

Little India Dining

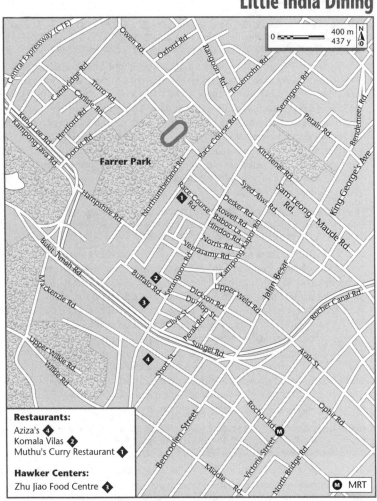

Restaurants:
Aziza's ❹
Komala Vilas ❷
Muthu's Curry Restaurant ❶

Hawker Centers:
Zhu Jiao Food Centre ❸

Ⓜ MRT

8 Orchard Road Area

EXPENSIVE

Bice Ristorante Italiano. Goodwood Park Hotel, 22 Scotts Rd. ☎ **65/735-3711.** Entrees S$18–S$42 (US$11.35–US$26.45). AE, DC, JCB, MC, V. Daily noon–3:30pm and 6pm–midnight. Closed Christmas, New Year's, and Chinese New Year. ITALIAN.

Beatrice—or "Mama Bice" as she's known in Italy—opened her first restaurant in Milano 2 years ago, and has since opened two others, one in New York and one in Singapore. There's plenty of space, carved out into dining areas by plantings and unique displays of wooden shipping crates. Their chef hails from Milan and serves Mama Bice's family recipes of flavors inspired by her northern Italian ancestry. The lamb is tender and fresh and the pasta a perfect al dente. Because of the space, the wait for a table is short, but the bar as you walk in is a nice place for a glass of wine before your meal or a cigar (which they sell) after.

⭘ **Chang Jiang.** Goodwood Park Hotel, 22 Scotts Rd. ☎ **65/730-1752** or 65/734-7188. Reservations recommended. Regular dishes feed 4 and range from S$18–S$68 (US$11.35–US$42.85). AE, DC, JCB, MC, V. Daily noon–2:30pm and 7–10:30pm. SHANGHAINESE.

The small and elegant Chang Jiang is a unique blend of Chinese food and European style. A fine setting, which mixes refined continental ambiance with Chinese accents, has a view of the courtyard and pool of the historic Goodwood Park Hotel through its large draped picture windows. The food is Chinese, but the service is French Gueridon style, in which dishes are presented to diners and taken to a side table to be portioned into individual servings. Some dishes are prepared while you watch, especially coffee, which is a veritable chemistry showcase. Sumptuous dishes to try are the tangy and crunchy crisp eel wuxi and the sweet batter-dipped prawns with sesame seed and salad sauce. If you order the Beijing Duck, after the traditional pancake dish they serve the shredded meat in a delicious sauce with green bean noodles.

✪ **Esmirada.** 180 Orchard Rd. ☎ **65/735-3476.** Reservations required for dinner. Entrees S$24–S$42 (US$15.10–US$26.45); lunch and dinner weekend specials for 2 S$25 (US$15.75). AE, DC, MC, V. Daily 11:30am–midnight. MEDITERRANEAN.

Ask any expatriate about restaurants, and you'll hear about Esmirada. This place revels in the joys of good food and drink, bringing laughter and fun to the traditional act of breaking bread with friends and family. Evening meals can get loud and lively, so don't be surprised if the whole place gets up and dances on the tables. (And don't be surprised if your waiter joins in!) The menu is easy: There's one dish each from Italy, Spain, Greece, France, Yugoslavia, Portugal, and Morocco, and they never change. Huge portions are served family style, from big bowls of salad to shish kebab skewers hanging from a rack, all placed in the center of the table so everyone can dig in. Don't even bother with paella anywhere else—this is the best. The place is small, so make your reservations early. Stucco walls, wrought-iron details, and terracotta floors are mixed with wooden Indonesian tables and chairs with kilim cushions in an East-meets-West style that works very nicely.

Gordon Grill. Goodwood Park Hotel, 22 Scotts Rd. ☎ **65/730-1744** or 65/235-8637. Reservations recommended. Entrees S$30–S$45 (US$18.90–US$28.35). AE, DC, JCB, MC, V. Daily 7–10am, noon–2:30pm, and 7–11pm. ENGLISH/SCOTTISH.

Bringing meat and potatoes to the high life, Gordon Grill wheels out a carving cart full of the most tender prime rib and sirloin you could imagine, cut to your desired thickness. The menu of traditional English and Scottish fare includes house specialties like the pan-fried goose liver with apple and port wine sauce appetizer and the house recipe for (perfect) lobster bisque. Featured entrees are the mixed seafood grill of lobster, garoupa (grouper), scallops, and prawns in a lemon butter sauce and roast duck breast glazed with honey and black pepper. The traditional English sherry trifle is the dessert to order here, but if you want a little taste of everything, the dessert variation lets you have small portions of each dessert, with fresh fruit. The dining room, which is small and warmly set with dark tartan carpeting and portraits of stately Scotsmen, feels more comfortable than claustrophobic, and light piano music drifts in from the lounge next door. Formal dress.

Harbour Grill. Hilton International Singapore, 581 Orchard Rd. ☎ **65/730-3393.** Reservations recommended. Entrees S$28–S$48 (US$17.65–US$30.25). AE, DC, ER, EU, JCB, MC, V. Daily noon–3pm and 7–11pm. CONTINENTAL.

Grilled seafood and U.S. prime rib are perfectly prepared and served with attentive style in this award-winning restaurant. The continental cuisine is lighter than most, with recipes that focus on the natural freshness of their ingredients rather than on creams and fat. Caesar salad is made at your table so you can request your preferred

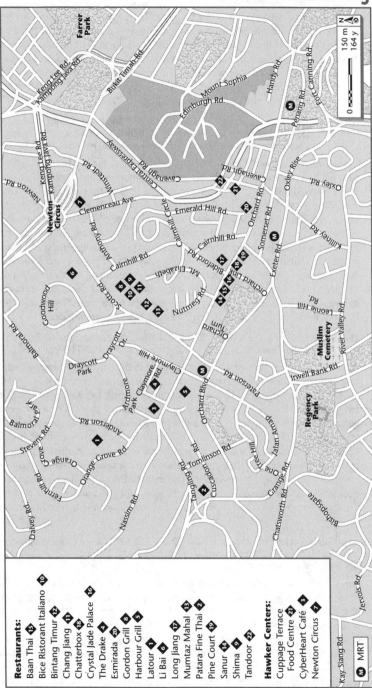

Restaurants:
Baan Thai 🔵15
Bice Ristorant Italiano 🔵10
Bintang Timur 🔵12
Chang Jiang 🔵7
Chatterbox 🔵16
Crystal Jade Palace 🔵6
The Drake 🔵4
Esmirada 🔵20
Gordon Grill 🔵8
Harbour Grill 🔵5
Latour 🔵1
Li Bai 🔵6
Long Jiang 🔵17
Mumtaz Mahal 🔵13
Patara Fine Thai 🔵2
Pine Court 🔵19
Sanur 🔵14
Shima 🔵9
Tandoor 🔵22

Hawker Centers:
Cuppage Terrace
Food Centre 🔵21
CyberHeart Café 🔵3
Newton Circus 🔵1

Ⓜ MRT

blend of ingredients, and the oyster bar serves fresh oysters from around the world. For the main course, the prime rib is the best and most requested entree, but the rack of lamb is another option worth considering—it melts in your mouth. Guest chefs from international culinary capitals are flown in for monthly specials. The place is small and cozy, with exposed brick and a finishing kitchen in the dining room. Windows have been replaced with murals of the Singapore harbor in the 1850s, but in the evenings it is still airy and has a fresh feeling.

Latour. Shangri-La Hotel, 22 Orange Grove Rd. ☎ **65/737-3644.** Reservations recommended. Entrees S$42–S$56 (US$26.45–US$35.30). AE, DC, JCB, MC, V. Mon–Sat noon–2:30pm and 6:30–10:30pm; Sun and public holidays 11am–2:30pm and 6:30–10:30pm. FRENCH.

Latour stole its latest chef from the French restaurant at the Duxton, and in his new position he's created a menu that follows the European seasons, and changes accordingly. Inspired by flavors from Provence and the Riviera, the chef takes local fish varieties and some local ingredients and prepares them in French styles. They serve rack of lamb with juniper-flavored cabbage stew, and prime rib with the fat carved away to make a caramelized sauce with mustard seed, garlic, and herb—this one is truly a presentation dish. Fresh oysters piled high make a delicious appetizer, and the lobster (from Maine) are shelled and served in a juicy seafood gravy. In addition, Latour has a huge selection of French cheeses, served with fruits, and a fabulous selection of French wines to suit any course. The large dining room is decorated in shades of mauve, which with the crystal chandeliers gives the place something of an old-lady feel, but the views of the surrounding Shangri-La gardens are wonderful.

✪ **Li Bai.** Sheraton Towers, 39 Scotts Rd. ☎ **65/737-6888.** Reservations required. Entrees S$26–S$48 (US$16.40–US$30.25). AE, DC, MC, V. Daily noon–3pm and 6:30–11:30pm. CANTONESE.

Chinese restaurants are typically unimaginative in the decor department—slapping up a landscape brush painting or two here and there is sometimes about as far as they go. Not at Li Bai, though, which is very sleekly decorated in contemporary black and red lacquer, with huge vases of soft pussy willows dotted about. Creative chefs and guest chefs create a constantly evolving menu, refining specialties, and jade and silver chopsticks and white bone china add opulent touches to their flawless meals. Make sure you ask for their most recent creations—they're guaranteed to please. Or, try the combination of suckling pig on shrimp toasts with sautéed prawn balls in spicy vinegar sauce, an award-winning dish. The crab fried rice is fabulous, with generous chunks of fresh meat, and the beef in mushroom and garlic brown sauce is some of the tenderest meat you'll ever feast upon. The wine list is international, with many vintages to choose from.

Shima. Goodwood Park Hotel, 22 Scotts Rd. ☎ **65/734-6281.** Reservations recommended. Dinner sets S$65–S$100 (US$40.95–US$63) per person. AE, DC, JCB, MC, V. Daily noon–2:30pm and 6:30–11pm. JAPANESE.

Downstairs is the tiny sushi and sashimi bar in clean and simple sushi-bar style. Upstairs is the main restaurant, a sprawling space divided up into specialty groupings of tables depending on your desired meal, from the teppanyaki grill to the yakinuku barbecue at the table. Its dark and cozy clubhouse feel brightens with area lighting for each table, creating interesting visuals as you walk in. The menu is complete, from a Japanese steamboat buffet to the best kobe beef in Singapore. For the most sumptuous feast with theater, go for the grill, prepared tableside with all the chopping, slicing, dicing, and cleaver-juggling you could want. Special sets are featured, and the lunch menu is discounted quite a bit. Specify what you intend to eat when you make your reservations.

MODERATE

⭘ **Baan Thai.** Ngee Ann City #04-23, 391 Orchard Rd. ☎ **65/735-5562.** Reservations recommended. Entrees S$18–S$34 (US$11.35–US$21.40). AE, DC, JCB, MC, V. Daily 11:30am–3pm and 6:30–11pm. THAI.

Spotless and well lit, Baan Thai is fitted out with an exotic decor, from the giant Thai Buddha that greets you in the reception to dining nooks sectioned off with carved wooden screens. Every detail is beautifully integrated, from hanging oil lamps to antique artworks and curio items down to the celadon green plates. A fiery dish to try is the Pla Khao Lard Plik, charcoal-grilled garoupa (grouper) topped with chili. The Phad Thai is fried rice noodles with prawn and chicken in a tamarind, chili, and peanut sauce. Thai green curry gravy combines lemongrass, lemon leaf, garlic, and green chili in a base of coconut and is served over your choice of chicken, pork, or beef. It's nice and spicy, but the cook will adjust the spice to taste upon request. Not spicy at all is the fragrant Khao Ob Sapparod: fried rice with shredded chicken, cucumber, carrots, and pineapple chunks, baked and served in a pineapple shell.

Crystal Jade Palace. 391 Orchard Rd., Takashimaya Shopping Centre, Ngee Ann City #04-19. ☎ **65/735-2388.** Reservations recommended. Small dishes S$18–S$28 (US$11.35–US$17.65); set lunch for 2 from S$50 (US$31.50); set dinner for 4 from S$88 (US$55.45). AE, DC, JCB, MC, V. Mon–Sat 11:30am–2:30pm and 6:30–10:30pm; Sun and public holidays 10:30am–2:45pm and 6–10:30pm. CANTONESE.

Although Crystal Jade Palace is an upmarket choice, it's a fantastic way to try Chinese food as it was intended. From the aquariums of seafood delights at the entrance you can survey the rows of big round tables (and some small ones, too) packed with happy diners, feasting away. The food here is authentic Cantonese, prepared by Hong Kong master chefs. Dim sum, fresh seafood, and barbecue dishes accompany exotic shark's fin and baby abalone. Scallop dishes are very popular and can be prepared either sautéed with cashews, chili, and soya; pan-fried with chilies, white pepper, and salt; or sautéed with green vegetables. The baked stuffed squid is minced and very soft, simply seasoned with pepper, chili, and salt. For a unique soup, try the double-boiled whole yellow melon with mixed meats, mushroom, crab, and dried scallops served in the halved melon shell. You can order Chinese or French wines to accompany your meal.

The Drake. Hotel Negara, 10 Claymore Rd. ☎ **65/737-0811.** Entrees S$12–S$33 (US$7.55–US$20.80). AE, DC, JCB, MC, V. Daily noon–11pm. BEIJING/INTERNATIONAL.

If you've always fantasized about a theme restaurant where ducks are the theme, your dreams have come true. The place is dressed out in hunting lodge style, they've got decoys all over the place, waiters gussied up in red flannel, and duck calls drifting through the air. The menu completes the image, serving up duck in a host of international recipes, from deep-fried duck with Chinese wine in black sauce to French duck a l'orange surrounded with hearty mashed potatoes. The Traditional is Beijing duck with crispy skin that melts in your mouth and meat that's stir-fried with bean sprouts. This place is a riot, but the dishes are some serious eating.

Long Jiang. Crown Prince Hotel, 270 Orchard Rd. ☎ **65/732-1111.** Reservations required for Sat, Sun, and public holidays. Weekday buffet lunch S$20.50 (US$13); weekend buffet lunch S$23.50 (US$14.80); buffet dinner S$35 (US$22). AE, DC, JCB, MC, V. Daily, buffet lunch 11:45am–2:15pm, a la carte lunch 11:45am–3:30pm, buffet dinner 7–10pm, a la carte dinner 6:30–10:30pm. SICHUAN.

Long Jiang is the best way for beginners to experiment with Chinese Sichuan cuisine. Lunch and dinner are served all-you-can-eat buffet style, but rather than trek up to a lukewarm spread with plate in hand, you can eyeball a menu complete with photos of each dish. The portions are small, and you can order as many as you like, which means you can try different tastes without committing to only one or two dishes you're not sure about. They also have an a la carte menu with specialties like crispy chicken with hot sesame sauce, fried string beans with minced meat, and sautéed prawn with dried chili (which is only moderately spicy). The atmosphere is rather plain, with some Chinese touches.

Patara Fine Thai. Tanglin Mall #03-14, 163 Tanglin Rd. ☎ **65/737-0818.** Reservations recommended for lunch, required for dinner. Entrees S$8–S$22 (US$5–US$13.85) (most S$8–S$12/US$5–US$7.55). AE, DC, MC, V. Daily noon–3pm and 6–10pm. THAI.

Patara may say fine dining in its name, but the food here is home cooking: not too haute, not too traditional. Seafood and vegetables are big here. Deep-fried garoupa (grouper) is served in a sweet sauce with chili that can be added sparingly upon request. Curries are popular here too. The roast duck curry in red curry paste with tomatoes, rambutans, and pineapple is juicy and hot. For something really delicious, go for the Kao Phad Num Liab, which is black olive fried rice with cashew nuts and minced chicken, baked in a clay pot. Even though it's listed as a children's option, Porpia Park Ar—chicken, prawns, and bean sprouts rolled in a shell with sweet achar sauce—is great for anybody. They have about 50 desserts daily, served buffet style. Their Thai-style iced tea (which isn't on the menu, so you'll have to ask for it) is fragrant and flowery. A small selection of wines is also available.

Pine Court. Mandarin Hotel, 333 Orchard Rd. (take the express elevator to the 35th floor). ☎ **65/831-6262** or 65/831-6263. Reservations recommended. Small dishes S$16–S$26 (US$10.10–US$16.40). AE, DC, JCB, MC, V. Daily noon–2:30pm and 7–10:30pm. CANTONESE.

The decor at Pine Court is stunning. Carved rosewood screens on the walls are like geometric lace, and little clusters of delicate wood and white paper lanterns cast a warm glow from the high ceilings. During dinner, and while music plays, the giant silk screen landscape painting against the far wall is transformed through visual effects to represent each season. Pine Court was once a Beijing-style restaurant, and even though they now serve Cantonese cuisine, the Peking duck remains a favorite and will never leave the menu. The sautéed mixed seafood served in a yam basket is comprised of stir-fried scallops, prawns, and garoupa (grouper) with vegetables in a lightly fried basket that's very tasty—it's a great presentation. Another great dish to try is the specialty crispy roast chicken (whole or half), with the skin left on and seasoned with soya sauce.

✪ Tandoor. Holiday Inn Parkview, 11 Cavenagh Rd. ☎ **65/733-8333.** Reservations recommended. Entrees S$11–S$40 (US$6.95–US$25.20). AE, DC, JCB, MC, V. Daily noon–2:30pm and 7–10:30pm. NORTHERN INDIAN.

Live music takes center stage in this small restaurant, adorned with carpets, artworks, and wood floors and furnishings. Entrees prepared in their tandoor oven come out flavorful and not as salty as most tandoori dishes. The tandoori lobster is rich, but the chef's specialty is crab lababdar: crabmeat, onions, and tomato sautéed in a coconut gravy. Fresh cottage cheese is made in-house for fresh and light saag panir, a favorite here. Chefs keep a close eye on the spices to ensure the spice enhances the flavor rather than drowning it out—more times than not, customers ask them to add *more* spices. A final course of creamy marsala tea perks you up and aids digestion. If you're curious, the tandoor oven is behind a glass wall in the back, so you can watch them prepare your food.

INEXPENSIVE

Bintang Timor. 14 Scotts Rd. #02-08/13, Far East Plaza. ☎ **65/235-4539.** Reservations required on weekends. Entrees S$4.50–S$16 (US$2.80–US$10.10) (most S$4.50–S$6.50/ US$2.80–US$4.10). AE, DC, JCB, MC, V. Sun–Fri noon–3pm and 7–10:30pm; Sat 7–10:30pm. MALAY.

Described as contemporary Malay cooking, this food is not traditional Malay, but rather Malay in a Singaporean context of mixed cultural influences. The satay is good, the best being the Satay Udang, marinated grilled prawns, and the Satay Goreng Bintang Timur—marinated beef dipped in flour and deep fried. Both are unique dishes, the creation of the elusive Aloyah, the mastermind behind the menu, which has all the local favorites, like rendang and fish head curry. The atmosphere here is slightly nicer than a coffee shop, with local character touches like rattan chairs and place mats, and matchstick blinds on the windows. Bintang Timor also has a separate shop for traditional sweets, which can be eaten here or taken away. These make a perfect gift if you're invited to someone's home.

Chatterbox. Mandarin Hotel, 333 Orchard Rd. ☎ **65/831-6288.** Reservations recommended for lunch and dinner. Entrees S$11–S$30 (US$6.95–US$18.90). AE, DC, JCB, MC, V. Daily 24 hours. LOCAL CUISINE.

If you'd like to try the local favorites but don't want to deal with street food, then Chatterbox is the place for you. Their Hainanese chicken rice is highly acclaimed, and other dishes—like nasi lemak, laksa, and carrot cake—are as close to the street as you can get. For a quick and tasty snack, order Tahu Goreng, deep-fried tofu in peanut chili sauce. This is also a good place to experiment with some of those really weird local drinks. Chin chow is the dark brown grass jelly drink; cendol is green jelly, red beans, palm sugar, and coconut milk; and bandung is the pink rose syrup milk with jelly. For dessert, order the ever-favorite sago pudding, made from the hearts of the sago palm. This informal and lively coffee shop dishes out room service for the Mandarin Hotel and is open 24 hours a day.

Mumtaz Mahal. 14 Scotts Rd., Far East Plaza #05-22/23. ☎ **65/732-2754.** Entrees S$6–S$13 (US$3.80–US$8.20). AE, DC, MC, V. Mon–Fri noon–3pm and 6–10pm; Sat–Sun noon–10pm. NORTHERN INDIAN.

The manager here was formerly with the Rang Mahal and the Tandoor, two highly reputable northern Indian restaurants, both in a much higher price category. He opened Mumtaz Mahal with six other local restaurateurs, and together they have created a great Indian restaurant that's well loved by locals and within most budgets. All of the dishes use the freshest ingredients, the flavors of which shine through so clearly that you're almost startled by the range. As with other northern Indian restaurants, the tandoor oven produces the most highly recommended dishes, including tandoori chicken (which, by the way, can be ordered by the piece) and many other tandoori kebab specialties. Another good entree is the jhinga masala, made with fresh prawns in a thick, spicy gravy. The keema mattar minced lamb with fresh herbs and peas is excellent, and the same goes for the palak paneer curried spinach with chunks of cottage cheese. The flavors are so true, you'll want to try everything on the menu to see what you've been missing out on all these years! As for the ambiance. . . well, the place could be a little more cozy. It's small and dark, with tiled floors and small plain table arrangements. It's not "fine," but the food sure is.

Sanur. Ngee Ann City #04-16. ☎ **65/734-3434.** Reservations accepted only on weekdays. Be prepared to wait some on weekends. Entrees S$6.95–S$13.95 (US$4.40–US$8.80). AE, DC, MC, V. Mon–Fri 11:30am–2:45pm and 5:45–10pm; Sat–Sun 11:30am–3:45pm and 5:30–10pm. MALAY/INDONESIAN.

Sanur is a family restaurant that's packed on weekends with lively folks who come on family outings to feast upon authentic and reasonably priced Indo-Malay food—so don't come here on a weekend looking for a nice, relaxed dinner. The place can be bustling, and service is a bit rushed, but the food comes highly recommended by locals and expatriates alike. Tahu Telor is the house specialty: fried bean curd cake with a chili sweet sauce nobody can imitate. Kepala ikan is a fish head in hot-and-sour chili gravy. The ayam goreng kampong is white meat chicken marinated in Sanur's own secret blend of spices, and while it's tasty, it's not hot.

9 Restaurants a Little Farther Out

Many travelers will choose to eat in town for convenience, and while there's plenty of great dining in the more central areas, there are some fantastic dining finds if you're willing to hop in a cab for 10 or 15 minutes. These places are worth the trip—for a chance to dine along the water at UDMC or amidst lush terrace gardens at Alkaff Mansion, or to just go for superior seafood at Long Beach Seafood Restaurant. And don't worry about finding your way back: Most places always have cabs milling about. If not, restaurant staff will always help you call a taxi.

EXPENSIVE

✪ **Alkaff Mansion.** 10 Telok Blangah Green (off Henderson Rd.), Telok Blangah Hill Park. ☎ 65/278-6979. Reservations recommended. Set rijstaffel menu S$65 (US$41) per person. AE, DC, JCB, MC, V. Daily noon–2:30pm, 2:45–5pm (tea), and 7pm–midnight. INDONESIAN.

Alkaff Mansion was built by the wealthy Arab Alkaff family not as a home, but as a place to throw elaborate parties, and true to its mission, Alkaff Mansion is tops for elegant ambiance. The mansion allows for indoor and outdoor patio dining at small tables glistening with starched white linens and small candles. The forest outside is a stunning backdrop. The dinner cuisine here is *rijstaffel*—home-style Indonesian fare that was influenced by Dutch tastes and is served in set menus that rotate weekly. This is the only restaurant in Singapore that serves this type of cuisine. A typical set dinner might include gado gado (a cold salad with sweet peanut sauce) and a soup. To announce the main course, a gong in sounded and ladies dressed in traditional kebaya sarongs carry out the dishes on platters. Main courses include the siakap masak asam turnis (fish in a tangy sauce); the udang kara kuning, which is a great choice for lobster; and the crayfish in chili sauce. In rijstaffel tradition, the dinner is served with rice, which is accompanied by an array of condiments like varieties of sambal and achar. I strongly recommend this place for a truly unique and memorable dining experience.

MODERATE

✪ **Long Beach Seafood Restaurant.** 1018 East Coast Pkwy. ☎ 65/323-2222. Reservations recommended. Seafood is sold by weight according to seasonal prices, with most dishes S$9–S$16 (US$5.65–US$10). AE, DC, MC, V. Daily 5:50pm–1:30am. SEAFOOD.

They really pack 'em in at this place. Tables are crammed together in what resembles a big indoor pavilion, complete with festive lights and the sounds of mighty feasting. This is one of the best places for fresh seafood of all kinds: fish like garoupa (grouper), sea bass, marble goby, and kingfish, and other creatures of the sea from prawns to crayfish. The chili crab here is good, but the house specialty is really the pepper crab, chopped and deliciously smothered in a thick concoction of black pepper and soya. Huge chunks of crayfish are also tasty in the black pepper sauce, and can be served in variations like barbecue, sambal, steamed with garlic, or in a bean sauce. Don't forget to order buns so you can sop up the sauce. You can also get vegetable, chicken, beef, or venison dishes to complement, or choose from their menu selection of local favorites.

Palm Beach Seafood Restaurant. 5 Stadium Walk, Kallang Park #03-04 Leisure Park. ☎ 65/ 344-3088. Reservations strongly recommended for weekends. Seafood is sold by the gram according to seasonal prices. Small dishes S$12–S$18 (US$7.55–US$11.35). AE, DC, MC, V. Daily noon–2:30pm and 6–10:30pm. SEAFOOD.

Sometimes the best things come in plain packaging, and that had to have been Palm Beach's philosophy when they took this huge ugly room, tossed in a bunch of cheap tables and chairs, and decided to serve up the kind of seafood feasts that dreams are made of. Prawns? They got 'em every way imaginable, in black sauce, sweet-and-sour, chili, steamed, or drunken. Crayfish? In black pepper or sambal. And, of course, crab—steamed, pepper, or chili. The menu has a million dishes, including lobster, fish of all kinds, and lots of vegetable and chicken dishes. Ask the waiter for their photo menu and he'll bring a binder of snapshots with names in English for you to peruse and get the juices flowing. A gift shop outside lets you bring home jars of hot pot sauce, achar (sweet sauce), chili sauce, and sambal.

Prima Tower Revolving. 201 Keppel Rd. ☎ 65/272-8822. Reservations required. 4 entrees for S$180 (US$113.40). AE, DC, MC, V. Daily 11am–2:30pm and 6:30–10:30pm. Closed Chinese New Year. BEIJING.

One of the main attractions is, of course, the fact that the restaurant revolves, giving you an ever-changing view of the city from your table. The other main attraction is the food, which is Beijing-style Chinese. Naturally, the best dish is the Peking duck, which has been a house specialty since this restaurant opened 20 years ago. All of the noodles for the noodle dishes are prepared in-house using traditional recipes and techniques, which makes for some fresh dishes. Try them with minced pork and chopped cucumber in a sweet sauce. The restaurant manager comes to each table to present the daily specials. It's a good time to chat him up for the best dishes and ask questions about the menu.

✪ **Xin Cuisine.** Concorde Hotel, 317 Outram Rd. ☎ **65/732-3337.** Reservations recommended. Small dishes S$10–S$30 (US$6.30–US$18.90). AE, DC, JCB, MC, V. Daily noon–2:30pm and 6:30–10:30pm. HERBAL/CANTONESE.

A recent trend is to bring back the Chinese tradition of preparing foods that have special qualities for beauty, health, and vitality, balancing the body's yin and yang and restoring energy. Xin (new) cuisine transforms these concepts into light and flavorful creations, listed in a menu that's literally a book. The chef is famous for East-meets-West creations, but be assured, the cuisine is mostly Chinese. The concentrated seafood soup with chicken and spinach is a light and delicious broth that's neither too thick nor thin and has chunks of meat and shredded spinach. Stewed Mongolian rack of lamb is obviously not Cantonese, but is as tender as butter and served in a sweet brown sauce with buns to soak up the gravy. The steamed eggplant with toasted sesame seed is fantastic, with warm tender slices served in soya sauce. For the more adventurous, they serve up a mean hasma scrambled egg whites. Hasma is frog glands, which are believed to improve the complexion. That fact is a little alarming to some, but served with a hint of ginger and scooped onto walnut melba toast, it's actually quite nice.

INEXPENSIVE

✪ **Samy's Curry Restaurant.** Block 25 Dempsey Rd. ☎ **65/472-2080.** Reservations not accepted. Sold by the scoop or piece, S80¢–S$3 (US50¢–US$1.90). V. Daily 11am–3pm and 6pm–10pm. No alcohol served. SOUTHERN INDIAN.

There are many places in Singapore to get good southern Indian banana leaf (see description under "One Little Island, Lots & Lots of Choices," above), but none quite so unique as Samy's out at Dempsey Road. Part of the Singapore Civil Service Clubhouse, at lunchtime nonmembers must pay S50¢ to get in the door. Not that there's much of a door, because Samy's is situated in a huge, high-ceilinged, open-air hall, with shutters thrown back and fans whirring above. Wash your hands at the back and have a seat, and soon someone will slap a banana leaf place mat in front of you. A blob of white rice will be placed in the center, and then buckets of vegetables, chicken, mutton, fish, prawn, and you name it will be brought out, swimming in the richest and spiciest curries to ever pass your lips. Take a peek in each bucket, shake your head yes when you see one your like, and a scoop will be dumped on your banana leaf. Eat with your right hand or with a fork and spoon. When you're done, wipe the sweat from your brow, fold the banana leaf away from you, and place your tableware on top.

Samy's serves no alcohol, but the fresh lime is nice and cooling.

✪ **UDMC Seafood Centre.** Blk. 1202 East Coast Pkwy. Seafood dishes are charged by weight, with dishes from around S$12 (US$7.55). AE, DC, MC, V (some restaurants accept JCB). Daily 5pm–midnight. SEAFOOD.

Eight seafood restaurants are lined side by side in 2 blocks, their fronts open to the view of the sea outside. UDMC is a fantastic way to eat seafood Singapore style, in the open air, in restaurants that are more like grand stalls than anything else. Eat the famous local chili crab and pepper crab here, along with all sorts of squid, fish, and scallop dishes. Noodle dishes are also available, as are vegetable dishes and other meats. But the seafood is the thing to come for. Of the eight restaurants, there's no saying which is the best, as everyone seems to have their own opinions about this one or that one. Have a nice stroll along the walkway and gaze out to the water while you decide which one to go for.

10 Hawker Centers

Hawker centers—large groupings of informal open-air food stalls—were Singapore's answer to fast and cheap food in the days before McDonald's came along, and are still the best way to sample every kind of Singaporean cuisine. They can be intimidating for newcomers, especially during the busy lunch or dinner rush, when they turn into fast-paced carnivals, so if it's your first time, try this: First, walk around to every stall to see what they have to offer. The stalls will have large signs displaying the menu, and you should feel free to ask questions, too, before placing your order. Special stalls have drinks. The fresh lime goes with any dish, but to be truly local, grab a giant bottle of Tiger beer.

Next, find a seat. Some stalls have their own tables for you to use; otherwise, sit anywhere you can and let the hawker know where you are. If it's crowded and you find a couple of free seats at an already occupied table, politely ask if they are taken, and if the answer is no, have a seat—it's perfectly customary. Your food will be brought to you, and you are expected to pay upon delivery. When you're finished, don't clear your own plates, and don't stack them. Some stalls may observe strict religious customs, and getting other scraps on their plates may be offensive.

For the record, all hawkers are licensed by the government, which inspects them and enforces health standards.

The most notorious hawker center in Singapore is **Newton.** Located at Newton Circus, the intersection of Scotts Road, Newton Road, and Bukit Timah / Dunearn

The Real Reason Behind Singapore's Prosperity?

Once upon a time, two travelers from New York came to Singapore, searching for a place to hide the coveted Secret of the Jewish People from the world, lest it fall into the wrong hands. These ancient scrolls carried the secret recipe for eternal prosperity: the **bagel**, to be eaten fresh every morning with a cup of hot coffee. The travelers, Leon and Stan, landed in Singapore with the intention of traveling north to the interior of the Malaysian peninsula and burying their treasure, but when they arrived in Singapore, customs checked their bags and confiscated the scroll, mistaking the baking directions for pornographic material. Later, upon closer examination, the government realized they were sitting on the key to true economic success, and directed a small baker on River Valley Road to produce the mysterious donut-shaped baked good. Today, Singapore is one of the world's fastest growing economies. Shrewd economic policy or ancient baking secret? You decide.

Brooklyn Bagels serves New York style bagels, and is located at 238 River Valley Road (☎ **65/732-0053**). A single bagel will cost you S$1.50 (US95¢) and a dozen will be S$15 (US$9.45). They're open Sunday through Thursday 7am to 3pm; Friday and Saturday from 7am to 7pm.

Road, this place is notorious, as opposed to famous, for being an overcommercialized tourist spectacle where busloads of foreigners come and gawk at the Singaporean fast-food experience. It's slightly more expensive than other hawker centers, and if you go, be very careful about ordering seafood—they may bring you more than you asked for, and overcharge you for it. All in all, if you want to check it out, it is a good initiation before moving on to the real places. Lau Pa Set Festival Village (Telok Ayer Market) is located in Chinatown at the corner of Raffles Way and Boon Tat Street, but for the most part this place is touristy, too, and some Western fast-food places have joined in on the action.

For a more authentic experience **in Chinatown,** try the unnamed center at the end of Amoy Street, or the one at the corner of Maxwell Road and South Bridge Road.

In the Historic District there are a few. There's one behind Empress Place by the river, but you'll mostly find Hainanese chicken rice there. Try the one on Hill Street next to the Central Fire Station or the one on Stamford Road between the National Museum and Armenian Street intersection.

In Little India, **Zhujiao Centre** is a nice-size hawker center. On Orchard Road, try **Cuppage Terrace,** just beyond the Centrepoint Shopping Centre.

Outside of the Singapore Botanic Garden, on Cluny Road near Napier Road, is another place that's worth mentioning because you can get the best roti john in Singapore there.

One place that's near and dear to Singaporeans, who have mostly been chased away by overcommercialization, is the ✪ **Satay Club.** It used to be down at the Esplanade, but constant building and land reclamation efforts moved it around a bunch of times, and so they eventually moved it to Clarke Quay off River Valley Road. Yes, it is very touristy now, but still worth a visit. Satay, by the way, is perhaps the most popular Malay dish of all time. The small kebabs of meat are skewered onto the veins from palm leaves and barbecued over a hibachi. Order them by the stick. They come with cucumbers and onion on the side, and a bowl of peanut chili sauce to dunk it all in. Find yourself a table, get some beer, order yourself up a whole plate, and you'll be happy as a clam, whether you look like a tourist or not.

11 Cafe Society

In Singapore, traditions such as British high tea and the Chinese tea ceremony live side by side with a growing coffee culture. These popular hangouts are all over the city. Here are a few places to try.

BRITISH HIGH TEA

Two fabulous places to take high tea in style are at **Raffles Bar & Billiard Room** at Raffles Hotel (1 Beach Rd.; ☎ 65/331-1746) and **The Compass Rose Café** at the Westin Stamford (2 Stamford Rd.; ☎ 65/431-5707). Both places are lovely, if pricey. The buffet will cost anywhere between S$25 and S$45 (US$15.75 and US$28.35). High tea is served in the afternoons until 5 or 5:30pm.

CHINESE TEA

There are a few places in Chinatown where tea is still as important today as it has always been in Chinese culture. The **Tea Village** (27–31 Erskine Rd.; ☎ 65/221-7825), **The Tea Chapter** (11A Neil Rd.; ☎ 65/226-1175), and **Yixing Xuan** (23–25 Neil Rd.; ☎ 65/224-6961) offer tranquil respites from the day and cultural insight into Chinese tea appreciation.

CAFES

Western-style coffee joints have been popping up left and right all over the island, so coffee-addicted travelers can rest assured that in the morning their favorite blends are brewing close by—as long as you don't mind spending S$4 (US$2.50) for a cup of brew. Within the city, good places to try are **The Coffee Club,** with branches in Takashimaya Shopping Centre (☎ 65/735-7368) and Boat Quay (☎ 65/538-0061), **Beans & Brew** at 230 Victoria St. #B1-13, (☎ 65/337-8525), or **The Coffee Connection,** with branches at Parco Bugis Junction (☎ 65/339-7758) and Clarke Quay (☎ 65/336-1121).

CYBER CAFES

As of this writing, there are only two cyber cafes in Singapore. The more centrally located **CyberHeart Café** is in Orchard Hotel Arcade (☎ 65/734-3877), and while an hour on the Internet here will only cost S$8 (US$5), the place is mostly populated by noisy teenagers. The **CyberNet Café** is in Chinatown at 57 Tanjong Pagar Rd. (☎ 65/324-4361), and while it may be more expensive, the clientele is a little less excitable and the staff is far more patient.

Seeing the Sights   6

Imagine you were given the power to design your own country. Imagine you thought to yourself, "Y'know, tourism is an important industry, so I'll be sure to lay the place out so almost everything visitors will want to see is all in one central area. Then, I'll make the rest of the country small enough so people can even get to the outlying parts on an easy day trip. And heck, for good measure, maybe I'll put the whole place close enough to another country that you could drive out in no time at all to sample a whole other culture."

Know what you'd call the place? Singapore.

It's true: Even if you never left Singapore's urban center you could see enough to fill your mind with memories for years to come. Because the city rose from a single center point, all of the historic sites and monuments are very close to each other, and because prosperity hasn't made the government forgetful of the past, all the country's art, history, and cultural museums have been housed in landmark buildings, placed respectfully in the heart of historic Singapore. As if that weren't enough, the homes, businesses, and places of worship erected by Singapore's early settlers still color the modern grid of city streets. There may be churches, temples, and mosques all over the island, but the urban center boasts the oldest and most spectacular ones. Add to this all the scenic parks and gardens, initiated by colonial agribusiness interests and preserved by the government's dedication to the natural habitat, and you have a remarkable thing: a distillation of hundreds of years of history and culture all beautifully arranged into a few square miles.

In this chapter I'll take you through Singapore's sights, from those in the major urban neighborhoods—the Historic District, Chinatown, Little India, Kampong Glam, and Orchard Road—to those outside the city, to the west, north, and east. There, you'll find large areas dedicated to nature reserves, a zoo and other wildlife attractions, theme parks, and sprawling temple complexes, all easily accessible by public transportation or a cab ride. As a kicker, I'll take you to Sentosa, a small island to the south that's packed from shore to shore with amusements, adventure theme parks, historic exhibits, nature displays, and outdoor activities for families.

A note: Many of the sights to see in Singapore are not of the "pay your fee and see the show" variety, but rather historic buildings, monuments, and places of religious worship. The city's historic

Urban Singapore Attractions

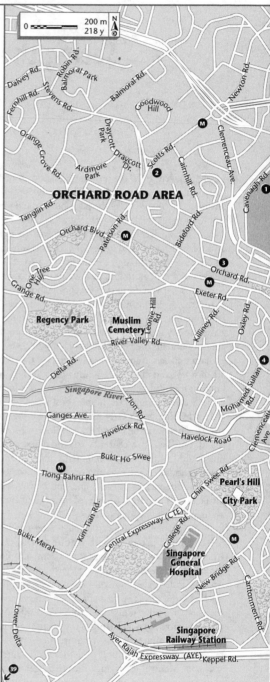

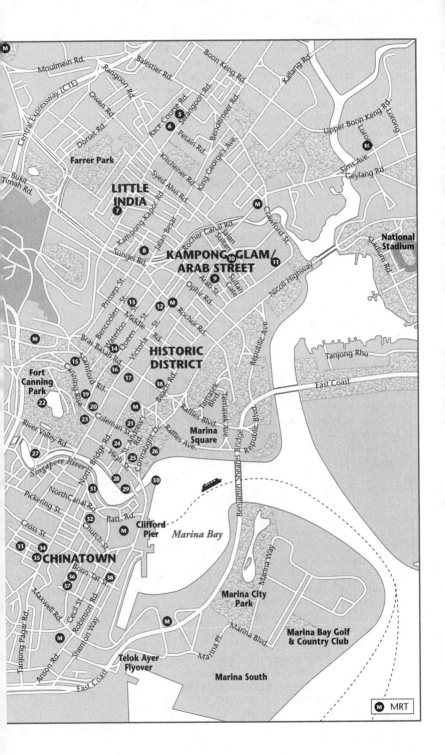

buildings, such as City Hall or Parliament House, must be appreciated from the outside, their significance lying in their unique architecture and historical context combined with the sensual effect of the surrounding city. Monuments and statues tell the stories of events and heroes important to Singapore both in the past and present. The places of worship listed in this chapter are open to the public and free of entrance charge. Expect temples to be open from sunup to sundown. Visiting hours are not specific to the hour, but unless it's a holiday (when hours may be extended), you can expect these places to be open during daylight hours.

1 The Historic District

Fort Canning Park. Major entrances are from the Hill Street Food Centre, Percival Rd. (Drama Centre), Fort Canning Aquarium, National Library Carpark, and Canning Walk (behind Park Mall). Free admission. Dhoby Gaut or City Hall MRT.

These days, Fort Canning Park is known for great views out over Singapore and for having the only remaining orange and coconut trees on the island, but in days past it served as the site of Raffles' home and later as a botanical garden. Its history may go back even further, though: Excavations over the years have unearthed ancient brick foundations that gave a certain credence to the island natives' belief that their royal ancestors lived and were buried on the site. After Raffles left the island for good, his house was occupied by the island's succeeding governors until around 1860, when it was torn down to make way for a fort. (The lookout kiosk stands on the former site.)

Fort Canning was built to quiet the fearful Europeans' demands for a defense against invasion. Instead, it quickly became the laughingstock of the island. The location was ideal for spotting invaders from the sea, but defending Singapore? Not likely. The cannons' range was such that their shells couldn't possibly have made it all the way out to an attacking ship—instead, most of the town below would have been destroyed.

The massive fort was demolished in 1907 and today the gate and the wall (Fort Gate and Fort Wall—catchy names) are the only reminders that it was ever here. The Fort Gate is a deep stone structure, and behind its huge wooden door is a narrow staircase that leads to the roof of the structure.

There is a *keramat,* or **sacred grave,** in the park. Because Fort Canning was the seat of power for each island ruler before Raffles' arrival, excavation sites have unearthed a few treasures and artifacts. This keramat is believed—with much debate—to be the final resting place of Iskander Shah (also known as Parameswara), an early ruler of Temasek (see chapter 1). Many still come to pray beside the grave.

Fort Canning was also the site of a **European cemetery.** To make improvements in the park, the graves were exhumed and the stones placed within the walls surrounding the outdoor performance field that slopes from the Music and Drama Society building. The large Gothic monument there was erected in memory of James Napier Brooke, infant son of William Napier, Singapore's first Law Agent, and his wife, Maria Frances, the widow of prolific architect George Coleman. Although no records exist, Coleman probably designed the cupolas as well as two small monuments over unknown graves. The Music and Drama Society building itself was built in 1938. Close by, in the wall, are the tombstones of Coleman and of Jose D'Almeida, a wealthy Portuguese merchant.

Beyond the performance field, outside the Gothic gate, is the ASEAN Sculpture Garden. Each sculpture was donated by a member of the Association of Southeast Asian Nations in 1982. It's a beautiful representation of regional unity.

Historic District Attractions

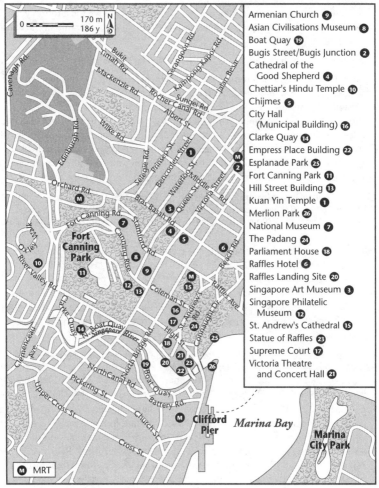

Armenian Church ⑨
Asian Civilisations Museum ⑧
Boat Quay ⑲
Bugis Street/Bugis Junction ②
Cathedral of the
    Good Shepherd ④
Chettiar's Hindu Temple ⑩
Chijmes ⑤
City Hall
    (Municipal Building) ⑯
Clarke Quay ⑭
Empress Place Building ㉒
Esplanade Park ㉕
Fort Canning Park ⑪
Hill Street Building ⑬
Kuan Yin Temple ①
Merlion Park ㉖
National Museum ⑦
The Padang ㉔
Parliament House ⑱
Raffles Hotel ⑥
Raffles Landing Site ⑳
Singapore Art Museum ③
Singapore Philatelic
    Museum ⑫
St. Andrew's Cathedral ⑮
Statue of Raffles ㉓
Supreme Court ⑰
Victoria Theatre
    and Concert Hall ㉑

Singapore Philatelic Museum. 23B Coleman St. ☎ **65/337-3888.** Admission S$2 (US$1.25). Tues–Sun 9am–4:30pm. Take the MRT to City Hall and walk toward Coleman St.

This building, constructed in 1895 to house the Methodist Book Room, recently underwent a S$7 million restoration and reopened as the Philatelic Museum in 1995. Exhibits include a fine collection of old stamps issued to commemorate historically important events, first day covers, antique printing plates, postal service memorabilia, and private collections. Visitors can trace the development of a stamp from idea to the finished sheet, and you can even design your own.

Hill Street Building. Hill St. at the corner of River Valley Rd., on Fort Canning Park.

Originally built to house the British Police Force, the building was sited directly across from Chinatown for easy access to quell the frequent gang fights. Later it became home to the National Archives and it is believed that inquisitions and torture were carried out in the basement during the Japanese Occupation. Former National Archive employees have claimed to have seen ghosts of tortured souls sitting at their desks.

Unfortunately, you are not allowed to wander inside to see the ghosties yourself. You'll have to satisfy yourself by appreciating the architectural beauty of the outside of the building.

✪ Armenian Church. 60 Hill St., across from the Grand Plaza Hotel.

No longer serving a much-diminished Armenian community, but lovingly maintained nevertheless, this chapel was the first permanent Christian church in Singapore. Designed by prolific architect George Coleman, most of its funding came from the thriving Armenian community. The church was consecrated in 1836 and underwent a few architectural changes in later years, and the last appointed priest serving the parish retired in 1936. Although regular Armenian services are no longer held, other religious organizations make use of the church from time to time. The cemetery in the back of the church is the burial site of many prominent Armenians.

✪ Asian Civilisations Museum. 39 Armenian St. ☎ **65/375-2510.** Adults S$3 (US$1.90), children 6–16 S$1.50 (US95¢), seniors (over 60) S$1 (US65¢); family ticket (max. 5 people) S$8 (US$5). Tues–Sun 9am–5:30pm. Free guided tours in English Tues–Fri 11am, Sat–Sun 11am and 2:30pm.

Just opened in 1997 and housed in the renovated Tao Nan School, this is the first branch of the Asian Civilisations Museum (the second is scheduled to open in 2000 in the Empress Place Building). Tao Nan (or ACM I) primarily focuses on the region's rich Chinese culture, displaying fine collections of jade, calligraphy, ceramics, furniture, and artworks, all offering visitors the chance to trace the archipelago's rich Chinese heritage. Changing exhibits in the temporary galleries represent the other Asian civilizations.

✪ National Museum. 93 Stamford Rd., across the street from Bras Basah Park. ☎ **65/375-2510.** www.museum.org.sg/nhb.html. Adults S$3 (US$1.90), children S$1.50 (US95¢), seniors (over 60) S$1 (US65¢); family ticket (max. 5 people) S$8 (US$5). Tues–Sun 9am–5:30pm. Free guided tours in English Tues–Fri 11am, Sat–Sun 11am and 2:30pm.

Originally called Raffles Museum, Henry McCallum's fine example of neo-Palladian architecture was opened in 1887 as the first of its kind in Southeast Asia, housing a superb collection of natural history specimens and ethnographic displays. In both 1907 and 1916, the museum outgrew its space and was enlarged. Renamed the National Museum in 1969, its collections went through a transformation, focusing on Singaporean history rather than that of the archipelago. Several years later, it became known as the Singapore History Museum. Twenty dioramas portray events from the settlement's early days to modern times. Included are tributes to Raffles, William Farquhar, and Rumah Baba, and a "typical turn-of-the-century Peranakan home" is open to visitors and allows you to envision how life was way back when.

Kuan Yin Temple. Waterloo St., about 1¹/₂ blocks from Bras Basah Rd. Open to the public during the day.

It's said that whatever you wish for within the walls of Kuan Yin Temple comes true, so get in line and have your wishes ready. It must work, as there's a steady stream of people on auspicious days of the Chinese calendar. The procedure is simple: Wear shoes easily slipped off before entering the temple. Light several joss sticks. Pray to the local god, pray to the sky god, then turn to the side and pray some more. Now pick up the container filled with inscriptions and shake it until one stick falls out. After that, head for the interpretation box office to get a piece of paper with verses in Mandarin and English to look up what your particular inscription means. (For a small fee, there are interpreters outside.) Now for the payback: If your wish comes true, be prepared to return to the temple and offer fruits and flowers to say thanks (oranges, pears, and apples are a thoughtful choice and jasmine petals are especially nice). Be careful what you wish for. Once you're back home and that job promotion comes through, your new manager will nix another vacation so soon. To be on the safe side, bring the goods with you when you make your wish.

✪ **Singapore Art Museum.** 71 Bras Basah Rd. ☎ **65/375-2510.** www.museum.org.sg/nhb.html. Adults S$3 (US$1.90), children S$1.50 (US95¢), seniors (over 60) S$1 (US65¢); family ticket (max. 5 people) S$8 (US$5). Tues–Sun 9am–5:30pm. Free guided tours in English Tues–Fri 11am, Sat–Sun 11am and 2:30pm.

The Singapore Art Museum (SAM) was officially opened in 1996 and houses an impressive collection of over 3,000 pieces of art and sculpture, most of it by Singaporean and Malay artists, which are regularly rotated to make up special exhibits. A large collection of regional pieces is also on display, and international exhibits are showcased regularly. Besides the main exhibit halls, the museum has a gift shop, cafe, conservation laboratory, an auditorium, and the E-mage Gallery, where multimedia presentations include not only the museum's own acquisitions, but other works from public and private collections in the region as well. Once a Catholic boys' school established in 1852, SAM has retained some visible reminders of its former occupants: Above the front door of the main building you can still see inscribed "St. Joseph's Institution," and a bronze-toned, cast-iron statue of St. John Baptist de la Salle with two children is standing in its original place.

Cathedral of the Good Shepherd. 4 Queen St., at the corner of Queen St. and Bras Basah Rd. Open to the public during the day.

This cathedral was Singapore's first permanent Catholic church. Built in the 1840s, it brought together many elements of a fractured parish. In the early days of the colony, the Portuguese Mission thought itself the fount of the Holy Roman Empire's presence on the island, and so the French Bishop was reduced to holding services at the home of a Mr. McSwiney on Bras Basah Road; a dissenting Portuguese priest held forth at a certain Dr. d'Ameida's residence; and the Spanish priest was so reduced that we don't even know where he held his services. These folks were none too pleased with their makeshift houses of worship and so banded together to establish their own cathedral—the Cathedral of the Good Shepherd. Designed in a Latin cross pattern, much of its architecture is reminiscent of St. Martin-In-The-Fields and St. Paul's in Convent Garden. The Archbishop's residence, in contrast, is a simple two-story bungalow with enclosed verandahs and a portico. Also on the grounds are the Resident's Quarters and the Priests' Residence, the latter more ornate in design, with elaborate plasterwork.

✪ **Chijmes (Convent of the Holy Infant Jesus).** 30 Victoria St.

Entering this bustling enclave of retail shops, restaurants, and offices, it's difficult to imagine this was once a convent which, at its founding in 1854, consisted of a lone, simply constructed bungalow. By late 1983, when the convent relocated to the suburbs, its many buildings of classrooms, living quarters, a chapel, and a rather large orphanage sprawled over the entire city block. The Singapore government, in planning the renovation of this desirable piece of real estate, wisely kept the integrity of the architecture, which is unique to the tropical climate. Be sure to visit the chapel (now a performance center) and imagine yourself cloistered in one of the most notable convents in Southeast Asia.

A note on the name: Chijmes is pronounced "Chimes"; the "Chij," as noted, stands for Convent of the Holy Infant Jesus, and the "mes" was just added on so they could pronounce it "Chimes."

✪ **Raffles Hotel.** 1 Beach Rd. ☎ **65/337-1886.**

Built in 1887 to accommodate the increasing upper-class trade, Raffles Hotel was originally only a couple of bungalows with 10 rooms, but, oh, the view of the sea was perfection. The owners, Armenian brothers named Sarkies, already had a couple of prosperous hotels in Penang and were well versed in the business, and it wasn't long before they added a pair of wings and completed the main building . . . and reading rooms, verandahs, dining rooms, and a grand lobby . . . and the Bar and Billiard Room . . . and a ballroom and a string of shops. By 1899, electricity was turning the cooling fans and providing the pleasing glow of comfort.

As it made its madcap dash through the twenties, the hotel was the place to see and be seen. Vacancies were unheard of. Hungry Singaporeans and guests from other hotels, eager for a glimpse of the fabulous dining room, were turned away for lack of reservations. The crowded ballroom was jumping every night of the week. It was during this time that Raffles' guest book included famous authors like Somerset Maugham and Noël Coward. These were indeed the glory years. But the lovely glimmer from the chandeliers soon faded with the stark arrival of the Great Depression. Raffles managed to limp through that dark time—and, darker still, through the Occupation—and later pull back from the brink of bankruptcy to undergo modernization in the fifties. But fresher, brighter, more opulent hotels were taking root on Orchard Road, pushing the "grand old lady" to the back seat.

The hotel was in limbo for a period of time due to legal matters, and in 1961 it passed through several financial institutions to land on the doorstep of the Development Bank of Singapore. It was probably this journey that saved the Raffles from a renovation nightmare. Instead, history-minded renovators selected 1915 as a benchmark and, with a few changes here and there, faithfully restored the hotel to that era's magnificence and splendor. Today, the hotel's restaurants and nightlife draw thousands of visitors daily to its open lobby, its theater playhouse, the Raffles Hotel Museum, and 65 exclusive boutiques. Its 15 restaurants and bars—especially the Tiffin Room, Raffles Grill, and Doc Cheng's (all reviewed in chapter 5)—are a wonder, as is its famous Bar and Billiards Room and Long Bar.

Bugis Street / Bugis Junction. Bugis MRT stop, across from Parco Bugis Junction shopping mall.

If you happened to visit Singapore in the seventies, and remember Bugis as a haven for transvestites and sex shows, you're in for a big surprise. Bugis Street ain't what it used to be. In place of the decadence is a giant shopping mall, Parco Bugis Junction. A little of the past still lingers at the **Boom Boom Room** (#02-04 New Bugis; ☎ 65/339-8187), where nightly shows feature the most beautiful transvestites belting out hits by Barbra Streisand and Judy Garland. (See chapter 9 for a full write-up.) There's also a night market with a few bargains on cheap chic, curio items, accessories, and compact discs.

The area around Bugis Street has a more benign history. The Bugis, fierce and respected warriors, were some of the first people to settle on Singapore in its early years. Raffles took note of their boatbuilding skills and, as part of his master town plan, included Bugis Town to attract more of them to the island.

✪ **St. Andrew's Cathedral.** Coleman St., between North Bridge Rd. and St. Andrew's Rd., across from the Padang. Open during daylight hours.

Designed by George Coleman, erected on a site selected by Sir Stamford Raffles himself, and named for the patron saint of Scotland, St. Andrew, and—guess what?—primarily funded by Singapore's Scottish community, the first St. Andrew's was the

Colonial Architecture 101

Three major players were influential in defining Singapore's early style. **George Drumgold Coleman,** an Irish architect who spent some time in Calcutta and later Java building private homes for wealthy merchants, visited Singapore (where he met Stamford Raffles), and returned to stay in 1826. By 1833, he'd been appointed Superintendent of Public Works. A prolific builder, his designs set the fashion for Singapore's architecture of the day. Only three of his buildings remain today, but they're all exceptional: **Parliament House** (Maxwell House, which unfortunately has been renovated beyond recognition), the **Armenian Church,** and the **Caldwell House** in Chijmes. Coleman also built many merchants' homes, offices, shops, and go-downs (shed-type warehouses), chiefly in a neo-Palladian style. Because the Singaporean climate was like that of the Mediterranean, he utilized many of that region's architectural elements, such as verandahs and porticos for shade, courtyard gardens for cool tranquillity, large windows and doors for air circulation, and tall ceilings to capture and hold the rising warm air. Local materials figured into his constructions, mostly timber from up-country jungles, locally quarried granite, and Chinese and Malacca bricks.

During this colonial period, Singapore served as the dumping ground for India's penal system, and prisoners were continually brought here to work in the quarries and brick foundries, and in the jungles, felling timber. Coleman had the idea to use these convicts for construction, and they played an important role in helping to shape Singapore's style, as many brought with them a superb knowledge of southern Indian plasterwork and construction skills.

Major J. F. A. McNair, a colonial engineer, continued Coleman's neo-Palladian style in his works, including the **Istana** and **Sri Temasek.** Following the English residence styles of India, he designed many fine country homes for the British expatriates, incorporating elements of the Italian Renaissance, a lifelong fascination.

Trained in London, **Regent Alfred John Bidwell** came to the Straits Settlements around 1895. Not long after his arrival in Singapore, he joined the prestigious architecture firm Swan and Maclaren. Bidwell had a thorough knowledge of what was fashionable for the times; for example, the Queen Anne style for his **Goodwood Hotel Tower Wing** also incorporated European influences then in vogue in Britain and on the continent. Bidwell was also responsible for designing the Main Building and the Bras Basah wings of the **Raffles Hotel,** keeping the integrity of the original edifice intact. Bidwell's renovations to the **Victoria Theatre and Concert Hall** remained true to the original design, built 50 years earlier in Victorian Revival style.

colonials' Anglican Church. Completed toward the end of the 1830s, its tower and spire were added several years later to accord the edifice more stature. By 1852, because of massive damage sustained from lightning strikes, the cathedral was deemed unsafe and was torn down. The cathedral that now stands on this site was completed in 1860. Of English Gothic Revival design, the cathedral is one of the few standing churches of this style in the region. The spire resembles the steeple of the Salisbury Cathedral—another tribute from the colonials to Mother England. Not only English residents but Christian Chinese, Indians, continental Europeans, and Malays consider this to be their center of worship.

The plasterwork of St. Andrew's inside walls utilized a material called *Madras chunam,* which, though peculiar, was a common building material here in the 1880s. Get this: A combination of shell lime (without the sand) was mixed with egg whites and coarse sugar or jaggery until it took on the consistency of a stiff paste. The mixture was thinned to a workable consistency with water in which coconut husks had steeped, applied to the surface, allowed to dry, and then polished with rock crystal or smooth stones to a most lustrous patina. Who would've thought?

The original church bell was presented to the cathedral by Maria Revere Belestier, the daughter of famed American patriot Paul Revere. The bell now stands in the Singapore History Museum.

City Hall (Municipal Building). St. Andrew's Rd., across from the Padang. Entrance to the visitor's gallery is permitted, but all other areas are off limits.

During the Japanese Occupation, City Hall was a major headquarters, and it was here in 1945 that Admiral Lord Louis Mountbatten accepted the Japanese surrender. In 1951, the Royal Proclamation from King George VI was read here declaring that Singapore would henceforth be known as a city. Fourteen years later, Prime Minister Lee Kuan Yew announced to its citizens that Singapore would henceforth be called an independent republic.

City Hall, along with the Supreme Court, was judiciously sited to take full advantage of the prime location. Magnificent Corinthian columns march across the front of the symmetrically designed building, while inside, two courtyards lend an ambiance of informality to otherwise officious surroundings. For all its magnificence and historical fame, however, the architect, F. D. Meadows, relied too heavily on European influence. The many windows afford no protection from the sun, and the entrance leaves pedestrians unsheltered from the elements. In defining the very nobility of the Singapore government, it appears the Singaporean climate wasn't taken into consideration.

Supreme Court. St. Andrew's Rd., across from the Padang. Closed to visitors, but worth seeing from the outside.

The Supreme Court stands on the site of the old Hotel de L'Europe, a rival of the Raffles Hotel until it went bankrupt in the 1930s. The court's structure, a classical style favored for official buildings the world over, was completed in 1939. With its spare adornment and architectural simplicity, the edifice has a no-nonsense, utilitarian attitude, and the sculptures across the front, executed by the Italian sculptor Cavaliere Rodolpho Nolli, echo what transpires within: Justice is the most breathtaking, standing 2.7 meters (9 ft.) high and weighing almost 4 tons. Kneeling on either side of her are representations of Supplication and Thankfulness. To the far left are Deceit and Violence. To the far right are a bull representing Prosperity and two children holding wheat, to depict Abundance.

Two and a half million bricks were used in building this structure, but take a moment to note the stonework: It's fake! Really a gypsum-type of plaster, it was applied by Chinese plasterers who'd fled from Shanghai during the Sino-Japanese conflict, and molded to give the appearance of granite.

While taking in the exterior, look up at the dome, which is a copy of the dome of St. Paul's Cathedral in London. The dome covers the courtyard, which is surrounded by the four major portions of the Supreme Court building.

The Padang. St. Andrew's Rd. and Connaught Dr.

This large field—officially called Padang Besar but known as the Padang—has witnessed its share of historical events. Bordered on one end by the Singapore

Recreation Club and on the other end by the Singapore Cricket Club, and flanked by City Hall, the area was once known as Raffles Plain. Upon Raffles' return to the island in 1822, he was angry that Farquhar had allowed merchants to move into the area he had originally intended for government buildings. All building permits were rescinded and a new site for the commercial district was planned for the area across the Singapore River. The Padang became the official center point for the government quarters, around which the Esplanade and City Hall were built. On weekends the Padang hosts cricket and rugby matches when they're in season (see chapter 10).

Today the Padang is mainly used for public and sporting events—pleasant activities—but in the 1940s it felt more forlorn footsteps when the invading Japanese forced the entire European community onto the field. There they waited while the occupation officers dickered over a suitable location for the "conquered." Presently, they ordered all British, Australian, and Allied troops as well as European prisoners on the 22 kilometer march to Changi.

Parliament House. 1 High St., at the south end of the Padang, next to the Supreme Court. Closed to the general public, but worth seeing from the outside.

Parliament House, built in 1826, is probably Singapore's oldest surviving structure, even though it has been renovated so many times it no longer looks the way it was originally constructed. It was designed as a home for John Argyle Maxwell, a Scottish merchant, but before it was completed, the government rented it to house the court and other government offices. In 1939, when the new Supreme Court was completed, the judiciary moved in; then, in 1953, following a major renovation, Maxwell's House was renamed Parliament House, and was turned over to the Legislature.

The original house was designed by architect George D. Coleman, who had helped Raffles with his Town Plan of 1822. Coleman's design was in the English neo-Palladian style. Simple and well suited to the tropics, this style was popular at the time with Calcutta merchants. Major alterations have left very little behind of Coleman's design, however, replacing it with an eclectic French classical style, but some of his work survives. Today, the building is being transformed once again, into part of a larger S$80 million Parliament Complex.

The bronze elephant in front of Parliament House was a gift to Singapore in 1872 from His Majesty Somdeth Phra Paraminda Maha Chulalongkorn (Rama V), Supreme King of Siam, as a token of gratitude following his stay in the previous year.

Victoria Theatre and Concert Hall. 9 Empress Place, at the southern end of the Padang. ☎ 65/339-6120.

Designed by colonial engineer John Bennett in a Victorian Revival style that was fashionable in Britain at the time, the theater portion was built in 1862 as the Town Hall. Victoria Memorial Hall was built in 1905 as a memorial to Queen Victoria, retaining the same style of the old building. The clock tower was added a year later. In 1909, with its name changed to Victoria Theatre, the hall opened with an amateur production of the *Pirates of Penzance*. Another notable performance occurred when Noël Coward passed through Singapore and stepped in at the last moment to help out a traveling English theatrical company who had lost a leading man. The building looks much the same as it did then, though of course the interiors have been modernized. It was completely renovated in 1979, conserving all the original details, and was renamed Victoria Concert Hall. It has since housed the Singapore Symphony Orchestra and various performance companies. (See chapter 9 for details.)

Statue of Raffles. Victoria Theatre and Concert Hall.

This sculpture of Sir Stamford Raffles was erected on the Padang in 1887 and moved to its present position after getting in the way of one too many cricket matches. During the Japanese Occupation, the statue was placed in the Singapore History Museum (then the Raffles Museum), and was replaced here in 1945. The local joke is that Raffles' arm is outstretched to the Bank of China building, and his pockets are empty. (In terms of wealth in Singapore, it's Chinese one; Brits nil.)

Empress Place Building. 1 Empress Place, at the southern end of the Padang next to the Parliament Building.

Standing as a symbol of British colonial authority as travelers entered the Singapore River, Empress Place Building housed almost the entire government bureaucracy around the year 1905, and was a government office until the 1980s, housing the Registry of Births and Deaths and the Citizenship Registry. Every Singaporean at some point passed through its doors. In the late eighties, the government offices moved out and the building was restored as an historical cultural exhibition venue.

The oldest portion is the part nearest Parliament House; it was designed by colonial engineer J. F. A. McNair and built by convict labor between June 1864 and December 1867. Four major additions and other renovations have been faithful to his original design. Inside, there are many surviving details, including plaster moldings, cornices, and architraves. It is currently being renovated as the second phase of the Asian Civilisations Museum.

Raffles Landing Site. North Boat Quay.

This polymarble statue was unveiled in 1972. It was made from plaster casts of the original 1887 figure located in front of the Victoria Theatre and Concert Hall (see above), and stands on what is believed to be the site where Sir Stamford Raffles landed on January 29, 1819.

ALONG THE RIVER

The Singapore River had always been the heart of life in Singapore even before Raffles landed, but for many years during this century life here was dead—quite literally. The rapid urban development that began in the 1950s turned the river into a giant sewer, killing all plant and animal life in it. In the mid-eighties, though, the government began a large and extremely successful cleanup project, and shortly thereafter, the buildings at Boat Quay and Clarke Quay were restored. Now the areas on both banks of the river offer entertainment, food, and pubs day and night. Future plans are in order to continue upriver with similar restoration projects, with the next big effort being made for Robinson Quay, just upriver from Clarke Quay. Plans call for it to host a nest of shops and restaurants focusing on the products, cuisine, and festivals of Spain, Greece, Turkey, and the south of France.

Boat Quay. Located on the south bank of the Singapore River between Cavenagh Bridge and Elgin Bridge.

Known as "the belly of the carp" by the local Chinese because of its shape, this area was once notorious for its opium dens and coolie shops. Nowadays, thriving restaurants boast every cuisine imaginable and the rocking nightlife offers up a variety of sounds—jazz, rock, blues, Indian, and Caribe—that are lively enough to get any couch potato tapping his feet. See chapters 5 and 9 for dining and nightlife suggestions, and remember to pronounce quay "key" if you don't want people to look at you funny.

Clarke Quay. River Valley Rd. west of Coleman Bridge.

The largest of the waterfront developments, Clarke Quay was originally named for the second governor of Singapore, Sir Andrew Clarke. In the 1880s, a pineapple cannery, iron foundry, and numerous warehouses made this area bustle. Today, with 60 restored warehouses and restaurants and a shopping section known as Clarke Quay Factory Stores, the Quay still hops. **River House,** formerly the home of a *towkay* (company president), is the oldest building. The **Bar Gelateria Bellavista** ice cream parlor (River Valley Road at Coleman Bridge) was once the ice house. The **Clarke Quay Adventure Ride** (☎ **65/337-1680**) on the Singapore River provides an historical panorama of Singapore and its people. (Tickets are S$5/US$3.15 adults, S$3/US$1.90 children and seniors; open daily from 11am to 10:30pm.) On Thursdays and Fridays from 6:30 to 8:30pm, enthusiasts can catch a Chinese opera performance and makeup demonstration that is a treat to watch. Get up early on Sunday, forgo the comics section and take in the flea market, which opens at 9am and lasts all day. Lots of bargains.

Merlion Park. South bank, at the mouth of the Singapore River, near the Anderson Bridge. Free admission. Daily 7am–10pm.

The Merlion is Singapore's half-lion, half-fish national symbol. The lion represents Singapore's roots as the "Lion City," while the fish represents Singapore's close ties to the sea. Bet you think a magical and awe-inspiring beast like this has been around in tales for hundreds of years, right? No such luck. Rather, he was the creation of some scheming mind at the Singapore Tourism Board in the early seventies. Talk about the collision of ancient culture and the modern world. Despite the Merlion's commercial beginnings, he's been adopted as the national symbol and spouts continuously every day at the mouth of the Singapore River from 10am to noon. Aside from the beastie himself, there's nothing to do in the park, and in fact, the best Merlion viewing can actually be done from Esplanade Park (see below).

Esplanade Park. Connaught Dr., on the marina, running from the mouth of the Singapore River along the Padang to Raffles Ave. Daily until midnight.

Esplanade Park and Queen Elizabeth Walk, two of the most famous parks in Singapore, were established in 1943 on land reclaimed from the sea. Several memorials are located here. The first is a fountain built in 1857 to honor **Tan Kim Seng,** who gave a great sum of money toward the building of a waterworks. Another monument, **the Cenotaph,** commemorates the 124 Singaporeans who died in World War I and was dedicated by the Prince of Wales. On the reverse side, the names of those who died in World War II have been inscribed. The third prominent memorial is dedicated to **Major General Lim Bo Seng,** a member of the Singaporean underground resistance in World War II who was captured and killed by the Japanese. His memorial was unveiled in 1954 on the tenth anniversary of his death.

Chettiar's Hindu Temple. 15 Tank Rd., close to the intersection of Clemenceau Ave. and River Valley Rd.

One of the richest and grandest of its kind in Southeast Asia, Chettiar's Hindu Temple is most famous for a **thoonganai maadam,** a statue of an elephant's backside in a seated position. It's said that there are only four others of the kind, located in four temples in India.

The original temple was completed in 1860, restored in 1962, and practically rebuilt in 1984. The many sculptures of Hindu deities and the carved Kamalam-patterned rosewood doors and arches and columns were executed by architect-sculptors imported from Madras, India, specifically for the job. The Hindu child god,

Lord Muruga, rules over the temple and is visible in one form or another wherever you look. Also notice the statues of the god Shiva and his wife, Kali, captured in their lively dance competition. The story goes that Kali was winning the competition, so Shiva lifted his leg above his head, something a woman wasn't thought capable of doing. He won and quit dancing—good thing, too, since every time Shiva did a little jig he destroyed part of the world.

Outside in the courtyard are statues of the wedding of Lord Muruga; his brother, Ganesh; another brother, Vishnu; and their father, Shiva; along with Brahma, the creator of all.

Used daily for worship, the temple is also the culmination point of Thaipusam, a celebration of thanks, and the Festival of Navarathiri (see chapter 2).

2 Chinatown / Tanjong Pagar

Wak Hai Cheng Bio Temple. 30–B Phillip St., at the corner of Phillip St. and Church St.

Like most of Singapore's Chinese temples, Wak Hai Cheng Bio had its start as a simple wood-and-thatch shrine where sailors, when they got off their ships, would go to express their gratitude for sailing safely to their destination. Before the major land reclamation projects shifted the shoreline outward, the temple was close to the water's edge, and so it was named "Temple of the Calm Sea Built by the Guangzhou People." It's a Teochew temple, located in a part of Chinatown populated mostly by the Teochews.

Inside the walls are two temple blocks, one for the Heavenly Emperor, the other for the Mother of Heavenly Sages. Look for the statue of the Gambler Brother, with coins around his neck. The Chinese pray to him for wealth and luck, and in olden days would put opium on his lips. This custom is still practiced today, only now they use a black herbal paste called *koyo*, which is conveniently legal.

Another unique feature inside the temple are the three-dimensional reliefs that depict scenes from Chinese operas.

Nagore Durgha Shrine. 140 Telok Ayer St., at the corner of Telok Ayer St. and Boon Tat St. ☎ 65/324-0021.

Although this is a Muslim place of worship, it is not a mosque, but a shrine, built to commemorate a visit to the island by a Muslim holy man of the Chulia people (a very early immigrant group from India), who was traveling around Southeast Asia spreading the word of Indian Islam. The most interesting visual feature is its facade: Two arched windows flank an arched doorway, with columns in between. Above these is a "miniature palace"—a massive replica of the facade of a palace, with tiny cutout windows and a small arched doorway in the middle. The cutouts in white plaster make it look like lace. From the corners of the facade, two 14-level minarets rise, with three little domed cutouts on each level and capped with onion domes. Inside, the prayer halls and two shrines are painted and decorated in shockingly tacky colors.

There is controversy surrounding the dates that the shrine was built. The government, upon naming the Nagore Durgha a national monument, claimed it was built sometime in the 1820s; however, Nagoreallauddeen, who is the 15th descendant of the holy man for whom the shrine is named, claims it was built many years before. According to Nagoreallauddeen, the shrine was first built out of wood and attap, and was later rebuilt from limestone in 1815, 4 years before the arrival of Sir Stamford Raffles. In 1818, rebuilding materials were imported from India to construct the present shrine. The government has no historical records to prove the previous existence of the shrine at that time. Nagoreallauddeen, who sits daily in the office just

Chinatown Attractions

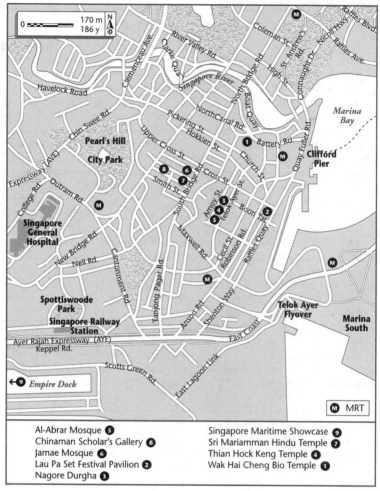

Al-Abrar Mosque **5**	Singapore Maritime Showcase **9**
Chinaman Scholar's Gallery **8**	Sri Mariamman Hindu Temple **7**
Jamae Mosque **6**	Thian Hock Keng Temple **4**
Lau Pa Set Festival Pavilion **2**	Wak Hai Cheng Bio Temple **1**
Nagore Durgha **3**	

to the right in the entrance hall, is fighting to have his date made official, and has covered the government plaque to the left of the front door, which declares the shrine a national monument. He'll tell you the whole story of the building and of his lineage if you ask, but he doesn't speak English, so grab a translator if you can.

✪ **Thian Hock Keng Temple.** 158 Telok Ayer St., ¹/₂ block beyond Nagore Durgha Shrine.

Thian Hock Keng, the "Temple of Heavenly Bliss," is the oldest Chinese temple in Singapore. Before land reclamation, when the shoreline came right up to Telok Ayer Road, the first Chinese sailors landed here and immediately built a shrine, a small wood-and-thatch structure, to pray to the goddess Ma Po Cho for allowing their voyage to be safely completed. For each subsequent boatload of Chinese sailors, the shrine was always the first stop upon landing. Ma Po Cho, the Mother of the Heavenly Sages, was the patron goddess of sailors, and every Chinese junk of the day had an altar dedicated to her.

The temple that stands today was built in 1841 over the shrine with funds from the Hokkien community, led by the efforts of two Malacca-born philanthropists, Tan

The Shophouses of Singapore

The shophouses that line many of Singapore's streets are perhaps the architectural feature travelers find most memorable about this city. These row houses were southern Asia's answer to urban commercial and residential buildings through the early 1800s and into the first half of the 20th century. Their design was perfect. Ground floors were occupied by shops or coffeehouses, while the upper floors were homes—an ideal situation for mom-and-pop operations. The rows of uniform buildings fit perfectly within the grid of the city streets, while inside air shafts and vents let air and sunlight circulate throughout. Out front, many of the shophouses featured ornately decorated facades, while the "five-foot-ways" (covered sidewalks) formed by the shophouses' projecting second stories shielded pedestrians from sun and rain.

Most of the shophouses were built between 1840 and 1960, and differ slightly depending on their year of construction. The earliest houses were built between 1840 and 1860. The style of architecture, imaginatively called the **Early Shophouse Style,** is easy to detect. These houses are low and squat, rising never more than two stories each. On the second floor, the one or two rectangular windows are plain, as are the facades. Sometimes the beam moldings give them a heavy appearance that's clumsy looking compared to the more delicate styles of the later shophouses. What minimal ornamentation exists sometimes reflects the ethnic background of the families who lived inside. Two good examples of this style are at 72 Arab St. and 68 Bussorah St., out in Kampong Glam.

As time went by, the high ceilings of the newer shophouses meant that the houses themselves gained in height. Windows started to show simple arches, and were adorned with timber shutters, sometimes with glass panels. Simple vents started to appear that were part functional and part decorative. This style, called the **First Transitional Shophouse Style,** can be seen at 118 Serangoon Rd. or 23 Kerbau Rd. in Little India.

Tock Seng and Tan Kim Seng. All of the building materials were imported from China, except for the gates, which came from Glasgow, Scotland, and the tiles on the facade, which are from Holland. The doorway is flanked by two lions, a male with a ball to symbolize strength, and a female with a cup to symbolize fertility. On the door are door gods, mythical beasts made from the combined body parts of many animals. Note the wooden bar that sits at the foot of the temple entrance (as do similar bars in so many Chinese temples). This serves a couple of purposes: First, it keeps out wandering ghosts, who cannot cross over the barrier. Second, it forces anyone entering the temple to look down as they cross, bowing their head in humility. Just inside the door are granite tablets that record the temple's history.

Ahead at the main altar is Ma Po Cho, and on either side are statues of the Protector of Life and the God of War. To the side of the main hall is a Gambler Brother statue, prayed to for luck and riches. From here you can see the temple's construction of brackets and beams, fitting snugly together and carved with war heroes, saints, flowers, and animals, all in red and black lacquer and gilded in gold. Behind the main hall is an altar to Kuan Yin, the Goddess of Mercy. On either side of her are the sun and moon gods.

To the left of the courtyard are the ancestral tablets. In keeping with Confucian filial piety, each represents a soul. Those with red paper are for souls still alive. Also in the temple complex is a pagoda and a number of outer buildings that at one time housed a school and community associations.

The transitional shophouse led into what is called the **Late Shophouse Style.** These houses were built between 1900 and 1940, and are the most ornamental of all of the shophouse styles. Second stories had three windows, sometimes separated by ornamental columns. They were decorated in bright colors with features borrowed from many different cultures. Chinese panel frescoes, wooden Malay fringes around the eaves, colorful ceramic tile work (many tiles were imported from Holland), and floral plasterwork make these shophouses stand out from the rest. Good examples of this style are found at 121 Serangoon Rd. in Little India and at 101 Jalan Sultan in Kampong Glam.

When the **Second Transitional Shophouse Style** came along late in the period of the Late Shophouse Style, designers began to pull away from the flamboyant decor of previous structures and concentrated on a more streamlined design. Elements of art deco began to creep in as ceramic tile designs combined with geometric window panels and balustrades. By the 1930s, the **Art Deco Shophouse Style** was in full swing, with classical streamlining of columns. No decorative tiles can be found on the facades, but the houses were made striking by their uniformity from house to house down an entire block. Usually this style of shophouse has a prominently displayed plaque with its date of construction. You can see this style at 148 and 150 Neil Rd. in Chinatown, and at 79 Serangoon Rd. in Little India.

One feature that was common to the houses, but is seen very rarely these days, is the **pintu pagar,** a type of front door that consisted of a pair of half doors, often intricately carved and painted, which had larger timber doors behind them. The pintu pagar design allowed the large doors to remain open during the day, letting in light and breezes yet ensuring a little privacy for the people inside. Along the same lines are the first-story windows, many of which have no glass, but just bars to keep out robbers and let air circulate.

Al-Abrar Mosque. 192 Telok Ayer St., near the corner of Telok Ayer St. and Amoy St., near Thian Hock Keng Temple.

This mosque was originally erected as a thatched building in 1827 and was also called Masjid Chulia and Kuchu Palli, which in Tamil means "hut mosque." In the 1850s the building that stands today was built. Even though the building faces Mecca, the complex conforms with the grid of city streets of the neighborhood. In the late 1980s, the mosque underwent major renovations which enlarged the mihrab and stripped away some of the ornamental qualities of the columns in the building. The one-story prayer hall was extended upward into a two-story gallery. Little touches like the timber window panels and fanlight windows have been carried over into the new renovations.

Lau Pa Set Festival Pavilion. 18 Raffles Quay, located in the entire block flanked by Robinson Rd., Cross St., Shenton Way, and Boon Tat St.

Though it used to be well beloved, the locals think this place has become an atrocity. Once the happy little hawker center known as Telok Ayer Market, it began life as a wet market. Now it's part hawker center, part western fast-food outlets, and all tourist.

It all began on Market Street in 1823, in a structure that was later torn down, redesigned, and rebuilt by G. D. Coleman. Close to the water, seafood could be unloaded fresh off the pier. After the land was reclaimed in Telok Ayer Basin in 1879, the market was moved to its present home, a James MacRitchie design that kept the original octagonal shape and was constructed of 3,000 prefab cast-iron elements brought in from Europe.

In the 1970s, as the financial district began to develop, the pavilion was dominated by hawkers who fed the lunchtime business crowd. In the mid-eighties, the structure was torn down to make way for the MRT construction and then meticulously put back together, puzzle piece by puzzle piece. By 1989, the market was once again an urban landmark, but it sat vacant until Scotts Holdings successfully tendered to convert it into a festival market. At this time, numerous changes were made to the building, which was renamed Lau Pa Sat ("Old Market") in acknowledgment of the name by which the market had been known by generations of Singaporeans.

Chinaman Scholar's Gallery. 14B Trengganu St. ☎ **65/222-9554.** Adults S$6 (US$3.80), children S$4 (US$2.50). Daily 9am–4pm.

The gallery's founder, Mr. Vincent Tan, opened this place in response to inquiries from Western friends who were curious about how the Chinese lived at home, behind closed doors. Located in a small space on the third story of an old shophouse, his gallery is filled with old items like clothing, kitchenware, photographs, and traditional musical instruments, many of which belonged to Mr. Tans' family. As you walk through, you can ask about any of the items, and Mr. Tan will bring to life their history and use. He can even play the musical instruments.

Before you stop by, be sure to telephone in advance. Mr. Tan is sometimes called away and has no assistant to keep the place open when he's gone.

✪ Sri Mariamman Hindu Temple. 244 South Bridge Rd., at the corner of South Bridge Rd. and Pagoda St.

As the oldest Hindu temple in Singapore, Sri Mariamman has been the central point of Hindu tradition and culture. In its early years, the temple housed new immigrants while they established themselves and also served as social center for the community. Today, the main celebration here is the Thimithi Festival in October or November. (See chapter 2.)

The shrine is dedicated to the goddess Sri Mariamman, who is known for curing disease, but as is the case at all other Hindu temples, the entire pantheon of Hindu gods are present to be worshipped as well. On either side of the gopuram are statues of Shiva and Vishnu, while inside are two smaller shrines to Vinayagar and Sri Ararvan.

The temple originated as a small wood-and-thatch shrine founded by Naraina Pillai, an Indian merchant who came to Singapore with Raffles' first expedition and found his fortune in trade. In the main hall of the temple is the small god that Pillai originally placed here.

✪ Jamae Mosque. 18 South Bridge Rd., at the corner of South Bridge Rd. and Mosque St.

Jamae Mosque was built by the Chulias, Tamil Muslims who were some of the earlier immigrants to Singapore, and who had a very influential hold over Indian Muslim life centered in the Chinatown area. It was the Chulias who built not only this mosque, but Masjid Al-Abrar and the Nagore Durgha Shrine as well. Jamae Mosque dates back to 1827, but wasn't completed until the early 1830s. The mosque stands today almost exactly as it did then.

While the front gate is typical of mosques you'd see in southern India, inside most of the buildings reflect the neo-classical style of architecture introduced in administrative buildings and homes designed by George Coleman and favored by the Europeans. A small shrine inside, which may be the oldest part of the mosque, was erected to memorialize a local religious leader, Muhammad Salih Valinva.

Singapore Maritime Showcase. World Trade Centre, #01-131 Harbour Promenade. ☎ **65/ 321-1053.** Adults S$4 (US$2.50), children S$2 (US$1.25). Tues–Fri 10:30am–6:30pm, Sat–Sun and public holidays 10:30am–8:30pm. SBS nos. 10, 30, 61, 84, 93, 97, 100, 131, 143, 145, 166, or TIBS no. 855. Singapore Trolley.

The central attraction here is the Maritime Odyssey ride, which retraces the growth of Singapore's port from the days of early traders through to the present and then projects well into the future (which, according to the Showcase, holds Barbie and Ken dolls living underwater in weird cubes). Spaceport Singapore is equally cheesy, and what can I say about one of the other attractions, the biggest Lego models in Singapore? The place is definitely intended for children, and there are some good laughs to be had, but you will not go home an empty shell if you miss this one.

3 Little India

Abdul Gafoor Mosque. 41 Dunlop St., between Perak Rd. and Jalan Besar.

Abdul Gafoor Mosque is actually a mosque complex consisting of the original mosque, a row of shophouses facing Dunlop Street, a prayer hall, and another row of houses ornamented with crescent moons and stars, facing the mosque. The original mosque, built in 1846, was called Masjid Al-Abrar, and is commemorated on a granite plaque above what could have been either the entrance gate or the mosque itself. It still stands, and even though it is badly dilapidated, retains some of its original beauty.

The surrounding shophouses were built in 1887 and 1903 by Shaik Abdul Gafoor, and their income paid for the building of the new mosque on the site 7 years later. A beautiful detail is the sunburst above the main entrance, its rays decorated with Arabic calligraphy.

Restoration of the shophouses is underway, including transformation of the facing shophouses into a religious school.

☺ Sri Veerama Kaliamman Temple. On Serangoon Rd. at Veerasamy Rd. Daily 8am–noon and 5:30–8:30pm.

This Hindu temple is primarily for the worship of Shiva's wife Kali, who destroys ignorance, maintains world order, and blesses those who strive for knowledge of God. The box on the walkway to the front entrance is for smashing coconuts, a symbolic smashing of the ego, asking God to show "the humble way." The coconuts have two small "eyes" at one end so they can "see" the personal obstacles to humility they are being asked to smash.

Inside the temple in the main hall are three altars, the center one for Kali (depicted with 16 arms and wearing a necklace of human skulls) and two altars on either side for her two sons—Ganesh, the elephant god, and Murugan, the four-headed child god. To the right is an altar with nine statues representing the nine planets. Circle the altar and pray to your planet for help with a specific trouble.

Around the left side of the main hall, the first tier of the gopuram tells the story of how Ganesh got his elephant head. A small dais in the rear left corner of the temple compound is an altar to Sri Periyachi, a very mean looking woman with a heart of gold. She punishes women who say and do things to make others feel bad. She also punishes men—under her feet is an exploiter of ladies.

Here's a bit of trivia: Red ash, as opposed to white, is applied to the forehead after prayers are made in a temple devoted to a female god.

Sri Perumal Temple. 397 Serangoon Rd., $^1/_2$ block past Perumal Rd. Best times to visit are between 7am and 11am or later, between 5pm and 7:30pm.

An Introduction to Hindu Temples

The gopuram is the giveaway—the tiered roof piled high with brightly colored stat- ues of gods and goddesses. Definitely a Hindu temple. So what are they all doing up there? It's because in India, what with the caste system and all, the lower classes were at one time not permitted inside the temple, so having these statues on the outside meant they could still pray without actually entering the temple. Further- more, while each temple is dedicated to a particular deity, all the gods are repre- sented, in keeping with the Hindu belief that although there are many gods, they are all one god. So everyone is up there, in poses or scenes that depict stories from Hindu religious lore. Sometimes there are brightly colored flowers, birds, and ani- mals as well—especially sacred cows. So why are some of them blue? It's because blue is the color of the sky, and to paint the gods blue meant that they, like the sky, are far-reaching and ever present.

There's no special way to pray in these temples, but by custom, most will pray first to Ganesh, the god with the elephant head, who is the remover of obstacles, especially those that can hinder one's closeness to god. Another interesting prayer ritual happens in the temple's main hall around a small dais that holds nine gods, one for each planet. Devotees who need a particular wish fulfilled will circle the dais, praying to their astrological planet god for their wish to come true.

The location of Hindu temples is neither by accident nor by Raffles' Town Plan. By tradition, they must always be built near a source of fresh water so that every morning, before prayer, all of the statues can be bathed. The water runs off a spout somewhere outside the main hall, from which devotees take the water and touch their heads.

Non-Hindus are welcome in the temples, to walk around and explore. Temple etiquette asks that you first remove your shoes, and if you need to point to some- thing, out of respect, please use your right hand, and don't point with your index finger.

Sri Perumal Temple is devoted to the worship of Vishnu. As part of the Hindu trin- ity, Vishnu is the sustainer balancing out Brahma the creator and Shiva the destroyer. When the world is out of whack, he rushes to its aid, reincarnating himself to show mankind that there are always new directions for development.

On the first tier to the left of the front entrance on the gopuram, statues depict Vishnu's nine reincarnations. Rama, the sixth incarnation, is with Hanumat, the monkey god, who helped him in the fierce battle to free his wife from kidnapping. Krishna, shown reclining amidst devotees, is the eighth incarnation and a hero of many Hindu legends, most notably the Bhagavad-Gita. Also up there is the half-and- half bird Garuda, Vishnu's steed. Inside the temple are altars to Vishnu, his two wives, and Garuda.

The temple was built in 1855, and was most recently renovated in 1992. Thaipusam is the main festival celebrated here (see chapter 2). During this festival, held in February, male devotees who had made vows over the year carry kavadi to show their thanks and devotion, while women carry milk pots in a parade from Sri Perumal Temple to Chettiar's Temple on Tank Road.

✪ **Temple of a Thousand Lights.** On Race Course Rd., 1 block past Perumal Rd. Daily 7:30am–4:45pm.

Thai elements influence this temple, from the stupa roofline to the huge Buddha in- side. Often this temple is brushed off as strange and tacky, but there are all sorts of

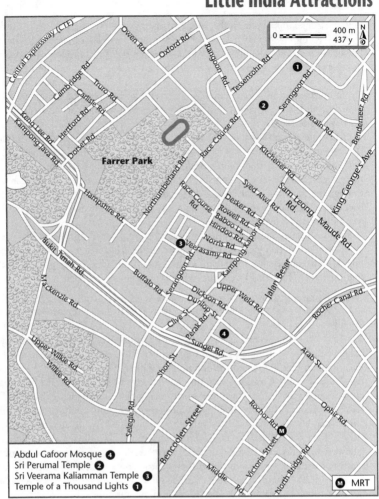

Abdul Gafoor Mosque ❹
Sri Perumal Temple ❷
Sri Veerama Kaliamman Temple ❸
Temple of a Thousand Lights ❶

Ⓜ MRT

surprises inside, making this place a veritable Buddha theme park. On the right side of the altar are statues of baby boddhisattvas for whom worshippers leave candy and toys. Around the base of the altar are murals depicting scenes from the life of Prince Siddhartha (Buddha) as he searches for enlightenment. Follow them around to the back of the hall and you'll find a small doorway to a chamber under the altar. Inside is another Buddha, this one shown at the end of his life, reclining beneath the Yellow Seraka tree. On the left side of the main part of the hall is a replica of a footprint left by the Buddha in Ceylon. Next to that is a wheel of fortune. For 50¢ you get one spin.

4 Arab Street / Kampong Glam

✪ **Sultan Mosque.** 3 Muscat St. Daily 9am–1pm and 2–4pm. No visiting is allowed during mass congregation Fri 11:30am–2:30pm.

Though there are over 80 mosques on the island of Singapore, Sultan Mosque is the real center of the Muslim community. The mosque that stands today is the second

Sultan Mosque to be built on this site. The first was built in 1826, partially funded by the East India Company as part of their agreement to leave Kampong Glam to Sultan Hussein and his family in return for sovereign rights to Singapore. The present mosque was built in 1928 and was funded by donations from the Muslim community. The Saracenic flavor of the onion domes, topped with crescent moons and stars, are complemented by Mogul cupolas. Funny thing, though: The mosque was designed by an Irish guy named Denis Santry, who was working for the architectural firm Swan and McLaren.

Other interesting facts about the mosque: Its dome base is a ring of black bottles; the carpeting was donated by a prince of Saudi Arabia and bears his emblem; and at the back of the compound, North Bridge Road has a kink in it, showing where the mosque invaded the nicely planned urban grid pattern. Also, if you make your way through the chink where the back of the building almost touches the compound wall, peer inside the makam to see the royal graves. They open the makam doors on Friday mornings and afternoons.

Sultan Mosque, like all the others, does not permit shorts, miniskirts, low necklines, or other revealing clothing to be worn inside. However, they do realize that non-Muslim travelers like to be comfortable as they tour around, and provide cloaks free of charge. They hang just to the right as you walk up the stairs.

✪ **Istana Kampong Glam.** Located at the end of Sultan Gate, 1 block past the intersection of Sultan Gate, Bagdad St., and Pahang St. This is a private residence, therefore no entry is permitted.

The Istana Kampong Glam hardly seems a fitting palace for Singapore's former royal family, but there's a fascinating controversial story behind its current state of sad disrepair. Sultan Hussein signed the original treaty in 1819 that permitted the British East India Trading Company to set up operations in Singapore. In 1824, Sultan Hussein, in a new treaty, signed over his sovereign rights to Singapore in return for Kampong Glam (which became his personal residence) and an annual stipend for himself and his descendants. Shortly after his death some 11 years later, his son, Sultan Ali, built the palace. The family fortunes began to dwindle over the years that followed, and a decades-long dispute arose between Ali's descendants over ownership rights to the estate. In the late 1890s, they went to court, where it was decided that no one had the rights as the successor to the sultanate, and the land was reverted to the state, though the family was allowed to remain in the house. Trouble is, since the place had become state owned, the family lost the authority to improve the buildings of the compound, which is why they've fallen into the sad state of disrepair you see today. Any day now, Sultan Hussein's family will be given the boot and the place will be spruced up to house Kampong Glam cultural exhibits.

It's not known who designed the Istana, but many believe it was George Coleman (see "Colonial Architecture 101," earlier in this chapter), who in addition to official buildings, contracted himself out for personal residences as well. The style certainly resembles signature elements found in some of his other works.

The house to the left before the main gate of the Istana compound is called Gedong Kuning, or Yellow Mansion. It was the home of Tenkgu Mahmoud, the heir to Kampong Glam. When he died, it was purchased by local Javanese businessman Haji Yusof the Belt Merchant. His descendants still live in the house.

Alsagoff Arab School. 121 Jalan Sultan, across from Sultan Plaza.

Built in 1912, the school was named after Syed Ahmad Alsagoff, a wealthy Arab merchant and philanthropist who was very influential in Singapore's early colonial

Arab Street & Kampong Glam Attractions

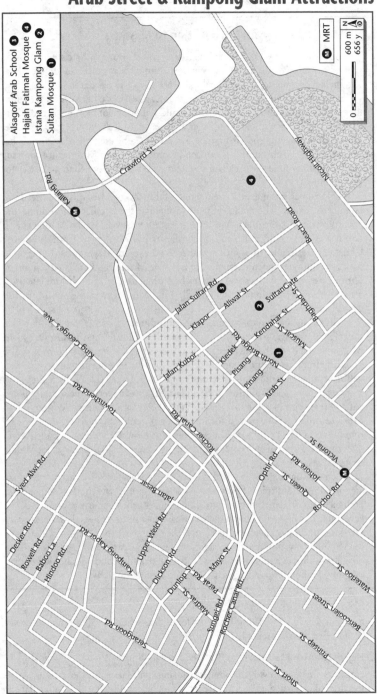

Sultan Mosque ❶
Istana Kampong Glam ❷
Hajjah Fatimah Mosque ❹
Alsagoff Arab School ❸

An Introduction to Mosques

To appreciate what's going on in the mosques in Singapore, here's a little background on some of the styles and symbols behind these exotic buildings. I have also included some tips that will help non-Muslims feel right at home.

The rule of thumb for Mosques is that they all face Mecca. Lucky for these buildings (and for Singaporean urban planners), most of the major mosques in Singapore have managed to fit within the grid of city streets quite nicely, with few major angles or corners jutting into the surrounding streets. One fine example of a mosque that obeys the Mecca rule but disregards zoning orders is Sultan Mosque in Kampong Glam. A peek around the back will reveal how the road is crooked to make way for the building.

The mosques in Singapore are a wonderful blend of Muslim influences from around the world. The grand Sultan Mosque has the familiar onion dome and Moorish stylings of the Arabic Muslim influence. The smaller but fascinating Hajjah Fatimah Mosque is a real blend of cultures, from Muslim to Chinese to even Christian—testimony to Islam's tolerance of other cultural symbols. On the other hand, the mosques in Chinatown, such as Jamae Mosque and the Nagore Durgha Shrine, are Saracenic in style, a style that originated in India in the late 19th century, mixing traditional styles of Indian and Muslim architecture with British conventionality.

Each mosque has typical features such as a **minaret,** a skinny tower from which the call to prayer was sounded (before recorded broadcasts), and a **mihrab,** a niche in the main hall, which faces Mecca and in front of which the imam prays, his voice bouncing from inside and resonating throughout the mosque during prayers. You will also notice that there are no statues to speak of. To the side of the main prayer hall there's always an **ablution area,** a place for worshippers to wash the exposed parts of their bodies before prayers, to show their respect. This is a custom for all Muslims, whether they pray in the mosque or at home. It is believed that the custom began in Islam's early days, before modern showers, and was intended to reduce the smell of so many people crammed into one small hall on those hot Middle Eastern days.

When visiting the mosques in Singapore, and anywhere else for that matter, there are some important rules of **etiquette** to follow. Appropriate dress is required. For both men and women, shorts are prohibited, and you must remove your shoes before you enter. For the ladies, please do not wear short skirts or sleeveless, backless, or low-cut tops. Also remember: Never enter the main prayer hall. This area is reserved for Muslims only. No cameras or video cameras are allowed, and remember to turn off cellular phones and pagers. Friday is the Sabbath day, and you should not plan on going to the mosques between 11am and 2pm on this day.

days and who died in 1906. It is the oldest girls' school in Singapore, and was the island's first Muslim school.

✪ **Hajjah Fatimah Mosque.** 4001 Beach Rd., past Jalan Sultan.

Hajjah Fatimah was a wealthy businesswoman from Malacca and something of a local socialite. She married a Bugis prince from Celebes, and their only child, a daughter, married Syed Ahmed Alsagoff, son of Arab trader and philanthropist Syed Abdul Rahman Alsagoff.

Hajjah Fatimah had originally built a home on this site, but after it had been robbed a couple times and later set fire to, she decided to build a mosque here and moved to another home.

Inside the high walls of the compound are the prayer hall, an ablution area, gardens and mausoleums, and a few of other buildings. You can walk around the main prayer halls to the garden cemeteries, where flat square headstones mark the graves of women and round ones mark the graves of men. Hajjah Fatimah is buried in a private room to the side of the main prayer hall, along with her daughter and son-in-law.

The minaret tower in the front was designed by an unknown European architect and could have been a copy of the original spire of St. Andrew's Cathedral. The tower leans a little, a fact that's much more noticeable from the inside. On the outside of the tower is a bleeding heart—an unexpected place to find such a downright Christian symbol. It's a great example of what makes this mosque so charming—all the combined influences of Moorish, Chinese, and European architectural styles.

5 Orchard Road Area

The Istana and Sri Temasek. Orchard Rd., between Claymore Rd. and Scotts Rd.

In 1859, the construction of Fort Canning necessitated the demolition of the original governors' residence, and the autocratic and unpopular governor-general Sir Harry St. George Ord proposed this structure be built as the new residence. Though the construction of such a large and expensive edifice was unpopular, Ord had his way, and design and construction went through, built mainly by convicts under the supervision of Major J. F. A. McNair, the colonial engineer and superintendent of convicts.

In its picturesque landscaped setting, Government House echoed Anglo-Indian architecture, but its symmetrical and cross-shaped plan also echoed the form of the traditional Malay istana (palace). During the Occupation, the house was occupied by Field Marshal Count Terauchi, commander of the Japanese Southern Army, and Major General Kawamura, commander of the Singapore Defense Forces. With independence, the building was renamed the Istana, and today it's the official residence of the President of the Republic of Singapore. Used mainly for state and ceremonial occasions, the grounds are open to every citizen on selected public holidays, though they're not generally open for visits. The house's domain includes several other houses of senior colonial civil servants. The colonial secretary's residence, a typical 19th-century bungalow, is also a gazetted monument and is now called Sri Temasek.

✪ **Peranakan Place.** Located at the intersection of Emerald Hill and Orchard Rd.

Emerald Hill was once nothing more than a wide treeless street along whose sides quiet families lived in typical terrace houses—residential units similar to the shophouse, with a walled courtyard in the front instead of the usual "five-foot-way." Toward Orchard Road, the terrace houses turned into shophouses, with their first floors occupied by small provisioners, seamstresses, and dried-goods stores. Across Orchard was Robinsons Department Store in a plain, boxy building.

As Orchard Road developed, so did Emerald Hill. A giant shopping mall—Centrepoint—was built close to the junction of the two roads, and Robinsons moved into more glitzy digs. Meanwhile, the buildings were all renovated. The shophouses close to Orchard became restaurants and bars and the street was closed off to vehicular traffic. Now it's an alfresco cafe, landscaped with a veritable jungle of potted foliage and peopled by colorful tourists—much different from its humble beginnings.

But as you pass Emerald Hill, don't just blow it off as a tourist trap. Walk through the cafe area and out the back onto Emerald Hill. All of the terrace houses have been redone, and magnificently. The facades have been freshly painted and the tiles polished, and the dark wood details add a contrast that is truly elegant. When these places were renovated, they could be purchased for a song, but as Singaporeans began grasping at their heritage in recent years, their value shot up, and now these homes fetch huge sums.

For a peek inside some of these wonderful places (and who doesn't like to see how the rich live?), go to a bookstore and look up *Living Legacy: Singapore's Architectural Heritage Renewed,* by Robert Powell. Gorgeous photographs take you inside a few of these homes and some other terrace houses and bungalows around the island, showing off the traditional interior details of these buildings and bringing their heritage to life.

Goodwood Park Hotel Tower Wing. 22 Scotts Rd., 1 block from Orchard Rd.

In 1861, with the Orchard Road area developing from a platation area into a residential district popular with Europeans, a prosperous German purchased a piece of land on Scotts Road to build a community clubhouse, to be called the Teutonia Club. The design was entrusted to Swan and McLaren and placed in the hands of R. A. J. Bidwell, who chose for the building the lively Dutch-, French-, and English-influenced Queen Anne style, which had emerged in England in the late 19th century. The L-shaped plan enclosed two large halls linked by a prominent projecting porte cochere at the corner. The halls had generous verandahs both front and back, which separated guests from service staff and ensured adequate ventilation.

The club officially opened on September 21, 1900, but toward the end of March 1915, as the reverberations of World War I spread around the world, some 300 German nationals in Penang and Singapore were classified as enemy aliens and, together with their families, shipped to be interned in Australia. Their possessions, including the clubhouse, were confiscated and liquidated at public auction. Three brothers purchased the club, renaming it Goodwood Hall after the famous Goodwood Racecourse and using it as a performance venue (for 2 nights in December 1922, ballerina Anna Pavlova performed there with her troupe) before converting it to a hotel in the late 1920s. During the Japanese Occupation the hotel was used by senior Japanese officers, and after the war the Army War Crimes Office conducted trials on the premises. Plans in the seventies that called for the replacement of the Tower Wing with a 16-story modern building, complete with bubble lift, were abandoned when it was vocally criticized by the public. Instead, a new tower, which faintly resembles the original, was built in 1978. It's only a replica, but for the record it's an official national monument. The hotel's public areas are open to nonguests.

6 The West Coast

The attractions grouped in this section are on the west side of Singapore, beginning from the Singapore Botanic Gardens at the edge of the urban area all the way out to the Singapore Discovery Centre past Jurong.

A handy way to get around to some of the major attractions on the West Coast is the **West Coast Attractions Shuttle Service.** Buses operate from 8:30am to 6:30pm daily at a frequency of about 20 minutes. There are two bus loops, a red and a blue, which you can catch at either the Lakeside or Jurong East MRT stations for trips to the Chinese and Japanese Gardens, Ming Village, Singapore Science Centre, and Omni Theatre, Tang Dynasty City, Jurong Crocodile Paradise, Jurong BirdPark, and Singapore Discovery Centre. Per trip it's between S70¢ and S$1.40 (US45¢ and US95¢) depending on where you're going, or S$2.50 (US$1.55) for a daily pass with unlimited rides. Ten percent discounts are also available for admission to attractions when you use the shuttle. They'll give you a coupon at one attraction that you can use at the next.

✪ **Jurong BirdPark.** 2 Jurong Hill. ☎ **65/265-0022.** Adults S$10.30 (US$6.90), children under 12 S$4.10 (US$2.50). Panorail: adults S$2.50 (US$1.55), children under 12 S$1 (US65¢). Mon–Fri 9am–6pm; Sat–Sun, and public holidays 8am–6pm. MRT to Boon Lay Station, transfer to SBS nos. 194 or 251.

Jurong BirdPark has a collection of 8,000 birds from over 600 species. Showcasing Southeast Asian species and other colorful tropical beauties, some of the breeds here are endangered. The over 20 hectares (49 1/2 acres) can be easily walked or, for a couple dollars extra, you can ride the panorail for a bird's-eye view (so to speak) of the grounds. The most fascinating attraction is the Waterfall Aviary, the world's largest walk-in aviary. It's an up close and personal experience with African and South American birds, plus a pretty walk through landscaped tropical forest and over babbling brooks. This is where you'll also see the world's tallest man-made waterfall, but the true feat of engineering here is the panorail station, built inside the aviary. Another smaller walk-in aviary is for Southeast Asian endangered bird species; at noon every day this aviary experiences a man-made thunderstorm. The daily guided tours and regularly scheduled feeding times are enlightening. Other bird exhibits are the flamingo pools, the World of Darkness (featuring nocturnal birds), and the penguin parade, a favorite for Singaporeans, who adore all things arctic.

Two shows feature birds of prey either acting out their natural instincts or performing falconry tricks. The **Fuji World of Hawks** is at 10am and the **King of the Skies** is at 4pm. The **All-Star Birdshow** is shown at 11am and 3pm, with trained parrots who race bikes and birds who perform all sorts of silliness, including staged birdy misbehaviors. Try to come between 9am and 11am for breakfast among hanging cages of chirping birds at the **Songbird Terrace.**

Jurong Crocodile Paradise. 241 Jalan Ahmad Ibrahim. ☎ **65/261-8866.** Adults S$6 (US$3.80), children under 12 S$3 (US$1.90). Daily 9am–6pm. MRT to Boon Lay Station, transfer to SBS nos. 194 or 251.

Just next door to Jurong BirdPark is the Jurong Crocodile Paradise, with over 2,500 crocs to see in action either in landscaped pens, in an enclosure for breeding, or in the underwater viewing areas. The crocodile paradise has been closed for renovations but will reopen sometime in 1998 with a brand-new modern facility—just in time, as the old place was starting to smell pretty bad. They'll have crocodile shows daily. Call ahead to verify times and also the cost of admission, which may change with the opening of the new facility.

Haw Par Villa. 262 Pasir Panjang Rd. ☎ **65/774-0300.** Adults S$16 (US$10), children S$10 (US$6.30). Daily 9am–6pm. MRT to Buona Vista and transfer to Bus no. 200.

In 1935, brothers Haw Boon Haw and Haw Boon Par—creators of Tiger Balm, the camphor and menthol rub that comes in those cool little pots—took their fortune and opened Tiger Balm Gardens as a venue for teaching traditional Chinese values. They made over a thousand statues and life-size dioramas depicting Chinese legends and historic tales and illustrating morality and Confucian beliefs. Many of these were gruesome and bloody and some of them were really entertaining.

But Tiger Balm Gardens suffered a horrible fate. In 1985, it was converted into an amusement park and reopened as Haw Par Villa. Most of the statues and scenes

Attractions in the West, East & North

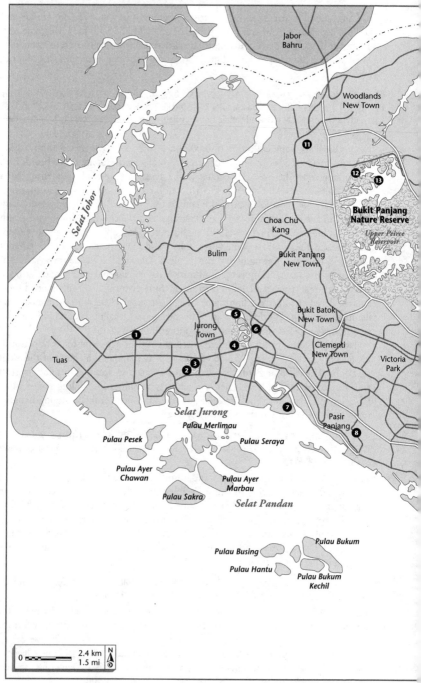

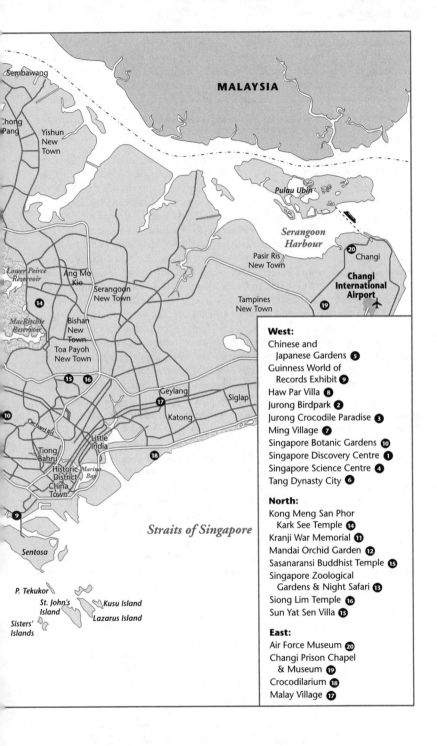

MALAYSIA

Sembawang

Chong Pang

Yishun New Town

Pulau Ubin

Serangoon Harbour

Pasir Ris New Town

Changi 🔟

Changi International Airport

Lower Peirce Reservoir

Ang Mo Kio

Serangoon New Town

Tampines New Town

🔟

🔟

MacRitchie Reservoir

Bishan New Town

Toa Payoh New Town

🔟 🔟

Geylang

Siglap

🔟

Katong

🔟

Orchard Rd.

Little India

Tiong Bahru

Marina Bay

Historic District

China Town

🔟

🔟

Straits of Singapore

Sentosa

P. Tekukor

St. John's Island

Kusu Island

Lazarus Island

Sisters' Islands

West:
Chinese and
  Japanese Gardens ❺
Guinness World of
  Records Exhibit ❾
Haw Par Villa ❽
Jurong Birdpark ❷
Jurong Crocodile Paradise ❸
Ming Village ❼
Singapore Botanic Gardens ❿
Singapore Discovery Centre ❶
Singapore Science Centre ❹
Tang Dynasty City ❻

North:
Kong Meng San Phor
  Kark See Temple 🔟
Kranji War Memorial 🔟
Mandai Orchid Garden 🔟
Sasanaransi Buddhist Temple 🔟
Singapore Zoological
  Gardens & Night Safari 🔟
Siong Lim Temple 🔟
Sun Yat Sen Villa 🔟

East:
Air Force Museum 🔟
Changi Prison Chapel
  & Museum 🔟
Crocodilarium 🔟
Malay Village 🔟

were taken away and replaced with rides. Well, business did not exactly boom. In fact, the park has been losing money fast. But recently, in an attempt to regain some of the original Tiger Balm Garden edge, they replaced many of the old statues, some of which are a great backdrop for really kitschy vacation photos. There are also two theme rides: the Tales of China Boat Ride and the Wrath of the Water Gods Flume.

Tang Dynasty City. 2 Yuan Ching Rd. ☎ **65/261-1116.** Adults S$15.45 (US$9.75), children under 12 S$10.30 (US$6.50). Daily 10am–6:30pm. MRT to Lakeside, then transfer to SBS nos. 154 or 240.

This theme park recreates Xian, the Chinese capital city during the Tang Dynasty (A.D. 618 to 907), the "Golden Age" of Chinese history for great achievements in the sciences, architecture, religion, and the arts, and for trade along the silk road. To build the reproduction city, around 80 workers who specialized in period buildings were brought in from China, as were all the green bricks and slates, roof tiles, 50,000 kilos of white jade, and almost S$5 million worth of antiques. As you make your way through the narrow streets you can check out the shops with artisans who carve chops (the stone stamps carved with Chinese characters that Chinese artists use to sign paintings and calligraphy) and eggshells (real eggshells, carved with intricate and delicate lace designs), and perform the tea ceremony. In some buildings you can walk upstairs, especially the three-story "pleasure home." The Buddhist temple that was built for the city has come into use as an actual temple for visitors to the park.

The wax museum has over 100 historical Chinese figures including Confucius and Ghenghis Khan. And if you think wax museums are creepy, you have to see the animated figures of Sun Yat Sen and Mao Zedong shouting propaganda. There are 2,000 reproduction terra-cotta warriors in an underground tomb display, plus Ghost Mansion, featuring Japanese-engineered illusions. Guided tours are conducted daily.

✪ Chinese and Japanese Gardens. Yuan Ching Rd. ☎ **65/265-5889.** Adults S$4.50 (US$2.80), children S$2 (US$1.25). Weekdays 9am–7pm; Sun and public holidays 8:30am–7pm; last admission 6pm daily. MRT to Chinese Garden or SBS nos. 335, 180, and 154.

The gardens are situated on two islands in Jurong lake, reached by an overpass, and are joined by the Bridge of Double Beauty. In the **Chinese Garden,** most of the area is dedicated to "Northern style" landscape architecture. The style of Imperial gardens, the Northern style integrates brightly colored buildings with the surroundings to make up for northern China's absence of rich plant growth and natural scenery. The Stoneboat is a replica of the stone boat at the Summer Palace in Beijing; inside the Pure Air of the Universe building are courtyards and a pond; and there is a seven-story pagoda—the odd number of floors symbolizing continuity. Around the gardens, special attention has been paid to the placement of rock formations to resemble true nature, and also to the qualities of the rocks themselves, which can represent the forces of yin and yang, male and female, passivity or activity, etc.

The Garden of Beauty is in Suzhou style, representing the Southern style of landscape architecture. Southern gardens were built predominantly by scholars, poets, and men of wealth. Sometimes called Black-and-White gardens, these were smaller, with more fine detail, and featured more subdued colors as the plants and elements of the natural landscape gave them plenty to work with. Inside the Suzhou garden are 2,000 pots of *penjiang* (bonsai) and displays of small rocks.

While the Chinese garden is more visually stimulating, the **Japanese garden** is intended to evoke feeling. Marble-chip paths lead the way so that as you walk you can hear your own footsteps and meditate on the sound. They also serve to slow the journey for better gazing upon the scenery. The Keisein, or "Dry Garden," uses white pebbles to create images of streams. Ten stone lanterns, a small traditional house, and a rest house appear nestled among two ponds with smaller islands joined by bridges.

There are toilets situated at stops along the way, as well as benches to have a rest or to just take in the sights. Paddleboats can be rented for S$5 (US$3.15) per hour just outside the main entrance.

✪ Singapore Botanic Gardens. Main entrance at corner of Cluny Rd. and Holland Rd. ☎ **1800/479-7100** toll-free in Singapore, or 65/471-9955. Free admission. Daily 5am–midnight. The National Orchid Garden: adults S$2 (US$1.25), children under 12 and seniors S$1 (US65¢). Daily 8:30am–6pm. MRT to Orchard. Take SBS nos. 7, 105, 106, 123, or 174 from Orchard Blvd.

Singapore's first botanic garden was started in 1822 at Fort Canning by Sir Stamford Raffles, and the present Botanic Garden was founded in 1859 by a horticulture society, which then turned it over to the government for upkeep. The garden was an important contributor to regional economic development when "Mad" Henry Ridley, then the garden's director, imported Brazilian rubber tree seedlings from Great Britain. He devised improved rubber-trapping methods and led the campaign to convince reluctant coffee growers to switch plantation crops. The garden has also pioneered orchid hybridization, breeding a number of internationally acclaimed varieties.

Carved out within the tropical setting is a rose garden, sundial garden with pruned hedges, a banana plantation, and a spice garden, and sculptures by international artists are dotted around the area. As you wander, look for the Cannonball tree, named for its cannonball-shaped fruit; Para rubber trees; teak trees; bamboos; and a huge array of palms, including the sealing wax palm—distinguished by its bright scarlet stalks—and the sago palm, which bears the pearl sago. The fruit of the silk-cotton tree is a pod filled with silky stuffing that was once used for stuffing pillows. Flowers like bougainvilleas and heliconias add beautiful color.

The **National Orchid Garden** is 3 hectares (7.4 acres) of gorgeous orchids growing along landscaped walks. The English Garden features hybrids developed here and named after famous visitors to the garden—there's the Margaret Thatcher, the Benazir Bhutto, the Vaclav Havel, and more. The gift shops sell live hydroponic orchids in test tubes for unique souvenirs.

The gardens have three lakes. Symphony Lake has an island band shell for "Concert in the Park" performances of the local symphony and international entertainers like Chris de Burg. Call visitor services at ☎ **65/471-9933**, or 65/471-9934 for performance schedules.

Guinness World of Records Exhibit. World Trade Centre, 2nd Floor. ☎ **65/271-8244.** Adults S$6 (US$3.80), children S$4 (US$2.50). Daily 10am–7pm.

Part of the international Guinness World of Records museums, this bizarre place is filled with wax replicas of all the human oddities you can imagine would be in the famous book.

Singapore Science Centre. Science Centre Rd., off Jurong Town Hall Rd. ☎ **65/560-3316.** www.sci-ctr.edu.sg/. Adults S$3 (US$1.90), children under 16 S$1.50 (US95¢). Tues–Sun and public holidays 10am–6pm. Take the West Coast Attractions bus (see above) or MRT to Jurong East then SBS nos. 66 or 335.

Featuring hands-on exhibits in true science-center spirit, you can play in the Atrium, Physical Sciences Gallery, Life Sciences Gallery, and the Hall of Science. Unfortunately, many of the exhibits are worn and tired from overuse and abuse. The Technology Gallery is one of the more interesting exhibits if you can wrestle the kids away from the machines, and the aromatics display, with blindfolded "guess the herb or spice" corner, is so popular they're thinking of upgrading it from temporary status. Singapore Airlines is redoing the new "On Wings We Fly" Aviation Gallery, which should be open soon. Also notable are the section on the cleaning of the Singapore River and showcased student projects from university students. The Omni Theatre is a five-story screening planetarium and the projection booth is encased in glass so you can check out how it works.

✪ Singapore Discovery Centre. 510 Upper Jurong Rd. ☎ **65/792-6188.** www.asianconnect.com/sdc. Adults S$9 (US$5.65), children under 12 S$5 (US$3.15). Simulator ride S$4 (US$2.50). Shooting Gallery S$3 (US$1.90). Tues–Fri 9am–7pm, Sat–Sun and public holidays 9am–8pm. MRT to Boon Lay; transfer to SBS nos. 192 or 193.

They originally planned to build a military history museum here, but had second thoughts that maybe the concept wouldn't bring the people running. What they came up with instead is a fascinating display of the latest military technology with hands-on exhibits that cannot be resisted. Designing tanks and ships is just one of the activities at 19 interactive information kiosks. Airborne Rangers is a virtual reality experience of parachuting from a plane and manipulating your landing to safety. In the motion simulator, feel your seat move in tandem with the fighter pilot on the screen. The Shooting Gallery is a computer-simulated combat firing range using real but decommissioned M16 rifles. Other attractions are an exhibit of 14 significant events in Singapore history, including the fall of Singapore, self-government, racial riots, and housing block development. And then there's Tintoy Theatre, where the robot Tintoy conducts an entertaining lecture on warfare! Tintoy fights a war, seeking the help of Sun Tzu and other ancient military tacticians. The IWERKS Theatre is a five-story IMAX projection. When you get hungry, there's a fast-food court.

You can also have a 30-minute bus tour of the neighboring Singapore Air Force Training Institute free with SDC admission. Inquire about tour times at the front counter.

Ming Village. 32 Pandan Rd. ☎ **65/265-7711.** Admission and guided tour free. Daily 9am–5:30pm. MRT to Clementi, then SBS no. 78. Ming Village offers a free Singapore Trolley shuttle from Paragon by Sogo on Orchard Rd. and from the Raffles Hotel bus stop at 9:20am and 9:30am respectively, and also at 10:30am and 10:40am respectively.

Tour a pottery factory that employs traditional pottery-making techniques from the Ming and Qing dynasties and watch the process from mold making, hand throwing, and hand painting to glazing each piece. After the tour, shop from their large selection of beautiful antique reproduction dishes, vases, urns, and more. Certificates of authenticity are provided, which describe the history of each piece. They are happy to arrange overseas shipping for your treasures, or if you want to carry it home, they'll wrap it very securely.

7 The North

The northern part of Singapore contains most of the island's nature reserves and parks. Here's where you'll find the Singapore Zoological Gardens, in addition to some sights with historical and religious significance. Despite the presence of the **MRT** in the area, there is not any simple way to get from attraction to attraction with ease. Bus transfers to and from MRT stops is the way to go—or you could stick to taxicabs.

Kranji War Memorial. Woodlands Rd., located in the very northern part of the island. MRT to Bugis. From Rochore Rd., take SBS no. 170.

Kranji Cemetery commemorates the men and women who fought and died in World War II. Prisoners of war in a camp nearby began a burial ground here, and after the war it was enlarged to provide space for all the casualties. The Kranji War Cemetery is the site of 4,000 graves of servicemen, while the Singapore State Cemetery memorializes the names of over 20,000 who died and have no known graves. Stones are laid geometrically on a slope with a view of the Strait of Johor. The memorial itself is designed to represent the three arms of the services.

○ Siong Lim Temple. 184–E Jalan Toa Payoh. Located in Toa Payoh New Town. Take MRT to Toa Payoh, then take a taxi.

This temple, in English "the Twin Groves of the Lotus Mountain Temple," has a great story behind its founding. One night in 1898, Hokkien businessman Low Kim Pong and his son had the same dream—of a golden light shining from the West. The following day, the two went to the western shore and waited until, moments before sundown, a ship appeared carrying a group of Hokkien Buddhist monks and nuns on their way to China after a pilgrimage to India. Low Kim Pong vowed to build a monastery if they would stay in Singapore. They did.

Laid out according to feng shui principles, the buildings include the Dharma Hall, a main prayer hall, and drum and bell towers. They are arranged in *cong lin* style, a rare type of monastery design with a universal layout so that no matter how vast the grounds are, any monk can find his way around. The entrance hall has granite wall panels carved in scenes from Chinese history. The main prayer hall has fantastic details in the ceiling, wood panels, and other wood carvings. In the back is a shrine to Kuan Yin, Goddess of Mercy.

Originally built amidst farmland, the temple became surrounded by suburban high-rise apartments in the 1950s and 1960s, with the Toa Payoh Housing Development Board New Town project and the Pan-Island Expressway creeping close by. The entire compound is currently under renovation, a fascinating process that involves some 30 to 50 expert craftsmen from China to take apart the buildings piece by piece, rebuild the rotten spots, and carefully reassemble it all.

○ Kong Meng San Phor Kark See Temple. Bright Hill Dr. Located in the center of the island to the east of Bukit Panjang Nature Preserve. Bright Hill Dr. is off Ang Mo Kio Ave. Take MRT to Bishan, then take a taxi.

The largest and most modern religious complex on the island, this place, called Phor Kark See for short, is comprised of prayer and meditation halls, a hospice, gardens, and a vegetarian restaurant. The largest building is the Chinese-style Hall of Great Compassion. There is also the octagonal Hall of Great Virtue and a towering pagoda. For 50¢ you can buy flower petals to place in a dish at the Buddha's feet.

If you're curious, there is a crematorium in the back of the complex. Arrive on Sundays after 1pm and wait for the funeral processions to arrive. Chairs line the side and back of the hall, and attendees do not mind if you sit quietly and observe, as long as you are respectful. The scene is not for the faint of heart, but is a touching moment of cultural difference and human similarity.

Sun Yat Sen Villa. 12 Tai Gin Rd., near Toa Payoh New Town. No phone. Free admission. Mon–Fri 9am–5pm, Sat–Sun and public holidays 9am–4pm. Take the MRT to Toa Payoh, then take a taxi.

Dr. Sun visited Singapore eight times to raise funds for his revolution in China, and made Singapore his headquarters for gaining the support of overseas Chinese in Southeast Asia. A wealthy Chinese merchant built the villa around 1880 for his mistress, and a later owner permitted Dr. Sen to use it. The house reflects the classic bungalow style, which is becoming endangered in modern Singapore. Its typical bungalow features include a projecting carport with a sitting room overhead, verandahs with striped blinds, second-story cast-iron railings, and first-story masonry balustrades. A covered walkway leads to kitchen and servants' quarters in the back.

Inside, the life of Dr. Sen is traced in photos and watercolors, from his birth in southern China through his creation of a revolutionary organization. Restorations are planned to convert it into the Sun Yat Sen Nanyang Memorial Hall.

Sasanaransi Buddhist Temple. 14 Tai Gin Rd., located next to the Sun Yat Sen Villa near Toa Payoh New Town. Daily 6:30am–9pm. Chanting: Sun 9:30am, Wed 8pm, and Sat 7:30pm. Take MRT to Toa Payoh, then take a taxi.

Known simply as the Burmese Buddhist Temple, it was founded by a Burmese expatriate to serve the overseas Burmese Buddhist community. His partner, an herbal doctor also from Burma, traveled home to buy a 10-ton block of marble from which was carved the 11-foot-tall Buddha who sits in the main hall, surrounded by an aura of brightly colored lights. The original temple was off Serangoon Road in Little India, and was moved here in 1991 at the request of the Housing Development Board. On the third story is a standing Buddha in gold, and murals of events in the Buddha's life.

Mandai Orchid Garden. Mandai Lake Rd., on the route to the Singapore Zoological Gardens. ☎ **65/269-1036.** Adults S$2 (US$1.25), children under 12 S50¢ (US30¢). Daily 8:30am–5:30pm. MRT to Ang Mo Kio and SBS no. 138.

Owned and operated by Singapore Orchids Pte. Ltd. for breeding and cultivating hybrids for international export, the gardens double as a Singapore Tourism Board tourist attraction. Arranged in English garden style, varieties are separated in beds that are surrounded by grassy lawn. Tree-growing varieties prefer the shade of the covered canopy. On display is Singapore's national flower, the Venda Miss Joaquim, a natural hybrid in shades of light purple. Behind the gift shop is the Water Garden, where a stroll will reveal many houseplants common to the West, as you would find them in the wild.

✪ **Singapore Zoological Gardens.** 80 Mandai Lake Rd., on the western edge of the Bukit Panjang Nature Reserve, on the Seletar Reservoir. ☎ **65/269-3411.** Adults S$9 (US$5.65), children under 12 S$4 (US$2.50). Discounts for seniors and handicapped. Daily 8:30am–6:30pm. MRT to Ang Mo Kio and take SBS no. 138.

They call themselves the Open Zoo because, rather than coop the animals in jailed enclosures, they let them roam freely in landscaped areas. Beasts of the world are kept where they are supposed to be using psychological restraints and physical barriers that are disguised behind waterfalls, vegetation, and moats. Some animals are grouped with other species to show animals coexisting as they would in nature. For instance, the white rhinoceros is neighborly with the wildebeest and ostrich—not that wildebeests and ostriches make the best company, but certainly contempt is better than boredom. Guinea and pea fowl, Emperor tamarins, and other creatures are free roaming and not shy; however, if you spot a water monitor or long-tailed macaque, know that they're not zoo residents—just locals looking for a free meal.

Major zoo features are the Primate Kingdom, Wild Africa, the Reptile Garden, the children's petting zoo, and underwater views of polar bears, sea lion, and penguins. Daily shows include primate and reptile shows at 10:30am and 2:30pm, and elephant and sea lion shows at 11:30am and 3:30pm. You can take your photograph with an orangutan, chimpanzee, or snake, and there are elephant and camel rides, too.

The literature they provide includes half-day and full-day agendas to help you see the most while you're there. The best time to arrive, however, is at 9am, to have breakfast with an orangutan, who feasts on fruits, putting on a hilarious and very memorable show. If you miss it, you can also have tea with him at 4pm. Another good time to go is just after a rain, when the animals cool off and become frisky.

✪ **Night Safari.** Singapore Zoological Gardens, 80 Mandai Lake Rd., on the western edge of the Bukit Panjang Nature Reserve, on the Seletar Reservoir. ☎ **65/269-3411.** Adults S$15.45 (US$9.75), children under 12 S$10.30 (US$6.50). Daily 7:30pm–midnight. Ticket sales close at 11pm. Entrance Plaza, restaurant, and fast-food outlet open from 6:30pm. MRT to Ang Mo Kio and take SBS no. 138.

Singapore takes advantage of its unchanging tropical climate and static ratio of daylight to night to bring you the world's first open-concept zoo for nocturnal animals. Here, as in the zoological gardens, animals live in landscaped areas, their barriers virtually unseen by visitors. These areas are dimly lit to create a moonlit effect, and a guided tram leads you through "regions" designed to resemble the Himalayan foothills, the jungles of Africa, and, naturally, Southeast Asia. Some of the free-range prairie animals come very close to the tram. The 45-minute ride covers almost $3\frac{1}{2}$ kilometers (2 miles), and has regular stops to get off and have a rest or stroll along trails for closer views of smaller creatures.

Staff are placed at regular intervals along the trails to help you find your way, though it's almost impossible to get lost along the trails; however, it is nighttime, you are in the forest, and it can be spooky. They are more or less to add piece of mind. They all speak English. Flash photography is strictly prohibited, and be sure to bring plenty of insect repellent. *A weirder tip:* Check out the bathrooms. They're all open-air, Bali style.

8 The East Coast

The East Coast is the region leading from the edge of Singapore's urban area to the tip of the east coast, at Changi Point. Eastern Singapore is home to the Changi International Airport, nearby Changi Prison, and the long stretch of East Coast Park along the shoreline. The **MRT** heads east in this region, but swerves northward at the end of the line. A popular **bus line** for east coast attractions not reached by MRT is the SBS no. 2, which takes you to Changi Prison, Changi Point, Malay Village, and East Coast Park (a short walk from Joo Chiat Centre).

Malay Village. 39 Geylang Serai, in the suburb of Geylang, an easy walk from the MRT station. ☎ **65/748-4700** or 65/740-8860. Free admission to village. Kampong Days and Cultural Museum: adults S$5 (US$3.15), children S$3 (US$1.90). Mon–Fri 10am–9pm, Sat–Sun and public holidays 10am–10pm. MRT to Paya Lebar.

In 1985, Malay Village opened in Geylang as a theme village to showcase Malay culture. The Cultural Museum is a collection of artifacts from Malay culture, which includes household items, musical instruments, and a replica of a wedding dais and traditional beaded ceremonial bed. Kampung Days lets you to walk through a kampung house (or Malay village house), as it would have looked in the 1950s and 1960s. The 25-minute Lagenda Fantasy show is more for kids, using multi-image projection, surround sound, and lights to tell tales from the Arabian Nights and the legend of Sang Nila Utama, the founder of Temasek (Singapore). The village has souvenir shops mixed with places that sell everything from antique knives to caged birds.

Two in-house groups perform **traditional Malaysian and Indonesian dances** in the late afternoons and evenings. Call on Saturday to find out if they'll be performing the Kuda Kepang in the evening. If you're lucky enough to catch it, it's a long performance but worth the wait because at the end the dancers are put in a trance and walk on glass, eat glass, and rip coconuts to shreds with their teeth (see chapter 1 for details). Arrive early because the place gets packed with locals.

✪ Changi Prison Chapel and Museum. 169 Sims Ave., off Upper Changi Rd., in the same general area as the airport. ☎ **65/743-7885**, or 65/543-0893 (museum gift shop). Free admission. Mon–Sat 9:30am–4:30pm. Closed public holidays. Changi Prison Chapel Sunday Service (all are welcome) 5:30–6:30pm. MRT to Tanah Merah station, then transfer to SBS no. 2.

Upon successful occupation of Singapore, the Japanese marched all British, Australian, and allied European prisoners to Changi by foot, where they lived in a prison camp suffering 3 years of overcrowding, disease, and malnutrition. Prisoners were cut off from the outside world except to leave the camp for labor duties. The hospital conditions were terrible; some prisoners suffered public beatings, and many died. In an effort to keep hope alive, they built a small chapel from wood and attap. Years later, at the request of former POWs and their families and friends, the government built this replica.

The museum displays sketches by W. R. M. Haxworth and secret photos taken by George Aspinall—both men POWs who were imprisoned here. Displayed with descriptions, the pictures, along with writings and other objects from the camp, bring this period to life, depicting the day-to-day horror with a touch of high morale.

Crocodilarium. 730 East Coast Pkwy., running along East Coast Park. ☎ **65/447-3722.** Adults S$2 (US$1.25), children under 12 S$1 (US65¢). Daily 9am–5pm. MRT to Paya Lebar or Eunos and take a taxi.

Head to the Crocadilarium if you're interested in seeing four types of crocodiles—from Singapore, Africa, Louisiana, and Caiman (South Africa)—and alligators from India. Of the total 1,800 crocodiles who reside here, 500 are on display. The Singapore crocodile, one of the largest, reaches a maximum size of 5.5 meters (6 yd.) and can weigh up to 500 kilograms (1100 lb.). They're pretty fierce because they have bigger heads, which means bigger mouths. However, midsize ones are the most dangerous to people because they have better mobility on land. Every so often the place picks up when a couple of them have a brutish fight. On a sweeter note, the Crocodilarium has approximately 400 births per year. Some young ones are on display—and they're very cute—but the Crocodilarium won't let you see the babies because they are delicate and spook easily. While many are intended for the booming pelt industry, some are just for show. A huge gift shop peddles crocodile products, which are made both in-house and imported from outside designers. Here you can also find ostrich hide, stingray skin, and antelope pelt goods.

The best way to get back to town is to ask the front counter to call you a cab.

Air Force Museum. Cranwell Rd. off Loyang Ave. Changi Camp. Free admission. Tues–Sun 10am–4:30pm. SBS nos. 2 or 9.

Established in 1988, this museum tracks the evolution of the Republic of Singapore Air Force with exhibits of historical artifacts and records and displays of aircraft, missiles, and dioramas with audiovisual effects.

9 Sentosa Island

In the 1880s, Sentosa, then known as Pulau Blakang Mati, was a hub of British military activity, with hilltop forts built to protect the harbor from sea invasion from all sides. Today, it has become a weekend getaway spot and Singapore's answer to Disneyland all rolled into one. If you tried to see everything, you'd need at least 3 days, but a day is just enough to see and do the best. If you want to get out of the city, the beaches are cooling and well stocked with activities, and resorts like the

Sentosa Island Attractions

Asian Village ③
Butterfly Park ⑥
Cable Car Plaza ⑤
Cinemania ⑬
Fantasy Island ⑫
Ferry Terminal ④
Fort Siloso ①
Images/Pioneers
  of Singapore ⑦
Maritime Museum ⑭
The Merlion ⑩
Orchid Garden ⑪
Underwater World ②
Volcanoland ⑨
Wonder Golf ⑧

△ Monorail Stations

■ Cable Car Station

Mount Faber
Scenic Park

Keppel Rd.

Tanjong
Beach

Central Beach

Siloso Beach

N

0   350 m
0   382 y

Beaufort are tranquil and romantic. If you're into the museum scene, there are some very well-presented historical exhibits and nature showcases. If you want to keep the kids happy, there's a water park, theme parks, and amusement rides. For your sense of adventure, you can never go wrong with Underwater World. Free with your Sentosa admission are the Fountain Gardens and Musical Fountain, the Enchanted Garden of Tembusu, the Dragon Trail Nature Walk, and the beaches.

You'll find a lot of people recommending Sentosa as a "must see" on your vacation. And while most travelers do visit the island for some part of their trip, it might not be the best way to spend your time if you're only in town for a few days. Basically, for those who like to do hard-core cultural and historical-immersion vacations, Sentosa will seem too contrived and cartoonish—just check out the Images of Singapore exhibit and go home. But for those who just want a good time, it delivers.

If you're spending the day, there are numerous restaurants and a couple of food courts. For overnights, the Rasa Sentosa Beach Resort and the Beaufort Sentosa, Singapore (see chapter 4) are popular hotel options.

GETTING THERE

Private cars are not allowed entry to the island, but there are more than a few ways to get to Sentosa. The cable car and ferry fares are exclusive of Sentosa admission charges, which you are required to pay upon arrival; bus fares include your admission charge. Admission is S$5 (US$3.15) for adults and S$3 (US$1.90) for children. Admission in the evenings is S$3 (US$1.90) for adults and S$1.80 (US$1.05) for children. Tickets can be purchased at the following booths: Mount Faber Cable Car Station; World Trade Centre Ferry Departure Hall; Cable Car Towers (next to the World Trade Centre); Cable Car Plaza (on Sentosa); Sentosa Information Booth 4 (at the start of the causeway, opposite Kentucky Fried Chicken); and at Sentosa Information Booth 3 (at the end of the causeway bridge, upon entering Sentosa). Many attractions require purchase of additional tickets, which you can get at the entrance of each.

BY CABLE CAR   Cable cars depart from the top of Mount Faber and from the World Trade Centre daily from 8:30am to 9pm at a cost of anywhere between S$5 and S$6.50 (US$3.15 and US$4.10) for adults, depending where you get on and off, and S$3 (US$1.90) for children. Plan at least one trip on the cable car because the view of Singapore, Sentosa, and especially the container port is really fantastic from up there. The round-trip cable car ticket is also good for a return on the ferry, in case you've had enough view.

BY FERRY   The ferry departs from the World Trade Centre on weekdays from 9:30am to 9pm at 20-minute intervals, and on weekends and public holidays from 8:30am to 9pm at 15-minute intervals. The round-trip fare is S$1.30 (US85¢), and one way is S80¢ (US50¢).

BY BUS   **SBS Leisure Pte. Ltd.** operates bus service to and from Sentosa. Service A operates between 7:15am and 11:30pm daily from the World Trade Centre (WTC) Bus Terminal. Services C and M run from the Tiong Bahru MRT Station between 7:20am and 11:30pm daily. Service E stops at Lucky Plaza, the Mandarin Hotel, Peranakan Place, Le Meridien Hotel, Plaza Singapura, and then Bencoolen Street, POSB Headquarters, Raffles City and Pan Pacific Hotel, and operates from 10am to 10:45pm daily. Fares run from S$6 to S$7 (US$3.80 to US$4.40) for adults and S$4 to S$5 (US$2.50 to US$3.15) for children, depending on which bus you catch and where. Fares are paid to the driver as you board and the Sentosa admission fee is included in your fare. The last bus out of Sentosa is 11:30pm.

BY TAXI Taxis are only allowed to drop off and pick up passengers at the Beaufort Sentosa, Singapore; Shangri-La's Rasa Sentosa Resort; and NTUC Sentosa Beach Resort. The taxi toll is S$3 (US$1.90) per entry from 7am to 10pm and is free from 10pm to 7am.

GETTING AROUND

Once on Sentosa, a free monorail operates from 9am to 10pm daily at 10-minute intervals to shuttle you around to the various areas. If you're staying at one of the island's major hotels, you can take advantage of their free shuttle services to get into town.

SEEING THE SIGHTS

The attractions that you get free with your Sentosa admission are the **Fountain Gardens** and **Musical Fountain,** the **Enchanted Garden of Tembusu,** the **Dragon Trail Nature Walk,** and the **beaches.**

The **Fountain Gardens,** just behind the Ferry Terminal, are geometric European-style gardens with groomed pathways and shady arbors. In the center is an amphitheater of sorts, the focus of which is a fountain—actually three fountains—which create water effects with patterns of sprays and varying heights. Regular shows throughout the day time the bursts to the sounds of everything from marches to Elton John. At night, they turn the lights on for color effects.

The **Flower Terrace** starts behind the Ferry Terminal through the Fountain Garden and creeps up the side of the steep hill beyond. The slope has a steep grade, but pathways meander to offer some relief from the climb. Still, in the heat, you're not taking this one fast.

The **Enchanted Garden of Tembusu,** in a corner of the Fountain Garden, is a shady grove of Tembusu trees and MacArthur palms. In the evenings, the garden is lit with tiny lights for a touch of romance.

The **Dragon Trail Nature Walk** takes advantage of the island's natural forest for a 1^1/$_2$-kilometer (1-mile) stroll through secondary rain forest. In addition to the variety of "dragons" to see (they're sculptures), there are also local squirrels, monkeys, lizards, and wild white cockatoos to try to spot.

There are three beaches, **Siloso Beach** on the western end and **Central Beach** and **Tanjong Beach** on the eastern end, each dressed in tall coconut palms and flowering trees. At Central Beach, deck chairs, beach umbrellas, and a variety of water-sports equipment like pedal boats, aquabikes, fun bugs, canoes, surfboards, and banana boats are available for hire at nominal charges. Bicycles are also available for hire at the bicycle kiosk at Siloso Beach. Shower and changing facilities, food kiosks, and snack bars are at rest stations. Siloso Beach is open at night for barbecue picnics, and has a really nice view of the tiny lights of ships anchored in the port. For beach activities like volleyball, check out the offerings at the Shangri-La's Rasa Sentosa Resort. Hotel guests get first dibs, but many activities and equipment are available to the public at reasonable charges.

All of the following attractions on Sentosa have admission charges separate from the Sentosa charge, and operating hours that differ from place to place.

Asian Village. ☎ 65/275-0338. Free admission. Daily 10am–9pm. Adventure Asia daily 10am–7pm. Monorail stop 1.

They set up this festival village around a tiny lake, with three zones representing the architectural moods of East, South, and Southeast Asia. Only there's no people. The original concept included bustling shops, street performers, traditional dance numbers, and regular shows in their auditorium, but not enough visitors came to the attraction, so most of the shops are empty and the dancers were laid off. You can paddleboat around the lake for S$5 (US$3.15) per half hour.

In the back of the village is Adventure Asia, with 10 rides tucked inside a shady grove. Ten bucks gets you unlimited rides—not a bad deal.

Maritime Museum. ☎ **65/270-8855.** Adults S$2 (US$1.90), children S50¢ (US30¢). Daily 10am–7pm. Closest to monorail stop 7, then walk along Gateway Ave.

Nautiphernalia buffs rejoice. It's a showcase devoted to Singapore's ever-important connection to the sea. From ship models to artifacts, sea charts, and photos, the museum tells the story of 14 centuries of maritime life.

✪ **Fantasy Island.** ☎ **65/275-1088.** Adults S$16 (US$10.10), children 3–12 S$10 (US$6.30). Daily 10am–7pm. Monorail stop 7.

If you have a few hours and a swimsuit, this place is a great time. Try out all kinds of water slides, water tunnels, surf rides, rapids, and a simulated lazy river running around the whole park. For the little ones, there are tree houses with water toys, special slides, and a kiddie pool. Changing rooms are available, there's a food outlet, and a first-aid team is on duty.

Cinemania. ☎ **65/373-0159.** Adults S$10 (US$6.30), children S$6 (US$3.80). Daily 11am–8pm. Monorail stop 7.

Cinemania is a 3-D audiovisual ride with motion simulator. They rotate three films at a time from a library of 25 titles like *Cosmic Pinball, Desert Duel,* and *Runaway Train.* Call ahead for titles and show times.

Sentosa Orchid Gardens. ☎ **65/278-1940.** Adults S$2.30 (US$1.45), free for children under 13. Daily 9:30am–6:30pm; last admission 6pm. Monorail stop 1; the Orchid Garden is to the east of the Fountain Gardens.

Located to the east of the Fountain Gardens, this place is more geared toward the theme-party scene, so you're better off at the National Orchid Garden at the Singapore Botanic Gardens or at Mandai Orchids to see the best collections.

The Merlion. ☎ **65/275-0388.** Adults S$3 (US$1.90), children S$2 (US$1.25). Daily 9am–10pm; last admission 9:30pm. Monorail stops 1 and 4.

Imagine if you will 12 towering stories of that half-lion, half-fish creature, the Merlion. That's a lot of mythical beast. Admission buys you an elevator ride to the ninth floor, where you can peer out the mouth, and to the top of its head for a 360° view of Singapore, Sentosa, and even Indonesia. Be at the Fountain Gardens at 7:30pm, 8:30pm, and 9:30pm nightly for the "Rise of the Merlion" show, where they light the thing up with 16,000 fiber-optic lights and shoot red lasers out its eyes. Poor Merlion. Hope this never happens to the national symbol of your home country.

VolcanoLand. ☎ **65/275-1828.** Adults S$10 (US$6.30), children under 12 S$6 (US$3.80). Daily 10am–8pm. Monorail stop 1 or 4.

It's hard to say whether VolcanoLand is entertaining or whether it's touristy and weird. The main attraction here is the ancient Central American "active volcano," a walk-through exhibit where you are taken on a journey to the center of the Earth with a mythological explorer and his Jules Verne–style robot buddy. Inside the "volcano" there's a multi-media show about the mysteries of life and the universe and a simulated volcano eruption. Besides its being completely contrived, the special effects creations are by far less cheesy than most. Outside the volcano in the rest of the small park are the not-very-politically-correct "Live Tribal Perfomances" like the Mayan Parade costume and dance ceremonies and the "Volcano Ritual Performance" to celebrate having survived the volcano.

✪ Images of Singapore. ☎ **65/275-0388.** Adults S$5 (US$3.15), children S$3 (US$1.90). Daily 9am–9pm; last admission 8:30pm. Monorail stop 4.

Images of Singapore is without a doubt one of the main reasons to come to Sentosa. There are three parts to this museum/exhibit, the Pioneers of Singapore and the Surrender Chambers—which date back as far as I can remember—and Festivals of Singapore, a recent addition.

Pioneers of Singapore is an exhibit of beautifully constructed life-size dioramas that place figures like Sultan Hussein, Sir Stamford Raffles, Tan Tock Seng, and Naraina Pillai, to name just a few pioneers, in the context of Singapore's timeline and their contributions to development. Also interesting are the dioramas depicting scenes from the daily routines of the different cultures as they lived during colonial times. It's a great stroll that brings history to life.

The powers that be have tried to change the name of the Surrender Chambers to the Sentosa Wax Museum, but it still hasn't caught on, because the Surrender Chambers are oh so much more than just a wax museum. The gallery leads you through authentic footage, photos, maps, and recordings of survivors to chronologically tell the story of the Pacific theater activity of World War II and how the Japanese conquered Singapore. The grand finale is a wax museum depicting, first, a scene of the British surrender and, last, another of the Japanese surrender.

Recently, Images of Singapore had added the Festivals of Singapore, another life-size diorama exhibit depicting a few of the major festivals and traditions of the Chinese, Malay, Indian, and Peranakan cultures in Singapore. For each group, wedding traditions are shown in complete regalia, with brief explanations of the customs. While this exhibit is not quite like being there and would be dull as a stand alone, it's not bad tacked on to the other two. Try to catch the video presentation at the end—a tribute to Singapore's strides in "cultural integration" in true "It's a small world after all" style.

WonderGolf Park. ☎ **65/275-2011.** Adults S$8 (US$5), seniors and students S$6 (US$3.80), children under 12 S$4 (US$2.50). Daily 9am–9pm. Monorail stop 4.

It's definitely miniature golf, but without the windmill. Instead, holes are made tricky using greens landscaped with rock designs and water features set on tiny terraces up the side of a steep slope. Two 18-hole and one 9-hole courses offer differing degrees of difficulty, and during the day it gets pretty hot. To get there, either hike up the Flower Terrace or climb down the catwalk from the Cable Car Station.

Butterfly Park and Insect Kingdom Museum of Singapore. ☎ **65/275-0013.** Adults S$5 (US$3.15), children S$3 (US$1.90). Daily 9am–7pm. Monorail stop 4.

The Butterfly Park is a walk-in enclosure for an up close view of some 60 live species of native butterflies, from cocoon to adult. At the Insect Kingdom, the exhibits are mostly dead, but extensive, with its collection carrying more than 2,500 bugs. Live ones to see include scorpions, tarantulas, and the very weird dead leaf mantis.

✪ Underwater World. ☎ **65/275-0030.** Adults S$13 (US$8.20), children S$7 (US$4.40). Daily 9am–9pm; last admission 8:30pm. Monorail stop 2.

Underwater World is without a doubt one of the most visited attractions here. Everybody comes for the tunnel: 83 meters of transparent acrylic tube through which you glide on a conveyor belt, gaping at sharks, stingrays, eels, and other creatures of the sea drifting by, above and on both sides. At 11:30am, 2:30pm, and 4:30pm daily, a scuba diver hops in and feeds them by hand. In smaller tanks you can view other unusual sea life like the puffer fish and the dragonlike weedy and leafy seadragons.

Then there's the latest display of bamboo shark embryos, developing within egg cases—need I say more?

✪ **Fort Siloso. ☎ 65/275-0388.** Adults S$3 (US$1.90), children S$2 (US$1.25). Daily 9am–7pm; last admission 6:30pm. Monorail stop 3.

Fort Siloso guarded Keppel Harbour from invasion in the 1880s. It's one of three forts built on Sentosa, and it later became a military camp in World War II. The buildings have been decorated to resemble a barracks, kitchen, laundry, and military offices as they looked back in the day. In places, you can explore the underground tunnels and ammunition holds, but they're not as extensive as you would hope they'd be.

Strolling & Touring
Around Singapore

7

Way back in the early 19th century, Sir Stamford Raffles had a vision for a multicultural Singapore, integrating diverse immigrant communities into one economy while creating separate ethnic neighborhoods within which they'd live. The Historic District was the center of the colonial administration, Chinatown was the heart of sea trade, Little India was the home of Indian commercial activities, and Kampong Glam was the focus of Islam and the Malay royalty. These neighborhoods were made official in his Town Plan of 1822, and amazingly enough, still stand 175 years later.

Modern Singapore, though, is bigger than its original neighborhoods, and what was once jungle has been cleared to create the popular suburban New Towns, which have simultaneously siphoned off many residents of the ethnic neighborhoods and, through the melting-pot effect, furthered the government's aim of molding a unified Singaporean national identity from the ethnic fragments. What are the neighborhoods like now? Many ethnic shops, restaurants, places of worship, and museums hold on, maintaining the ties between the areas and the Chinese, Indian, and Malay communities, but even this situation is under attack—curiously, by a plan designed to enshrine the neighborhoods' ethnicities.

Recognizing the importance of Singapore's individual cultures—if only for the tourist revenues they generate—the Urban Redevelopment Authority has instituted the Tourism 21 plan, whose aim it is to preserve these cultural nooks in the city by restoring buildings, adding tourist touches, and turning each area into a Thematic Zone. Does this sound like Disney to you? It does to me. The plan has already begun to take hold in Chinatown, where, sadly, most of the lifestyle that made that neighborhood come alive has been forced out by the newly renovated buildings' newly high rents. What's taken their place? A lot of bland souvenir shops. At the risk of sounding alarmist, here's my prognosis: Now is perhaps the last time when a traveler to Singapore can see the remaining neighborhoods untouched by meddling government planners. You've picked a good time to go.

In this chapter, I've tailored four walking tours to the four big ethnic neighborhoods: the Historic District, Chinatown, Little India, and Arab Street and Kampong Glam. The walking tours map out the most convenient route to see all the sights in each neighborhood. While the larger sights are described in greater detail in chapter 6, in between these places lie interesting features of the city—the small details that locals take for granted and visitors take home as treasured memories. I've pointed out some of the more interesting features along the routes, and provided some information of what these small details reveal about Singapore and its people. At the end of the chapter, I've also provided write-ups on some of the more respectable tour services, if you feel you want to take a guided tour.

One final note: Though these neighborhoods were always ethnic enclaves, they were never ethnic fortresses, so no matter where you go, you'll find influences from many cultures mixed into the scene. In the Historic District, for instance, Christian churches and Hindu and Chinese temples coexist. In Chinatown, there are Indian mosques and Hindu temples. Likewise, Little India's got Chinese, Burmese, and Muslim places of worship. What I'm saying is, don't plan to visit Little India and expect to feel like you're in downtown Dehli. You're in Singapore, and in Singapore, the big mix is the essence of life.

1 Walking Tours

WALKING TOUR 1
The Historic District

Start: Fort Canning Park
Finish: City Hall MRT, Stamford Road
Time: 5 hours (excluding museum tours but including an hour for lunch)
Best Times: Anytime

When Raffles first sailed up the Singapore River he saw a small fishing and trading village along the banks and a thick overgrowth of jungle and mangrove forest creeping up a gentle hill that overlooked the harbor. Over time, the left bank of the river would be reclaimed and built up for sea trade, the right bank would be cleared for the center of government activity, and high atop the hill, he'd build his home, Government House.

The Town Plan of 1822 set aside this district, referred to in this book as the Historic District but also called the Colonial District or the City Centre. The central point was **The Padang,** a large field for sports exercises and ceremonies. Around the field, government buildings were erected, each reflecting preferred British tastes of the day. European hotels popped up, as well as cultural centers, and the Esplanade by the marina became a lively focal point for the European social scene.

The oldest part of the city is **Fort Canning Park,** the hill where Raffles built his home. Its history predates Raffles, with excavation sites unearthing artifacts and small treasures from earlier trading settlements and a sacred shrine that's believed to be the final resting place of Iskander Shah, founder of the Sultanate of Malaysia. It is here that the walking tour begins. (See chapter 6 for more details on most of these sights.)

1. Begin at **Fort Canning Park.** If you follow Canning Rise to the top of the hill, you'll be at the Battle Box, from which you can pick up the path and follow it through the historic sites in the park. You'll finish at the entrance after the Music and Drama Academy. Walk down Canning Rise to Hill Street.

On your right just before Hill Street is the:

2. Philatelic Museum. Housed in a restored 1895 building, the museum presents stamps issued to commemorate important events, first day covers, antique printing plates, postal service memorabilia, and private collections.

Historic District Walking Tour

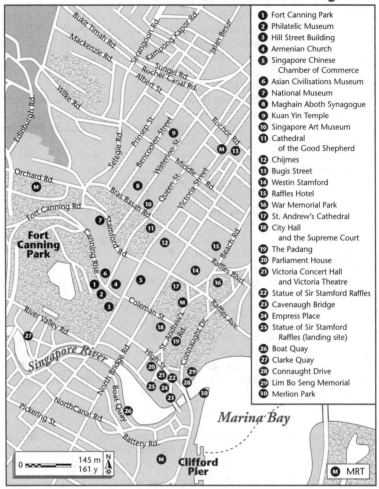

1. Fort Canning Park
2. Philatelic Museum
3. Hill Street Building
4. Armenian Church
5. Singapore Chinese
   Chamber of Commerce
6. Asian Civilisations Museum
7. National Museum
8. Maghain Aboth Synagogue
9. Kuan Yin Temple
10. Singapore Art Museum
11. Cathedral
    of the Good Shepherd
12. Chijmes
13. Bugis Street
14. Westin Stamford
15. Raffles Hotel
16. War Memorial Park
17. St. Andrew's Cathedral
18. City Hall
    and the Supreme Court
19. The Padang
20. Parliament House
21. Victoria Concert Hall
    and Victoria Theatre
22. Statue of Sir Stamford Raffles
23. Cavenaugh Bridge
24. Empress Place
25. Statue of Sir Stamford
    Raffles (landing site)
26. Boat Quay
27. Clarke Quay
28. Connaught Drive
29. Lim Bo Seng Memorial
30. Merlion Park

M MRT

At Hill Street, turn right and you'll pass the fire station on your right, followed by the Hill Street Food Centre. One block along Hill Street and on your right is the:

3. **Hill Street Building.** Originally built to house the British Police Force and later the home of the National Archives, it's rumored that the Japanese conducted tortures here during the Occupation.

Turn around and backtrack. On your left after you pass Canning Rise at #60 is the:

4. **Armenian Church.** Designed by George Coleman, the church was consecrated in 1836 and was the first permanent Christian church in Singapore. The cemetery in the back of the church holds the graves of many prominent Armenians.

A ways down across the street at #47 is the:

5. **Singapore Chinese Chamber of Commerce.** The organization was founded in 1906, but this building wasn't built until 1964. It has two fascinating dragon murals, which deserve close inspection.

Walk straight on until you reach Stamford Road. Turn left and 1 block along, at the corner of Stamford Road and Armenian Street, is the **MPH building,** with one of the largest English bookstores in Singapore.

A detour down Armenian Street will take you to the **Substation** on your right, one of the hubs of the Singapore visual and performing arts communities. Just beyond the Substation is the:

6. **Asian Civilisations Museum.** Housed in the old Tao Nan School building, this first branch of a planned two-branch museum focuses on the Malaysian archipelago's rich Chinese heritage, presenting displays of fine jade, calligraphy, ceramics, furniture, and artworks.

Backtrack to Stamford Road and turn left. Up a way on your left is the:

7. **National Museum.** Focusing on Singaporean history, the museum's collection includes 20 dioramas that portray events from the settlement's early days to modern times.

Cross the street and cut through **Bras Basah Park** on Bencoolen Street. *Bras Basah* literally means "dried rice," and it was so named because this was a place to which wet rice was brought to lay out to dry. In the park today you can find rickshas lined up waiting for business. At the corner of Bencoolen Street and Bras Basah Road, turn right.

For a short side trip, turn left onto Waterloo Street; 2 blocks down on your left is the:

8. **Maghain Aboth Synagogue.** Built in 1878, it was the first synagogue in Singapore. Farther down Waterloo Street on your left is:

9. **Kuan Yin Temple.** This place is famous for granting your most fervent wishes, so read the instructions in chapter 6 and get on-line.

Back on Bras Basah Road, on your left will be the:

10. **Singapore Art Museum.** The museum houses a large collection of art and sculpture, most of it by Singaporean and Malay artists.

Also along Bras Basah Road, farther on your right at the corner of Bras Basah and Queen Street is the:

11. **Cathedral of the Good Shepherd.** Built in the 1840s by various congregations, it was Singapore's first permanent Catholic cathedral.

One more block along Bras Basah and you'll take a right onto Victoria Street. Turn right, and on your left will be:

12. **Chijmes.** Once a large convent and orphanage, this place has turned all the way around and now houses retail shops, restaurants, and a performance space.

For another side trip, from Chijmes, take Victoria Street back past the intersection of Bras Basah and walk about 6 blocks to:

13. **Bugis Street.** Once full of sex shows and decadence, Bugis has cashed in and become a shopping center, though you can still catch a transvestite review at the **Boom Boom Room** (see chapter 9).

Back on Bras Basah, turn right from Chijmes or left from Bugis Street. To your right is the towering:

14. **Westin Stamford.** (See chapter 4.) The tallest hotel in the world, it sits atop Raffles City Shopping Centre. On your left is the **Raffles Hotel Arcade.** If you follow Bras Basah to the corner at Beach Road and turn left, you'll be at the entrance of the:

15. **Raffles Hotel.** (See chapters 4, 6, and 9.) Built in 1887, Raffles is a living, breathing slice of British colonial history that's still going strong as the 21st century looms. If nothing else, take a stroll through the lobby. If you have more time, check out the museum or have a Singapore Sling in the place they originated, the famous Long Bar.

☕ **TAKE A BREAK** For a no-muss, no-fuss local lunch I'd recommend **Rendezvous** in Raffles City. For a more upscale meal, the buffet at Raffles' **Tiffin Room** is lovely. If it's the afternoon, you could catch high tea at the **Raffles Bar & Billards Room,** or, for a few dollars more, take your tea at the **Compass Rose,** at the top of the Westin Stamford. The view is to die for. (See chapter 5 for details on all of these.)

From Raffles Hotel, backtrack on Beach Road and continue past the intersection at Bras Basah. On your left is:

16. War Memorial Park. This memorial was erected for the Singaporeans who lost their lives during the Japanese Occupation. Because of its four columns, it is called "the chopsticks," each chopstick representing a group—Chinese, Malays, Indians, and Europeans and other races—who died.

As you pass War Memorial Park, bear right onto St. Andrew's Road and look to your right to see:

17. St. Andrew's Cathedral. An earlier church designed by George Coleman stood on this site until it was struck by lightning and torn down in 1852. The present structure dates from 1860 and is of English Gothic Revival design—it's one of the few standing churches of this style in the region.

Follow St. Andrew's Road to:

18. City Hall and the Supreme Court. Both will be on your right. Both were built in a very official-looking classical style, on a very official-looking piece of real estate. Check out the sculptures that stand along the front of the Supreme Court. Ever wonder what Justice, Supplication, Thankfulness, Deceit, Violence, Prosperity, and Abundance look like? Here's your chance to find out.

Across the street from these buildings is:

19. The Padang. It may only look like a playing field to you, but as the center around which the city was built, it has a great deal of historic significance.

After the Supreme Court, as you round the curve, bear left. Just ahead is the:

20. Parliament House. The seat of Singapore's Legislative Assembly, it is probably the oldest building in the country, having been built in 1826 (though it's been substantially altered since). The bronze elephant you see out front was an 1872 gift from the King of Siam.

As you continue round the curve of St. Andrew's Road, you'll see the:

21. Victoria Theatre and Concert Hall. The theater portion was built in 1862 as the Town Hall, and the concert hall was built in 1905 as a memorial to Queen Victoria. Today, the Singapore Symphony Orchestra and various other companies call it home.

Cut around to the front of the theater to see the first:

22. Statue of Sir Stamford Raffles. Dating from 1887, the statue stood in the Padang until it got in the way of the cricket matches.

From the statue you can look across the water to see:

23. Cavenagh Bridge. Constructed in 1869, it linked the government center with Commercial Square across the river. It was named after Orfeur Cavenagh, who was governor of Singapore from 1859 until 1867.

From Cavenagh Bridge you can walk up the bank of the river and pass:

24. Empress Place. It will be on your right. The building once housed almost the entire government bureaucracy of Singapore, and at press time it was being converted to house branch II of the Asian Civilisations Museum.

Walk a block or two along the river to the second:

25. Statue of Sir Stamford Raffles. This statue was made from plaster casts of the original 1887 figure located in front of the Victoria Theatre and Concert Hall (see above), and stands on what is believed to be the site where Sir Stamford Raffles landed on January 29, 1819. This is a great place to appreciate the Singapore River.

Across the river is:

26. **Boat Quay.** It's known as "the belly of the fish." It takes a little bit of imagination to see it, but from this point as you look upstream and down, the shape of the river resembles a fish, with Boat Quay sitting at its belly. According to Chinese feng shui, it is this belly—the luckiest part of the fish—that's made Boat Quay a commercial success throughout its history.

For a detour, upriver is:

27. **Clarke Quay.** A former cannery and warehouse area, Clarke Quay is now home to 60 restored warehouses that contain retail shops and restaurants. Just before it is **Elgin Bridge,** built in 1862 and named after Lord Elgin, a British High Commissioner who merely passed through Singapore in 1857 on his way to China.

Also at this point along the river, examine the trees to find a fragment of the old metal pipe banister that once marked the edge of the water. When they built up this side of the river, they cut the banister, but a small portion was embedded in the trunk of the tree, and still remains. The tree is now about 20 yards from the water's edge.

Return from your detour back to the Raffles landing site. At this point you are behind the Parliament Building. To the right side is Parliament Lane. Follow this back to St. Andrew's Road. Turn right and follow the curve around the Padang to:

28. **Connaught Drive.** Connaught follows along the edge of the Padang, while on its other side is a park called **Queen Elizabeth Walk.** At the beginning of Queen Elizabeth Walk is **Anderson Bridge,** linking the Historic District to Collyer Quay. If the bridge is to your right, look slightly left to see the:

29. **Lim Bo Seng Memorial.** The statue was erected in memory of Major General Lim Bo Seng, a member of the Singaporean underground resistance in World War II who was captured and killed by the Japanese.

On the other side of Anderson Bridge is:

30. **Merlion Park.** Here you can see Singapore's national symbol, the Merlion—half-fish, half-lion, and all-around symbol of prosperity.

WALKING TOUR 2
Chinatown

Start: Wak Hai Cheng Bio Temple on Phillip Street
Finish: Yue Hua Chinese Emporium on Eu Tong Sen Road
Time: 3 to 4 hours (maybe more, depending on the heat, how much time you take for lunch, and how much you'd like to dawdle)
Best Times: Start in the morning to give yourself enough time to see all you want without being rushed. Any day of the week should be fine.

When the first Chinese junk landed in Singapore sometime around 1821, the sailors aboard rushed to the shore and prayed to Kuan Yin, the Goddess of Mercy, for bringing them safely to their destination. A small shrine was built on the shore, which became the first stop all Chinese sailors made as they landed ashore. It was no Thian Hock Keng Temple, but hey, they had to start somewhere.

These Chinese and other merchants set up warehouses along the western bank of the Singapore River, and business offices, residences, clan associations, and coolie houses began to fill the area behind Boat Quay. In 1822, when Sir Stamford Raffles

Chinatown Walking Tour

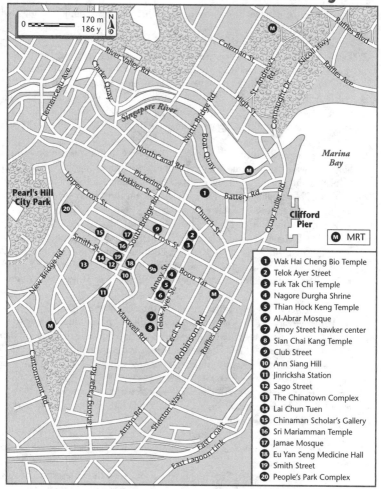

1	Wak Hai Cheng Bio Temple
2	Telok Ayer Street
3	Fuk Tak Chi Temple
4	Nagore Durgha Shrine
5	Thian Hock Keng Temple
6	Al-Abrar Mosque
7	Amoy Street hawker center
8	Sian Chai Kang Temple
9	Club Street
10	Ann Siang Hill
11	Jinricksha Station
12	Sago Street
13	The Chinatown Complex
14	Lai Chun Tuen
15	Chinaman Scholar's Gallery
16	Sri Mariamman Temple
17	Jamae Mosque
18	Eu Yan Seng Medicine Hall
19	Smith Street
20	People's Park Complex

developed his Town Plan, he reserved this area for the Chinese, naming it Chinatown, a name which has stuck.

As you tour Chinatown, you may be surprised to see a Hindu Temple and even a couple of mosques. Although the area was predominantly Chinese, many Hindus and Muslims settled here, drawn by fresh water at Spring Street (as Hindu temples must always be built near a water supply and Muslims require water for ablution before prayers) and by commerce.

For a long time, Chinatown remained basically unchanged, but that's changed recently as the Urban Redevelopment Authority has come in to renovate many of the more interesting places along the Chinatown walk. During the course of the walking tour, I'll show the contrast between the old and the new, and describe some of the effects of the URA's plan.

The tour begins on Phillip Street at:

1. Wak Hai Cheng Bio Temple. Built by Chinese sailors, its name means "Temple of the Calm Sea Built by the Guangzhou People." It's a Teochew temple, located in a part of Chinatown (from here to Boat Quay) that was populated mostly by the Teochews.

From here, cross Church Street to:

2. **Telok Ayer Street.** Telok Ayer Street once ran along the seashore. Everything to your left was water before major land reclamation schemes in the 1800s extended the shoreline. As you walk down Telok Ayer Street, on your right at #76 is:

3. **Fuk Tak Chi Temple.** It's a tiny and smoky Taoist temple with incense sellers inside.

Continue along Telok Ayer and on your right as you pass Boon Tat Street you'll see:

4. **Nagore Durgha Shrine.** Built to commemorate a visit to the island by a Muslim holy man who was traveling around Southeast Asia spreading the word of Islam, there's a continuing dispute over exactly how old the place is. If you can find a translator, Nagoreallauddeen, the 15th descendant of the holy man, will tell you his side of the dispute—he's here every day.

A little farther down on the right is:

5. **Thian Hock Keng Temple.** The oldest Chinese temple in Singapore, it's another one built originally by Chinese sailors and dedicated to the goddess Ma Po Cho. Note the wooden bar that runs across the entrance, keeping out wandering ghosts and, coincidentally, forcing you to bow as you enter—or at least to look down, so you don't trip.

Still farther down Telok Ayer Street, on the right, is the:

6. **Al-Abrar Mosque.** Also known as Kuchu Palli (small mosque) and as Masjid Chulia, the original mosque on this site was a thatched hut that was probably erected not long after 1827. The present brick structure was erected in the 1850s.

Just past Al-Abrar Mosque on the right is **Amoy Street.** Turn onto Amoy and as you walk up on your left you'll see the:

7. **Amoy Street hawker center.** This place gets crowded at lunchtime, serving professionals in the many advertising and public relations firms that have settled in the restored shophouses along Amoy.

Next to the hawker center is the:

8. **Sian Chai Kang Temple.** Another small shrine, this one is painted bright red and is open in the front.

Continue along Amoy Street, and when you reach the intersection of Amoy and Boon Tat Street, look at the decrepit **shophouse** on the corner. The side is exposed to reveal trees that are taking root in the crumbling walls of the structure. This is a great example of the shophouse in its worst unrenovated state. This one looks too far gone to even be considered for renovation and might eventually be torn down.

Continue up Amoy Street to Cross Street. Turn left and walk a ways. To the left will be:

9. **Club Street.** Club Street was a famous social spot for wealthy Chinese businessmen, and as you walk a couple blocks down you'll come across a side street, also called Club Street (9a). At the end of this short lane is a mansion known as the **Chinese Weekly Entertainment Club,** which was built in 1892 as a gentlemen's club for Chinese millionaires.

Turn back to the original Club Street and continue down to Ann Siang Hill and turn left.

10. **Ann Siang Hill.** The shophouses on Ann Siang Hill are gorgeous examples of decorative local architecture and all of the influences on it. Some of these old buildings, like #7, still have two-part pintu pagar doors—small, saloon-style swinging

panels that allow air circulation while providing privacy and large doors right behind them that are only used to lock up. Some of the tile work on these houses is stunning. Take a look at #26 and #24 through #19. Also at #19 you can see the square peephole above the door where the people sleeping upstairs can peer down to see who's at the door.

Ann Siang Hill is also home to many **clan associations.** These family guilds were created in the early 1800s to support new Chinese immigrants to Singapore by helping them to find work and send money home. For the established Chinese clan members, the associations distributed news from the mainland, served social functions, and settled disputes.

Ann Siang Hill branches off into two roads. Stay to the right and walk a block until it turns into Kadayana Lur Street. Continue straight until you hit Maxwell Road, where you'll make a right and head for the intersection of Maxwell and South Bridge Road. It's a large intersection, but as you look to your left the triangular white building is the old:

11. **Jinricksha Station.** This was the depot for the thousands of rickshas that once served as regular public transportation. The building has now been converted into restaurants.

☕ **TAKE A BREAK** For a side trek, turn toward Jinricksha Station and bear right down Neil Road. Along Neil Road are a couple of Chinese teahouses—**The Tea Chapter** and **Yixing Xuan** (see chapter 5)—where you can relax and take in a traditional Chinese tea ceremony. At #51 is a complex of shophouses and inside is a small exhibit of photographs of old Tanjong Pagar. If you're in the mood for something more substantial than tea, stop into **Chen Fu Ji Fried Rice,** at 7 Erskine Road near South Bridge Road. This is the best fried rice in the world. Trust me.

From the intersection at Jinricksha station, cross South Bridge Road and turn to the right. Walk along South Bridge Road until you reach Sago Street, and turn left.

12. **Sago Street.** This street was named after factories here, which once prepared sago, a starchy staple from the sago palm that is used as a base for many Chinese recipes, especially pudding. Sago Street also became known for its funeral parlors and hospices. Many elderly Chinese would come to this place to die so as not to invite bad spirits and fortune associated with death into their families' homes.

At the end of Sago Street, across Trengganu Street, is:

13. **The Chinatown Complex.** This is a large market filled with row after row of stalls selling souvenirs, luggage, household items, clothing, leather goods, and more. Feel free to bargain. In the back toward the left is a row of stores, a few of which sell large collections of incense, Chinese teapots, antique jade, and carvings. If you're curious, there's a huge wet market in the basement where you can peruse the exotic fruits and vegetables, dried foodstuffs, and meats, seafood, and poultry.

Back on Trengganu Street, walk down until you reach Smith Street. At the corner here you'll find:

14. **Lai Chun Tuen.** This Cantonese opera house once staged Chinese opera performances regularly. The building is currently undergoing a complete overhaul.

While we're on the subject of overhauling, this whole area of Chinatown (Sago Street, Smith Street, Trengganu Street, Temple Street, and Pagoda Street) is being converted by the Urban Redevelopment Authority into a **Chinatown Thematic Zone.** Automobile traffic will be cut off from these streets, and a promenade for tourists will take over. Ask any of the local Chinese around here and they'll tell you with sad reminiscence about all the craftsmen—the incense makers, lantern makers, calligraphers, chop cutters, kite makers, and others—who once handcrafted their wares in the shops. Almost all have been chased away since restoration of the shops pushed rents far beyond their reach. One look now and you'll see the coming of the future: Most of the artisans' shops have been replaced by souvenir shops.

Some of the shops, though, are worth taking a look inside. **Zhen Lacquer Gallery** (#1 Trengganu) has a great collection of East Asian and Southeast Asian arts and crafts, which make good gifts. **Toh Foong** (#5 Temple St.) is on the expensive side but has a large collection of antique porcelain and china, as well as curio items. **Keng Sin Gift Shop** (#30 Temple St.) has regulation souvenirs in the front of the store. Ask them about their watch collection. **D'Art Station** (#65 Pagoda) has bamboo birdcages of all shapes and sizes and a good collection of Chinese teapots and teas.

If you're still on Trengganu Street, look for #14B, where you'll find the:

15. **Chinaman Scholar's Gallery.** Up on the third story, Mr. Vincent Tan's gallery offers a peek inside a Chinese home, displaying such items as clothing, kitchenware, photographs, and traditional musical instruments.

From the gallery, continue left down Trengganu Street until you reach Pagoda. Turn right and ask yourself, "Who chose these awful colors to paint these shophouses anyway?"

☕ **TAKE A BREAK**   At #39 Pagoda St. is the peanut man, who sells the best peanuts in Singapore.

As you walk down Pagoda Street, approaching on the right-hand corner of Pagoda and South Bridge Road, you can't miss the colorful statuettes on the gopuram of the:

16. **Sri Mariamman Temple.** The oldest Hindu temple in Singapore, it was originally a small wood-and-thatch shrine founded by Naraina Pillay, an Indian merchant who came to Singapore with Raffles' first expedition. In the main hall of the temple you can see the small god that Pillai originally placed here.

Turn left on South Bridge and walk 1 block. On your left you'll see the:

17. **Jamae Mosque.** Behind the typical-looking gate, the mosque itself has the neoclassical style that was popular in the 1830s, when it was built. A small shrine inside memorializes Muhammad Salih Valinva, a local religious leader.

Backtrack down South Bridge until you reach Smith Street on your right. Across South Bridge Road is the:

18. **Eu Yan Seng Medicine Hall.** Open from 8:30am to 6pm Monday through Saturday, this place has been around for 80 years, prescribing cures like swallow's nests; animal gall bladders, glands, and penises; dried insects; amphibians; reptiles; and worms. Some of the staff speak English and they're used to inquisitive tourists, so you can ask all the questions you want about the remedies and the ailments they cure.

Cross back over South Bridge Road and up:

19. **Smith Street.** After you pass the intersection at Trengganu, keep your eye to the right-hand side of the street. At #48 is another Chinese medicine shop, followed by a shop that sells every kind of soy product imaginable. One shop farther is a shop that sells incense and paper products. Here you can find Hell money and paper replicas of luxury items, which the Chinese burn for their ancestors (it's believed the items then rise to heaven for their ancestors to enjoy). Traditional

(at your service)

To reach the other side of the world the easy way, use **AT&T DIRECT**℠ SERVICE. Simply dial the access number for the country you're in (for a list of AT&T Access Numbers, take the wallet card provided) and you'll be connected to English-speaking operators and get AT&T's quick, clear connections. Plus, you can use your AT&T Calling Card or any of these major credit cards. Now, what could be easier than that?

It's all within your reach.

paper items included shoes and coats, but today you'll find paper luxury cars and cellular phones.

At the end of Smith Street is New Bridge Road / Eu Tong Sen Road. Cross using the overpass to:

20. People's Park Complex. Do some shopping. Farther down Eu Tong Sen Road is People's Park Centre, where Yue Hua Chinese Emporium is located.

WALKING TOUR 3
Little India

Start: Corner of Hastings Road and Serangoon Road
Finish: Leong San See Temple, Race Course Road
Time: 2 to 3 hours
Best Times: Don't go on a Sunday, which is the only day off for workers—so Serangoon Road gets packed. Tour buses usually arrive around 10am, so it may be better to get here earlier. If you arrive at 8 to 8:30am, you can have a local breakfast in Zhu Jiao Centre.

Little India did not develop as a community planned by the colonial authorities like Kampong Glam or Chinatown, but came into being because immigrants to India were drawn to business developments here. In the late 1920s, the government established a brick kiln and lime pits here that attracted Indian workers, and the abundance of grass and water made the area attractive to Indian cattle traders. On the site of the present Zhu Jiao Centre at the eastern end of Serangoon Road, indigenous bamboo grew, which was used to build fences, and a natural spring provided holy water for religious purposes.

Many of the street names in Little India reflect the cattle industry that once thrived here. Serangoon Road has a few stories behind its name. One of the more popular ones dates back to when Malay traders would use this route to come into town to trade. Serangoon Road used to run all the way to Pongol to the far northeast side of the island, and bandits would sometimes enter town on this road to loot. As they traveled the road, the Malay traders would beat drums to scare away dangerous animals and also to alert soldiers to stand guard against bandits who might rob them. *Serang* in Malay means "attack," and if you combine that with the beat of the drum, you get *serang-gong*.

The tour begins on the corner of Hastings Road and Serangoon Road, where there's a stone plaque carved with Tamil writing. The animal head on the plaque could be a cow, indicating the cattle industry of the early settlers here. The symbols on the plaque stand for Vishnu, Shiva, and Brahma, the Hindu trinity.

Across Serangoon Road is:

1. Zhu Jiao Centre. The hawker stalls in the front part—half designated for Chinese food and the other half for Indian—are a good place to stop for a cup of coffee. The crescent moon and star on some of the signs indicate where food is halal, following the strict dietary laws of Islam. Walk through the stalls to the back, where you'll find a wet market. These open-air markets are named wet markets because workers there hose down the concrete floor every morning before business. A walk through the separate sections reveals the strange world of local fruits, Chinese vegetables, local and imported dried fish, mushrooms and chilies, and meats, poultry, and seafood.

At one time they slaughtered the chickens here, but government sanitation laws drove the business to factories. If you're adventurous, hang around early to see if you can meet up with a poultry truck driver who's willing to let you hitch a ride on his delivery route for one of the most unusual tours around the island.

Exit out the side to Buffalo Road and head away from Serangoon Road. **Komala Vilas** (see chapter 5) is at #12-14 Buffalo Road. If you don't have lunch plans, come back for their dosai.

At the corner of Buffalo Road and Kerbau Road (Malay for "cow") is:

2. **#37 Buffalo Road.** It's a little shop that sells batik from Sri Lanka, flowers made into prayer garlands, and betel leaves for red dye. All the ingredients for chewing betel can be found here: the betel nut, leaf, and chalk, which are combined and chewed, staining the mouth crimson red.

Turn right on Kerbau Road, down what looks almost like a back alley, and into an open courtyard. Directly to your right, #37 Kerbau Road is called:

3. **Tan House.** It's a residence that has been restored in perfect Peranakan style and is a great example of the mixed cultural influences in local architecture. Above the windows in the front are Chinese vents called *bienfu*. Shaped like bats, the bienfu are symbols of good luck. Other Chinese influences are the bamboo engravings on the shutters to symbolize strength and the green tiles above the porch to keep the rain water from running off just outside the front door. This is good feng shui, as it keeps the money close. The green wooden lacelike detail just beneath the eaves is Malay influenced. The columns are European, as are the Edinburgh curved windows.

Continue through the courtyard toward Serangoon Road and you'll hit the small intersection where Kerbau meets:

4. **Bellilios Lane.** The street's namesake was a wealthy and influential cattle trader around the turn of the century. The squat shophouses here were once used as stables on the first floor and residences on the second. Remain on Kerbau. Across the street as you walk toward Serangoon, notice the shops, which hang bits of Indian-style "feng shui." The *Asmi* (a spiritual advisor; the Tamil version of the feng shui master) employ their own superstitions to protect their shops from evil influences. Pumpkins, shells, charcoal, limes, limestone, and even preserved umbilical cords (wrapped in a string like an egg) are hung high, and scary images of gods are placed around the door. These shops always have altars, and before daily business begins, shop owners prepare the altar, burn incense, and offer prayers.

Cross over Serangoon to:

5. **Campbell Lane.** Here you'll find shops with Indian arts and crafts, plus souvenirs. You can find feathers from the peacock—the Hindu guardian of the gates of Heaven and Hell, whose feathers are not plucked but are harvested as they fall out naturally—clay pots that cook the best traditional curries, jugs for water that double as percussion instruments, and decorative dot stickers for adorning ladies' foreheads (by the way, these do not mean that the lady is married). Here you can also find the white powder that's applied to the forehead after prayer, which is made from camphor and cow dung. (Shiva's chariot was drawn by a cow, and the dung symbolizes respect and serves as a reminder that all people will end up as ash. Camphor is a germ killer.)

The best of the souvenir shops is **Kuna's** (#3 Campbell Lane), where you'll find a great variety of handicrafts at fairly reasonable prices. Before you get into any shopping, it's good to know that when Indians shake their heads from left to right it is affirmative.

Across the street is:

6. **Little India Arcade.** Its 26 prewar shophouses have been restored to house shops with clothing, fabrics, jewelry, and ceremonial items.

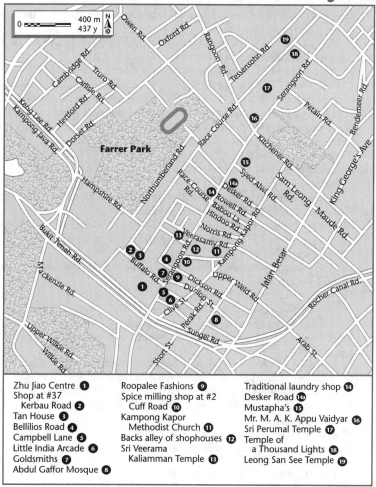

Zhu Jiao Centre ❶	Roopalee Fashions ❾	Traditional laundry shop ⓮
Shop at #37	Spice milling shop at #2	Desker Road ⓮ₐ
Kerbau Road ❷	Cuff Road ❿	Mustapha's ⓯
Tan House ❸	Kampong Kapor	Mr. M. A. K. Appu Vaidyar ⓰
Bellilios Road ❹	Methodist Church ⓫	Sri Perumal Temple ⓱
Campbell Lane ❺	Backs alley of shophouses ⓬	Temple of
Little India Arcade ❻	Sri Veerama	a Thousand Lights ⓲
Goldsmiths ❼	Kaliamman Temple ⓭	Leong San See Temple ⓳
Abdul Gaffor Mosque ❽		

Back out on Serangoon Road you'll find about a million:

7. Goldsmiths. They're all on the up and up, and charge the going rate for gold. This is one of the best places in Singapore to buy the stuff. At this end of Serangoon Road the jewelry is predominantly Indian filigree styling, which has different patterns to represent different Indian races. Toward the other end, selections turn more modern. Inside, check out the nine stone rings. Gemstones are placed in a grid pattern according to lucky horoscope prescriptions worked out by the Asmi.

Make a right onto Dunlop Street and follow it until you reach the:

8. Abdul Gafoor Mosque. Actually a mosque complex, it consists of the original mosque, a row of shophouses facing Dunlop Street, a prayer hall, and another row of houses facing the mosque. Most of the complex is from the late 19th century.

Backtrack to Serangoon Road or take the parallel Upper Dickson Road for a different view. Back on Serangoon Road, as you walk down you can shop for a **sari,** traditional attire for southern Indian women. Shop #84/86 is:

9. Roopalee Fashions. The ladies here will show you how to wrap the thing around yourself (or your wife). Northern Indian women's attire—*salwar kameez,* with long pants and elegant tunic—are better quality here than in India because all the better products are reserved for export.

Now's a good time to look in the gutter for red paint splashes, which are actually spit marks from betel nut chewers.

When you hit Cuff Road on the right, turn off and look for:

10. **#2 Cuff Road.** This is a spice milling shop with an authentic (and very loud) electric Indian spice mill. If you make it inside, be prepared to sneeze. On the porch at #2 Cuff Road, if you look up you'll see a square peephole in the ceiling. This was so people sleeping upstairs could see who's at the door in the night. It's very rare to find one of these, now that these old places are being restored.

At the end of Cuff Road is:

11. **Kampong Kapor Methodist Church.** The church is attended almost exclusively by Peranakans.

Across the street from the spice mill, walk through the back alley to see the:

12. **Back alley of shophouses.** The square patches on the backs of the buildings are where they'd collect the "honey buckets," as some of these places didn't have plumbing until the 1970s. Back alleys like this were introduced in 1915 to provide escape from fires.

When you reach Veerasamy Road, head back up to Serangoon, and just across the road you can't miss the:

13. **Sri Veerama Kaliamman Temple.** In front of the temple is a box in which worshippers smash coconuts, a symbolic smashing of the ego to ask to be shown the humble way and for the removal of personal obstacles. The coconuts have two tiny carved "eyes" so the coconut can "see" the obstacle to smash.

☕ **TAKE A BREAK** OK, it's curry break time. Walk northward on Serangoon Road to Race Course Lane, onto which you'll make a left. Follow this to the end, where you'll find Race Course Road and **Muthu's Curry Restaurant,** at #76/78. It ain't elegant, but you can't beat the price, and restaurants don't come much more authentic.

Cross Serangoon Road again and keep walking down until you reach the **coffee shop** at the corner of Norris Road, where you can watch chepatis being made.

Farther along at #270 Serangoon Road is:

14. **Singapore's one and only traditional laundry shop.** They no longer use charcoal-filled irons, but heavy old electric ones plugged in the ceiling. Catch a glimpse of the Chinese guy who's been working here since 1930. The varicose veins on his legs are one of this walking tour's more edifying sights.

14a. **Desker Road.** The more curious among you might want to take a walk down **Desker Road,** famous for its prostitution houses. Male travelers won't have any problems walking in this area, and curious women shouldn't have trouble if accompanied by a man. Women may want to stay away at night. Off Serangoon Road, turn right on Desker. The intersection of Lembu Road is where transvestites and prostitutes hang around in the evening. Across from Lembu Road, turn off Desker into the alley and at the first walkway intersection, turn left down the narrow alley behind the 2 blocks of buildings. As you walk, if you can peer in the rooms, you can find women waiting for business. Along the way, you'll find stands with people selling pornographic videotapes and displays with everything from aphrodisiacs to enlargement devices, birth control pills, and other related finds. Don't approach unattended displays—rumors have it the authorities plant sting operations here. In the evenings, there's a salesman here with a real sideshow-style sales technique for his wares. Other vendors have displays with Buddhist charms and amulets, and some even have household tools. Go figure. The alley lets out into a street that will let you backtrack to Serangoon Road.

At the corner of Syed Alwi Road is:

15. Mustapha's. This is a popular department store where you can find Indian fabrics, gold jewelry, and inexpensive appliances. (See chapter 8.)

Remain on Serangoon and cross Kitchener Road. The next left is Perumal Road. At #8, on the right, is:

16. Mr. M. A. K. Appu Vaidyar. The good doctor prescribes ayurvedic medicines (Sri Lankan mixtures of imported herbs and minerals) such as aphrodisiacs for men and women, immune boosters for children, and ointments for thick hair. Tell him what ails you and he'll find you some goo, with the help of a book to translate to English. Consultation costs vary, but can be as low as S$12 (US$7.55). Don't forget to take off your shoes.

Back out on Serangoon Road, just a half a block on the left is:

17. Sri Perumal Temple. The rear building on the temple grounds is a wedding hall. Ask the attendants if there's a wedding, and if there is, feel free to watch. You'll probably be invited for a meal. If you accept (which is absolutely customary, by the way), give a token gift to the couple—an envelope with money in odd amounts like S$21 or S$31 (never an even amount, for luck reasons) is customary. The best time to find weddings are on Saturdays and Sundays around 6 or 7pm.

At this point you can either backtrack down Perumal Street or cut through the blocks of housing estates to Race Course Road where on your right you'll find the:

18. Temple of a Thousand Lights. The temple shows influences of Thai architecture, and contains such elements as a replica of a footprint left by the Buddha in Ceylon, statues of baby boddhisattvas for whom worshippers leave candy and toys, and a wheel of fortune that you can spin for 50¢.

Across the street is the small and sleepy:

19. Leong San See Temple or Dragon Mountain Temple. Built in 1926, this Chinese Buddhist temple is darker and more serene than the Temple of a Thousand Lights.

WALKING TOUR 4
Arab Street & Kampong Glam

Start: The corner of Arab Street and Beach Road
Finish: Hajjah Fatimah Mosque on Beach Road
Time: About 2 hours, but depending on what kind of shopping frenzy you get into, and how long you want to stop for breaks, it may stretch to 3 or more
Best Time: Any day but Sunday, when Arab Street is closed

Kampong Glam is the traditional heart of Singaporean Muslim life. Since early colonial days, the area has attracted Muslims from diverse ethnic backgrounds, fusing them into one community by their common faith and lifestyle.

The name Kampong Glam is a combining of the Malay word for "village" (kampung) and the glam tree, which at one time grew in abundance in the area. Related to the eucalyptus, the glam tree produced an extract that was made into *minyak kaku putih,* an ointment used for treating ailments from earaches to arthritis, and as first aid for dressing wounds.

In 1819, the British made a treaty with Sultan Hussein Shah, then sultan of Singapore, to cede Singapore to the British East India Trading Company. As part of the agreement, the sultan was offered a stipend and given Kampong Glam as a settlement for his palace and subjects. The sultan's original settlement began at Beach Road, which was then at the water's edge, and extended back to the Rochore River, which is now Rochore Canal. From side to side, it stretched from what is now Rochore Road to Jalan Sultan. Sultan Hussein built his palace, Istana Kampong Glam, at the end of Sultan Gate and named the area Kota Raja, Malay for "The King's enclave." Over time, as parcels of land were sold off for burial grounds, schools, mosques, or farms, the area shrunk. Now all that remains of Kota Raja is the Istana itself.

Trade grew in the area as a wave of merchants and tradesmen moved in to serve and provision the large numbers of pilgrims who debarked from here on their journey to Mecca. Blacksmiths set up shops on Sultan Gate and Beach Road and provided ships with anchors, pulleys, and hooks. Tombstone carvers also made a killing in the area, due to the proximity of many local burial grounds.

Although the ethnic Arab population in Singapore has never reached large proportions, their influence is immediately obvious through such Kampong Glam street names as Bussorah Street, Muscat Street, Baghdad Street, Arab Street, and Haji Lane. This walking tour takes you down these streets, where elements of Muslim life still thrive—the regular prayers at the Sultan Mosque, mom-and-pop shops selling Malay and Muslim cultural and religious items, and stalls selling halal food. Unfortunately, some elements of Kampong Glam are slowly disappearing. The Istana, for instance, will soon be transformed into a modern museum (a sad event for many locals, to whom the structure has remained a symbol of Malay glories past), and you'll probably arrive just in time to see the last remains of the blacksmithing and tombstone-carving businesses, whose sad decline is testimony to the growing modernization of Singapore's industrial power.

At the corner of Arab Street and Beach Road is:

1. **Hishamuddin and Co.** With millions of baskets hanging and stacked all along the sidewalk, this shop has been captured by many a tourist camera and picture postcard.

    As you gaze down the rest of this seemingly ordinary street, this shop looks a lot more fun than the others, but don't let looks deceive: This street is one of the most treasured shopping places in Singapore, for travelers and locals alike. Arab Street shops have the best selection of fabrics, from silks to batiks. You'll also find large selections of sarongs, leather goods, jewelry, and curio treasures. Good thing there are money changers everywhere.

2. **Shopping Break.** If you're reading this at home, you'll think, "But the tour just started," but if you're standing on the corner of Arab Street, and I went and dragged you off right away, you'd be mad at me. Let's just get this over with right now.

    For interesting jewelry, brassware, and leather bags, try **Rishi Handicrafts** (58 Arab St.). **Aljunied Brothers** (#91) has a good selection of batik dresses, shirts, carpets, place mats, tablecloths, and other linens.

    C. Rashiwala Bros. (100 Arab St.) is a Malay wedding shop selling all you'd need to stage a ceremony, from traditional-style clothing to fancy bridal suite dressings. Check out the little carpets with built in compasses so you always know where Mecca is!

    Sham Sudeen Djamal & Co. (108 Arab St.) has open boxes and buckets containing spices of all kinds, many of which are surprisingly recognizable. **Kim Lee and Company** (#109) is fun for sewing notions and beads.

    Goldsmiths here have Western styles of jewelry as well as Javanese-influenced necklaces and brooches for Malay clothing. **Nam Hing Lin Kee Jewellery Pte. Ltd.** (159 Arab St.) is a reputable shop.

Arab Street & Kampong Glam Walking Tour

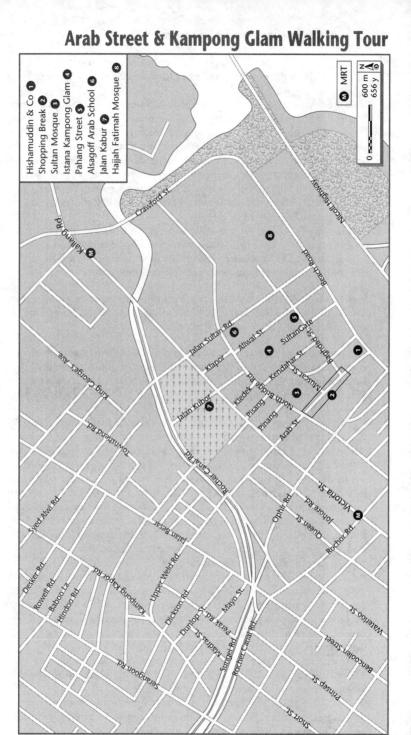

Hishamuddin & Co ❶
Shopping Break ❷
Sultan Mosque ❸
Istana Kampong Glam ❹
Pahang Street ❺
Alsagoff Arab School ❻
Jalan Kubur ❼
Hajjah Fatimah Mosque ❽

Ⓜ MRT

N

0 — 600 m
0 — 656 y

187

Arab Street is one of the best places to buy loose stones, but don't buy them on the street; buy them in the shops. **Bril Diamonds Pte. Ltd.** (123 Arab St.) is a good place to start.

Just off Arab Street are a couple of other noteworthy shops. **Singalang Jaya** (9 Baghdad St.) has an amazing selection of handmade *songkok,* the hats worn by Muslim men. **Jamal Kazura Aromatics** (728 North Bridge Rd.) sells alcohol-free perfumes in fragrant oil bases, as well as aromatics for burning, in scents of fruits, woods, and knock-offs of popular designer fragrances. (Why are they oil-based? Remember, Muslims cannot use alcohol in any form—not even in perfumes.)

Once you have taken in the shopping, the cultural portion of the tour begins. Off Arab Street, about midway between Beach Road and North Bridge Road is Muscat Street. Take it to reach the:

3. **Sultan Mosque.** This is the real center of Singapore's Muslim community, the present mosque was built in 1928 and was funded by donations from the Muslim community. The Saracenic and Mogul flavors of the architecture mask the fact that an Irish guy named Denis Santry actually designed the structure.

☕ **TAKE A BREAK**   If the shopping's got you worn out already, stop in **Zam Zam's** (☎ 65/298-7011) at 697/699 North Bridge Rd., behind Sultan Mosque, for a cool drink or a quick meal of murtabak.

Continue down Muscat to Kandahar Street. Make a right, then a left as soon as you see an opening in the compound wall to place you on the grounds of the:

4. **Istana Kampong Glam.** It may not look like much now, but this was the residence of the sultan of Singapore, and had remained the home of his descendants for over 150 years.

Exit Istana Kampong Glam through Sultan's Gate and follow to the intersection at **Baghdad Street** on your right and **Pahang Street** on your left. Just past this intersection on the right you can still see two remaining foundings at #37 and #39, where there was once a thriving community of metal workers who pounded out hardware for the merchant ships of yesterday. There was also a booming tombstone-carving trade here, a result of the many surrounding graveyards, but that is now completely extinct. Backtrack up Sultan Gate and take a peek around the corner of Baghdad Street to see if any discarded tombstones are still lying around. Interestingly enough, many of the tombstones that were carved here were made by Chinese artisans who had learned to mimic Arabic script.

Next, head across the intersection to:

5. **Pahang Street.** The entire row of refurbished blockhouses to the left has been owned since the houses were built in 1935 by Arab philanthropist Syed Abdul Rahman Taha Alsagoff. Some small details have been replaced, including the hanging Javanese lamps. As you head down Pahang Street towards Jalan Sultan, keep your eyes peeled for back alleyways, which are great places to see the older buildings, with their crumbling walls and makeshift add-ons.

When you reach Jalan Sultan, turn left. A ways up to the left is the:

6. **Alsagoff Arab School.** Established in 1912, it's the oldest girls' school in Singapore, and was the island's first Muslim school.

Deep in the back alley just beyond the school are street-side barbers. If you want a rare treat, have a shave and a haircut in a back alley. Better than one of those high-style salons you've been going to, don't ya think?

Continue up Jalan Sultan till you reach Victoria Street, and turn left onto it. Along Victoria is a road called:

7. Jalan Kabur. Literally translated as "Cemetery Road," you can find along both its sides a number of ancient royal tombs as well as the graves of Kampong Glam's early settlers. The somewhat serene and peaceful atmosphere of the cemetery, with its shady trees, offers a stark contrast to the rest of Kampong Glam.

Backtrack down Jalan Sultan until you get to Beach Road. Turn left and follow Beach till, on your left, you see:

8. Hajjah Fatimah Mosque. Named for a wealthy businesswoman and socialite from Malacca, the mosque contains a prayer hall, ablution area, gardens and mausoleums, and a few other buildings. Hajjah Fatimah herself is buried in a private room to the side the main prayer hall, along with her daughter and son-in-law.

2 Organized Tours

Many private outfits provide guided tours (in English) that can take you around to see the sights.

BUS TOURS   Trolley tours of urban Singapore are offered by **Singapore Explorer** (☎ 65/339-6833 or 65/338-9205); RMG Tours (☎ 65/220-1661), offers 3¹/₂-hour tours that take in sights throughout the country; **Holiday Tours and Travel** (☎ 65/733-3226), runs half- and full-day tours of major attractions; and **Singapore Sightseeing Tour East** (☎ 65/332-3755; www.singnet.com.sg/~sstep), offers unique theme tours such as a cultural tour through the major historical districts, the Founding Footsteps of Raffles Tour, and the Shop Till U Drop Tour, as well as more standard sightseeing tours.

BOAT & FERRY TOURS   **Eastwind Organisation** (☎ 65/533-3432 or 65/532-4740), sails Chinese junks along the Singapore River, out into the harbour, and around Singapore's southern islands; **Singapore River Boat** (☎ 65/339-6833 or 65/338-9205), offers a half-hour tour that departs from the Clarke Quay Jetty; **Singapore River Cruises & Leisure** (☎ 65/336-6119 or 65/227-6863), offers a half-hour water taxi tour that takes you up and down the Singapore River and out into the harbour; and **Watertours** (☎ 65/533-9811), offers a junk cruise, a catamaran cruise, and also a trip aboard the *Admiral Cheng Ho,* an exact replica of a famous and very ornate Imperial vessel from the Ming Dynasty.

A CABLECAR TOUR   **Singapore Cable Car** (☎ 65/270-8855) offers a neat way to see some of Singapore on the way to Sentosa—even if you turn around and come straight back. If you depart from Mount Faber Park, the ride is longer, cruising over green forest growth and bungalows before meeting the Cable Car Towers (at the World Trade Centre) and heading out over Keppel Harbour. They operate from 8:30am to 9pm daily and cost up to S$6.50 (US$3.80) for adults and S$3 (US$1.90) for children.

PERSONAL TOURS   For the ultimate in-depth sightseeing experience, you can hire a personal guide from **The Registered Tourist Guides Association of Singapore** (☎ 65/339-2110), which handles training and licensing of all of the official tour guides in Singapore. These people are the experts. They usually handle groups, but are perfectly willing to take small groups and individuals around the city. Rates are from S$35 to S$50 (US$22 to 31.50) per hour, depending on the expertise of the tour guide you request.

8 Shopping

In Singapore, shopping is a sport—from the practiced glide through haute couture boutiques to skillful back-alley bargaining to win the best prices on Asian treasures. The shopping here is always exciting, with something to satiate every pro shopper's appetite.

From its humble beginnings as an operation for the British East India Trading Company, Singapore has always been a trading mecca. When Sir Stamford Raffles first set foot on its shore, he envisioned a free port to serve as a go-between for trade from China in the north and Indonesia to the south to Europe and India to the west. In the early days of maritime trade, the Northeast Monsoon from November to March would blow in junks from China, Indo-China, and Siam, while during the autumn months, the Southwest Monsoon would escort in Bugis and Indonesian traders. Boat Quay was in its trading glory, with spices, silks, gold, tin, rattan, and, of course, opium.

Today, the focal point of shopping in Singapore is **Orchard Road,** a very long stretch of glitzy shopping malls packed with Western clothing stores, from designer wear to cheap chic, and many other mostly imported finds. Singaporeans have a love-hate relationship with Orchard Road. As the shopping malls developed, they brought hip styles into the reach of everyday Singaporeans, adding a cosmopolitan sheen to Singapore style. But Orchard Road also ushered in a new culture of obsessive consumerism. One working mother told me about her school-age son who spent a month working at a job for S$200 a week, only to take all his earnings down to Orchard Road and squander it on a pair of S$800 jeans. You can see this kind of blatant image-consciousness in the throngs of teenagers that crowd the malls on weekends and school holidays.

Even to outsiders, Orchard Road is a drug; however, most of the clothing and accessories shops sell Western imports, and while the prices may be bargain-basement for Japanese visitors, the rest of us will find that the prices of Western brand-name fashions are no less expensive than at home. And it's all the same stuff you can get at home, too. I tried to find a unique gift to bring for a Singaporean friend, something they could not get in Singapore, so I went to the gift shop at the Metropolitan Museum of Art in New York City. Sure enough, as soon as I got to Singapore I found that the Met had opened two outlets on Orchard Road.

In the seventies, before the malls, Singapore was truly a shopping heaven. Local and regional handicrafts were skillfully made by local artisans, who by now have almost all been squeezed out of their quaint shops by rising real estate prices. And who can forget Thieves' Market, a sprawling series of awning-covered back alleys that teemed on weekends with table displays of antique finds from the region; brass and gems from Thailand; jade and ivory from China; batiks from Indonesia; and knockoff luggage, clothing, watches, leather goods, and pirate recordings, all for a bargain. The government shut the place down in the late eighties when the sale of drugs started to take the place of other goods, and as the government became more aware of copyright violation practices.

Nostalgia aside, there are still some nifty shopping areas around, like the places on **Arab Street,** the night market out at **Bugis Street,** and at the small flea market in **Chinatown,** where you can pick up odd items for bargains. Anybody who's been around Singapore long enough will tell you that most of the really juicy bargains went the way of the dodo when the huge shopping malls came to town, but if you know the prices of certain items that you'd like, some comparison shopping may save you a little money. In this chapter, I'll give you some tips on where to find the better merchandise, competitive prices, and memorable shopping experiences.

1 Singapore Shopping Tips

HOURS   Shopping malls are generally open from 10am to 8pm Monday through Saturday, with some stores keeping shorter Sunday hours. The malls sometimes remain open until 10pm on holidays. Smaller shops are open from around 10am to 5pm Monday through Saturday, but are almost always closed on Sundays. Hours will vary from shop to shop. Arab Street is closed on Sundays.

PRICES   Almost all of the stores in shopping malls have fixed prices. Sometimes these stores will have seasonal sales, especially in July, when they have the month-long **Great Singapore Sale,** during which prices are marked down, sometimes up to 50% or 75%. In the smaller shops and at street vendors, prices are never marked, and people will quote you higher prices than the going rate, in anticipation of the bargaining ritual. These are the places to find good prices, if you negotiate well. Which leads me to . . .

BARGAINING   Also called haggling, this standard Asian routine is difficult at first for many Westerners, who are accustomed to accepting fixed prices without an argument. For tips on mastering the process, see the "Getting in Touch with Your Inner Haggler" feature in this chapter.

GST TOURIST REFUND SCHEME   When you shop in stores that display the blue "Tax Free for Tourists" logo, the government will refund the goods and services tax (GST) you pay on purchases totaling S$300 (US$189) or more. Upon request, the sales clerk will fill out a refund form, which you retain with your receipt. If you've purchased up to S$300 at the same store, but on different dates, you can still claim the refund for all of the items. Have the sales clerk help you fill out the form. When you leave Singapore, present your refund forms at Customs along with your passport, and let them see the goods you've purchased to show that you're taking them out of the country with you. Customs will stamp the forms, which you then present at any of the Cash Refund Counters in the airport for an on-the-spot cash refund—or, if you like, you can mail in the stamped form to receive a check or a direct transfer of the amount to your bank account. Certain restrictions apply—if you've been working in Singapore, for instance, or fail to take the items out of the country within

Urban Singapore Shopping

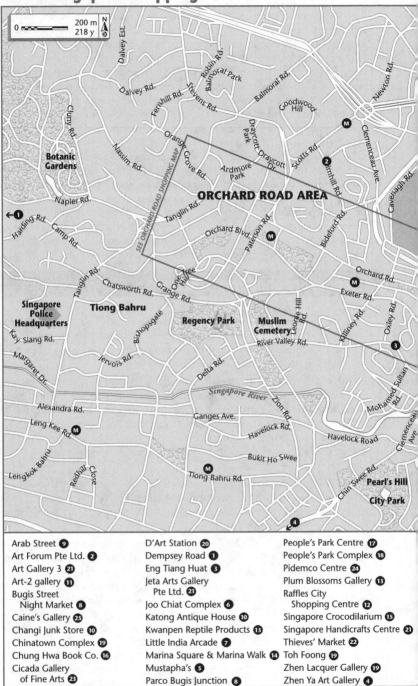

Arab Street **9**
Art Forum Pte Ltd. **2**
Art Gallery 3 **21**
Art-2 gallery **11**
Bugis Street
  Night Market **8**
Caine's Gallery **25**
Changi Junk Store **10**
Chinatown Complex **19**
Chung Hwa Book Co. **16**
Cicada Gallery
  of Fine Arts **23**

D'Art Station **20**
Dempsey Road **1**
Eng Tiang Huat **3**
Jeta Arts Gallery
  Pte Ltd. **21**
Joo Chiat Complex **6**
Katong Antique House **10**
Kwanpen Reptile Products **13**
Little India Arcade **7**
Marina Square & Marina Walk **14**
Mustapha's **5**
Parco Bugis Junction **8**

People's Park Centre **17**
People's Park Complex **18**
Pidemco Centre **24**
Plum Blossoms Gallery **13**
Raffles City
  Shopping Centre **12**
Singapore Crocodilarium **15**
Singapore Handicrafts Centre **21**
Thieves' Market **22**
Toh Foong **19**
Zhen Lacquer Gallery **19**
Zhen Ya Art Gallery **4**

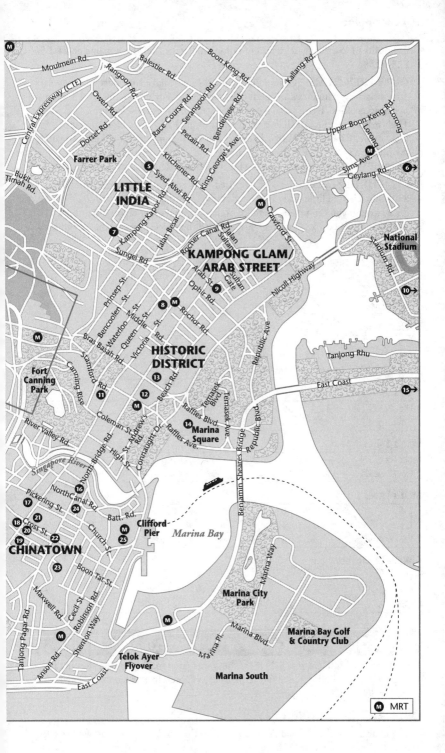

2 months of the purchase date. For complete details, call the hot line at ☎ 65/ 225-6238.

DUTY-FREE ITEMS   Changi International Airport has a large duty-free shop that carries cigarettes, liquor, wine, perfumes, cosmetics, watches, jewelry, and other designer accessories. There's also a chain of duty-free stores in Singapore called **DFS.** Their main branch is at Millenia Walk, next to the Pan Pacific Hotel down by Marina Square (☎ 65/332-2118). The store is huge and impressive, but unfortunately, the only truly duty-free items are cigarettes and liquor—everything else carries the standard 3% GST. Feel free to apply for the Tourist Refund Scheme here, though.

CLOTHING SIZES   Those of you used to shopping in big-and-tall stores will unfortunately find little ready-to-wear clothing in Singapore that'll fit you—but that doesn't mean you can't take advantage of the many excellent tailors around town. If you wear a regular size, however, this chart will help you convert your size to local measures.

Ladies' Dress Sizes

U.S.	8	10	12	14	16	18
U.K.	30	32	34	36	38	40
Continental	36	38	40	42	44	46

Ladies' Shoes

U.S.	5	$5^1/_2$	6	$6^1/_2$	7	$7^1/_2$	8	$8^1/_2$	9
U.K.	$3^1/_2$	4	$4^1/_2$	5	$5^1/_2$	6	$6^1/_2$	7	$7^1/_2$
Continental	35	35	36	37	38	38	38	39	40

Men's Suits

U.S. & U.K.	34	36	38	40	42	44	46	48
Continental	44	46	48	50	52	54	56	58

Men's Shirts

U.S. & U.K.	14	$14^1/_2$	15	$15^1/_2$	16	$16^1/_2$	17	$17^1/_2$
Continental	36	37	38	39	40	41	42	43

Men's Shoes

U.S.	7	$7^1/_2$	8	$8^1/_2$	9	$9^1/_2$	10	$10^1/_2$	11	$11^1/_2$
U.K.	$6^1/_2$	7	$7^1/_2$	8	$8^1/_2$	9	$9^1/_2$	10	$10^1/_2$	11
Continental	39	40	41	42	43	43	44	44	45	45

Children's Clothes

U.S.	2	4	6	8	10	13	15
U.K.	1	2	5	7	9	10	12
Continental	1	2	5	7	9	10	12

2 The Shopping Scene, Part I: Western-Style Malls

Orchard Road is the biggie, as I've said, but other good mall spots are at Marina Bay, Bugis Junction, Raffles City, and at the Raffles Hotel. In this section, I'll give you the lowdown on the hot spots.

ORCHARD ROAD AREA

The malls on **Orchard Road** are a tourist attraction in their own right, with smaller boutiques and specialty shops intermingled with huge department stores. **Takashimaya** and **Isetan** are upmarket department stores from Japan. **Lane**

Getting in Touch with Your Inner Haggler

In Singapore, many shopkeepers cling to the old tradition of not fixing prices on their merchandise, instead making every item's purchase a little performance piece by insisting their customers bargain for it. For Westerners who are unaccustomed to this tradition, bargaining can be embarrassing and frustrating at first—after all, you don't know the protocol; you're just not sure what to do. All it takes is a little practice, though, and soon you'll be bargaining with the best of 'em. I've seen many Westerners go into their first market like lambs to the slaughter, only to loosen up after a few encounters and begin to enjoy the process for the sport it really is.

The most important thing to remember when bargaining is to keep a friendly, good-natured banter between you and the seller. Getting him or her mad won't save you a dime, and if you get 'em really riled up, they won't sell you anything at any price and will just throw you out. But don't let that scare you; just be nice and patient, and you'll get where you want to go.

One important tip for bargaining is to first have an idea of the value of what you're buying. This can be difficult for unusual items, but a little comparison shopping here may help you out. Try to look like you live in Singapore. A lot of the local European and North American residents shop at these places, so you won't look out of place. If a salesperson asks you where you are from, don't smile and say London or San Francisco, but toss out a blasé "Tampines" (pronounced *"tampin-ees"*) or "Holland Village" without even looking up. If they think you're a local, they'll try to get away with less.

A simple "How much?" is the place to start, to which they'll reply with their top price. Let the bidding begin! It's always good to come back with a little smile and ask "Is that your best price?" They'll probably come down a bit, but if it's obvious they're trying to soak you, tell them you'll pay a price that's about half of what they had originally offered; otherwise, just knock about 30% or 40% off. The standard reaction from them will always be to look at you like you're a crazy person for even suggesting such a discount, but don't falter! This is standard technique. For each little bit their price comes down, bring yours up just a bit until you reach a price you like. If you're having trouble talking them down, try these strategies: When buying more than one item, ask for a generous discount on the less expensive item. If you've seen it cheaper elsewhere, tell them. Or you can pull the old, "But I only have 20 dollars" ploy. (Just make sure you don't turn around and ask them to change a 50!) Try anything, even if it's just a wink and a little "Don't you have any special discounts for ladies shopping on Wednesdays?"

Some people have said that once you start the bargaining ritual, it's rude to walk away and not purchase the item. Here's a news flash: It's your money, and if you still don't feel comfortable shelling it out, then don't do it under any feeling of obligation. Besides, the final bargaining strategy is to just politely say "No thank you" and walk away. You'll be surprised at how fast prices can come down as you're walking out the door.

Crawford comes out of the West, as does **K-Mart**. **John Little Pte. Ltd.** is one of the oldest department stores in Singapore, followed by **Robinson's,** and **Tang's** is historic, having grown from a cart-full of merchandise nurtured by the business savvy of local entrepreneur C. K. Tang. Boutiques range from the younger styles of **Stussy** and **Guess?** to the sophisticated fashions of **Chanel** and **Yves Saint Laurent.** You'll also find antiques, oriental carpets, art galleries and curio shops, Tower Records and HMV music stores, MPH and Times bookstores, video arcades, and scores of restaurants, local food courts, fast-food joints, and coffeehouses—even a few discos, which open in the evenings (see chapter 9). It's hard to say when Orchard Road is not crowded, but it's definitely a mob scene on weekends, when kids don't have classes and come to hang around, looking for fun.

Centrepoint. 176 Orchard Rd.

Centrepoint is home to Robinson's department store, which first opened in Singapore in 1858. There are about 150 other shops in this mall. On the ground floor are fast-food outlets, and on the fourth level are two large English bookstores, Times and MPH.

Far East Plaza. 14 Scotts Rd.

Far East Plaza is a bustle of little shops that sell everything from CDs to punk fashions, luggage to camera equipment, eyewear to souvenirs. Mind yourself here: Most of these shops do not display prices, but rather gauge the price depending on how wealthy the customer appears. If you must shop here, use your shrewdest bargaining powers. It may pay off to wear something that's seen better days.

The Heeren. Orchard Rd.

Thanks to the opening of a Singapore branch of Britain's HMV music stores, the Heeren is the latest hangout joint for teens. The front entrance of the mall is lined with towers of video monitors flashing and blaring the latest in American and British chart toppers. There also happens to be a nice cafe to the side, with a garden for enjoying a cup of coffee, tea, or a snack. At the midway point along the Orchard Road stretch, it's a recommended stop for a break.

Hilton Shopping Gallery. 581 Orchard Rd.

The shopping arcade at the Hilton International Hotel is the most exclusive shopping in Singapore. Gucci, Donna Karan, Missoni, and Luis Vuitton are just a few of the international design houses that have made this their Singapore home.

Lucky Plaza. 304 Orchard Plaza.

The map of this place will take hours to decipher, as there are somewhere over 400 stores here. (No kidding.) It's basically known for sportswear, camera equipment, watches, and luggage. If you buy electronics, please make sure you get an international warranty with your purchase. Also, like Far East Plaza, Lucky Plaza is a notorious rip-off problem for tourists. Make sure you come here prepared to fend off slick sales techniques. It may also help to take the government's advice and avoid touts and offers that sound too good to be true.

Ngee Ann City / Takashimaya Shopping Centre. 391 Orchard Rd.

Takashimaya is another Japanese department store import, but Ngee Ann City has many more smaller boutiques to attract shoppers. Alfred Dunhill, Chanel, Coach, Tiffany & Co., Royal Copenhagen, and a Waterford and Wedgwood boutique are found here, along with many other local and international fashion shops.

Orchard Towers. 400 Orchard Rd.

This mall is a mix of smaller shops dealing in cheap chic clothing, jewelry, eyewear, tailoring, books, and more. There's a 7-Eleven on the ground floor for Americans experiencing screwy homesickness, and a Jason's Supermarket at the back, specializing in imported foods.

Orchard Road Shopping

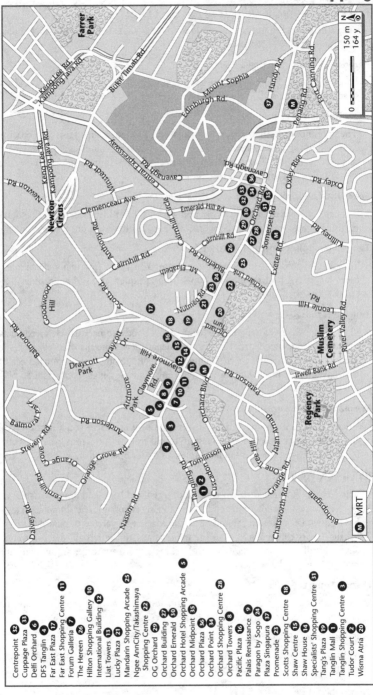

Centrepoint **32**
Cuppage Plaza **33**
Delfi Orchard **6**
DFS Tanglin **4**
Far East Plaza **17**
Far East Shopping Centre **11**
Forum Galleria **7**
The Heeren **26**
Hilton Shopping Gallery **10**
International Building **12**
Liat Towers **13**
Lucky Plaza **21**
Mandarin Shopping Arcade **25**
Ngee AnnCity/Takashimaya Shopping Centre **22**
OG Orchard **29**
Orchard Building **27**
Orchard Emerald **30**
Orchard Hotel Shopping Arcade **5**
Orchard Midpoint **35**
Orchard Plaza **36**
Orchard Point **34**
Orchard Shopping Centre **28**
Orchard Towers **8**
Pacific Plaza **16**
Palais Renaissance **9**
Paragon by Sogo **24**
Plaza Singapura **37**
Promenade **23**
Scotts Shopping Centre **18**
Shaw Centre **15**
Shaw House **14**
Specialists' Shopping Centre **31**
Tang's Plaza **19**
Tanglin Mall **1**
Tanglin Shopping Centre **3**
Tudor Court **2**
Wisma Atria **20**

197

Palais Renaissance. 390 Orchard Rd.

Shops here include upmarket boutiques like Krizia and Guerlain. More shops are expected to move in soon.

Paragon by Sogo. 290 Orchard Rd.

Paragon by Sogo is another upmarket shopping mall. Emanuel Ungaro, Escada, Van Cleef et Arpels, and the Paloma Picasso Boutique are some of its resident stores.

Shaw House. 350 Orchard Rd.

The main floors of Shaw House are taken up by Isetan, a large Japanese department store with designer boutiques for men's and women's fashions, accessories, and cosmetics. On the fifth level is the Lido Theatre, a cinema complex showing new releases from Hollywood and around the world.

Specialists' Shopping Centre. 277 Orchard Rd.

The anchor store in this smaller shopping mall is John Little, Singapore's oldest department store, which opened in 1845. The prices, however, are very 1990s.

Tanglin Shopping Centre. Tanglin Rd.

Tanglin Shopping Centre is unique and fun. You won't find many clothing stores here, but you'll find shop after shop selling antiques, art, and collectibles—from curios to carpets.

Tang's Plaza. 320 Orchard Rd.

C. K. Tang was an entrepreneur who once sold goods from a cart. He saved his pennies and later opened C. K. Tang, a small department store that did very well. Now, Tang's is a department store that competes with all the other international megastores that have moved in. The beauty is that Tang's is truly Singaporean, and its history is a local legend.

Wisma Atria. 435 Orchard Rd.

Wisma Atria is a favorite hangout for the younger set. Here you'll find everything from Nine West Shoes to a Levi's store mixed in with numerous eyewear, cosmetics, and high- and low-fashion boutiques, all under one roof.

MARINA BAY

The Marina Bay area arose from a plot of reclaimed land, and now boasts the giant Suntec City convention center and all the hotels, restaurants, and shopping malls that have grown up around it. Shopping in the Marina Bay area is popular for everyone because of its convenience, with the major malls and hotels all interconnected by covered walkways and pedestrian bridges, making it easy to get around with minimal exposure to the elements.

Marina Square. 6 Raffles Blvd.

Marina Square is a huge complex that, in addition to a wide variety of shops, has a cinema, fast-food outlets and cafes, pharmacies, and convenience stores.

Millenia Walk. 9 Raffles Blvd.

Millenia Walk is smaller than Marina Square, but has more upmarket boutiques like Fendi, Guess?, and Liz Claiborne, to name a few.

AROUND THE CITY CENTRE

While the Historic District doesn't have as many malls as the Orchard Road area, it still has some good shopping. Raffles City is a very large mall, and convenient because it sits right atop the City Hall MRT stop. One of my favorite places to go, however, is the very upmarket Raffles Hotel Shopping Arcade, where I like to window shop and dream about actually being able to afford some of the stuff on display.

Parco Bugis Junction. Victoria St.

Here you'll find restaurants—both fast food and fine dining—mixed in with clothing retailers, most of which sell fun fashions for the younger set.

Raffles City Shopping Centre. 252 North Bridge Rd.

Raffles City S.C. is located right on top of the City Hall MRT station, which makes it a very well-visited mall. Men's and women's fashions, books, cosmetics, and accessories are sold in shops here, along with gifts.

Raffles Hotel Shopping Arcade. 328 North Bridge Rd.

These shops are mostly haute couture; however, there is the Raffles Hotel gift shop for interesting souvenirs. For golfers, there's a Jack Nicklaus signature store.

3 The Shopping Scene, Part II: Multicultural Shopping

For shopping malls that are a little out of the ordinary, try the **People's Park Complex** in Chinatown (1 Park Rd.) for Chinese goods and housewares, jade, and jewelry at good prices. Down Eu Tong Sen Street from People's Park Complex is **People's Park Centre** (101 Upper Cross St.). Look there for Yue Hua, an emporium for imported Chinese goods. Across the street from People's Park is the **Chinatown Complex,** with vendor stalls selling inexpensive souvenirs, cheongsams (those sexy Chinese sleeveless dresses with the Mandarin collar and side slits), leather goods, luggage, and household items.

Also in the Chinatown vicinity, you'll find **Pidemco Centre** (95 South Bridge Rd.), which is wall-to-wall goldsmiths and jewelers.

In Chinatown, along Smith, Trengganu, and Pagoda streets, you can shop for Chinese handicrafts, art, curio items, and souvenirs (although not at the best prices). Ask around and you may find some collections of special designer watches and bags.

Holland Village (Holland Road Shopping Centre, 211 Holland Ave.; SBS no. 77 from Orchard Road) is where all the expatriates shop, and is a good place for pottery, rattan goods, ethnic handicrafts, and souvenirs at slightly lower prices than you'll find in town.

Joo Chiat Complex out on Geylang Road is the place to go for modern silk, cotton, and polyester fabrics, and for other Malay and Muslim goods. Take the MRT to Paya Lebar and walk down Geylang Road.

Small shops line the sides of **Arab Street,** where you can find Indonesian handicrafts, batik sarongs, rattan goods, jewelry, leather goods, spices, and some good bargaining.

On Serangoon Road in **Little India,** you'll find gold in Western and Indian designs, Indian-style fashions, watches, luggage, and Indian arts and handicrafts. At the corner of Serangoon Road and Hastings Road is the **Little India Arcade,** with 26 shops full of clothing and crafts. Down Serangoon Road is **Mustapha's,** a favorite with the locals for Indian silk, gold jewelry, and cheap household appliances *(watch out, though:* they don't have international warranties).

OUTDOOR MARKETS

A few outdoor markets still exist, though it ain't like the old days. At the Bugis MRT station, across from Parco Bugis Junction, is a **night market** (which is also open during the day) for cheap chic, some curio items, accessories, and compact discs. **In**

Chinatown, on the corner of South Bridge Road and Cross Street you'll find what people sometimes refer to as **Thieves' Market,** which is a flea market of mostly attic finds laid out on blankets. Feel free to bargain like mad at these places.

4 Best Buys

Basically, almost anything that you can buy in Singapore you can buy at home for a comparable price. There are, however, some things you can get here that are real steals. Following is a list of some of your better buys in Singapore. Later in the chapter, I'll suggest specific shopping locations or stores for each type of item.

ANTIQUES   Antiques are fun to shop for in Singapore. Once upon a time, the locals preferred new over old furnishings, but lately a resurgence of interest in heritage has made wealthy locals dig through their attics, jacking up prices for the old treasures they find. A stroll through some of the antique shops will still uncover beautiful and unusual treasures, and—inflated prices and all—you won't get a better price back home.

ART GALLERIES   Art galleries display fascinating pieces of Singaporean traditional and modern works, and there are galleries that specialize in regional work and even in Chinese reproduction pieces. Pottery is also great shopping here, from delicate antique pieces to reproductions to regulation household blue and white (blue-and-white glaze bowls, plates, and cups depicting Chinese landscape scenes, bamboo, birds, etc., and available at prices that are truly worth writing home about).

EYEGLASSES, LUGGAGE & WATCHES   A few other things to add to your shopping list are eyeglasses, which in Singapore are dirt cheap compared to anywhere else; luggage, which can be bargained down in price (even the good designer knockoffs!); and watches, which can also be bargained for (again, even the good designer knockoffs).

FABRICS   Exquisite fabrics like Chinese silk, Thai silk, batiks, and inexpensive gingham are very affordable and the selections are extensive. If you have time, see if you can have something tailored. There are many fine men's tailors for suits and slacks made to fit. For the ladies, the ultimate souvenir is to order a **cheongsam,** the Chinese dress with the Mandarin collar, frog clasps, and high slits up the side! Readymade ones of lesser-quality silk and sateens are really cheap and fun, but a tailored full-length dress from the silk of your choosing is an elegant addition to your formal attire.

On another note, if you've ever dreamed of owning a sarong or sari, you can get them in Singapore for very reasonable prices.

JEWELRY & ACCESSORIES   Crocodile skin products are well made and affordable at a couple of specialty shops (see below). Jewelry is also a bargain. Gold, which is sold at the day's rate, is fashioned into both modern styles and to Chinese and Indian tastes. Loose stones, either precious or semiprecious, are abundant in many reputable shops, and can be set for you during your stay.

ORIENTAL CARPETS   While you're in Singapore, you may wish to browse around in an oriental carpet shop. Museum-quality handmade carpets from all over Asia make their way to store showcases in Singapore, and even if you're not in the market per se, these rugs are as much fine art as any painting or sculpture, and a walk through a good carpet store can bring history and culture to life.

PEWTER   Malaysia is home to the world's largest pewter manufacturer, **Royal Selangor,** which has in its collection over a thousand different tableware and gift items in both contemporary and traditional styles. There are several outlets in Singapore, and catalogs for you to take with you.

SOUTHEAST ASIAN HANDICRAFTS   Naturally, Southeast Asian handicrafts are all cheaper here than as imports in the West. But if you plan to shop for these things, and Singapore is merely a stop on a list of other Southeast Asian destinations, don't buy that Indonesian mask here; instead, wait until you get to Jakarta for the best selection and price. The downside, however, is that sometimes countries export the finest merchandise, saving only the shoddier varieties for domestic sales.

SPICES   You may not think to buy spices on your holiday, but if the fancy strikes you to shop for some, you'll marvel at the selection, quality, and prices. Nutmeg, black pepper, ginger, curry, and saffron are just a few of the Southeast Asian spices used every day in Western kitchens and marked up every day at Western stores. Small quantities will fit snugly in your suitcase, and can make surprising gifts for the gourmets in your life. Besides, maybe you'll get a delicious meal in return!

5 Shopping A to Z

ANTIQUES

At the northern tip of Orchard Road is the mellow **Tanglin Shopping Centre** (Tanglin Road), whose quiet halls are just packed with little antique boutiques. Tanglin is a quiet place, which adds to the museum feel as you stroll past window displays of paintings, pottery, tapestries, and curio items made of jade or brass—all kinds of excellent, quality collectibles and gifts. Some good shops are **Malaysia Arts & Crafts Pte. Ltd.** (Basement 1; ☎ 65/737-4747), **Tzen Gallery** (Basement 1; ☎ 65/734-4339), **Antique Junction** (Level 1; ☎ 65/735-2816), **Antiques of the Orient Pte. Ltd.** (Level 1; ☎ 65/735-6315), and **Ling Antique House** (Level 3; ☎ 65/732-1422). There are many more, though. This is a place to really explore.

Just next to Tanglin Shopping Centre is Tudor Court, where you'll find **Lopoburi Arts & Antiques** (☎ 65/735-2579) and its large selection of Buddha sculptures.

To get an eyeful of some local furnishings in antique Indonesian, Chinese, and Peranakan styles, take a taxi out to **Dempsey Road** and walk up the hill to the warehouses. Inside each warehouse is a dealer, with enticing names like **Vintage Palace Pte. Ltd.** (Blk. 7 #01-03/04; ☎ 65/479-2181), **Asia Passion** (Blk. 13 #01-02; ☎ 65/473-1339), **Yesterdays Antiques & Curios** (Blk. 13 #01-03A; ☎ 65/476-4831), **Journey East Pte. Ltd.** (Blk. 13 #01-04; ☎ 65/473-1693), and **Eastern Discoveries** (Blk. 26 #01-04; ☎ 65/475-1814). There are over a dozen places here, each specializing in different wares. Some have large furniture pieces, from carved teak Indonesian-style furniture to authentic pieces from mainland China. Some have smaller items, like antique baskets, carved scale weights from the old opium trade, or collections of Buddha statues. There are also oriental carpet shops mixed in. The stores on Dempsey Road are all open daily from around 10:30am to 6:30pm, and close for lunch at midday. As with all of the antique shops in Singapore, they'll help you locate a reliable shipper to send your purchases home.

Other places of interest are out in **Geylang.** The **Katong Antique House** (208 East Coast Rd.; ☎ 65/345-8544), carries a unique collection of old items from Peranakan homes and closets, including the exquisitely embroidered *kebayas* (blouses) and fine Peranakan beaded slippers. Call the proprietor beforehand to schedule an appointment. Cross the street and walk up Joo Chiat Road to Duku Road; off Duku take the first left on Everitt. At No. 4 is the showroom for the **Changi Junk Store** (☎ 65/348-4917), where you'll find items like Chinese, Peranakan, and Indonesian

---

Shopping for Peranakan Antiques

Singapore is a dream come true for the antique collector. Recent trends toward cosmopolitan tastes brings to Singapore a wide selection of antiques from China, Burma, Thailand, and Indonesia; however, if it's local pieces you're interested in, you want to look at Peranakan furniture. Also called Malacca or Straits-Chinese furniture, these pieces are what you'd find in the wealthy Peranallan homes of Singapore and Malaysia. The style can be divided into three types. The first is the **blackwood and rosewood furniture** that was traditionally made by Chinese cabinetmakers. Some of these pieces have mother-of-pearl inlaid patterns in floral designs. The second type is the carved or reddish brown lacquer **namwood furniture,** with elaborate carvings that are sometimes gilded in gold. The third type is the **European-inspired furniture** made out of teakwood. Although these pieces have an overall Western form, upon closer examination you'll find that they have distinctly Chinese motifs.

The blackwood and rosewood pieces are made using traditional Chinese joinery techniques. Mechanical fasteners and pegs are not used, but rather, the pieces are held together by complex mortise and tenons. This furniture can be identified by its use of elaborate carvings, inlays, and, in some cases, marble tabletops and chair seats. Most styles copy Chinese furniture styles from the Ming and Ching dynasties and are imported from China. In this style, you'll find chairs, stools, settees, opium beds, tea tables, half round tables, and altar tables.

Namwood is less dense than blackwood or rosewood, and carves very easily. When namwood is finished it is almost always painted and lacquered because of its soft density and coarse texture. These pieces generally don't appear in as good condition as other pieces because the wood shrinks with age and requires repairs. This furniture was reserved primarily for ceremonial pieces, including altar tables, carved screens, and gilded decorations. You can also find chairs, tables, opium beds, and wedding cabinets.

Teakwood furniture is very European in styling and construction technique. Mechanical fasteners are used, and you'll often see features such as turned legs, although some pieces use traditional Chinese joinery methods and carved legs. What distinguishes teakwood furniture from European furniture is that the carvings and decorations are Chinese mixed in with familiar Queen Anne cabriole legs and aspects of Chippendale and Hepplewhite. In teakwood you'll find chairs, dining tables, tea tables, wardrobes, cabinets, and bureaus.

---

carved wood panels, large old cabinets, chairs, and tables. Most of the pieces are in desperate need of refinishing and maybe a few minor repairs, but for a bargain hunter who's handy with lacquer thinner and steel wool, there are some real diamonds in the rough here.

CROCODILE PRODUCTS

Crocodile and other reptile-skin products are really big in Singapore. On Orchard Road, high fashions created from these skins are for sale at **Kwanpen Reptile Products** at Raffles Hotel Arcade (☎ **65/334-0601**).

Probably the favorite places to go for crocodile are **Jurong Crocodile Paradise** (241 Jalan Ahmad Ibrahim; ☎ **65/261-8866**) and **Singapore Crocodilarium** (730 East Coast Pkwy.; ☎ **65/447-3722**). They both have showrooms filled with crocodile goods, as well as pelts from other exotic beasts.

EYEGLASSES

Eyeglasses? Why would anyone want to buy eyeglasses on their holiday? Because in Singapore they're dirt cheap, that's why. For the price of one pair of frames with prescription lenses in the United States, I can get a pair of prescription glasses, a pair of prescription sunglasses, contact lenses, and even have my old frames re-lensed. If you can beat that at home, do it. If not, take advantage while you can.

The reason why they're so cheap is because the government does not have as strict regulations on optometry as they have in the West. However, I assure you the larger prescription firms are very good at what they do. You'll get a cheap price, but not cheap quality. Go to **Capitol Optical,** which has many branches. Centrally located ones are at #03-132 Far East Plaza (☎ **65/736-0365**), #01-77 Lucky Plaza (☎ **65/ 734-4166**), and 435 Orchard Rd. #03-39 (☎ **65/732-2401**).

FABRICS

Most fabrics are sold by the meter and there is no standard width, so make sure you inquire when you're purchasing off the bolt. **Chinese silks** are found at places like the **China Silk House** (Tanglin Shopping Centre, Level 2, Tanglin Road; ☎ **65/ 235-5020**); or in **Centrepoint** (176 Orchard Rd.; ☎ **65/733-0555**), which has one of the largest selections on the island. High-quality Chinese silks are also at **Yue Hua** in the People's Park Centre (see above), which also has exceptional tailoring services for cheongsams (see above), as well as ready-made silk fashions. Other silk dealers are in almost every mall in the Orchard Road area.

For silk and other fabrics, check out **Arab Street. Asher Fabrics** (119 Arab St.; ☎ **65/293-6892**) has silks from Thailand, India, China, and Italy. Also see **Basharahil Bros.** (101 Arab St.; ☎ **65/296-0432**) for silks. **Aljunied Bros.** (91 Arab St.; ☎ **65/293-2751**) has a large selection of cotton batiks, ready-made clothing, and household linens. You can also try **Batik Emporium** (136 Arab St.; ☎ **65/ 297-2955**), **Bian Swee Hin & Co.** (107 Arab St.; ☎ **65/293-4763**), **Goodwill Trading Company** (56 Arab St.; ☎ **65/298-3205**), or **VK Mohd Hussein** (132 Arab St.; ☎ **65/296-8246**).

For other finds, a few shops along Serangoon Road in Little India have some fine **Indian silks.** The largest selection is at Mohd Mustapha & Samsuddin Co., Pte. Ltd., more commonly known as **Mustapha's** (320 Serangoon Rd.; ☎ **65/299-2603**). **Joo Chiat Centre** in Geylang has many, many small to midsize fabric shops. You can find silks, batiks, cottons, and polyesters at unbeatable prices.

FINE ART

Singapore has a huge number of art galleries and shops that are both a pleasure to look at and—if you've got the wherewithall —a prime hunting ground for serious art, both antique and contemporary. Some of the best galleries include **Art-2,** 45 Armenian St., The Substation (☎ **65/338-8713**), for works by young Singaporean artists; **Cony Art Pte. Ltd.,** 160 Orchard Rd., #04-15 Orchard Point (☎ **65/738-6672** or 65/738-6676), for antique Oriental ceramics and Han and Qing Dynasty porcelains; **Plum Blossoms Gallery,** 328 North Bridge Rd., #02-37 Raffles Hotel Arcade (☎ **65/334-1198**), for Tibetan carpets; and **Zhen Ya Art Gallery,** 1 Maritime Sq., #01-110 Expo Gateway, World Trade Centre (☎ **65/ 271-5450**), for Chinese paintings and calligraphy.

JEWELRY

For upmarket jewels and settings, the most trusted dealer in Singapore is **Larry Jewelry (S) Pte. Ltd.** (Orchard Towers, Level 1, 400 Orchard Rd.; ☎ **65/732-3222**) but be prepared to drop a dime.

For gold jewelry, the place to go is **Pidemco Centre** (95 South Bridge Rd.). With 20 or so goldsmiths who also carry jade and precious stones, this is a great starting point for good prices and reputable salespeople.

Peek in the window displays of the gold shops along **Serangoon Road** and you'll see all kinds of Indian-style gold necklaces and bangles. Each Indian ethnic group has its own traditional patterns, all of them featuring intricate filigree. Indian gold is more reddish in color, and the delicate designs are brilliant and very unusual.

Loose gemstones can be purchased on Arab Street. A nice selection is at **Nam Hing Lin Kee Jewelry Pte. Ltd.** (150 Arab St.; ☎ 65/294-3623). Also good is **Bril Diamonds Pte. Ltd.** (123 Arab St.; ☎ 65/291-2236).

LUGGAGE

The malls on Orchard Road have everything from Luis Vuitton to cheap knockoffs. Unfortunately, most luggage shops are located in Far East Plaza and Lucky Plaza, two shopping malls that are notorious for ripping off tourists (see above). However, if you know what you want, how much it's worth, and how much you're willing to pay, I say try your luck. If you're savvy, you'll come away with a bargain.

In your wanderings on **Serangoon Road** and **Arab Street** you'll also find some luggage places; otherwise, stick to the malls.

ORIENTAL CARPETS

Once you've walked on a hand-knotted Turkoman in your bare feet, trailed your fingers along the pile of an antique Heriz, or admired the sensuous colors of a Daghostani, you'll never look at broadloom again with the same attitude. And best yet, they come in a range of sizes and prices to suit most any room and wallet. Think of your purchase as an investment—even the new carpets coming out of Turkey and other Middle Eastern countries increase in value. Ask that of your wall-to-wall. Still don't want to splurge? Check out the "mini rugs," which measure about a foot square. They're very inexpensive, fit in your luggage, and, once home, drape nicely over the arm of a sofa or look elegant on the hall table.

Many shops also carry **kilims** (woven carpets). These tribals lend a primitive elegant ambiance to most any decorating scheme. Antique camel bags, tent door hangings (how did you think the nomads maintain their privacy?), and other colorful pieces are offered at reasonable prices.

Most shopkeepers are a hospitable bunch. Get them talking about their merchandise and they'll often invite you to have a tea or a cool drink. They know the background of every rug and many have wonderful stories to tell. It's an afternoon well spent, even if it's just to impress your friends back home.

Ask anyone in Singapore where to shop for carpets, and they'll send you to **Hassan's Carpets** (#03-01/06 Tanglin Shopping Centre; ☎ 65/737-5626), which has been a fixture in Singapore for generations. Hassan's is stocked with over US$5 million of museum-quality carpets. In fact, Hassan's supplied all of the carpets for the restoration of Raffles Hotel.

If you want to see still more carpets, you can take a taxi out to Dempsey Road to **Kashmir Carpet House** (Blk. 6E; ☎ 65/732-0969); **Tehran Carpet Gallery** (14–4 Dempsey Rd.; ☎ 65/474-8474); **Jehan Gallery** (Blk. 26 #01-01/02; ☎ 65/475-0003); or **Tandis Gallery** (Blk. 26 #01-05; ☎ 65/475-7220).

PEWTER

Royal Selangor, the famous Malaysian pewter manufacturer since 1885, rode high on the Malaysian tin business at the turn of the century, pewter being a tin alloy. This firm is based in Kuala Lumpur and has eight showrooms in Singapore. The most centrally located are at #01-27 Raffles Hotel Arcade (☎ **65/334-1183**); #02-38 Raffles City Shopping Centre (☎ **65/339-3958**); #02-40 Paragon by Sogo, 290 Orchard Rd.(☎ **65/235-6633**); and #02-127 Marina Sq. (☎ **65/339-3115**).

POTTERY

For pottery, there are a few ways to go. Antique porcelain items can be found in Chinatown. Try **Toh Foong** (5 Temple St.; ☎ **65/223-1343**). For antique reproductions try **Ming Village** (32 Pandan Rd.; ☎ **65/265-7711**). For modern houseware potteries and large pots, go to Holland Village. **Sin Seng Huat Arts and Crafts** (16 Lorong Mambong, off Holland Road; ☎ **65/466-9266**) also sells small baskets and rattan furnishings.

The ultimate in pottery shopping, however is a place the locals refer to as the "pottery jungle." **Thow Kwang Industry Pte. Ltd.** is a taxi ride away at 85 Lorong Tawas off Jalan Bahar (☎ **65/265-5808**). This backwoods place has row after row of pots, lamps, umbrella stands—you name it. There's even a room with antique pieces.

SOUTHEAST ASIAN HANDICRAFTS

Pottery, baskets, puppets, and batiks are just some of the more unusual crafts to be found among all the tacky stuff in the usual souvenir shops. Some areas, such as **Little India** (Serangoon Road) and **Arab Street,** specialize in the stuff, but a trip to the **Singapore Handicrafts Centre** (Chinatown Point, 133 New Bridge Rd.) will provide one-stop shopping for the traveler. With about 50 souvenir shops under one roof, you'll be hard-pressed not to find something of interest. Also be sure to check out the daily demonstrations of traditional crafts at Marina Square.

A gold-plated orchid is something you don't find every day, but you do find them every day at **Rises** (Singapore Botanic Gardens gift shop, Cluny Road; see chapter 6 for full Gardens information; ☎ **65/475-5104**). The process was developed in the 1970s and is exclusive to Singapore. Different orchid species make up the pins, earrings, and pendants, and the choices are extensive.

In Chinatown, the **Zhen Lacquer Gallery** (1 Trengganu St.; ☎ **65/222-2718**) has, in addition to Chinese lacquerware, many unusual gift items from around the region, some of which are antiques. In the market for a wooden birdcage? **D'Art Station** (#65 Pagoda St.; ☎ **65/225-8307**) has an extensive collection in different sizes and prices, as well as a large selection of Chinese teapots and imported teas. For handmade paper and calligraphy brushes, plus a nifty assortment of old chops (stamps) try **Chung Hwa Book Co.** (71 South Bridge Rd.; ☎ **65/532-2045**), and if you want to find an oriental musical instrument, go to **Eng Tiang Huat** (284 River Valley Rd.; ☎ **65/734-3738**), whose displays also include *wayang* (Chinese opera) props and costumes (great as wall hangings). The owners love to demonstrate their wares.

Lim's Arts & Crafts (211 Holland Ave., #02-01 Holland Road Shopping Centre; ☎ **65/467-1300**) is a great place for souvenirs at some of the lower prices in town. If unique and comfortable batik fashions sound good to you, head for local designer **Peter Hoe's** boutique, at 30 Victoria St., #01-05 Chijmes (☎ **65/339-6880**).

SPICES

Since the early days of Singapore trade, spices have been a main traffic item. Still today, spices in the West can carry steep price tags and can be lacking in freshness and potency. Not only is spice shopping in Singapore a great way to save money and give your home-cooking some flair, but it's a lot of fun investigating the strange nuts, roots, and powders in boxes and burlap sacks, to see if you can guess them all. One of my favorite spice shops is **Shamsudeen Djamal & Co.** (☎ **65/291-4390**), out at #108 Arab St., which has all the offerings in full display.

9 Singapore After Dark

What do you want to do tonight? Do you want to go out for a cultural experience and find a traditional dance or music performance or a Chinese opera, or do you want to put on your finery and rub elbows with society at the symphony? If it's live performance you're looking for, you have your choice not only of the local dance and theater troupes but of the many West End and Broadway shows that come through on international tours. Or you may want to try a local performance—smaller theater groups have lately been hitting nerves and funny bones through stage portrayals of life in the Garden City. Singapore has successfully transformed itself into a center for the arts in this part of the world, and is beginning to achieve a level of sophistication you'd come to expect from a major Western city.

If wilding it up is more your speed, there's all kinds of nighttime revelry going on. Society may seem puritanical during the daylight hours, but once the night comes, the clubs get crazy. Sure, the discos and bars may be a little Mary Poppins–like for travelers coming from large Western cities, but when you relax and go with the flow you'll have a great time.

The best place to start is **Boat Quay,** the strip of renovated shophouses turns into a veritable mall of bars, karaoke lounges, discos, and cafes after 9 or 10 in the evening. As you stroll along the river, you can hear the hip-hop, reggae, jazz, blues, rap, techno, disco—you name it—pouring from each door. It seems like there's a million places here, and, without a doubt, you're bound to find at least some of them appealing.

A quieter place with a bizarre collection of clubs is **Mohamed Sultan Road.** A few of these places try to speak to a smaller, trendier audience, but for a fun bar, I recommend trying the Next Page.

Then there's **Orchard Road.** The area around the Scotts Road and Orchard Road intersection has a tremendous number of nightclubs, each with its own favorite clientele and all with high prices of admission. This area is the hub of the wealthier Singaporean club hoppers, who buy VIP memberships that let them sit in special quarters. Half the fun of Orchard Road at night is watching all these people. On weekends, between the jet-setters and the wannabes, the area is sometimes more crowded at midnight than it is at noon.

Orchard Towers is an intriguing place. There is a number of clubs inside, each of which has a reputation as a place to meet women of the world. One place is frequented by Filipino ladies, another by Indonesian ladies, and so on. These discos are about as sleazy as Singapore gets, so I've only listed one of them—Top Ten—in this book.

1 Tips on Singapore Nightlife

INFORMATION   Major cultural festivals are highly publicized by the STB, so one stop by their office will probably fill your evening agenda for your whole trip. Another source is the *Straits Times,* which lists events around town, as well as the *New Paper,* which also lists musical events like local bands and international rock and pop tours. Both of these papers also provide cinema listings and theater reviews.

TICKETS   Telephone bookings for **Ticket Charge** outlets are through ☎ 65/ **296-2929,** or stop by their locations at Centrepoint Shopping Centre, Tangs department store, or Wisma Atria shopping mall on Orchard Road. SISTIC ticket outlets are at Forum Shopping Centre, Parco Bugis Junction, Raffles City Shopping Centre, Specialist Shopping Centre, Takashimaya, and Victoria Concert Hall. The main telephone number is ☎ **65/348-5555.** These are also excellent places to learn about performances, or you can call the performance venues direct at the numbers provided in this chapter.

HOURS   Theater and dance performances can begin anywhere between 7:30 and 9pm. Be sure to call for the exact time. Many bars open in the late afternoon, a few as early as lunchtime. Disco and entertainment clubs usually open around 6pm, but generally don't get lively until 10 or 11pm. Closing time is at 1 or 2am on weekdays, 3am on weekends.

DRINK PRICES   Because of the government's added tariff, alcoholic beverage prices are high everywhere, whether in a hotel bar or a neighborhood pub. "House pour" drinks (generics) are between S$10 and S$13 (US$6.30 and US$8.20). A glass of house wine will cost between S$10 and S$15 (US$6.30 and US$9.45), depending on if it's a red or a white. Local draft beer (Tiger), brewed in Singapore, is on average S$10 (US$6.30). Almost every bar and club has a happy hour before 7:30pm and discounts can be up to 50% off for house pours and drafts. Most of the disco and entertainment clubs charge steep covers, but they will usually include one drink. Hooray for ladies' nights—at least 1 night during the week—when those of the feminine persuasion get in for free.

DRESS CODE   Many clubs will require smart casual attire. Feel free to be trendy, but stay away from shorts, T-shirts, sneakers, and torn jeans. Be forewarned that you may be turned away if not properly dressed. Many locals dress up for their night on the town, either in elegant garb or trend-setting threads, although a certain amount of respectability is always expected.

SAFETY   You'll be fairly safe out during the wee hours in most parts of the city, and even a single woman alone has little to worry about. Occasionally, groups of young men may cat call, but by and large those groups are not hanging out in the more cosmopolitan areas. On the weekends, police set up barricades around the city to pick up drunk drivers, so if you rent a car, be careful about your alcohol intake, or appoint a designated driver. Otherwise, you can get home safely in a taxi, which fortunately aren't too hard to find even late at night, with one exception: When Boat Quay clubs close, there's usually a mob of revelers scrambling for cabs. (Note that after midnight, a 50% surcharge is added to the fare, so make sure you don't drink away your ride home!)

Urban Singapore Nightlife

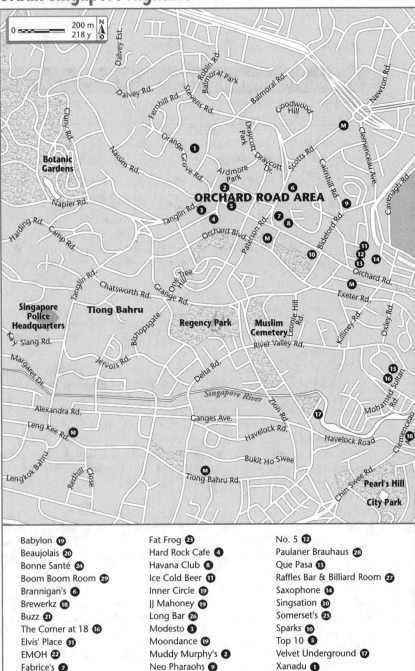

Babylon ⑲
Beaujolais ⑳
Bonne Santé ㉔
Boom Boom Room ㉙
Brannigan's ⑥
Brewerkz ⑱
Buzz ㉑
The Corner at 18 ⑯
Elvis' Place ㉛
EMOH ㉒
Fabrice's ⑦

Fat Frog ㉓
Hard Rock Cafe ④
Havana Club ⑧
Ice Cold Beer ⑪
Inner Circle ⑲
JJ Mahoney ⑲
Long Bar ㉖
Modesto ③
Moondance ⑲
Muddy Murphy's ②
Neo Pharaohs ⑨
Next Page ⑮

No. 5 ⑫
Paulaner Brauhaus ㉘
Que Pasa ⑬
Raffles Bar & Billiard Room ㉗
Saxophone ⑭
Singsation ㉚
Somerset's ㉕
Sparks ⑩
Top 10 ⑤
Velvet Underground ⑰
Xanadu ①
Zouk ⑰

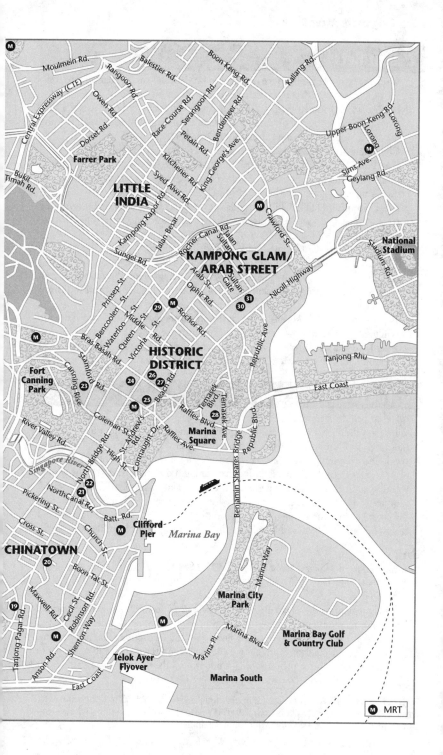

2 Best Bets

- **Wildest Party:** At **Elvis' Place** they had to put banisters on the bar on the weekends to keep the crazy people from tumbling behind into the sink.
- **Best Arty Hangout:** At the **Fat Frog** you can meet folks from the scene at the Substation arts center next door. At **EMOH** there's a more grassroots attempt to bring the arts to popular attention: Bring Your Own Poetry.
- **Chairman Mao's Favorite Bar:** He always has a smile at the **Next Page.**
- **Best Place for an Afternoon Beer: No. 5** is cool and dark—a refreshing contrast to the scorching heat outside. In the afternoons it's so quiet that you'd never know there's madness going on just outside on Orchard Road.
- **Most Hopping Dance Club: Buzz** hasn't the glitzy freak show of Zouk nor the trendy hipness of **Neo Pharaohs,** but I'll bet you'll hear a hundred songs that are all favorites.
- **Best Use of Day-Glo Decor: Zouk.** Period.
- **Too Cool for School:** A veteran of Zouk and Velvet Underground decided to open his own club to show the city how to do it right. **Neo Pharaohs** is just in time to save the Singapore club scene from Top 40 mediocrity and industrial numbness.
- **Best Show:** The drag queens at **Boom Boom Room** win the prize here. The club is all that remains of the once-thriving sex industry on Bugis Street.
- **Best Live Music:** International performers take the stage at **Fabrice's** to add African, Latin, and American spice to a night on the town.

3 The Bar & Club Scene

Like hip people everywhere, Singaporeans love to go out at night, whether it's to lounge around in a cozy wine bar or to jump around on a dance floor until 3 in the morning. And Singaporeans have become pretty eclectic in their entertainment, so you'll find everything from jazz to Elvis, from "garage" to techno, worldbeat, or just plain rock. The truth is, the nightlife is happening. Local celebrities and the young, wealthy, and beautiful are the heroes of the scene, and their quest for the "coolest" spot keeps the club scene on its toes. The listings here are keyed in to help you find the latest or most interesting place. *A tip:* At press time, the most happening bar and club were the Next Page and Neo Pharaohs, respectively. Start from there.

BARS

Brannigans. Hyatt Regency, 10–12 Scotts Rd. ☎ **65/730-7107.** No cover. Draft beer and house-pours around S$10 (US$6.30). Sun–Thurs 5pm–2am, Fri–Sat 5pm–3am. Happy hour nightly 5–8pm.

In the basement of the Hyatt Regency is Brannies. Known by local and expatriate barflies for its promise of alcohol-induced fun, the bar always takes center stage, no matter what the DJ is spinning or the house bands are covering. The place is jam-packed with regular customers of all ages and backgrounds who come to drink, dance to pop and rock, do the pick-up thing, slink around the dark seating areas, or chat up a professional woman or two. Feel free to get a little rowdy.

Elvis' Place. #B1-13 The Concourse Shopping Mall, 298 Beach Rd. ☎ **65/299-8403.** No cover. Draft beer and house-pours from S$9 (US$5.65). Mon–Thurs 4pm–1am, Fri–Sat 4pm–3am. Happy hour nightly 4–8:30pm with half-price drafts.

Welcome to the delightful world of Elvis Wee, Singapore's resident Elvis Presley tribute artist. Elvis (Mr. Wee) is a local celebrity, known for his tribute performances and large collection of memorabilia. He hangs out at the bar and loves to talk about Elvis, life, and the world, and is very gracious when you ask for a photo or autograph. As for the bar, it's no bigger than a postage stamp, but on Friday and Saturday nights the place rocks so hard, Elvis and his crew had to put railings on the bar to keep the folks from falling into the sink. It's truly a United Nations crowd here, and even though Mr. Wee hung up his cape last year on Elvis' birthday (he needed a break), the crowd is more than happy to fill in where he left off. Whether you love the King or not, you've got to love a place that gets down like this.

The Fat Frog. 45 Armenian St. (behind the Substation). ☎ **65/338-6201.** No cover. Limited menu. Draft beer around S$9 (US$5.65). Tues–Sun 11:30am–midnight.

The patio in the back of this place is bigger than the air-conditioned bar inside, but beers are reasonable and the clientele is friendly. The main attraction is its location—behind the Substation, a hub for Singapore's visual and performing arts scene, making this place a good stop after a show. Sometimes you can even run into performers and other majors from the local scene. Inside is a bulletin board promoting current shows, performances, and openings. Around the patio courtyard walls are murals by local painters on themes that rotate regularly.

Hard Rock Café. #02-01, 50 Cuscaden Rd. ☎ **65/235-5232.** Cover S$12 (US$7.55). Cover includes first drink. Draft beer from S$8 (US$5). Daily 6pm–1am.

The Hard Rock Café in Singapore is like the Hard Rock Café in your hometown. You probably don't go to that one, so don't bother spending your vacation time in this one either. Not that it's all bad—the Filipino house band is pretty good, if you like that sort of thing. Basically, it's nothing more than a tourist pick-up joint. Bring mace.

Ice Cold Beer. 9 Emerald Hill. ☎ **65/735-9929.** No cover. Draft beer from S$9 (US$5.65). Sun–Thurs 5pm–2am, Fri–Sat 5pm–3am. Happy hour nightly 5–9pm.

Well, well, well, what have we here? It's Singapore's answer to a frat bar, complete with wall-to-wall girlie posters and beer ads. The place gets its name from the actual bar, which is a glass ice cooler filled with bottled beer. Your evening's entertainment includes a DJ spinning pop and rock from the 1970s and 1980s, but I assure you, dancing rarely happens, 'cause the place is filled mostly with *guys*. There are darts, pool, and upstairs is a comfy laser disc screening room, where you can pick a sofa or comfy chair, order a beer, and kick back to a second-run flick. There are two or three shows daily, with a schedule on the wall. By the way, the foot-long hot dogs are really 9 inches.

JJ Mahoney. 58 Duxton Rd. ☎ **65/225-6225.** No cover. Draft beer from S$8 (US$5), with house-pours just slightly more. Sun–Thurs 5pm–1am, Fri–Sat and the eve of public holidays 5pm–2am. Happy hour nightly 5–8pm.

If you're looking for a real bar-type bar, JJ Mahoney comes pretty close. You have the tile floor, the dark wood bar and paneling, stools lining the sides, and everyday people sidled up for another round. The first floor is a nice place to hang out and meet people (until about 10:30, when the band kicks in with contemporary but rather loud music), and will broadcast soccer games from time to time. The second floor, up a wide hardwood staircase, has small tables where you can order drinks and play games like Scrabble, Yahtzee, chess, and checkers. The third floor is reserved for KTV, a karaoke lounge where you're less apt to get suckered into paying for double-priced, watered-down drinks for con women.

✪ **Long Bar.** Raffles Hotel Arcade, Raffles Hotel, 1 Beach Rd. ☎ **65/337-1886.** No cover. Draft beer S$9 (US$5.65), Singapore Sling S$16 (US$10), Sling with souvenir glass S$25

(US$15.75). Sun–Thurs 11am–1am, Fri–Sat 11am–2am. Happy hour nightly 6–9pm, with special deals on pitchers of beer and mixed drinks.

Here's a nice little gem of a bar, even if it is touristy and expensive. With tiled mosaic floors, large shuttered windows, electric fans, and punkah fans moving in waves above, Raffles Hotel has tried to retain much of the charm of yesteryear, so you can enjoy a Singapore Sling in its birthplace and take yourself back to when history was made. And truly, the thrill at the Long Bar is tossing back one of these sweet juicy drinks while pondering the Singapore adventures of all the famous actors, writers, and artists who came through here in the first decades of the century. If you're not inspired by the poetry of the moment, stick around and get juiced for the pop/reggae band at 9.

Muddy Murphys. #B1-01/01-06 Orchard Hotel Shopping Arcade, 442 Orchard Rd. ☎ 65/735-0400. No cover. Draft beer and house-pours around S$12.50 (US$7.85). Sun–Thurs 10am–1am, Fri–Sat 10am–2am. Happy hour daily 10am–7:30pm (happy hour begins earlier, but the discount is not as great as other places).

This is one of a few Irish bars in Singapore. Located on two levels in the shopping mall, on the upper level you have the more conservative business set having drinks after the 9-to-5 gig, while downstairs the party lasts a little longer and gets a little more lively. Irish music rounds out the ambiance created by the mostly Irish imported trappings around the place. Occasionally they'll even have an Irish band. There is a limited menu for lunch, dinner, and snacks.

✪ The Next Page. 15 Mohamed Sultan Rd. ☎ 65/235-6967. No cover. Small snack menu available. Draft beer S$6.50 (US$4.10). Daily 2pm–3am. Happy hour daily 2–9pm.

Few bars stand out for ambiance like the Next Page, which is a freaky Chinese dream in an old Singaporean shophouse. Creep through the pintu pagar front door and pass the opium bed in the front hall into the main room, its old walls of crumbling stucco washed in sexy Chinese red, lanterns glowing crimson in the air shaft rising above the island bar, to the left of which is a giant portrait of a smiling Mao Zedong. It's a delightfully sick twist of Chinese decadence. Far out. The crowd is mainly young professionals who by late night have been known to dance on the bar (and not only on weekends). In the back is more seating, darts, and a pool table.

✪ No. 5. 5 Emerald Hill. ☎ 65/732-0818. No cover. Draft beer and house-pours S$9 (US$5.65). Sun–Thurs noon–2am, Fri–Sat noon–3am. Happy hour daily noon–9pm, including S$5 (US$3.15) drafts, house-pours, and house wine.

Down Peranakan Place there are a few bars, one of which is No. 5, a cool, dark place just dripping with Southeast Asian ambiance, from its old shophouse exterior to its partially crumbling interior walls hung with rich wood carvings. The hardwood floors and beamed ceilings are complemented by seating areas cozied with Oriental carpets and kilim throw pillows. Upstairs is more conventional table-and-chair seating. The glow of the skylighted air shaft and the whirring fans above make this an ideal place to stop for a cool drink on a hot afternoon. In the evenings, it's a good place to mix and mingle with locals and expatriates.

MICROBREWERIES

✪ Brewerkz. #02-07 Riverside Point, 30 Merchant Rd. ☎ 65/438-7438. No cover. Sun–Fri 5pm–midnight, Sat 5pm–1am. Happy hour nightly 5–9pm with 2-for-1 beers.

Microbreweries are a recent trend in Singapore. After the success of Paulaner Brauhaus (see below), Brewerks came along, with over twice as many home brews and an airy, contemporary style, like a giant IKEA room built around brewing kettles and copper pipes. Brewerkz features five tasty brew selections from recipes created by their English brewmaster: Nut Brown Ale, Red Ale, Wiesen, Bitter, and Indian Pale Ale (which, by the way, has the highest alcohol content). A pint'll set you back about S$12 (US$7.55), while the sampler set of 2-ounce portions of each beer is S$13 (US$8.20). At the time of writing, Brewerkz had only a partial license, which limited its hours. The closing hours have probably since been extended.

Paulaner Brauhaus. #01-01/02-01/03-01 Millenia Walk, 9 Raffles Blvd. ☎ **65/337-7131.** No cover. Sun–Thurs 11:30am–2am, Fri–Sat 11:30am–3am. Happy hour nightly 5:30–9pm for 20% off drafts.

You won't find any polka night here, but you will find beer brewed on the premises by a German brewmaster. Two beers, one dark and one light, are served up daily from copper kettles that rise above the bar. Live folk or pop performances take place in front of the kettles nightly. Upstairs, the Polish/German restaurant gives way to disco with live pop music at 10:30pm, when the German banners and knickknacks are transformed by flashing disco balls. A draft is only S$10 (US$6.30), and every Thursday is ladies night in the disco, where women are served three free drinks after 10pm.

JAZZ BARS

✪ **Raffles Bar & Billiards Room.** Raffles Hotel, 1 Beach Rd. ☎ **65/331-1746.** No cover. Daily 11:30am–1am.

Talk about a place rich with the kind of elegance only history can provide. Raffles Bar & Billiards began as a bar in 1896 and over the decades has been transformed to perform various functions as the hotel's needs dictated. In its early days, legend has it that a patron shot the last tiger in Singapore under a pool table here. Whether or not the tiger part is true, one of its two billiards tables is an original piece, still in use after 100 years. In fact, many of the fixtures and furniture here are original Raffles antiques, including the lights above the billiards tables and the score boards, and are marked with small brass placards. In the evenings, a jazzy little trio shakes the ghosts out of the rafters, while from 6pm to 1am nightly people lounge around enjoying single malts, cognacs, coffee, port, Champagne, chocolates, and imported cigars. Expect to drop a small fortune. From 11:30am to 2:30pm, a S$40 (US$25.20) per person seafood buffet is served; from 3:30 to 6pm is high tea.

Saxophone. 23 Cuppage Terrace. ☎ **65/235-8385.** No cover. Draft beer and house-pours from S$9 (US$5.65). Daily 6pm–2am. Happy hour nightly 6–8pm, including half-price drafts (not honored on the patio).

For a not-so-high-brow jazz evening, try Saxophone, a hole-in-the-wall place with live jazz and blues every day except Monday from 10 or 10:30pm till around 12:30am. Inside is tiny, but there's an outside patio and an upstairs restaurant that serves French cuisine. Saxophone also has some interesting local pieces of art hung here and there. Above the bar, check out the old poster from the seventies, displaying how men are supposed to wear their hair.

Somerset's Bar. Level 3 Raffles City Shopping Centre, 2 Stamford Rd. ☎ **65/431-5332.** No cover. Draft beer from S$11 (US$6.95), cocktails from S$14 (US$8.80). Daily 5pm–2am. Happy hour nightly 5–8:30pm.

Somerset's is a big, well-lit lounge with a long bar and plenty of small tables and chairs. They feature at least two sets of live music every night: country, pop, and rock from 6:15 to 8:15pm except Saturday, and a more jazzy set from 9pm to around 1am every night. From time to time they've hosted internationally renowned performers like bassist Eldee Young, pianist Judy Roberts, and vocalist Nancy Kelly.

DISCOS

⭐ **Buzz.** 88 Circular Rd. ☎ **65/536-9557.** No cover. Selected bottled beers from S$6 (US$3.80). Mon–Thurs 6pm–1am, Fri 6pm–2am, Sat 7pm–2am, Sun 7pm–1am.

Buzz isn't as glitzy and high profile as some of the other dance clubs in Singapore, but everyone who goes out at night knows about it. Its many regulars come back again and again to dance to eighties music, which sometimes includes a tune or two you'd never thought you'd hear again. Wednesday is ladies' night, when women can enjoy their first two beers or house-pour cocktails on the house. Thursday is "Guys Night Out," featuring a "naughty but nice" lingerie show.

⭐ **Fabrice's.** Marriott Hotel basement, 320 Orchard Rd. ☎ **65/738-8887.** Cover Sun–Thurs S$15 (US$9.45), Fri–Sun and on eve of public holidays S$20 (US$12.60). Cover charges include 1 free drink. Draft beer and house-pours from around S$11 (US$6.95). Daily 9pm–3am.

Here's a funky little disco catering to the world-beat crowd. It's all dressed in African mud cloth, South American tapestries, and masks from all over, and throw pillows and chairs surround little tables glowing with tiny candles. The small dance floor throbs with people grooving to DJ funk and dance rhythms in between sets by world-beat bands from Latin America, the United States, and Africa. The house band and style rotates frequently, and bands are given Monday nights off. Tuesday is ladies' night, with no charge for women. There's no happy hour, but something they call "Detox Hour" from 11pm to midnight, when drinks are two for one. Hmmm.

Modesto. #01-01A Orchard Parade Hotel, 1 Tanglin Rd. ☎ **65/732-7808.** Cover for men only S$18 (US$11.35) after 10pm. Daily 6:30pm–3am.

Modesto is a funky hip-hop dance place catering to younger crowds, even though the minimum age to get in is 21 for women and 23 for men. It's small but flashy, and it's always busy. The DJ plays fast dance tracks with some light rap thrown in. Modesto requests you dress smart casual. Happy hours from 6 to 8pm have 50% off specials on drafts and house-pour cocktails, and from 8 to 10pm the specials are 30% off. Tuesday and Friday are ladies' nights, when women get two free drinks.

⭐ **Neo Pharaohs.** 56 Cairnhill Rd. ☎ **65/736-3098.** No cover. Draft beer and house-pours S$8 (US$5). Daily 7pm–3am. Happy hour nightly 7–9pm.

I admit I have a fascination with places that are so cool they don't even have a sign to tell people where they are. This is the case with Neo Pharaohs, the latest and most fashionable nightclub on the scene. In a shophouse on Cairnhill Road, overshadowed by the gaudy neon lights of Club Porsce, the only distinguishing markings are a couple of gargoyles and a red lantern on the front porch. Inside is a series of little rooms connected by staircases and hallways. The first floor is a bar, on upper levels are cozy seating areas and private nooks, and on the top floor is a disco. The owners have tried to get away from what is tried-and-true in Singapore, and have replaced Day-Glo disco decor with draped red velvet and deep hues in a sexy and modern Moroccan and Tunisian style of design. The music isn't the typical techno or eighties revival either, but "garage," which the owner and creative force describes as a more heady mix of rhythm and grooves mixed with some world music, but absolutely no heavy house and techno. Guest DJs from abroad provide a regular flow of inspiration. These days this is the place to be seen, as most of the Singaporean jet set have moved their parties to this address. Expect there to be a cover charge by early 1998.

Sparks. #08-00 Ngee Ann City, 391 Orchard Rd. ☎ **65/735-6133.** Cover Sun–Thurs S$15 (US$9.45), Fri–Sat and eve of public holidays S$25 (US$15.75). Cover includes first drink. Draft beer and house-pours around S$10 (US$6.30). Mon–Fri 6:30pm–3am, Sat–Sun and eve of public holidays 7pm–3am.

Sparks has recently been accused of being a weekend hangout for young thugs and junior druggies. True, it does cater to a younger crowd, but either way, it's a huge and impressive disco with three separate rooms, a giant video screen, and a fantastic light show, plus KTV (Karaoke Television) rooms. On the main stage is a live band playing oldies and Top 40 nightly at 9pm. When the DJ kicks in, it's fast techno dance music. If you want a KTV room, sign up early. Happy-hour specials are discounts on the cover; weekday entry before 8pm is only S$8 (US$5.05) and Friday before 8pm it's S$10 (US$6.30). There's no happy hour on public holidays. Wednesday is ladies' night, with no cover charge for women.

Top Ten. #05-18A Orchard Towers, 400 Orchard Rd. ☎ 65/732-3077. Cover Sun–Thurs S$17.15 (US$10.80), Fri S$22.90 (US$14.50), Sat and eve of public holidays S$28.60 (US$18). Daily 5pm–3am. Happy hour nightly 5–9pm.

Even though it's one of the sleaziest joints in Singapore, Top Ten has one of the highest cover charges. The huge space is like an auditorium, with a stage and dance floor at one end, seating areas on levels grading up to the top of the other end, and a lighted cityscape scene surrounding the whole thing. A cover band plays three sets of pop 7 days a week, but people don't come here for the decor or even the music: Top Ten is a notorious pick-up joint for Asian women. Bring your wallet. All drinks are 50% off. Tuesday night is ladies' night and women don't have to pay the cover.

Velvet Underground. Jiak Kim St. ☎ 65/738-2988. Cover S$20 (US$12.60). Daily 6pm–3am.

Part of the Zouk family (see below), Velvet Underground opened 4 years ago as an intimate alternative to the circus atmosphere next door at Zouk's larger disco. It is also a disco, but with an older, more sophisticated clientele, and disco decor that's not so crazy to the eye. Actually, you'd be surprised the things they do with gold lamé these days. It's a groovy place, but be prepared to deal with the Zouk mobs outside, as Velvet Underground is just to the side of the club compound's main entrance. Unfortunately, Velvet Underground will close at the same time as Zouk, in December 1998.

Xanadu. Shangri-La Hotel, Orange Grove Rd. ☎ 65/737-3644. Cover after 9pm Sun–Thurs, women S$11 (US$6.95), men S$13 (US$8.20); after 9pm Fri–Sat, women S$16 (US$10), men S$20 (US$12.60). Draft beer S$9 (US$5.65). Mon–Thurs 6pm–2am, Fri–Sat and eve of public holidays 6pm–3am.

Known as a disco for a more mature crowd, Xanadu has been on the scene for a while now. It's spacious and the air is not as smoky as other places. The dance floor is large, with a mellower selection of dance and pop music and a live Top 40 cover band nightly from 8:30pm onward. The minimum age is 23 years for men and women, and dress is smart casual. There's no cover charge for guests of the Shangri-La Hotel. From 6 to 8:30pm, the happy hour includes specials on draft beer and half-price house-pour mixed drinks.

Zouk. Jiak Kim St. ☎ 65/738-2988. www.zoukclub.com.sg. Cover S$15 (US$9.45). Daily 6pm–3am.

Zouk was one of the first big clubs to come along. Set in three old warehouses, the club is three parts: a patio wine bar, the small space-age ambient Phuture bar, and a large maze of a disco in glaring shades of Day-Glo and disco lights. Zouk has enjoyed much success since it opened; on weekends, it packs literally thousands of partiers, who come to dance to techno and house music and hear famous international performers like Grace Jones, Björk, and Cyndi Lauper. Unfortunately, Zouk has lost its lease to housing developers, who want to build apartment houses on its site along the

Singapore River. They will remain open until December 1998, and I've included it in this book because if you have a chance to get there, you'll have Singapore bragging rights for at least a decade—"I remember Zouk . . ."

CABARET

Boom Boom Room. #02-04 New Bugis St. ☎ **65/339-8187.** Cover Wed–Thurs S$17 (US$10.75), Fri–Sat S$23 (US$14.50); no cover Mon–Tues. Sun–Thurs 8pm–2am, Fri–Sat 8pm–3am.

Bugis Street was once a seedy nightspot teeming with drag queens, transvestites, and sex performers a la Bangkok, but that's all gone since the government cleaned up the area and opened a night market. What does remain, however, is the Boom Boom Room, a rather antiseptic version of the shenanigans of days gone by, but still a fun night out with female impersonators and somewhat bawdy vaudeville acts. Performances by local TV stars Kumar and Leena are the highlights of the show, while Monday and Tuesday are reserved for new acts, to give stage experience to up-and-coming impersonators. Shows start on Monday and Tuesday at 10:30pm, Wednesday and Thursday at 10:45pm, and Friday and Saturday at 11pm. Drinks are moderately priced.

GAY & LESBIAN NIGHTSPOTS

Aside from the bars, clubs, and discos listed below, many clubs feature a gay and/or lesbian night as either a closed or public party. Sometimes the night is an official event planned by the club, sometimes it's an unofficial event planned by the patrons. On Wednesdays, Zouk is said to be a popular gay hangout, as is the Velvet Underground on Saturdays. Call **Neo Pharaohs** (☎ **65/736-3098**) to find out about planned events, gay and lesbian nights, or fetish nights. In addition to these places, there are a couple of gay bars that have asked to remain unlisted in this book, so ask around for a better sense of the scene in Singapore. Also, try the Web for sites on gay and lesbian life in Singapore—the site www2.best.com/~utopia/tipsing.htm provides links to other Singaporean gay and lesbian sites.

Babylon. 52 Tanjong Pagar Rd. ☎ **65/227-7466.** No cover. Draft beer from S$9.50 (US$6). Mon–Thurs 7pm–2am, Fri–Sat and the eve of public holidays 7pm–3am, Sun 7pm–midnight. Happy hour nightly 7–8:30pm.

Babylon is a small, gay karaoke club, comparable in size to Inner Circle (see below), though with a slightly nicer atmosphere. The crowd at this bar is younger and might not be as open as at Inner Circle, but try it out anyway.

Inner Circle. 78 Tanjong Pagar Rd. ☎ **65/222-8462.** No cover. Mon–Thurs 7pm–midnight, Fri 7pm–1am, Sat 7pm–2am. Happy hour Sun–Thurs 7–8:30pm.

Inner Circle is a karaoke bar for gay men. It's pretty small and dark, with a tiny bar, a large karaoke screen, and not much more to write home about. Most of the clientele are Singaporeans, but the staff is very friendly and open, and assure me that Westerners, although not frequent guests, are very welcome and will definitely have a good time.

Moondance. 62 Tanjong Pagar Rd. ☎ **65/324-2911.** Cover Thurs S$13 (US$8.20), Fri–Sat S$16 (US$10). Cover includes first drink. Draft beer around S$10.50 (US$6.60). Mon–Sat 6pm–3am.

Located in Tanjong Pagar, this disco isn't exclusively gay or lesbian, but has a large following of gay and lesbians mixed in with their regular crowd. Thursday night is Lesbian Night, and Moondance gets very crowded. The dance floor is packed with people who request songs from the DJ *and actually get to hear them.* Friday's Gay Night is equally popular. As far as the ambiance goes, it's dark and spacy inside. The walls are flat black with Day-Glo planets, stars, and galaxies. It's too small to compete with places like Zouk or Velvet Underground, but it's a nice detour from the mainstream. From 6 to 10:30pm the place is a karaoke lounge; after 10:30pm it's a disco. Happy hour is from 6 to 9pm, with specials like half-price house-pour drinks and 25% off all others.

KARAOKE

JJ Mahoney. 58 Duxton Rd. ☎ **65/225-6225.** No cover. Draft beer from S$8 (US$5), with house-pours just slightly more. Sun–Thurs 5pm–1am, Fri–Sat and the eve of public holidays 5pm–2am. Happy hour nightly 5–8pm.

JJ Mahoney is also listed under bars, but if you're looking for a nice place for karaoke, up on the third floor there's an intimate little lounge with friendly staff who'll spin from many books filled with all the tunes you could ever want to squeak out.

Singsation Theme Karaoke. The Plaza Hotel, 7500A Beach Rd. ☎ **65/298-0011.** No cover. Drinks from S$10 (US$6.30). Daily 6pm–1am.

Singsation has 18 theme rooms, from cozy log cabins to a drive-in movie setting to the interior of an airplane, complete with seats and an aisle. There's also a large room for those who like to croon to a bigger crowd.

WINE BARS

Beaujolais. 1 Ann Siang Hill. ☎ **65/224-2227.** No cover. Daily noon–1am.

This little place is smaller than small, but its charm makes it a favorite place for loyal regulars. In a shophouse built on a hill, the five-foot way is more like a patio than a sidewalk. Two tables outside and two tables inside don't seem like much room, but there's more seating upstairs. They believe that wine should be affordable, and so their wines are very moderately priced per glass and bottle.

✪ **Bonne Sante.** #01-13 The Gallery, Chijmes, 30 Victoria St. ☎ **65/338-1801.** No cover. Sun–Thurs 5pm–2am, Fri–Sat 5pm–3am.

Tucked in a quaint little courtyard in the back of Chijmes is one of the more recent wine bars on the scene. Tables and chairs are set around the shady courtyard to take advantage of the architectural splendor of the old nunnery, while inside is a contemporary bar dressed in shiny black offset by warm natural tones, subtle lighting tricks, and leafy plants. Bonne Sante has somewhere between 250 and 275 labels from Australia, France, Chile, South Africa, California, and more. Wine by the glass is around S$10 to S$15 (US$6.30 to US$9.45) for white selections and S$10 to S$25 (US$6.30 to US$15.75) for reds. Champagne is also sold by the glass for S$15 (US$9.45). Bottles range from around S$50 (US$31.50) up to as high as S$2,000 (US$1,248.20). A small menu of Asian finger food is served. Look for monthly promotions for featured countries, regions, or grapes.

The Corner at 18. 18 Mohamed Sultan Rd. ☎ **65/737-1518.** No cover. Sun–Thurs 6pm–2am, Fri–Sat 6pm–3am.

This is one of the newer wine bars in town, and has not a hint of pretension. It's at the end of a long strip of bars along Mohamed Sultan Road, and by the time you make it to the Corner at 18, you won't know what to order anymore, so it's a good thing they have a small menu of hot items, along with draft beer and a nice selection of wines. What's more, the bartender may entertain you with astounding bar magic tricks.

Que Pasa. 7 Emerald Hill. ☎ **65/235-6626.** No cover. Sun–Thurs 6pm–2am, Fri–Sat 6pm–3am.

One of the mellower joints along Peranakan Place is this little wine bar, with a small collection of some 70 to 100 labels but plenty of atmosphere and a nice central location that makes it a well-attended spot. It's another bar in a shophouse, but this one has as its centerpiece a very unusual winding stairway up the air shaft to the level above. The walls are lined with wine bottles and artworks for sale. In the front you can order Spanish-style finger food—tapas, anyone?—and cigars. The place is a basic cafe, but the VIP club on the upper floor is a formal living room, complete with wing chairs and board games. Wines are from France, Australia, Chile, California, New Zealand, and Germany. Bottles are priced at S$40 (US$25.20) and up. White and red wines sold by the glass will only set you back between S$8 and S$10 (US$5 and US$6.30).

A CIGAR BAR

Havana Club. Lobby level Marriott Hotel, 320 Orchard Rd. ☎ **65/834-1088.** Daily 10am–midnight.

In a tiny living-room setting in the corner of the Marriott lobby, you can sit and gnaw your stogie or take it away. They have over 200 kinds of cigars, including Cubanos, ranging from S$4 to S$80 (US$2.50 to US$50.40). They also serve a small selection of cognacs.

4 The Performing Arts

Singapore is no cultural backwater. Professional and amateur theater companies, dance troupes, opera companies, and musical groups offer a wide variety of not only Asian performances, but Western as well. Broadway road shows don't stop in San Francisco, where the road ends, but continue on to include Singapore in their itineraries—*Cats, Phantom of the Opera,* and *Les Misérables* have played to sell-out audiences. Each of the three tenors—Domingo, Pavarotti, and Carreras—has played the town, and Yo-Yo Ma brought down the house. Winton Marsalis, Tito Puente, and Michael Jackson have been equally as successful. The Merce Cunningham Dance Company and the Bolshoi Ballet have both graced the boards and the New York Philharmonic, under the baton of maestro Zubin Mehta, thrilled Singaporeans and visitors alike.

International stars make up only a small portion of the performance scene, though. Singapore theater comprises four distinct language groups—English, Chinese, Malay, and Indian—and each maintains its own voice and culture. The **Chinese Theatre Circle** has performed worldwide and participated in the Edinburgh Festival. **TheatreWorks,** an English-language theater, regularly presents contemporary original plays and has become an innovator of alternative theater.

The Singapore Symphony Orchestra, just 18 years old, gives concerts any jaded New Yorker or Londoner would find inspiring. Singapore's own artists, such as U.S.-based violinist Siow Lee Chin and former Air Supply lead guitarist Rex Goh, to name just two, have garnered critical acclaim worldwide.

Around town, impromptu stages feature irregularly scheduled performances of traditional entertainments. **Wayangs** (Chinese operas) are loud, gaudy, and much fun to watch. Gongs and drums herald the lavishly costumed, heavily made-up actors, who perform favorite Chinese tales in the original language. Don't worry about trying to follow the story line; the actions more than make up for any language barrier. Performances are especially numerous during the Festival of the Hungry Ghosts in August (see chapter 2).

You also might be fortunate enough to happen upon a production as simple as one I saw, in which two "old Chinese gents" sat on a park bench talking about ancient times. The performance was so realistic that an elderly man, overjoyed to find compatriots, sat himself down between the two and joined the conversation. The two actors carried on in true show biz fashion and included the old man, much to the delight of the audience.

A CONCERT HALL

Victoria Theatre and Concert Hall. Empress Place. ☎ **65/339-6120.**

The Victoria is home to the Symphony Orchestra, and other international and local performances, including musicals, festivals, and dance groups. Home-grown companies that regularly stage productions at the Victoria include **The People's Association Indian Orchestra** (☎ **65/440-9353**) and the **Indian Fine Arts Society Orchestra** (☎ **65/270-0722**), as well as the **Nanyang Academy of Fine Arts Chinese Orchestra** (☎ **65/338-9176**), famous for its rendition of folk tunes and classical Chinese music using traditional instruments. They treat Singaporeans and visitors alike to four performances a year. Call for schedule information.

CULTURAL SHOWS

ASEAN Night. Mandarin Hotel, Orchard Rd. ☎ **65/737-4411.** Reservations recommended. Tues–Sun dinner at 7pm, show at 7:45pm.

A little bit of everything from Singapore, Indonesia, Thailand, Malaysia, Brunei, and the Philippines. Traditional music and dance bring the culture of these ASEAN (Association of Southeast Asian Nations) countries to your table at poolside. It's a good bargain at about S$50 (US$31.50) with dinner or S$26.25 (US$16.50) for show only. You have to eat anyway, so why not throw in the flavors of all of Southeast Asia?

Instant Asia. Singa Inn Seafood Restaurant, 920 East Coast Pkwy. ☎ **65/345-1111.** S$35–S$40 (US$22–US$25.20) per person for meals. Shows nightly at 7pm.

The show, free to diners, is a 45-minute melange of Indian, Malay, and Chinese dance. After the regular performances, audience members are invited to join the troupe. This is a good chance to get a shot of Uncle John with a python around his neck.

Raffles Jubilee Hall. 328 North Bridge Rd. ☎ **65/331-1732.** Admission S$5 (US$3.15). Daily 10am, 11am, 12:30pm, 1pm.

An audiovisual history of Sir Stamford Raffles and the founding of Singapore is presented hourly in the 392-seat theater.

Tai He Lou Theatre. Tang Dynasty City, 2 Yuan Ching Rd. ☎ **65/261-1116.** Performance and meal S$30 (US$18.90).

Chinese dancers and gymnasts perform during a buffet lunch between noon and 1pm. The charge for lunch and performance is exclusive of the theme park entrance/ tramway fee of S$15.45 (US$9.75). See chapter 6 for more info on Tang Dynasty City.

10 Singapore's Outdoors

The famous image of Singapore, promulgated by the convention board and recognizable to business travelers everywhere, is of the towering cityscape along the water's edge—but there's a reason they call this place the Garden City. Not only are there picturesque gardens and parks nestled within the urban jungle, but the urban jungle is nestled within *real* jungle. While it's true that most of the wooded areas have been replaced by suburban housing, it's also true that thousands of acres of secondary rain forest have survived the migration of Singaporeans to the suburbs. Better yet, there are still some areas with primary rain forest, some of which are accessible by paths.

In general, think *subtle* when you think about outdoor activities here. As I've said before, the beaches and scuba-diving opportunities here are not the best (that's what Malaysia is for—see chapters 11 through 16), and, on the other end of the spectrum, the island doesn't have anything that could really pass for climbable mountains or raftable rivers. Likewise, spectator sports are not well developed in Singapore. There's horse racing, rugby, and cricket, but beyond that, there are very few other regular activities.

What it does have are spectacular gardens, from the well-groomed Botanical Garden (see chapter 6) to nature preserves like Bukit Timah and Sungei Buloh, where tropical rain forest and mangrove swamps are close enough to the city for you to fit in a morning or afternoon visit. On the one hand, it's fascinating to see how these areas survive amidst rapid urbanization. On the other, it's fun to check these places out and be back to the hotel in time to dress for dinner.

1 Parks & Nature Reserves

In the late 1800s, the colonial government began to section off reserves of forest to preserve the habitats of local species of plants and animals. The first of these was the Bukit Timah Nature Reserve, which was established in 1883. In 1990, Singapore passed a National Parks act which established the National Parks Board to oversee not only the national parks, but also the Singapore Botanical Gardens and Fort Canning Park. The mission of the board is to preserve and promote the nature reserves as a sanctuary for wildlife, a place for plant conservation, and a resource for education and outdoor recreational activities. Today, in addition to Bukit Timah, the nature reserve system includes MacRitchie, Seletar, Pierce, and Upper Pierce reservoirs. With the exception of Bukit Timah, these places are located in the central part of the island.

While the Sungei Buloh Nature Park is not under the jurisdiction of the National Parks Board, it too serves to conserve wildlife for educational and recreational purposes.

Bukit Timah Nature Reserve. Neo 177 Hindhede Dr. ☎ **1800/468-5736.** Free admission. Daily 7am–7pm. MRT to Newton, then TIBS no. 171 or SBS no. 182 to park entrance.

Bukit Timah Nature Reserve is pure primary rain forest. Believed to be as old as one million years, it's the only place on the island with vegetation that exists exactly as it was before the British settled here. The park is over 81 hectares (202 acres) of soaring canopy teeming with mammals and birds and a lush undergrowth with more bugs, butterflies, and reptiles than you can shake a vine at. Here you can see over 700 plant species, many of which are exotic ferns, and mammals like long-tailed macaques, squirrels, and lemurs. There's a visitor center and four well-marked paths. One path leads to Singapore's highest point. At 163 meters (535 ft.) above sea level, don't expect a nosebleed, but some of the scenic views of the island are really nice. Along another walkway is Singapore's oldest tree, estimated to be 400 years old. Also at Bukit Timah is Hindhede Quarry, which filled up with water at some point, so you can take a dip and cool off during your hike.

Sungei Buloh Nature Park. Neo Tiew Crescent. ☎ **65/669-0377.** Adults S$1 (US65¢); children under 12, students, and seniors S50¢ (US35¢). Mon–Fri 7:30am–7pm, Sat–Sun and public holidays 7am–7pm. MRT to Kranji, SBS no. 925 to Kranji Reservoir Dam. Cross causeway to park entrance.

Located to the very north of the island, Sungei Buloh is out of the way, and not the easiest place to get to, but it is a beautiful park devoted to the wetland habitat and mangrove forests that are so common to the region. The park, which is 87 hectares (218 acres) has constructed paths and boardwalks through tangles of mangroves, soupy marshes, grassy spots, and coconut groves. Of the flora and fauna, the most spectacular sights here are the birds, of which there are somewhere between 140 and 170 species in residence or just passing through for the winter. Of the migratory birds, some have traveled from as far as Siberia to escape the cold months from September to March. Bird observatories are set up at different spots along the paths. Also, even though you're in the middle of nowhere, Sungei Buloh has a visitor center, a cafeteria, and souvenirs.

MacRitchie Nature Trail. Central Catchment Nature Reserve. No phone. Free admission. From Orchard Rd. take SBS no. 132 from the Orchard Parade Hotel. From Raffles City take SBS no. 130. Get off at the bus stop near Little Sisters of the Poor. Next to Little Sisters of the Poor, follow the paved walkway, which turns into the trail.

Of all the nature reserves in Singapore, the Central Catchment Nature Reserve is the largest at 2,000 hectares (5,000 acres). Located in the center of the island, it's home to four of Singapore's reservoirs: MacRitchie, Seletar, Pierce, and Upper Pierce. The rain forest here is secondary forest, but the animals don't care; they're just as happy with the place. There's one path for walking and jogging (no bicycles allowed) that stretches 3 kilometers (1.8 miles) from its start in the southeast corner of the reserve, turning to the edge of MacRitchie Reservoir then letting you out at the Singapore Island Country Club.

East Coast Park. East Coast Pkwy. No phone. Free admission. MRT to Bedok, SBS no. 31, or on Sun and public holidays SBS no. 401.

Singapore Outdoors

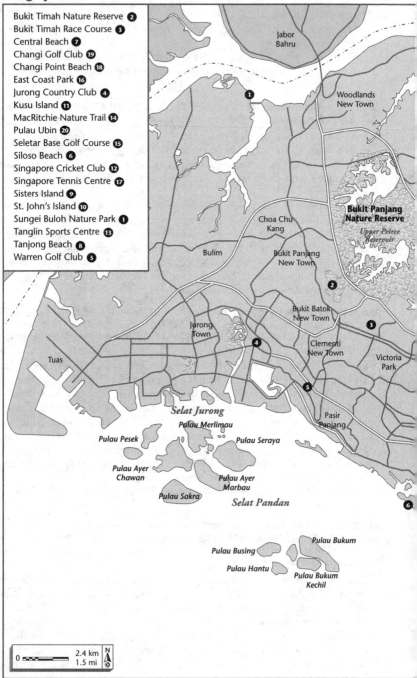

Bukit Timah Nature Reserve **2**
Bukit Timah Race Course **3**
Central Beach **7**
Changi Golf Club **19**
Changi Point Beach **18**
East Coast Park **16**
Jurong Country Club **4**
Kusu Island **11**
MacRitchie Nature Trail **14**
Pulau Ubin **20**
Seletar Base Golf Course **15**
Siloso Beach **6**
Singapore Cricket Club **12**
Singapore Tennis Centre **17**
Sisters Island **9**
St. John's Island **10**
Sungei Buloh Nature Park **1**
Tanglin Sports Centre **13**
Tanjong Beach **8**
Warren Golf Club **5**

Jabor
Bahru

Woodlands
New Town

**Bukit Panjang
Nature Reserve**

*Upper Peirce
Reservoir*

Choa Chu
Kang

Bukit Panjang
New Town

Bulim

Bukit Batok
New Town

Jurong
Town

Clementi
New Town

Victoria
Park

Tuas

Selat Jurong

Pasir
Panjang

Pulau Merlimau

Pulau Pesek

Pulau Seraya

*Pulau Ayer
Chawan*

*Pulau Ayer
Marbau*

Pulau Sakra

Selat Pandan

Pulau Bukum

Pulau Busing

Pulau Hantu

*Pulau Bukum
Kechil*

0   2.4 km
     1.5 mi   N

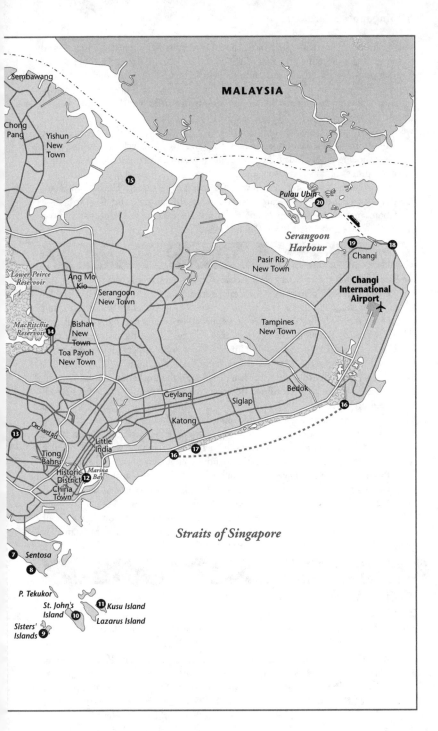

Sembawang

MALAYSIA

Chong Pang

Yishun New Town

15

Pulau Ubin **20**

Serangoon Harbour

Pasir Ris New Town

19 Changi **18**

Changi International Airport

Lower Peirce Reservoir

Ang Mo Kio

Serangoon New Town

MacRitchie Reservoir **14**

Bishan New Town

Toa Payoh New Town

Tampines New Town

Geylang

Siglap

Bedok

16

Katong

13

Orchard Rd.

Tiong Bahru

Little India

Historic District **12**

China Town

Marina Bay

16 **17**

Straits of Singapore

7 *Sentosa*

8

P. Tekukor

St. John's Island **10**

11 *Kusu Island*

Lazarus Island

Sisters' Islands **9**

East Coast Park is a narrow strip of reclaimed land, only 8.5 kilometers long, tucked in between the shoreline and East Coast Parkway. It's a hangout for Singaporean families on the weekends. Moms and Dads barbecue under the trees while the kids swim at the beach, which is nothing more than a narrow lump of grainy sand sloping into yellow-green water with more seaweed than a sushi bar. Paths for bicycling, in-line skating, walking, or jogging run the length of the park, and are crowded on weekends and public and school holidays. On Sundays, you'll find kite flyers in the open grassy parts. The lagoon is the best place to start for bicycle and in-line skate rentals, canoeing, and windsurfing. A couple of outfits, listed later in this chapter, offer equipment rentals and instruction.

East Coast Park is home to a few other interesting places. **UDMC Seafood Centre** (see chapter 5) is located not far from the lagoon, and **Big Splash**—Singapore's first water park with water slides, wave pools, and river rides—is not too far away, at 902 East Coast Pkwy.(☎ 65/345-6762).

2 Beaches

Besides the beach at East Coast Park (see above) is the smaller beach at Changi Village, called **Changi Point.** From the shore, you can have a panoramic view of Malaysia, Indonesia, and other islands that belong to Singapore. The beach is calm, and frequented mostly by locals who set up camps and barbecues to hang out all day. There's kayak rentals along the beach, and in Changi Village there's a hawker center where you can have a fresh seafood lunch when you get hungry. To get there take SBS no. 2 from either the Tanah Merah or Bedok MRT stations.

The beaches on **Sentosa** are wild with families on the weekends and public holidays. There are three beaches: **Siloso Beach** on the western end, and **Central Beach** and **Tanjong Beach** on the eastern end. They are more meticulously landscaped than Changi Point, and have a greater range of facilities, including shower and changing facilities, food kiosks, and snack bars at regularly spaced rest stations. Siloso Beach is open at night for barbecue picnics, and has a few bars along the water. About once a month, rumors spread throughout the island about a party on the beach that lasts until the sun comes up. They are never publicized, but are anticipated by the many folks looking for an alternative to the bar scene at night. Ask around at the bars, and they'll let you know if there's something going on.

On **Kusu** and **St. John's islands** there are quiet swimming lagoons, a couple of which have stunning views of the city. Some people head out to **Sisters Island** for swimming, but the trip is a bit expensive for just a dip.

3 Sports & Recreation

BICYCLE RENTAL

Bicycles are not for rent within the city limits, and traffic does not really allow for cycling on city streets, so sightseeing by bicycle is not recommended for city touring.

AT EAST COAST PARK   Bicycles can be rented at East Coast Park from **Ling Choo Hong** (☎ 65/449-7305), near the hawker center at Carpark E; **SDK Recreation** (☎ 65/445-2969), near McDonald's at Carpark C; or **Wimbledon Cafeteria & Bicycle Rental** (☎ 65/444-3928), near the windsurfing rental places. All of these are open 7 days from about 9am to 8 or 9pm. Rentals are all in the neighborhood S$4 to S$5 (US$2.50 to US$3.15) per hour. Identification may be requested.

ON SENTOSA ISLAND   On Sentosa there are a few rental places. Try **SDK Recreation** (☎ 65/272-8738), located at Siloso Beach off Siloso Road, a short walk from Underwater World (see chapter 6). It's open daily from around 10am to 6:30 or 7pm. Rental for a standard bicycle is S$4 (US$2.50) per hour. A mountain bike ranges from S$5 to S$7 (US$3.15 to US$4.40) per hour. Identification is required.

IN PULAU UBIN   One favorite place where the locals go for mountain-biking sorts of adventures is Pulau Ubin, off the northeast coast of Singapore. When you get off the ferry, there are a number of places to rent bikes. The shops are generally open between 8am and 6pm and will charge between S$5 and S$8 (US$3.15 and US$5) per hour, depending on which bike you choose.

BILLIARDS

The snooker and billiards halls are usually open from 10am to around midnight to 2am, depending on the day of the week. Charges range from S$5 to S$10 (US$3.15 to US$6.30) per hour, and many places offer discounts during weekday hours. A couple of good bets are **Master Cue Snookarium,** 1018 East Coast Pkwy. #01-01 (☎ 65/441-6183), and **Super Cue Marina South,** 15 Marina Grove, Marina South (☎ 65/221-1010), a part of Super Bowl Ltd., where you'll also find bowling, a games arcade, and a food court.

CANOEING

Canoes, kayaks, and plastic Funyaks (or banana boats, as they are sometimes called) are available to rent at the beach at **Changi Village,** East Coast Parkway near the lagoon, and on **Sentosa Island's Central Beach,** where you can also rent pedal boats and aquabikes. Rental spots are open from around 9am to 6pm daily, and charge between S$6 and S$12 (US$3.80 and US$7.55) per hour depending on what you rent. Life preservers are also available.

Be sure to ask about the parameters in the water before you paddle away. Out at the beach at Changi Village, you can see Indonesia and Malaysia, but that doesn't mean you can row there. Patrols will stop you if you try to tool around in foreign waters.

IN CHANGI   In Changi, try **American Unsinkable Kayak** on the beach (☎ 65/563-9015).

ON SENTOSA ISLAND   On Sentosa, try **Boathouse Watersports** at 60 Siloso Beach Walk (☎ 65/275-1053 or 65/275-0667).

AT EAST COAST PARK   At East Coast Park, head for the lagoon, where there are a few outlets that can hook you up.

GOLF

Golf is a very popular sport in Singapore. There are quite a few clubs, and though some of them are exclusively for members only, many places are open for limited play by nonmembers. All will require you bring a par certificate.

Most hotel concierges will be glad to make arrangements for you, and this may be the best way to go. Also, it's really popular for Singaporeans to go on day trips to Malaysia for the best courses. See chapters 14 and 15 for more information about golfing in Malaysia.

Changi Golf Club. 20 Netheravon Rd. ☎ 65/545-5133.

Nonmembers can play at this private club only on weekdays. The 9-hole course is par 34, and you can play 9 holes for S$41.20 (US$26) or 18 (play it twice) for S$82.40

(US$52). They have club and shoe rentals for around S$20 and S$10 (US$12.60 and US$6.30) respectively. A caddy for 18 holes is S$25 (US$15.75). There's no need for advanced booking, and if you walk in at the right time they will set you up with other players. The course opens at 7:30am. Last tee is 4:30pm.

Jurong Country Club. 9 Science Centre Rd. ☎ **65/560-5655.**

Nonmembers can play 7 days a week, but must call in advance for a booking at this 18-hole course. Greens fees are S$120 (US$75.60). Par for the course is 72. Clubs, carts, and caddies are available for S$25 (US$15.75) each. First tee is between 7:15 and 8:45am. Second tee is between noon and 1:30pm.

Seletar Base Golf Course. 244 Oxford St., 3 Park Lane. ☎ **65/481-4745.**

This 9-hole, 35-par course is open for nonmembers 7 days a week. Greens fees are S$45 (US$28.35) on weekdays and S$60 (US$37.80) on weekends, and you can have a trolley for a S$6 (US$3.80) deposit. Club rental from the pro shop is S$15 (US$9.45). First tee is at 7am except for Monday through Thursday, when first tee is at 11am. Last tee is 5pm.

The Warren Golf Club. 50 Folkestone Rd. #01-00. ☎ **65/777-6533.**

Nonmembers are welcome at the Warren on weekdays only, and no reservation is necessary. It's a 9-hole course with a S$83 (US$52.30) flat fee for either 9 or 18 holes. Club rental is S$12 (US$7.55), a trolley is S$7 (US$4.40), and a caddy is anywhere between S$18 and S$32 (US$11.35 and US$20.15). First tee is 7am, last tee is 4:30pm, and there's no tee between 3 and 4pm each day. Friday mornings are reserved for ladies, while Friday afternoons are for gentlemen only.

IN-LINE SKATE RENTALS

East Coast Park has long stretches of paved pathways along the beach that make for some very scenic skating. Rentals are available from **Ling Choo Hong** (☎ **65/449-7305**), near the hawker center at Carpark E; and **SDK Recreation** (☎ **65/445-2969**), near McDonald's at Carpark C, for S$7 (US$4.40) per hour, including protective wear. Both are open from 9am to 8 or 9pm daily.

SCUBA DIVING

The locals are crazy about scuba diving, but are more likely to travel to Malaysia and other Southeast Asian destinations for good underwater adventures. Why's that? The most common complaint is that the water surrounding Singapore is really silty—sometimes to the point where you can barely see your hand before your face. Also, the waters around Singapore can be very choppy in places. Still, many travelers who are stopping in Singapore en route to popular diving destinations in Southeast Asia will complete the certificate training course through a scuba firm in Singapore. The best place to try for a beginner certification course is at **Sea Dive,** 10 Jalan Serene #02-115 (☎ **65/487-3178**), which also organizes diving trips and offers classes up to advanced levels. **Club Aquanaut,** 190 Clemenceau Ave., #05-33 Singapore Shopping Centre (☎ **65/334-3454**), also arranges diving trips. You'll need international scuba certification to participate.

TENNIS

Out at East Coast Park, the **Singapore Tennis Centre** on East Coast Parkway (☎ **65/442-5966**) has courts that are open to the public. If you want to stay closer to town, you can play at the **Tanglin Sports Centre** on Minden Road (☎ **65/473-7236**). Court costs are between S$10 and S$15 (US$6.30 and US$9.45). In addition, a number of **hotels** have tennis facilities for guests. See the individual hotel write-ups in chapter 4 for details.

WATERSKIING

The Kallang River has been the venue for international waterskiing tournaments. Contact the **Cowabunga Ski Centre,** Kallang Riverside Park, 10 Stadium Lane (☎ 65/344-8813), where you can arrange lessons for adults and children and waterskiing by the hour or by the ride. Call in advance for a reservation. The cost is anywhere from S$65 to S$85 (US$41 to US$53.55) per hour. Be aware that they keep weird hours: Tuesday from 2 to 7pm; Wednesday through Friday noon to 6:30pm; and on Saturdays, Sundays, and public holidays they're open from 9:30am to 7pm. They're closed on Mondays.

WINDSURFING & SAILING

You'll find both windsurf boards and sailboats for rent at the lagoon in **East Coast Park.** Most places are open from 9am to around 7pm daily. The charge for a board is S$20 (US$12.60) for 2 hours and for a sailboat is around S$20 (US$12.60) for 1 hour. Deposits will be required. **Sailspirit,** 1210 East Coast Pkwy. (☎ 65/445-5108), offers rentals only, while the **East Coast Sailing Centre,** 1210 East Coast Pkwy. (☎ 65/449-5118) offers basic instruction as well as rental.

4 Spectator Sports

CRICKET

Cricket season is from March to September, and at the **Singapore Cricket Club,** matches are played every Saturday at 11:30am and Sunday at 11am. The clubhouse is reserved for club members; however, all are welcome to watch from the sides. The Cricket Club is located at the Esplanade, Connaught Drive (☎ 65/338-9271).

HORSE RACING

Races are held on selected Saturdays and Sundays at the **Bukit Timah Race Course** at Singapore Turf Club out on Bukit Timah Road (☎ 65/460-3400). The races follow the Malaysian circuit, and so are only held every 4 to 6 weeks. Admission to the stands is S$5.15 and S$10.30 (US$3.25 and US$6.50). There's an air-conditioned "members club" that foreign passport holders can watch from for a S$20.60 (US$13) fee (provided your foreign passport isn't from Malaysia). The club asks that you dress "smart casual," and refrain from wearing shorts or T-shirts in the stands.

RUGBY

The rugby season runs from September to March. Games are held at the **Singapore Cricket Club,** the Esplanade, Connaught Drive (☎ 65/338-9271), on Saturdays at 5:30pm. Visitors are welcome to watch the games, but only club members are allowed to view from the clubhouse.

5 The Surrounding Islands

There are 60 smaller islands ringing Singapore that are open for full- or half-day trips. The ferry rides are cool and breezy, and provide interesting up close views of some of the larger ships docked in the harbor. The islands themselves are small and, for the most part, don't have a lot going on. The locals basically see them as little escapes from the everyday grind—peaceful respites for the family.

KUSU & ST. JOHN'S ISLANDS

Kusu Island and St. John's Island are both located to the south of Singapore proper, about a 15- to 20-minute ferry ride to Kusu from the World Trade Centre, 25 to 30 minutes to St. John's.

Its name meaning "Tortoise Island" in Chinese, there are many popular legends about how **Kusu Island** came to be. The most popular ones involve shipwrecked people, either fishermen or monks, who were rescued when a tortoise turned himself into an island. Kusu Island was originally two small islands and a reef, but in 1975, reclaimed land turned it into a (very) small getaway island. There are two places of worship: a Chinese temple and a Malay shrine. The Chinese temple becomes a zoo during "Kusu Season" in October, when thousands of Chinese devotees flock here to pray for health, prosperity, and luck. There are two swimming lagoons (the one to the north has a really beautiful view of Singapore Island), picnic facilities, toilets, and public telephones.

Historically speaking, **St. John's Island** is an unlikely place for a day trip. As far back as 1874, this place was a quarantine for Chinese immigrants sick with cholera; in the 1950s, it became a deportation holding center for Chinese Mafia thugs; and later it was a rehab center for opium addicts. Today you'll find a mosque, holiday camps, three lagoons, bungalows, a cafeteria, a huge playing field, and basketball. It's much larger than Kusu Island, but not large enough to fill a whole day of sightseeing. Toilets and public phones are available.

Ferries leave at regular intervals and make a circular route, landing on both islands. Tickets are available from the desk at the back of the World Trade Centre. Adult tickets are S$6.20 (US$3.90) and tickets for children under 12 are S$3.10 (US$1.95). During "Kusu Season"—the month of October—thousands of people make their way to Kusu Island to pray in the temple there, and during this month the ferry departs from Clifford Pier. To get to the World Trade Centre, take MRT to Tanjong Pagar, then SBS nos. 10, 97, 100, or 131. For Clifford Pier, take the MRT to Raffles and walk through Change Alley. *A small tip:* There's a Cold Storage in the World Trade Center where you can pick up water and provisions for the trip.

SISTERS ISLAND

Sisters Island, just to the west of St. John's, is not visited as regularly as the other islands because no regular ferry service has operations there. However, at **Clifford Pier** you can hire one of the water taxis—the bumboats hired by ships in the harbor for cargo and crew shuttles—to take you there. The taxi dispatchers are on the ground level, lined up with tables, folding chairs, and CB radios. Feel free to bargain, but the trip will probably cost you around S$50 (US$31.50). Basically, people go to Sisters Island to swim. Sisters is also a popular destination for divers, who hire boats and come for advanced scuba outings.

PULAU UBIN

Located off the northeast tip of Singapore, Pulau Ubin has industry (mining), some Malay kampungs, and trails throughout the island for hiking and mountain biking (rentals are available at the ferry pier). You can eat fresh seafood at a few restaurants, and there are public toilets. Rumor has it that during the Occupation, the Japanese brought soldiers here to be tortured, and so some believe the place is haunted.

To get there, take SBS no. 2 to Changi Village. Walk past the food court down to the water and find the ferry. There's no ticket booth, so you should just approach the captain and buy your ticket from him—it'll cost you about S$1.50 (US95¢). The boats leave regularly, with the last one returning from the island at 9pm.

Getting to Know Malaysia

11

There are so *many* reasons to come to Malaysia. Come here to submerse yourself in traditional Malay culture or to shop in modern malls. Come to stretch out and relax on sprawling beaches. Come to scuba dive in the blue waters, and see life in some pristine coral reefs off the east coast and on the islands. Inland, you can visit national nature reserves with mysterious tropical forests; rivers, both lazy and quick, that are waiting to be explored; mountains waiting to be climbed; and caves waiting to be crept around in. History is richest in the city of **Malacca,** where early-18th-century trade brought cultures together over time to build one of the most eclectic cities you'll ever see. **Johor Bahru** and **Kuala Lumpur** (typically known as "KL") are testimony to the economic success of Malaysia. These cities, while full of their own history, are modern and cosmopolitan. For a taste of everything, there's **Penang,** where beaches, nature, history, and culture collide. What's more, you'd be hard-pressed to find better choices of food outside Penang.

The Tourism Board is catching on to the money that tourism brings into the country and has become much better about promoting the various destinations and attractions than ever before—a trend that is likely to increase as more and more visitors come here each year.

The following chapters cover destinations in peninsular Malaysia—specifically Kuala Lumpur, the capital city; Johor Bahru, the southernmost city on the peninsula; Malacca, one of the oldest cities in Malaysia; Desaru, a golfing resort; Mersing and Tioman Island, for some of the best scuba in peninsular Malaysia; Kuantan and Cherating, for the beach resorts; Genting and Cameron Highlands, for a vacation in hill resorts; and Penang, for a taste of every walk of life that has made Malaysia an international crossroads. Johor is only a skip across the water by bus, train, or ferry, and getting to the more northerly destinations from Singapore is easy by air. Airports in Kuala Lumpur, Penang, Kuantan, Johor, Malacca, and Tioman have service direct to and from Singapore. Call the **Malaysia Airlines office** in Singapore at ☎ **65/336-6777** for more information, or consult the "Getting There" section in chapter 12.

1 The Lay of the Land

Malaysia is all over the place. Put together, peninsular Malaysia and the two states on Borneo, Sabah and Sarawak—approximately 240

Peninsular Malaysia

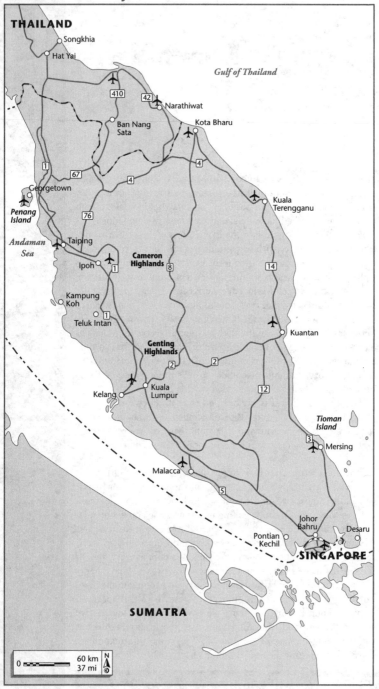

THAILAND

Songkhia

Hat Yai

Gulf of Thailand

410

42

Narathiwat

Ban Nang
Sata

Kota Bharu

1

67

4

4

Georgetown

Kuala
Terengganu

Penang
Island

76

Andaman
Sea

Taiping

Cameron
Highlands

8

14

Ipoh

1

Kampung
Koh

Teluk Intan

1

Genting
Highlands

Kuantan

2

2

Kelang

Kuala
Lumpur

12

Tioman
Island

3

Mersing

Malacca

5

Johor
Bahru

Desaru

Pontian
Kechil

SINGAPORE

SUMATRA

0   60 km
           37 mi

N

4-0277

kilometers (150 miles) east across the South China Sea—cover a total of 336,700 square kilometers (202,020 sq. miles) of land. Peninsular Malaysia makes up about 465,000 square kilometers (134,680 sq. miles) of this area, and contains 11 of Malaysia's 13 states: Kedah, Perlis, Penang, and Perak are in the northwest; Kelantan and Terengganu in the northeast; Selangor, Negeri Sembilan, and Melaka are about midway down the peninsula on the eastern side; Pahang, along the east coast, sprawls inward to cover most of the central area (which is mostly forest preserve); and Johor covers the entire southern tip from east to west. The 2 remaining states of the 13 are Sarawak and Sabah, both located on Borneo. Destinations I've covered in this book are in the following states: Johor Bahru, Desaru, and Mersing are in Johor; Pulau Tioman (Tioman Island), Kuantan, Cherating, and the Cameron and Genting Highlands are in Pahang; Malacca is in Melaka; and of course Penang is in Penang. Kuala Lumpur, although it appears on a map to be located in the center of the state of Selangor, is actually a federal district, a la Washington, D.C., in the United States.

Peninsular Malaysia shares its north border with Thailand. In the south, just over the Strait of Johor, is Singapore, connected by a vehicular causeway. Over there on Borneo you've got Sarawak and Sabah neighboring Indonesia's Kalimantan. In a tiny nook cut out of the Sarawak coast is the oil-rich Sultanate of Brunei.

The major cities of the peninsula are more or less along the coasts. Many were built on old trade or mining settlements, and fall near one another of Malaysia's many rivers.

Over 70% of Malaysia is covered in tropical evergreen forest, estimated to be some of the oldest tropical forests in the world. The diverse terrain allows for a range of forest types, such as montane forests, sparsely wooded tangles at higher elevations, lowland forests, the dense tropical jungle type of forest, mangrove forest along the waters' edge, peat swamp forest along the waterways, and a host of other types. On the peninsula, there are three national forests: Taman Negara (or "National Forest") and Kenong Rimba Park, both lying inland in the middle of the land mass, and Endau Rompin National Park, located toward the southern end of the peninsula. Each of these parks has a world of adventure, whether you prefer quiet nature walks to observe fascinating wildlife or hearty adventure like white-water rafting, mountain climbing, caving, and jungle trekking.

Peninsular Malaysia is surrounded by the South China Sea on the east coast and the Strait of Malacca on the west. The peninsula's east coast has a living coral reef, good waters, and gorgeous tropical beaches, and its more southerly parts have beach resort areas. By way of contrast, the waters in southern portions of the Strait of Malacca are choppy and unclear from shipping traffic, and are hardly ideal for diving or for the perfect Bali Hai vacation. But once you get as far north as Penang, the waters become beautiful again—go to the beach and have a drink with an umbrella in it.

2 Malaysia Today

The Malaysia of today enjoys a peaceful melting pot of races—Malay, Chinese, Indians, Eurasians, and various indigenous peoples living in Sabah and Sarawak. Freedom of religion is the practice, with the majority of Malays following Islam and other groups practicing Christianity, Buddhism, and Hinduism.

Within a stable political climate, Malaysia's economy has gained strong headway. Up until the devaluation of the Ringgit Malaysia (the country's currency) in mid-1997, the country's economy had grown steadily, making it one of the most developed of all the Association of Southeast Asian Nations (ASEAN) countries. Its economy is built upon the manufacturing sector in electronics and rubber products, as well as on agriculture and mining. Exports in raw rubber and timber also add to the coffers.

The government is headed by a prime minister and his cabinet. Malaysia also has a constitutional monarch, called the Yang Di Pertuan Agong (The King), who is selected for a rotating 5-year term from among Malaysia's nine traditional kings.

3 A Look at the Past

Ask any savvy restaurateur and he'll tell you the three keys to success: location, location, location.

Take a place like Malaysia. Back in the early days of sea exploration, trade was the major fuel lighting the fires of adventurers. To the west of Malaysia you had the Indians, and later the Arabs and Europeans, and to the east you had the Chinese (and later, most unfortunately, the Japanese). Malaysia was right in the middle.

The earliest documented modern civilization here has been unearthed by archaeologists in Kedah, in the north. Evidence points to this group having been Hindu-Buddhist traders who lived in the area around A.D. 300. Recorded history didn't come around until the Malay Annals were written in the 17th century. These tell the story of Parameswara, also known as Iskander Shah, ruler of Temasek (Singapore), who was forced to flee to **Malacca** around A.D. 1400, where he set up a trading port and gave it the name it still bears today. Malacca grew in population and prosperity, attracting Chinese, Indian, and Arab traders. With the Arabs came Islam, and the rule of Malacca was turned into a sultanate under the leadership of Iskander Shah's son. The word of Islam quickly spread throughout the entire peninsula.

The next major event in Malay history came in 1511, when the Portuguese decided they wanted a piece of Malacca's action. They conquered the city in only 30 days, chased the sultanate south to Johor, built a fortress that forestalled any more trouble from the populace, and set up Christian missionaries. The Portuguese stuck around until 1641, when the Dutch came-a-conquerin', looking to expand their trading power in the region.

For the record, Malacca originally attracted foreign invaders because of its success as a trading port, but neither the Portuguese nor the Dutch were able to continue the great trading tradition of the past. After the Portuguese took over, the town fell asleep economically, and has yet to reawaken.

Meanwhile, back in the north, Francis Light of the British East India Company landed on the island of **Penang** and cut a deal with the sultan of Kedah to cede it to the British. By 1805, Penang had become the seat of British authority in Southeast Asia, but the establishment served less as a trading cash cow and more as political leverage in the race to beat out the Dutch for control of the Southeast Asian trade routes.

The British had Penang and Bencoolen and were in the process of building a new port, Singapore, along the trade routes. The Dutch, who were basically centered around Indonesia, agreed to trade Malacca to the British in exchange for Bencoolen, located at the southern end of Sumatra. In 1824, with the Treaty of London, the exchange was official. In 1826, the British East India Company formed the Straits Settlements, uniting Penang, Malacca, and Singapore under Penang's control. In 1867, power over the Straits Settlements shifted from the British East India Company to the British colonial rule in London.

Kuala Lumpur came to life in 1857 as a settlement at the crook of the Klang and Gombak rivers, about 35 kilometers (21 miles) inland from the west coast. Tin miners came inland to prospect and set up a trading post, which flourished. Forty years later, in 1896, it became the capital of the British Malayan territory.

In 1941, during World War II, the Japanese conquered Malaysia en route to Singapore. Life for Malays during the 4-year occupation was a constant and almost unbearable struggle to survive hunger, disease, and separation from the world.

After the war, when the British sought to reclaim their colonial sovereignty over Malaysia, they found the people thoroughly fed up with foreign rule. The struggle for independence served to unite Malay and non-Malay residents from throughout the country. By the time the British agreed to Malaysian independence, the states were already united. On August 31, 1957, Malaysia was cut loose, and Kuala Lumpur was named its official capital.

4 Malaysian Culture

The mix of cultures in Malaysia is the result of centuries of immigration, especially from China and India, and of the Malays' generally tolerant view toward other races and religions. Early waves of foreigners brought wealth from around the world, their own unique cultural heritage, and Islam. It is interesting, however, that for the most part each culture remains intact; that is, none have been homogenized. Traditional temples and churches exist side by side with mosques.

Likewise, traditional art forms of the various cultures are still practiced, most notably in the areas of dance and cultural performances. Chinese opera, Indian dance, and Malay martial arts are all very popular cultural activities here. **Silat,** originating from a martial arts form (and still practiced as such by many), is a dance performed by men and women. Religious and cultural festivals are open for everyone to appreciate and enjoy.

Traditional Malaysian music is a trip. Very similar to Indonesian music, it is heavy on rhythms, the constant beating of drums underneath the light repetitive melodies of the stringed gamelan (no relation at all to the Indonesian metallophone gamelan), will put you in a trance with its simple beauty.

5 Cuisine

Malaysian food is delicious, but in multicultural Malaysia, as in Singapore, so is the Chinese food, the Peranakan food, the Indian food . . . the list goes on. In the major cities you'll find hawker stalls, fine dining establishments, and everything in between. In chapter 5 I have provided detailed descriptions of the various cuisines you will find in Malaysia.

Planning a Trip to Malaysia

12

Whether you're planning a quick hop across from Singapore or a full-blown trip through the countryside, Malaysia has a wide range of activities to offer travelers. While Malacca has superior historical sightseeing, Tioman Island is best for scuba diving. The best shopping is in Kuala Lumpur, but you won't find nature trails like you will at Taman Negara in the middle of the capital.

There's also a variety of ways to enter Malaysia, whether you come in by car, bus, or train from Singapore, fly into one of the international airports in Kuala Lumpur or Penang, or take a train from Bangkok. In this chapter I'll run through your options and get you started.

1 Visitor Information & Entry Requirements

The **Malaysia Tourism Board (MTB)** can provide useful information by way of pamphlets and advice prior to your trip, but keep in mind they are not yet as sophisticated as the Singapore Tourism Board. Much of the information they provide is vague, broad-stroke descriptions with few concrete details that will be useful for the traveler.

Overseas offices are located as follows:

IN THE U.S.
- **New York:** 595 Madison Ave., Suite 1800, New York, NY 10022 (☎ **212/754-1113;** fax 212/754-1116)
- **Los Angeles:** 818 W. 7th St., Suite 804, Los Angeles, CA 90017 (☎ **213/689-9702;** fax 213/689-1530)

IN CANADA
- **Vancouver:** 830 Burrard St., Vancouver, B.C., Canada V6Z 2K4 (☎ **604/689-8899;** fax 604/689-8804)

IN AUSTRALIA
- **Sydney:** 65 York St., Sydney, NSW 2000, Australia (☎ **02/299-4441;** fax 02/262-2026)
- **Perth:** 56 William St., Perth, WA 6000, Australia (☎ **09/481-0400;** fax 09/321-1421)

Malaysian Ringgit Conversion Chart

RM	S$	US$	Can$	Aust$	NZ$	U.K.£
.10	.05	.04	.05	.05	.06	.02
.20	.11	.08	.11	.10	.11	.05
.50	.27	.20	.27	.25	.28	.11
1.00	.55	.40	.55	.50	.56	.23
2.00	1.10	.80	1.10	1.00	1.12	.46
5.00	2.75	2.00	2.75	2.50	2.80	1.15
10.00	5.50	4.00	5.50	5.00	5.60	2.30
20.00	11.00	8.00	11.00	10.00	11.20	4.60
50.00	27.50	20.00	27.50	25.00	28.00	11.50
100.00	55.00	40.00	55.00	50.00	56.00	23.00
500.00	275.00	200.00	275.00	250.00	280.00	115.00
1000.00	550.00	400.00	550.00	500.00	560.00	230.00

IN THE U.K.

- **London:** 57 Trafalgar Sq., London, WC2N 5DU, UK (☎ **071/930-7932;** fax 071/930-9015)

IN SINGAPORE

- 10 Collyer Quay, #01-06, Ocean Building (☎ **65/532-6321**)

Within Malaysia, offices are in **Kuala Lumpur, Penang,** and **Johor Bahru.** See "Visitor Information" in chapters 14, 15, and 16 for exact addresses. The official Web site of the Malaysia Tourism Board is **http://tourism.gov.my.**

ENTRY REQUIREMENTS

To get into the country you must have a valid passport. Citizens of the United States do not need visas for tourist and business visits not exceeding 3 months. Citizens of Canada, Australia, New Zealand, and the U.K. do not require a visa for tourist or business visits not exceeding 1 month.

If you are traveling from an area infected with yellow fever, you will be required to show proof of yellow fever vaccination. Contact your nearest Malaysia Tourism Board (MTB) office to find out the specific areas that fall into this category.

CUSTOMS REGULATIONS

You can enter Malaysia with 1 liter of hard alcohol and 1 carton of cigarettes. Currency-wise, you are not supposed to bring in more than RM10,000 (US$4,000), and you're not supposed to leave with more than RM5,000 (US$2,000). Naturally, you should not try to leave with any birds or animals, especially endangered ones. Some tourists buy such creatures without being told it is illegal to bring some of them out of the country. Taxes and tariffs are the same for all visitors.

Certain items—such as clothing, jewelry, chocolates, spirits, alcohol, and tobacco products—may be dutiable when you enter the country. Customs officials may ask you to pay a deposit for "temporary importation." When you leave, you'll have to show these items with your receipts (to prove you didn't sell them in some back alley) and they'll give you your deposit back. If you plan to eat your chocolates, smoke

What Things Cost in Kuala Lumpur

Taxi from the airport to the city center (fixed)	RM30 (US$12)
Local telephone call (3 min.)	10 sen
Double room at an expensive hotel	RM450 (US$180)
Double room at a moderate hotel	RM200 (US$80)
Double room at an inexpensive hotel	RM100 (US$40)
Dinner for one, with wine, at an expensive restaurant	RM100 (US$40)
Dinner for one, with wine, at a moderate restaurant	RM35 (US$14)
Dinner for one at a hawker center coffee shop	RM2 (US80¢)
Bottle of beer	RM5–RM12 (US$2–US$4.80)
Coca-Cola	RM1–RM6 (US40¢–US$2.40)
Roll of film	RM8–RM10 (US$3.20–US$4)
Admission to National Museum	RM1 (US40¢)
Movie ticket	RM5–RM9 (US$2–US$3.60)

your cigarettes, or drink your drinks, they probably won't ask to see the empty little brown cups, the stubbed-out butts, and the empties.

2 Money

Malaysia's currency is the **Malaysian ringgit.** It's also commonly referred to as the Malaysian dollar, and prices are marked as RM (a designation I've used throughout this book). Notes are issued in denominations of RM1, RM2, RM5, RM10, RM20, RM50, RM100, RM500, and RM1000. One ringgit is equal to 100 sen. Coins come in denominations of 1, 5, 10, 20, and 50 sen, and there's also a 1 ringgit coin.

At the time of this book's writing, the Malaysian currency had been seriously de-valued due to the Southeast Asian monetary crisis, to the point where RM1 = only US22¢—as opposed to its normal value of approximately US40¢. I've chosen to give conversions in this book that reflect a noncrisis state of affairs, going on the philosophy that if you're going to be surprised by a different conversion rate, it might as well be a good surprise, with the conversion going in your favor. There-fore, the conversions used in these chapters are as follows: US$1 = RM2.50, Ca-nadian $1 = RM1.85, British Pound 1 = RM4.30, Australian $1 = RM2, New Zealand $1 = RM1.80.

Before you begin budgeting your trip, I suggest you obtain the latest conversions so you don't suffer any shocks—unpleasant or pleasant—at the last minute. A neat and easy money conversion program can be found on the Internet through CNN's Web site at **www.cnn.com/TRAVEL/CURRENCY**.

EXCHANGING MONEY

Currency can be changed at banks and hotels, but you'll get a more favorable rate if you go to one of the money changers that seem to be everywhere. It's just like Singapore: The money changers are in shopping centers, in little lanes, and in small stores—just look for signs. The money changers are often men in tiny little booths with a lit display on the wall behind them showing the latest exchange rates. All major currencies are accepted usually, and there is never a problem with the U.S. dollar.

GETTING CASH ON THE SPOT

Kuala Lumpur, Penang, and Johor Bahru have quite a few **automatic teller machines** (ATMs) scattered around, but they're few and far between in the smaller towns. Generally, you'll want to carry cash and/or traveler's checks.

TRAVELER'S CHECKS

Generally, travelers to Malaysia will never go wrong with **American Express** and **Thomas Cook** traveler's checks, which can be cashed at banks, hotels, and licensed money changers. Unfortunately, they are often not accepted at smaller shops. Even in some big restaurants and department stores, many cashiers don't know how to process these checks, which might lead you to a long and frustrating wait.

CREDIT CARDS

Credit cards are widely accepted at hotels and restaurants, and at many shops as well. Most popular are American Express, MasterCard, and Visa. Some banks may also be willing to advance cash against your credit card, but you have to ask around because this facility is not available everywhere.

3 When to Go

There are two peak seasons in Malaysia, one in winter and another in summer. The peak winter tourist season falls from the beginning of December to the end of January, covering the major winter holidays—Christmas, New Year's Day, Chinese New Year, and Hari Raya. Tourist traffic slows down from February through the end of May, then picks up again in June. The peak summer season falls in the months of June, July, and August, and can last into mid-September. After September it's quiet again until December. Both seasons experience approximately equal tourist traffic, but in summer months that traffic may be spread out a little more.

CLIMATE

Climate considerations will play a role in your plans. If you plan to visit any of the east coast resort areas, the low season is between November and March, when the monsoon tides make the water too choppy for water sports and beach activities. Likewise on the west coast, the rainy season is from April through May, and again from October through November.

The temperature is basically static year-round. Daily averages for the temperature are between 67°F and 90°F (21°C and 32°C). Temperatures in the hill resorts get a little cooler, averaging 67°F (21°C) during the day and 50°F (10°C) at night.

The clothing recommendations I gave for Singapore in chapter 2 apply just as well to Malaysia.

PUBLIC HOLIDAYS & EVENTS

Malaysia celbrates 12 public holidays: New Year's Day, Thaipusam, Chinese New Year, Hari Raya Aidil Fitri, Labour Day, Vesak Day, the King's Birthday, Awal Muharam, Hari Raya Aidil Adha, National Day, Deepavali, and Christmas. Most of the religious holidays—Chinese New Year and Thaipusam, for example—correspond to the listing for Singapore holidays in chapter 2. Others—such as the King's Birthday (June 5), Labour Day (May 1), and National Day (August 31)—are distinctly Malaysian.

During Malaysia's official public holidays, expect government offices to be closed, as well as some shops and restaurants, depending on the ethnicity of the shop owner or restaurant owner. Also count on public parks, shopping malls, and beaches to be more crowded, as locals will be taking advantage of their time off. Of the 12 public holidays, only 5 (New Year's Day, Labour Day, the King's Birthday, National Day, and Christmas) fall on the same day every year. The other holidays will vary from year to year according to the lunar calendar.

4 Tips for Travelers with Special Needs

TRAVELERS WITH DISABILITIES   Most of Malaysia's infrastructure provides poor access for disabled travelers. International hotel chains will be more likely to provide accommodating facilities. While public toilets in these hotels will have special facilities for wheelchairs, forget most of the public toilets everywhere else. They're impossible.

SENIORS   Seniors can take advantage of special rates for airlines and international hotel chains. Few attractions offer discounts for seniors.

GAY & LESBIAN TRAVELERS   Malaysia is still very conservative when it comes to alternative lifestyles. Generally, people are closemouthed when you ask about gays or lesbians in Malaysia. Proceed with caution.

STUDENTS   Students with an international student card can get discounts at some public attractions (such as museums), but basically, unless you're obviously a young student (not past your teens), you'll have to pay adult fees.

There is a special train fare on the Keretapi Tanah Melayu Berhad (KTM) railways system for international student cardholders. For RM80 (US$32), cardholders can have 7 days unlimited travel with the Eurotrain.

5 Getting There

BY PLANE

Malaysia has international airports in Kuala Lumpur, Penang, and Johor Bahru. About 45 airlines fly to Malaysia. Major airlines include Air New Zealand, Ansett Australia, British Airways, Canadian Airlines, Malaysia Airlines, Quantas Airlines, Singapore Airlines, and Virgin Atlantic Airways.

American readers will notice there are no American carriers directly servicing Malaysia. Generally, there's just not enough passenger and cargo business to justify the routes; however, if you have frequent-flyer miles to use, or would like to fly a route that will allow you to accumulate miles on an existing account, call your carrier and they can route you there on a partner carrier.

An airport departure tax is levied on all flights. The tax is RM5 (US$2) for domestic flights and RM40 (US$16) for international flights.

KUALA LUMPUR   The **Sultan Abdul Aziz Shah, Subang International Airport** (☎ **603/746-1833**) operates out of three terminals: Terminal 1 (T1) is for international flights; Terminal 2 (T2) handles flights between Singapore and Kuala Lumpur, which includes flights to Sarawak and Sabah that originate in KL and transfer at Singapore's Changi Airport; Terminal 3 (T3) handles all other domestic flights.

The opening of the first phase of a new airport, **Kuala Lumpur International Airport (KLIA),** is scheduled for the first half of 1998. KLIA will be a huge airport complex in Sepang, located 53 kilometers (32 miles) outside of Kuala Lumpur. The first phase will operate two runways with a large terminal building. The entire complex will be completed and fully functional by the year 2012, and will have the capacity to handle up to 60 million passengers a year in its final operational status. The airport will feature 216 check-in counters, ATM self-check-in kiosks, state-of-the-art security systems, and train access to the Kuala Lumpur city center. The ultimate plan is to make Kuala Lumpur a hub for international travel in Southeast Asia.

PENANG　The airport in Penang is rather uncreatively called **Penang International Airport** (☎ **04/834-411**). The airport handles international and domestic flights from one terminal.

BY TRAIN

The **Keretapi Tanah Melayu Berhad (KTM)** is Malaysia's rail system, running express and local trains four times a day from Bangkok, Thailand, down the west coast of Malaysia, with stops in and between Butterworth (for Penang), Kuala Lumpur, Malacca, Johor Bahru, and ending in Singapore. The **Kuala Lumpur Central Railway Station** is on Jalan Hishamuddin (☎ **03/274-7435**); the **Johor Bahru railway station** is at Jalan Campbell (☎ **07/223-3040**); and the **Singapore Railway Station** is on Keppel Road in Tanjong Pagar (☎ **65/222-5165**).

For an idea on **fares,** the trip from Bangkok to KL is around RM148.30 (US$59.20) for first-class passage and RM66.30 (US$26.50) for second class (no third class is available from Bangkok). The trip takes about 35 hours. From Singapore to Kuala Lumpur, the trip lasts 6 hours and the fare is around RM60 (US$24) for first class, RM26 (US$10.40) for second class, and RM14.80 (US$6) for third class. If you're in Singapore and you just want to hop a train to Johor Bahru, the fare is only RM4.20 (US$1.75) first class, RM1.90 (US80¢) second class, and RM1.10 (US45¢) third class. The trip is a mere half hour to 40 minutes. Tickets can be purchased at any of the railway stations along the route.

To save you some money, KTM has a **Railpass** that allows you unlimited travel in Singapore and Malaysia. The pass for adults is RM140 (US$55) for 10 days or RM300 (US$120) for 30 days. A pass for a child between 4 and 12 years is RM70 (US$28) for 10 days and RM150 (US$60) for 30 days.

If you have an international student identification, you can travel on the **Eurotrain Explorer Pass–Malaysia.** It lets you make unlimited second- or third-class trips on all KTM trains in peninsular Malaysia and Singapore for 1 week for just RM75 (US$32). These passes may be purchased at any train terminal.

There is also a daily **mail train** between Singapore and Kuala Lumpur, which leaves Singapore at 8:15am daily and costs about RM23.50 (S$14.80/US$9.40)— half the cost, but it takes 10 hours one way.

On the other end of the spectrum, the **Eastern & Orient Express (E&O)** operates a route between Bangkok, Kuala Lumpur, and Singapore. Traveling in the luxury style of the Orient Express, the entire journey takes about 42 hours from start to finish. Compartments come in Sleeper (approximately RM3,120/S$2,000/US$1,248 per person double occupancy), State (RM4,395/S$2,790/US$1,758 per person double occupancy), and Presidential (RM8,175/S$5,190/US$3,270 per person double occupancy). All fares include meals on the train. Overseas reservations for the E&O Express can be made through a travel agent.

BY BUS

From Singapore, there are many bus routes to Malaysia from the **Ban Sen Terminal** at the corner of Queen Street and Arab Street in Kampong Glam.

The **Singapore–Johor Bahru Express** (☎ **65/292-8149**) takes less than an hour and departs at 10- to 15-minute intervals from 6:30am to midnight. Fares are about RM3.25 (S$2.10/US$1.30) one way.

The **Kuala Lumpur–Singapore Express** (☎ **65/292-8254**) departs Kuala Lumpur three times daily and takes just under 6 hours for the trip. Fare for Normal Coach is RM27.40 (S$17.30/US$10.95), and for Deluxe Coach is RM34.60 (S$22/US$13.85). It is worth your while to pay the higher fare for deluxe—the fare isn't that much more, but the buses are cleaner and the seats re-cline very far back.

The **Malacca–Singapore Express Sdn Bhd** (☎ **65/293-5915**) departs eight times daily and takes 4¹/₂ hours to complete. The fare is RM17.35 (S$11/US$6.95).

BY FERRY

You can get to Malaysia from Singapore by ferry if you go out to **Changi Point.** The ferry will take you across the Strait of Johor to Tanjung Belungkor on the southeast-ern shore of Malaysia. The trip takes 45 minutes, and the boat leaves four times daily, at 8:15am, 11:15am, 2:15pm, and 5:15pm. Check-in time is 1 hour before depar-ture. The one-way fare for adults is S$15 (US$9.45), for children ages 12 to 18 (stu-dents) is S$13 (US$8.20), and for children under 12 is S$9 (US$5.65). Round-trip is S$24 (US$15.10) for adults, S$21 (US$13.25) for students, and S$15 (US$9.45) for children. Contact **FerryLink (S) Pte. Ltd.** (in Singapore; ☎ **65/543-3600** or 65/733-6744).

Ferries to Tioman Island are also available except from November to March, dur-ing the monsoon. From the Singapore Tanah Merah Ferry Terminal, you can catch a ferry to the Berjaya Jetty at Tioman every day except Wednesday. The ferry leaves at 8:30am, but check-in time is 1 hour before departure. The trip takes about 3¹/₂ hours. Contact **Auto Batam Ferries and Tours Pte. Ltd.** (in Singapore; ☎ **65/ 542-7105**).

BY CAR

For convenience, driving to Malaysia from Singapore can't be beat. You can go where you want to go, when you want to go there, and without the hassle of public transportation—but it is quite expensive. In Singapore, to rent a car you must have an International Driver's License obtained in your home country before your trip. Avis and Hertz both have branches at Singapore's Changi Airport and in town. You can rent the car, take it into Malaysia, and bring it back, or you can drop it off some-where on the peninsula for an extra fee. (See details in chapter 3. For road tips in Malaysia, see chapter 13.)

13 Learning Your Way Around Malaysia

The modernization of Malaysia has made travel here more convenient than ever, so whether it's by plane, train, bus, taxi, or self-drive, traveling around the peninsula is easy. In fact, it's convenient enough for you to plan to hop from city to city and not waste too much precious vacation time. This chapter will help your logistical planning with tips on how to plan a trip that's more holiday and less frustration.

1 Getting Around Peninsular Malaysia

By and large, all the modes of transportation between cities are reasonably comfortable, so you don't have to choose your journey based upon this parameter. What you will need to consider is how much time you have to get from place to place, and just how much you'd like to see in between destinations. Forgive me for stating the obvious, but while air travel is the quickest means of transport, you miss out on the flavor of the countryside—the time you spend gazing out the window of a train or taking a slow drive on winding roads could make for the most relaxing travel experience. Another consideration is price. Although air travel is not too costly between cities, you can't beat the S$14.80 (US$9.40) mail train trip from Singapore to Kuala Lampur.

BY AIR

Pelangi Air, Technology Resources Tower, 18th floor, 161B Jalan Ampang, KL (☎ **03/262-4453**), and **Berjaya Air,** Lot 205, 2nd floor, Plaza Berjaya, KL (☎ **03/232-5797**), offer domestic flights around Malaysia, with airports located in KL, Penang, Kuantan, Johor Bahru, Tioman Island, Taman Negara, Malacca, and several other destinations. Fares are reasonable, running approximately as follows (all fares for one-way domestic travel): KL to Johor Bahru, RM93 (US$37.20); KL to Kuantan, RM74 (US$29.60); KL to Penang, RM104 (US$41.60); Johor Bahru to Kuantan, RM93 (US$37.20).

AIRPORTS

- **Johor Bahru:** Senai Airport; ☎ **07/599-4500**
- **Kuala Lumpur:** Sultan Abdul Aziz Shah, Subang International Airport; ☎ **03/746-1833**
- **Kuantan:** Sultan Maj Ahmed Shah Airport; ☎ **09/538-2923**

- **Malacca:** Batu Berenadam Airport; ☎ **06/538-2923**
- **Penang:** Penang International Airport; ☎ **04/834-411**
- **Tioman Island:** Tioman Airport; ☎ **11/344-038**

BY RAIL

The **Keretapi Tanah Melayu Berhad (KTM)** is Malaysia's railway system. Trains run from north to south between Bangkok and Singapore, with stops in between including Butterworth (for Penang Island), Kuala Lumpur, Malacca, and Johor Bahru. There is a second line that branches off this line at around the midpoint between Johor Bahru and KL and heads northeast to Kota Bahru.

TRAIN STATIONS

- **Johor Bahru:** Johor Bahru Railway Station, Jalan Campbell; ☎ **07/223-3040**
- **Kuala Lumpur:** Central Railway Station, Jalan Hishamuddin; ☎ **03/274-7435**
- **Malacca:** Tampin Station (located 38km north of the city); ☎ **06/411-034**
- **Butterworth:** Butterworth Station, Jalan Bagan Dalam; ☎ **04/331-2796**

BY BUS

Malaysia's intercity coach system is very good and inexpensive. Fares are charged according to the distance you travel. Air-conditioned express bus service will cost you more, but since the fares are so inexpensive, it's well worth your while to spring the couple dollars extra for the comfort.

BUS STATIONS

- **Johor Bahru:** Johor Bahru Bus Terminal, off Jalan Gertak Merah, near Orchid Plaza
- **Kuala Lumpur:** The **Putra Bus Station** (☎ **03/442-9530**), opposite the Putra World Trade Centre, for east coast express buses; **Pekeliling Bus Station** (☎ **03/442-1256**), on Jalan Tun Razak, for east coast service; **Podium Block** (☎ **03/292-7519**), at the Holiday Inn City Centre on Jalan Raja Laut, for executive coaches to Penang and Johor Bahru; **Pudu Raya Bus Terminal** (☎ **03/230-0145**) at Jalan Cheng Lock for north- and southbound buses, and buses to and from Singapore
- **Malacca:** Jalan Tun Ali (no phone)
- **Butterworth (Penang):** Butterworth Bus Terminal, Jalan Pantai, near the ferry terminal and railway station (no phone)

BY TAXI

You can take taxis between cities and states. Rates depend on the distance you plan to travel. They are fixed, and stated at the beginning of the trip. In Kuala Lumpur, go to the second level of the **Pudu Raya Bus Terminal** to find cabs that will take you outside the city. For taxis to destinations outside KL, call the **Kuala Lumpur Outstation Taxi Service Station,** 123 Jalan Sultan, KL (☎ **03/238-3525**). A taxi from KL to Malacca will cost you approximately RM100 (S$64/US$40), KL to Cameron Highlands RM150 (S$96/US$60), KL to Butterworth RM200 (S$128/US$80), KL to Johor Bahru RM200 (S$128/US$80).

BY CAR

Back in the seventies, there was some trouble with roadside crime—bandits who'd stop cars and hold up the travelers inside. Fortunately for drivers in Malaysia, this is a thing of the past. In the mid-1990s, Malaysia opened the **North-South Highway,** running from Bukit Kayu Hitam in the north on the Thai border and Johor

Bahru at the southern tip of the peninsula. The highway has made travel along the west coast of Malaysia easy. There are rest areas with toilets, food outlets, and emergency telephones placed at intervals along the way. There's a toll, which varies depending on the distance you're traveling.

Driving along the **east coast** of Malaysia is actually much more pleasant than driving along the west coast. The highway is narrower and older, but it brings you through oil palm and rubber plantations, and the essence of kampung Malaysia permeates throughout. Often as you get near villages you'll have to slow down and swerve past cows and goats, which are really quite oblivious to oncoming traffic. You have to get very close to honk at them before they move.

The speed limit on highways is 110 kilometers per hour. On the minor highways the limit ranges from 70 to 90 kilometers per hour. Do not speed, as there are traffic police strategically situated around certain bends. It is a well-known fact that many of the police who stop drivers to book them for speeding or other minor offenses will let the perpetrator of the offense go for a bribe. The amount to offer varies from RM50 to RM150 (US$20 to US$60), with the variance depending on the severity of your offense, the crookedness or audacity of the police officer, and your bargaining skills. It is not uncommon for Singaporeans and other tourists to be stopped despite not having flouted any road rules. If you really feel you've not broken any laws, stand your ground and ask for a proper traffic summons. This applies to the whole of Malaysia, in cities and along major highways.

Distances between major towns are: From **KL to Johor Bahru,** 368 kilometers (221 miles); from **KL to Malacca,** 144 kilometers (86 miles); from **KL to Kuantan,** 259 kilometers (155 miles); from **KL to Butterworth,** 369 kilometers (221 miles); from **Johor Bahru to Malacca,** 224 kilometers (134 miles); from **Johor Bahru to Kuantan,** 325 kilometers (195 miles); from **Johor Bahru to Mersing,** 134 kilometers (80 miles); from **Johor Bahru to Butterworth,** 737 kilometers (442 miles).

To **rent a car** in Malaysia, all you need is an International Driver's License. While there are desks for major car rental services at the international airports in Kuala Lumpur and Penang, there are additional outlets, as follows:

- **Johor Bahru: Avis,** Tropical Inn Hotel (☎ 07/224-4824); **National Car Rental,** Lian Shong Building, Ground Floor (☎ 07/223-0503)
- **Kuala Lumpur: Avis,** 40 Jalan Sultan Ismail (☎ 03/242-3500); **Hertz,** Komplex Antarabangsa (☎ 03/248-6433); **National Car Rental,** Jalan Sultan Ismail, Shop 9, Ground Floor, President House (☎ 03/248-0522)
- **Penang: Avis,** 388 Bukit Ferringhi Rd. (☎ 04/649-8891); **Budget Rent-A-Car,** Lapangan Terbang Bayan Lepas (☎ 04/649-8891); **National Car Rental,** Lot 201E/F Bayan Lepas (☎ 04/262-9405)

HITCHHIKING

Hitchhiking is not advisable, especially for women. You almost never see people hitchhiking in Malaysia.

2 Suggested Itineraries

IF YOU HAVE 2 DAYS   Go to **Penang.** It has great history, beaches, food, and a laid-back atmosphere. All the better if you're coming from or on the way to Thailand, because Penang is close to the Thai border.

IF YOU HAVE 4 DAYS   If it's shopping and nightlife you want, then a couple of days in **KL** followed by a couple of days in **Penang** would be good. If you just want to relax, a couple of days in Penang followed by a couple of days at **Cameron Highlands** would be nice. Those who just want to get away from it all should head straight to **Tioman.**

IF YOU HAVE 1 WEEK   Start in **Tioman** or **Kuantan** to unwind at the beach for 2 or 3 days, then spend a couple more days in the **Cameron Highlands** (or Genting, if you prefer theme parks and casinos). From there, head to **KL** to see what it is all about.

Alternately, start in **Malacca** for 2 days to take in the history, head for **KL** for another couple of days, then round off the trip in **Penang.**

IF YOU HAVE 2 WEEKS   A good way to break up the trip to see as much as you can would be to spend 3 days in **Tioman,** 2 days in **Kuantan,** 2 days in **Cameron Highlands,** 2 days in **Malacca,** 2 days in **KL,** and 3 days in **Penang.**

3 Tips on Accommodations

Peak months of the year for hotels are December, January, and February and July, August, and September. You will need to make reservations well in advance to secure your room during these months. The Commonwealth Games, an international sporting competition with participation of some 63 or more countries, will be held in Kuala Lumpur in September 1998, so the city is expected to be crammed then.

TAXES & SERVICE CHARGES   All the nonbudget hotels charge 10% service charge and 5% government tax. As such, there is no need to tip. But bellhops still tend to be tipped at least RM2 (US80¢) and car jockeys or valets should be tipped at least RM4 (US$1.60) or more.

4 Tips on Dining

I strongly recommend eating in a **hawker stall** when you can, especially in Penang, where the local food is absolutely delicious. Chapter 5 of this book gives an overview of Malaysian food, and some other cuisines you can expect to find in Malaysia. The chapter also gives tips on how to navigate a hawker center.

Also, many Malaysians eat with their hands off banana leaves when they are having *nasi padang* or *nasi kandar* (rice with mixed dishes). This is absolutely acceptable. If you choose to follow suit, wash your hands first and try to use your right hand, as the left is considered unclean (traditionally, it's the hand used to wash after a visit to the toilet). If you're eating at hawker stalls, it is advisable to go for freshly cooked hot or soupy dishes. Don't risk the precooked items.

Also, avoid having ice in your drink in the smaller towns, as it may come from a dubious water supply. If you ask for water, either make sure it's boiled or buy mineral water.

TAXES & SERVICE CHARGES   A 10% service charge and a 5% government tax are levied in proper restaurants, but hawkers charge a flat price.

5 Tips on Shopping

Shopping is a huge attraction for tourists in Malaysia. In addition to modern fashions and electronics, there are great local handicrafts. In each city section, I've listed some great places to go for local shopping.

For **handicrafts,** prices can vary. There are many handicraft centers, such as the **Karyaneka** in KL, 186–188 Jalan Raja Chulan (☎ **03/243-1868**), where these

Visiting Malaysia's Places of Worship

In Malaysia there are no designated hours for visiting mosques, temples, or churches. You may feel uncomfortable visiting in evening hours, and truly I don't recommend it, but during daylight hours feel free to go at any time. If you are unsure whether entry is permitted when you arrive, there will always be an office or caretaker available who can answer your questions and reassure you that it is fine to enter. Also, you may be uncomfortable entering a place of worship belonging to a religion other than your own if worship services are being conducted. Many religions don't mind spectators, but again, the caretaker can let you know if it would be proper to enter. By and large, you may wish to avoid mosques on Fridays between noon and 2:30pm, which are the hours for Friday afternoon prayers. Other than that, you should be fine.

goods can be astronomically priced, but you are assured of the quality. Alternatively, you could hunt out bargains in markets and at roadside stores in little towns, which can be much more fun.

Batik is one of the most popular arts in Malaysia, and the fabric can be purchased just about anywhere in the country. Batik can be fashioned into outfits and scarves or can be purchased as sarongs. Woven cloths in silks and metallic threads, called *songket,* are gorgeous, and are either made into traditional clothing styles or sold by the piece.

Traditional wood carvings have become popular collector's items. Statues and masks are carved by the Mah Meri tribe on the west coast in the state of Selangor. These carvings are traditionally used to cast off evil spirits and cure illness, and have become well sought-after by tourists.

Malaysia's **pewter products** are popular. Selangor Pewter is the brand that seems to have the most outlets and representation. You can get anything from a pewter picture frame to a pewter mug.

Silver designs are very refined, and jewelry and fine home items are still made by local artisans, especially in the northern parts of the peninsula. In addition, craft items such as **wayang kulit** (shadow puppets) and **wau** (colorful Malay kites, like the one on the cover of this book) make great gifts and souvenirs.

TAXES & SERVICE CHARGES   At dining/drinking establishments and hotels, be prepared to pay an additional 10% service charge and 5% government charge on top of your bill. Sales taxes, however, are hard to figure out because not all shops are consistent. Some will charge the government charge, while others won't. When shopping for imported goods—say, designer clothing or luggage—be prepared to pay the extra 5%. If the goods are locally produced, tax is often not charged, or is included in the tagged price.

FAST FACTS: Malaysia

American Express   In **Kuala Lumpur,** the American Express office is at Mayflower / American Express Travel on the 2nd floor, MAS Building, Jalan Sultan Ismail (☎ 03/261-0007). In **Penang,** Mayflower / Acme Travel in the Tan Cheong Building, 274 Victoria St. (☎ 04/262-3724). In **Johor Bahru,** Mayflower / Acme Tours, Wisma Tan Cheong, N027 2-F, Jalan Tun Abdul Razak (☎ 07/

224-1357). In **Kuantan,** Mayflower/Acme Tours, Tan Cheong Building, A7348, Jalan Beserah (☎ **09/513-1866**).

Area Codes   See "Telephones & Faxes," below.

Business Hours   Banks are open from 10am to 2pm Monday through Friday and 9:30 to 11:30am on Saturday. Government offices are open from 8am to 12:45pm and 2 to 4:15pm Monday through Friday and from 8am to 12:45pm on Saturday. Smaller shops like provision stores may open as early as 6 or 6:30am and close as late as 9pm, especially those near the wet markets. Many such stores are closed on Sunday afternoons and Saturday evenings and are busiest before lunch. Other shops open 9:30am to 7pm. Department stores and shops in malls tend to open later, about 10:30am or 11am till 8:30pm or 9pm throughout the week. Bars, except for those in Penang and the seedier bars in Johor Bahru, must close at 1am. Apparently, some close their doors and party on, but they never advertise this because places caught doing so have had their licenses suspended or equipment taken away in police raids. Your best bet would be to find a person in a disco or pub who looks like a real party animal and ask if he knows where to go after 1am.

Customs   See "Customs Regulations" in chapter 12.

Dentists & Doctors   Consultation and treatment fees vary greatly depending on whether the practitioner you have visited operates from a private or public clinic. The standard of treatment at some of the public clinics is known to be rather dubious, but then so are the standards of some of the small private clinics. However, it is still safer to go to a private doctor or dentist. Your best bet is to visit a private medical center if your ailment appears serious. These are often expensive but being virtual mini-hospitals, they have the latest equipment. If you just have a flu, it's quite safe to go to a normal MD. The fee at a private center ranges from RM20 to RM45 (US$8 to US$18).

Call ☎ **999** for emergencies. Find out about emergency evacuation services in your own country before coming over.

Drug Laws   As in Singapore, the death sentence is mandatory for drug trafficking (defined as being in possession of more than 15 grams of heroin or morphine, 200 grams of marijuana or hashish, or 40 grams of cocaine). For lesser quantities you'll be thrown in jail for a very long time and flogged with a cane.

Electricity   The voltage used in Malaysia is 220–240V at 50 cycles. The three-point square plugs (exactly the same as Singapore) are used. Buy an adapter if you plan to bring any appliances. Many larger hotels can provide adapters upon request.

Etiquette   Malaysia is becoming increasingly conservative. It's nowhere close to what it's like in the Middle East or India, but except for KL and maybe Penang and Johor Bahru, skimpy clothes are bound to garner disapproving glares. Don't dress to flash flesh, especially you ladies. You can wear contemporary clothes, but crop tops, short shorts, and miniskirts are frowned upon unless you're at a nightspot. Still, you're not about to get stoned and you're unlikely to be molested if you do dress like that—though you can expect to be rather insolently checked out.

People do shake hands, but don't use your left hand. Sometimes, you'll notice people giving you a really limp handshake and then seeming to wipe their hand on their chest. Don't be offended. The Malay-style handshake is a light touch of palm to palm, after which the hand is touched to the heart. It is a lovely symbolic gesture.

People in Malaysia seldom give each other the hug and peck on the cheek common to Westerners. It's not customary and you really shouldn't try it as it may cause some awkwardness. Respect each person's private space. Don't get too close, especially to members of the opposite sex. They may get the wrong idea.

Hitchhiking   It's not common among locals and I don't really think it's advisable for you either. The buses between cities are very affordable, so it's a much better idea to opt for those instead.

Language   The national language is Bahasa Malaysia, although English is widely spoken. Chinese dialects and Tamil are also spoken.

Liquor Laws   Liquor is sold in pubs and supermarkets in all big cities, or in provision stores. You'll hardly find any sold at Tioman though, so bring your own if you're headed there and wish to imbibe. A recent ruling requires pubs and other nightspots to officially close by 1am.

Newspapers & Magazines   English-language papers the *New Straits Times, The Star, The Sun,* and *The Edge* can be bought in hotel lobbies and magazine stands. Of the local magazines, *Day & Night* has great listings and local "what's happening" information for travelers.

Telephones & Faxes   Most hotels have International Direct Dialing service and will charge extra for calls made to use the service.

Local calls can be made from **public phones** using coins or phone cards. Half the public phones (the coin ones) don't seem to work in Malaysia. It's frustrating to have coins swallowed only to find that the phone isn't working, and won't give your money back.

One point about public phones that can be confusing is some phones take only 20 sen or 50 sen coins while others take 10 sen coins. Those that take the larger coins usually have an option for follow-on calls. If you've only spoken a short time and need to make another call, don't hang up after the first call; instead, just press the follow-on button and you can make another local call.

International calls can be made from phones that use cards, or from a telecom office.

- **To place a call from your home country to Malaysia,** dial the international access code (011 in the U.S., 0011 in Australia, 0170 in New Zealand, 00 in the U.K.), plus the country code (60), plus the Malaysia area code (Cameron Highlands 5, Desaru 7, Genting Highlands 9, Johor Bahru 7, Kuala Lumpur 3, Kuantan 9, Malacca 6, Mersing 7, Penang 4, Tioman 9), followed by the six- or seven-digit phone number (for example, from the U.S. to Kuala Lumpur, you'd dial 011+60+3+000-0000).
- **To call Malaysia from Singapore** via an operator, dial ☎ **109;** to call direct, dial the international access code (005) plus Malaysia's country code (60) plus the city code and the number (for example, to call Kuala Lumpur, you'd dial 005+60+3+000-0000).
- **To call Singapore from Malaysia,** dial the international access code (001), plus Singapore's country code (65), plus the seven-digit phone number (for example, 001+65+000-0000).
- **To place a call within Malaysia,** you must use area codes if calling between states. Note that for calls within the country, area codes are all preceded by a zero (i.e., Cameron Highlands 05, Desaru 07, Genting Highlands 09, Johor Bahru 07, Kuala Lumpur 03, Kuantan 09, Malacca 06, Mersing 07, Penang 04, Tioman 09).

- **To place a direct international call from Malaysia,** dial the international access code (001), plus the country code of the place you are dialing, plus the area code, plus the residential number of the other party.
- **To reach the international operator,** dial ☎ **108.**

International country codes are as follows: for the U.S. and Canada 01, for the U.K. 44, for Australia 61, and for New Zealand 62. Singapore's is 65.

Television   Guests in larger hotels can get satellite channels such as HBO, Star TV, or CNN. Internet cafes are becoming popular in the big cities, allowing you to access the major American news networks through the Internet. Local TV station TV3 shows English-language comedies, movies, and documentaries.

Time   Malaysia is 8 hours ahead of Greenwich mean time, 16 hours ahead of U.S. Pacific standard time, 13 ahead of eastern standard time, and 2 hours behind Sydney. It is the same time as Singapore. There is no daylight saving time.

Tipping   People don't tip, except bellhops and car jockeys. For these, an amount not less than RM4 (US$1.60) is okay.

Toilets   To find a public toilet, ask for the *tandas.* In Malay, *lelaki* is male and *perempuan* is female.

Water   Water in Kuala Lumpur is supposed to be potable, but most locals boil the water before drinking it—and if that's not a tip-off, I don't know what is. Elsewhere, just be safe and buy mineral water to drink. It costs about RM2 to RM2.50 (US80¢ to US$1) for a 1-liter bottle.

14 | The East Coast & Tioman Island

Most of the land covered in this chapter is in the state of Johor, the southernmost state in Malaysia. Johor Bahru, the capital, is a small and modern city, and the first stop in Malaysia for travelers coming over the causeway from Singapore. Along the east coast, Desaru is built on weekend visits by Singaporeans looking for family fun and golf. North of Desaru, Tioman Island is a scuba and beach lovers' paradise. (Tioman is actually in the state of Pahang, but is most easily accessed through Mersing, which is in Johor.)

Just north of Johor is Pahang, the largest state in Malaysia (covering about 35,960 sq. km). Despite all that space, only about a million people live here, which means travelers can experience some marvelously unspoiled inland jungle forests—which promise adventures in trekking, climbing, and river rafting—and beautiful beaches that stretch all the way up the coast. Much of Taman Negara, Malaysia's national forest preserve, is in this state, as are the hill resorts Cameron Highlands and Genting Highlands. (As the hill resorts are most commonly accessed from Kuala Lumpur, however, I've written about them in chapter 15.)

1 Johor Bahru

Johor Bahru, the capital of Johor, is at the southern tip of the Malaysian peninsula, where Malaysia's North-South Highway comes to its southern terminus. Since it's just over the causeway from Singapore, a very short drive by car or bus, it's one of the most popular points of entry to Malaysia. Johor Bahru is not the most fascinating destination in Malaysia, but for a short day visit from Singapore or as a short stopover en route to other Malaysian destinations, there's some good shopping and sightseeing.

While, ounce for ounce, Malacca's got the best historical life of any other city in Malaysia, Johor Bahru has some significance of its own. In 1511, when the Portuguese captured Malacca, the sultanate there relocated to Johor Bahru. In 1641, it aligned itself with the Dutch until the British came along and signed a treaty with Sultan Ali of Johor. The terms of the treaty gave Dato' Temenggong Daing Ibrahim control over Johor. His son, Sultan Abu Bakar, inherited control in 1866. Under his leadership, Johor adopted a constitution and instituted a modern government. The economy thrived, and Sultan Abu Bakar became known as "The Father of Modern Johor." It was Sultan Abu Bakar who built the Istana Besar, now the Royal

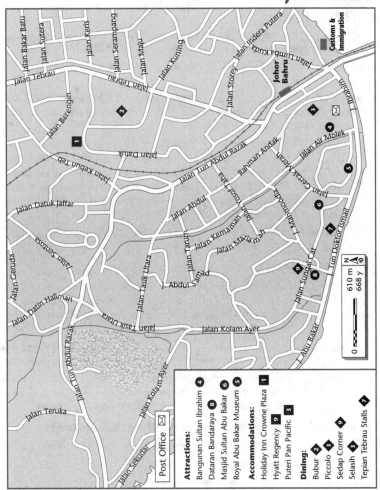

Attractions:
Bangunan Sultan Ibrahim **4**
Dataran Bandaraya **8**
Masjid Sultan Abu Bakar **6**
Royal Abu Bakar Museum **5**

Accommodations:
Holiday Inn Crowne Plaza **1**
Hyatt Regency **9**
Puteri Pan Pacific **3**

Dining:
Bubur **2**
Piccolo **1**
Sedap Corner **9**
Selasih **3**
Tepian Tebrau Stalls **7**

Abu Bakar Museum, which holds the historical treasures of the sultanate. The present sultan is His Majesty Sultan Iskander, who has held the title since 1981.

Today, Johor Bahru is a city of Malays, Chinese, and Indians, as well as other groups—not at all dissimilar to the cultural makeup of Singapore. Its proximity to Singapore makes the city the most cosmopolitan among its southern Malaysian neighbors. You're more likely to find colorful nightlife here, for instance, but the big attraction for tourists and Singaporeans is the shopping. Local handicrafts here are far less expensive than in Singapore, and what with the recent blow to the Malaysian Ringgit, bargaining (in the near future at least) may lead to even greater rewards for foreigners.

VISITOR INFORMATION

There are two offices of the **Malaysia Tourism Board** in Johor Bahru: at the Tanjung Puteri Tour Bus Complex (☎ **07/224-9485**) and at No. 1, 4th floor, Tun Abdul Razak Complex, Jalan Wong Ah Fook (☎ **07/224-0288**). The **Johor Tourist Association** is at the Holiday Inn Crowne Plaza (☎ **07/332-3800**).

GETTING THERE

BY CAR   If you arrive by car, you'll clear immigration at the **Customs Complex** (Jalan Bukit Meldrum, just past the Singapore-Malaysia causeway).

BY BUS   The **Johor Bahru Bus Terminal** is off Jalan Gertak Merah, near Orchid Plaza.

BY TRAIN   The Keretapi Tanah Melayu Berhad (KTM) trains arrive and depart from the **Johor Bahru Railway Station** (Jalan Tuk Abdul Raza, opposite Merlin Tower; ☎ **07/223-3040**).

BY PLANE   The **Senai Airport** in Johor Bahru has regular flights to major cities in Malaysia and to and from Singapore. The airport tax is RM20 (US$8) for international flights and RM5 (US$2) for domestic. For reservations on **Malaysian Airlines** flights call ☎ **07/334-1003** in Johor Bahru. A taxi from the airport to the city center will run you RM25 (US$10) per person, but for RM4 (US$1.60) you can pick up a shuttle from the Malaysian Airlines office at Plaza Pelangi on Jalan Kuning.

BY FERRY   There is also a FerryLink service from Singapore's Changi Point to Tanjung Belungkor. (See information under "Getting There" in chapter 12.)

SEEING THE SIGHTS

The sights in Johor Bahru are few, but there are some interesting museums and a beautiful istana and mosque. Johor Bahru is a fabulous place to stay for a day, especially if it's just for a day trip from Singapore, but to stay for longer may be stretching the point.

Royal Abu Bakar Museum. Grand Palace, Johor. Jalan Tun Dr Ismail. ☎ **07/223-0555.** Adults RM26.29 (US$10.50), children under 12 RM11.27 (US$4.50). Sat–Thurs 10am–5pm.

Also called the Istana Besar, this gorgeous royal palace was built by Sultan Abu Bakar in 1866. Today it houses the royal collection of international treasures, costumes, historical documents, and fine art from the family collection.

Bangunan Sultan Ibrahim (State Secretariat Building). Jalan Abd Ibrahim.

The State Secretariat is housed in this building, which was built in 1940.

Masjid Sultan Abu Bakar. Jalan Masjid.

This mosque was built after the death of Sultan Abu Bakar in 1897.

Dataran Bandaraya. Centered around Jalan Wong Ah Fook. ☎ **607/332-3800**.

Dataran Bandaraya, the City Square, is a new building where the tourism assocation holds promotional festivals from time to time.

ACCOMMODATIONS

Several international chains have accommodations in JB. Most are intended for the business set, but holiday travelers will find the accommodations very comfortable.

The Holiday Inn Crowne Plaza. Jalan Dato Sulaiman, Century Garden, 80990 Johor Bahru, Johor. ☎ **800/465-4329** from the U.S. and Canada, 800/221066 from Australia, 0800/442222 from New Zealand, 0800/987121 from the U.K., or 07/332-3800. Fax 07/331-8884. 350 units. A/C MINIBAR TV TEL. RM370–RM410 (US$148–US$164) double; RM420–RM460 (US$168–US$184) Club Floor. AE, DC, JCB, MC, V.

While this hotel is not walking distance from the city center, it was the first five-star business-class hotel in Johor Bahru, and is larger than the other hotels in the city. It is comfortable and not overly formal, with furniture wrapped in traditional fabrics, wood paneling details, and marble floors in the lobby. VCRs are available upon request, with RM15 (US$6) video rentals. Services include airport shuttle and valet service. Facilities include a midsize outdoor pool; fitness center with sauna, steam bath, and massage; one squash court; and a business center, and there is a shopping complex attached. Discount packages are available.

The Hyatt Regency. Jalan Sungai Chat, P.O. Box 222, 80720 Johor Bahru, Johor. ☎ **800/233-1234** or 07/222-1234. Fax 07/223-2718. 400 units. A/C MINIBAR TV TEL. RM360–RM420 (US$144–US$168) double; RM500–RM550 (US$200–US$220) Executive Floor; RM1,000–RM4,000 (US$400–US$1,600) suite. AE, DC, JCB, MC, V.

The Hyatt is near the City Square, but likes to fancy itself as a city resort, focusing on landscaped gardens and greenery around the premises. The deluxe rooms are located better than the others, with views of Singapore and fabulous sunsets. Facilities include fitness center with sauna, Jacuzzi, and massage; two-level outdoor pool; two tennis courts; and a business center. Discount packages are available.

The Puteri Pan Pacific. "The Kotaraya," P.O. Box 293, 80730 Johor Bahru, Johor. ☎ **07/223-3333**, or 800/8533 toll-free in Malaysia. Fax 07/223-6622. 460 units. A/C MINIBAR TV TEL. RM350–RM450 (US$140–US$180) double; RM450–RM1,600 (US$180–US$640) suite. AE, DC, JCB, MC, V.

The good news is it's located in the heart of the city, near attractions and shopping. The bad news is it is a very busy hotel and human traffic makes it noisy and somewhat on the run-down side. Nevertheless, little traditional touches to the decor make the Pan Pacific unique. Facilities include an outdoor pool, tennis and squash courts, fitness center, saunas, steam room, and business center. The Pacific Plus package offers a better rate.

DINING

The majority of the fine dining in Johor Bahru is in the hotels. Outside the hotels you have some great local-style cuisine, both Malay and Chinese, and wonderful seafood from the city's hawker stalls.

Bubur. 191 Jalan Harimau, Century Garden. ☎ **07/335-5891.** Reservations held for a half hour only. Entrees RM7–RM12 (US$2.80–US$4.80). AE, MC, V. Daily 11am–5am. Closed 4 days into the Chinese New Year. TAIWAN CHINESE.

For fast, inexpensive eats you can even order to take away, try this place. It's a family restaurant, so it can get pretty lively. The staff is quick and attentive without being imposing. Best dishes are the traditional braised pork in soya sauce and the grilled pomfret (a type of fish) in black bean sauce.

Piccolo. Hyatt Regency, Jalan Sungai Chat. ☎ **07/222-1234.** Entrees RM20–RM58 (US$8–US$23.20). AE, DC, JCB, MC, V. Daily 11:30am–2:30pm and 6:30–10:30pm. ITALIAN.

Perhaps one of the most popular places for the expatriate community in Johor Bahru, the poolside ambiance has a very tropical and relaxed feel to it. Under the timber awning, the high ceiling and bamboo chick blinds give it a balcony feel. By the pool, the subtle lighting and lush foliage make it very romantic. For a good dish, try the grilled seafood.

Sedap Corner. 11 Jalan Abdul Samad. ☎ **07/224-6566.** Reservations recommended. Entrees RM4.50–RM24 (US$1.80–US$9.60) (most dishes no more than RM6/US$2.40). No credit cards. Daily 9am–9:45pm. THAI/CHINESE/MALAY.

Sedap Corner is very popular with the locals. It's dressed down in metal chairs and Formica-top tables, with a very coffee-shop feel. Local dishes like sambal sabah, otak otak, and fish head curry are house specials, and you don't have to worry about it being too spicy.

Selasih. The Puteri Pan Pacific, "The Kotaraya." ☎ **07/223-3333**, ext. 3151. Reservations recommended. Buffet lunch RM22 (US$8.80); Buffet dinner RM35 (US$14). AE, DC, JCB, MC, V. Daily 11:30am–2:30pm and 6:30pm–10:30pm. MALAY.

For a taste of Malaysian cuisine, Selasih has a daily buffet spread of over 70 items, featuring regional dishes from all over the country. Every night, the dinner buffet is accompanied by traditional Malay music and dance performances. For extra value, seniors over 55 receive a 50% discount and children under 12 pay only RM1 for each of their years.

HAWKER CENTERS

The **Tepian Tebrau Stalls** in Jalan Skudai (along the seafront) and the stalls near the **Central Market** offer cheap local eats in hawker-center style.

SHOPPING

The **Johor Craftown Handicraft Centre** on Jalan Skudai off Jalan Abu Bakar has, in addition to a collection of local crafts, demonstration performances of handicraft techniques. At **MAWAR Complex** on 562 Jalan Sungei Chat, in the Mawar House is **Karyaneka,** selling batik and other textiles, baskets, wood carvings, and pottery. **Johorcraft,** on Jalan Johor Bahru and Kota Tinggi, is another handicraft center. **JOTIC,** 2 Jalan Ayer Molek, is a supermall with tourist information, cultural performances, exhibits, demonstrations of crafts, and food stalls.

2 Johor's Outdoors

In addition to its cities and towns, Johor also has some beautiful nature to take in, which is great if you have only a short time to see Malaysia and can't afford to travel north to some of the larger national parks.

Johor Endau Rompin National Park is about 488 square kilometers (293 sq. miles) of lowland forest. There's camping in four sites and jungle trekking through 26 kilometers (16 miles) of trails and over rivers to see diverse tropical plant species, colorful birds, and wild animals. Take the North-South Highway (from either Johor Bahru or Kuala Lumpur) to Kluang. Travel to Kahang, where you can pick up a four-wheel-drive vehicle to the visitors center and park entrance. For more information, contact the National Parks (Johor) Corporation, JKR 475, Bukit Timbalan, Johor Bahru (☎ **07/223-7471**). It's advised that you obtain an entry permit in advance of your visit.

The Waterfalls at Lombong, near Kota Tinggi, measuring about 34 meters (112 ft.) high, are about 56 kilometers (34 miles) northeast of Johor Bahru. You can cool off in the pools below and enjoy the area's chalets, camping facilities, restaurant, and food stalls.

GOLF

Johor is a favorite destination for golf enthusiasts. The **Royal Johor Country Club** and **Pulai Springs Country Club** are just outside Johor Bahru and offer a range of country club facilities, while other courses are a bit more traveling time, but offer resort-style accommodations. Greens fees will vary from weekends to weekdays and depend on whether you're a guest or just visiting for the day. You'll pay anywhere between RM50 and RM250 (US$20 and US$100).

One note of caution: If you play in Johor, especially at the Royal Johor Country Club, don't wear yellow. As the official color of the sultan, he is the only one allowed to wear it on the courses.

- **Royal Johor Country Club,** 3211, Jalan Larkin, 80200 Johor Bahru, Johor (☎ **07/223-3322;** fax 07/224-0729)
- **Palm Resort Golf & Country Club,** Jalan Persiaran Golf off Jalan Jumbo, 81250 Senai, Johor (☎ **07/599-6222;** fax 07/599-6001)
- **Desaru Golf & Country Club,** Tanjung Penazar, 81907 Kota Tinggi, Johor (☎ **07/822-1445;** fax 07/822-1855)
- **Tanjung Puteri Golf & Country Club,** Pasir Gudang, 81700 Johor Bahru, Johor (☎ **07/251-3533;** fax 07/251-3466)
- **Starhill Golf & Country Club,** 6.5 KM, Maju Jaya, Kempas Lama, 81330 Sekudai, Johor Bahru, Johor (☎ **07/556-6325;** fax 07/556-7327)
- **Kukup Golf Resort,** Pekan Penerok, 82300 Pontian Johor, Johor (☎ **07/ 696-0952;** fax 07/696-0961)
- **Tioman Island Golf Club,** Pulau Tioman, P.O. Box 4, 86807 Mersing, Johor (☎ **09/445-445;** fax 09/445-716)
- **Pulai Springs Country Club,** 64 Jalan Padi Satu, Bandar Baru Uda, 81200 Johor Bahru, Johor (☎ **07/520-7222;** fax 07/520-7999)
- **Sebana Golf & Marina Resort,** P.O. Box 102, Bandar Penawar Post Office, 81900 Kota Tinggi, Johor (☎ **07/825-2028;** fax 07/825-2033)

3 Desaru

Desaru is an odd sort of place, a man-made holiday resort town where once you reach the resorts' outer areas, you're pretty much in the middle of nowhere. The advantage of Desaru is that it's not far from Singapore, so you can get there and back pretty fast (which makes it popular with Singaporeans, who come to play golf or for weekend getaways). The disadvantage is that there are far more fabulous places to go for idyllic beaches, good scuba, and golf. The beaches are okay, but the water could be cleaner, and there's a strong undertow that makes it somewhat dangerous for swimmers. What's more, there are plans underway to develop Desaru further, and investors are lining up to dump tons of money and turn the town into what will undoubtedly be a very contrived, soulless resort area.

GETTING THERE

BY CAR   You can reach Desaru over well-laid roads by car and bus from Johor Bahru.

BY FERRY   From Singapore's Changi Ferry Terminal, 30 Changi Ferry Rd., there's a FerryLink service (☎ **65/545-3600;** fax 65/542-9615) that lets you off in Malaysia at the **Tanjong Belungkor Ferry Terminal** (☎ **07/251-7404,** 07/251-7407, or 07/ 251-7408; fax 07/251-7414). One-way passenger fares from Singapore are S$18 (US$11.35) for adults, S$11 (US$6.95) for children; round-trip fares are S$24 (US$15.10) for adults, S$15 (US$9.45) for children. From Tanjong Belungkor to Singapore, the one-way adult fare is RM32 (US$12.80), child RM20 (US$8); round-trip adult RM44 (US$17.60), child RM27 (US$10.80). You can even bring your car or a bike. Vehicle fares for a car from Singapore one way are S$24 (US$15.10), round-trip S$32 (US$20.15); from Tanjong Belungkor to Singapore, it's one way RM44 (US$17.60), round-trip RM58 (US$23.20). Bicycle from Singapore one way is S$5 (US$3.15), round-trip S$7 (US$4.40); from Tanjong Belungkor to Singapore one way it's RM9 (US$3.60), round-trip RM13 (US$5.20). Ferries depart Singapore daily at 8:15am, 11:15am, 2:15pm, and 5:15pm, and depart Tanjong Belungkor at 9:45am, 12:45pm, 3:45pm, and 6:45pm. Contact your accommodations to arrange for shuttle service to Desaru.

ACCOMMODATIONS

Desaru Golden Beach Resort. P.O. Box 50, Tanjung Penawar, 81907 Kota Tinggi, Johor. ☎ **07/822-1101.** Fax 07/822-1480. 57 units, 115 villas. A/C MINIBAR TV TEL. Weekdays RM150–RM200 (US$60–US$80) double; RM350 (US$140) suite; RM170 (US$68) villa, RM370 (US$148) villa suite. Weekends RM220–RM280 (US$88–US$112) double; RM420 (US$168) suite; RM240 (US$96) villa, RM450 (US$180) villa suite. AE, DC, JCB, MC, V.

Desaru Golden Beach Resort is part of the Desaru resort complex, comprised of 12 hotels and many golf courses, located along 17 kilometers (10 miles) of sandy beach. This hotel is casual and comfortable, with a tropical open-air concept lobby with a high timbered ceiling to allow for cool breezes. The standard rooms face the parking area and garden, while the superior rooms face the sea, and are assigned on a first-come, first-served basis. These rooms are casual and comfortable, though certain details (like the bathrooms) are old, and not in a charming way. The villas, which are nestled between trees and the beach, are brand new. Facilities include a large outdoor pool, access to the fitness center at Desaru Perdana Beach Resort, a Jacuzzi, two outdoor tennis courts, water-sports equipment, and bicycle rental.

The main attraction here besides the beach is golfing. Greens fees for hotel guests are RM70 (US$28) on weekdays and RM110 (US$44) on weekends. The resort complex has 45 holes, not including the 18-hole signature Robert Trent Jones Jr. course.

Desaru Perdana Beach Resort. P.O. Box 29, Bandar Penawar, 81900 Kota Tinggi, Johor. ☎ **07/822-2222.** Fax 07/822-2223. 229 units. Package 1 includes standard sea-view rm and American breakfast: weekdays RM210 (US$84) double, RM288.75 (US$115.50) triple; weekends RM262.50 (US$105) double, RM341.25 (US$136.50) triple. Package 2 includes standard sea-view rm, American breakfast, ferry service, and jetty transfer: weekdays RM337.75 (US$135.10) double, RM476 (US$190.40) triple; weekends RM381.50 (US$152.60) double, RM519.75 (US$207.90) triple. AE, DC, MC, V.

Also part of the Desaru beach resort area, the Desaru Perdana Beach Resort is another favorite for golfers. It is newer than the Desaru Golden Beach Resort, and is a classy mix of louvered sliding and glass doors and rattan furnishings. Expect five-star quality service and huge rooms with balconies. Ask for the sea-view rooms. Facilities include a large outdoor pool, a small fitness center, Jacuzzi, sauna, tennis courts, water-sports equipment, and a souvenir shop.

Desaru Tennis Ranch Hotel. P.O. Box 20, Tanjung Penawar, Desaru, 81907 Kota Tinggi, Johor. ☎ **07/822-1211** or 07/822-1213. Fax 07/822-1937. 36 chalets. A/C TV. Weekdays RM165 (US$66) standard double, RM225 (US$90) superior double; RM225 (US$90) family; RM290 (US$116) suite. Weekends RM200 (US$80) standard double, RM270 (US$108) superior double; RM270 (US$108) family; RM375 (US$150) suite. AE, DC, MC, V.

Just next to the beach is this small group of basic, quiet, kampung-like chalets. The chalets have a living room, a verandah, and a kitchenette, and some have wood floors while others have cement. You could say it has a rustic charm, but if you're fussy about having things clean and new, this is not the place for you. Rooms have refrigerators, but only 10 have telephones. Guests of the chalets can use the sports and exercise facilities at the Desaru Golden Beach Hotel. Bring your room key for identification purposes.

DESARU OUTDOORS

It goes without saying that many visitors come for the golf. Guests at the **Desaru Golf & Country Club,** P.O. Box 57, Tanjung Penawar, 81907 Kota Tinggi, Johor (☎ **07/822-2333;** fax 07/822-1855), can play on the 45 holes and the 18-hole Robert Trent Jones Jr. course. Greens fees for 18 holes on weekends and public holidays are RM150 (US$60), and are RM90 (US$36) Monday through Friday. Nine holes after 4pm weekends and public holidays cost RM55 (US$22) and on weekdays RM45 (US$18). Greens fees are discounted for guests of the Desaru Golden Beach Hotel. Club rentals, shoes, trolleys, and buggies are available for rent, and caddy fees range from RM12 (US$4.80) for a trainee to RM20 (US$8) for the best they've got. Be sure to confirm your reservation 2 weeks beforehand.

At the hotels in Desaru you can arrange hikes in the nearby jungle and horseback riding.

For water sports, check out the **Happy Sports Centre** on the sea between the Desaru Golden Beach Hotel and Desaru Chalet (☎ 10/775-6506). They're open from 9:30am to 5:30pm daily with rentals of jet skis, go-karts, windsurf boards, inner tubes, sailboats, and kayaks. They can also arrange boat rides, parasailing, waterskiing, fishing trips, and speedboat rides.

A little off the beaten track is **Tanjung Balau Fishing Village,** 5.2 kilometers (3.12 miles) from Desaru, which is a tourist spot where visitors can see the life of local fishermen and their families by the sea. You can join in on the fishing activities, traveling out to sea for a day's work, and then stay in one of five dormitories. For bookings, call ☎ **07/822-1201,** or fax 07/822-1600. Or contact the Tourism Manager, KEJORA Headquarters, Jalan Dato' Onn, Bandar Penawar, 81900 Kota Tinggi, Johor, Malaysia.

Also in the village, visit the **Fisherman Museum,** with displays of generations of equipment and fishing techniques.

4 Mersing

Mersing is not so much a destination in itself, but more a jump-off point for ferries to the islands on the east coast of Malaysia, such as Tioman, Dayang, Sibu, or Aur. Nobody really stays in Mersing unless they've missed the boat—literally. There are a couple of good seafood restaurants in town, but otherwise it's just a small, relaxed fishing town.

GETTING THERE

BY BUS   Air-conditioned buses leave **Singapore** at 9am and 10am daily from Lavender Street Junction, off Kallang Bahru. For information, call **Pan Malaysia** at ☎ **65/294-7035.** Tickets are S$13.10 (US$8.25) to Mersing. Air-conditioned buses leave **Kuala Lumpur** from Pudu Raya Bus Station, on Jalan Cheng Lock (☎ **03/230-0145**) and from the Kelang Bus stand on Jalan Sultan Mohamed. It costs around RM16 (US$6.40). A night bus leaves at 10:30pm and arrives in Mersing at 5:30am.

ACCOMMODATIONS

Mersing has no world-class accommodations or resorts. The places you'll find here are basic accommodations for those just passin' through. Aside from the two places below, other budget accommodations can be found along Jalan Endau, near the beach. Most have shared bathrooms with no television, air-conditioning, or telephones, and rates vary from RM15 to RM20 (US$6 to US$8), cash only.

Mersing Inn. 38 Jalan Ismail, next to the Parkson supermarket, 86800, Mersing, Johor. ☎ **07/799-2288.** Fax 07/799-1919. 40 units. RM55 (US$22) double. MC.

The rooms are small but clean, but some do not have air-conditioning, so be sure to specify. Likewise, some don't have televisions or telephones. The one "luxury"? Private baths for each room.

Timotel. 839 Jalan Endau, 86800, Mersing, Johor. ☎ **07/799-5888.** Fax 07/799-5333. 50 units. A/C MINIBAR TV TEL. RM120–RM180 (US$48–US$112) double; RM240–RM270 (US$96–US$108) suite. AE, MC.

This motel, one of the newest and most pleasant in Mersing, has clean and neat rooms and modern conveniences like room service and laundry service. The hotel provides free transfers to and from the jetty. There's a fitness center, and bicycle rental can be arranged.

DINING

Like the hotels in Mersing, none of the restaurants are particularly "fine." There is, however, some pretty good seafood to be eaten here, if you don't mind a really low-key and colloquial dining experience. Neither of the places below has a phone, and if they did they probably wouldn't use them for silly things like taking reservations. Just head on down and find a table.

Ee lo Restoran. Jalan Abu Bakar, next to the roundabout beside the newspaper shop. No phone. Meals from RM5–RM10 (US$2–US$4). No credit cards.

This place is pretty popular for the backpacker set, who come for the chicken rice and roasted pork. It's an old coffeehouse, and although the hygiene levels may seem dubious, the food is tasty. The steamed prawns are succulent, and they have an unusual dish—stir-fried vegetables in milk—which is quite tasty. Lunch for two will run you RM30 (US$12).

Mersing Seafood Restaurant. Jalan Ismail, next to the Shell station. No phone. Noodle dishes RM5 (US$2); other dishes RM10 (US$4) and up. No credit cards.

You won't need a reservation, even though it gets crowded on weekends. The service is lousy and the place is a little grubby, but the food is so good nobody seems to care. Prices will range according to season. Some great dishes to try are the deep-fried squid stuffed with salted egg yolk, the bamboo or asparagus clams fried in chili sauce, or the sautéed garlic prawns.

5 Tioman Island

Tioman Island is without a doubt the most popular destination on Malaysia's east coast. For the record, it's really in the state of Pahang, but is covered in the Johor section of the book because it is most commonly accessed through Mersing, which is in Johor. The island is only 39 kilometers (23.4 miles) long and 12 kilometers (7.2 miles) wide, but has sandy beaches, clear water with sea life and coral reefs, and jungle mountain-trekking trails with streams and waterfalls. Its idyllic setting was the location for the 1950s Hollywood film *South Pacific*.

Despite heavy tourist traffic, Tioman has retained much of its tropical island charm, perhaps by virtue of the fact that few large hotels have been built on it. However, some parts are becoming very commercial, particularly **Kampung Tekek,** which is where you arrive at either the main jetty or the airport. A paved stretch of road runs up the west coast, between Tekek and **Berjaya Tioman Beach Resort** (the largest and most modern resort on the island), and this area is more built up than the rest of the island. "Built up" is really a relative term; however, if you trek overland from Tekek to the east coast, you'll find beaches that are more peaceful and serene.

Activity is spread throughout the kampungs along the shores of the island. Each of these places has some sort of accommodations facilities (most of them very basic) with some access to canteens or restaurants. On the west coast to the north of Tekek is **Kampung Air Batang,** more popularly called ABC, which retains much

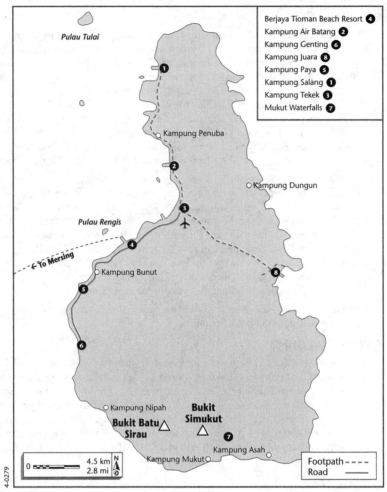

Berjaya Tioman Beach Resort **4**
Kampung Air Batang **2**
Kampung Genting **6**
Kampung Juara **8**
Kampung Paya **5**
Kampung Salang **1**
Kampung Tekek **3**
Mukut Waterfalls **7**

Pulau Tulai

1

Kampung Penuba

2

○ Kampung Dungun

Pulau Rengis

3

4

← To Mersing

○ Kampung Bunut

8

5

6

○ Kampung Nipah   **Bukit Simukut**

Bukit Batu Sirau △   △   **7**

Kampung Asah ○

Kampung Mukut ○

0   4.5 km
     2.8 mi   N

Footpath ----
Road ———

4-0279

picturesque ambiance even though it is one of the more popular spots. Farther north is **Kampung Salang,** which also gets pretty crowded. ABC and Salang are also the headquarters for a few of the scuba-diving operations. To the south of Tekek, still on the west coast, is the **Berjaya Tioman Resort.** Farther south are **Kampungs Paya** and **Genting.** On the east coast is **Kampung Juara.** If you want the most secluded area of the island, Juara is best. In order to reach it you must trek across the center of the island or take the water bus around to the jetty there. At Juara, the beach is a long, dazzling crescent of sand and the water is very clear.

There is a small local population on the island living in the kampungs, but at almost any given time there are more tourists, most of whom come from Singapore and other parts of Malaysia, than locals. Most come for the scuba and beaches, but from November through February you won't find many tourists. Monsoon tides make Tioman hard to access by ferry, and not the most perfect vacation in the tropical balmies.

GETTING THERE

BY PLANE   Flights to Tioman originate from **Singapore, Kuala Lumpur, Kuantan,** and **Johor Bahru.** From Singapore's Seletar Airport, **Pelangi Air** (☎ 65/ 336-6777), a division of Malaysia Airlines, has daily flights departing at 11am and 1:20pm and arriving at 11:40am and 2pm, respectively. The trip costs approximately RM115 (US$46) one way. From Kuala Lumpur's Terminal 3, Pelangi Air operates two flights daily, departing at 9am and 10:40am for a cost of RM141 (US$56.40). The flight lasts only 1 hour and 10 minutes. Pelangi Air flights from Kuantan's Sultan Ahmad Shah Airport depart at 11:30am daily. They cost RM79 (US$31.60), and the flight is 40 minutes. Daily flights from Johor Bahru's Sultan Ismail International Airport depart daily at 1:20pm for a 40-minute flight. The Pelangi Air flight costs RM100 (US$40).

BY FERRY   Ferries depart Mersing from the Mersing Jetty, a short walk from the center of town, located just next to the R&R Plaza. There are many operators to choose from, and if you take the time to wander in each place, you may be able to get a better fare. Boats leave Mersing Jetty at intervals that depend on the tide. The trip takes around 1½ hours and can cost between RM20 and RM25 (US$8 and US$10), depending on the power of the boat you hire. Try to get to the jetty within office hours. You'll be besieged by people offering the services of their craft, but take time to step into the offices around the jetty that have brochures.

BY CHARTER PLANE   Also at R&R Plaza, a three-seater charter plane can make the trip for RM55 (US$22) per person.

GETTING AROUND

Walking between some kampungs is pretty difficult when there's no path. Generally the west coast is a little better, and there's a regular path that cuts through the island from Tekek to Juara. Basically the best way to get around is by hiring sea buses. Each kampung has a jetty, and operators come by frequently throughout the day. Tickets are sold at booths near the jetties, where you can also get schedules. Hiring a speedboat will cost RM75 (US$30), but will rush your trip. For a regular speed bumboat it costs anywhere between RM10 and RM50 (US$4 and US$20), depending on where you're going.

USEFUL TIPS

MONEY   There are money changers who accept traveler's checks in Tekek at the airport, by the jetty, and at Berjaya Tioman Resort. Other places will take traveler's checks, and some of the smaller accommodations now accept them as payment. The best idea for a better rate is to cash them at a bank on the mainland before you go.

TELEPHONES   There are public phones at Tekek, ABC, and Salang, which you can use with phonecards bought on the island. Most guest houses have nothing more than cellular phones, which they will allow guests to use—at a price.

DINING   You won't find fantastic food on the island. Most cuisine is simple sandwiches, burgers, fish-and-chips, and some breakfast foods. There are provisions shops here and there, but prices are marked up. Bring some food and beverages from the mainland if you want to save some pennies. Alcohol is served in very few places, so bring your own beverages if you intend to imbibe. At Salang, the Sunset Bar serves drinks, but closes at midnight. The Berjaya Tioman Resort also serves alcohol, as do some other hotels that have recently opened.

VISIBILITY   Bring a flashlight, as it can be a little dark after sunset.

ACCOMMODATIONS

Unless you stay at the Best Western Berjaya Tioman Beach Resort, expect to be roughing it a little. For some travelers, the Berjaya Tioman, with its wonderful modern conveniences, is what it takes to make a tropical island experience the most relaxing. Your shower is always warm, you can order food to your room, and you can arrange any activity through the concierge in the lobby. For others, though, real relaxation comes from an escape from modern distractions. The small hotels in the kampungs have very minimal facilities and little to no conveniences such as hot showers and telephones. Why would you want to stay in them? Because they're simple, quiet, close to the beach, and less touristy than the resort. The downside is that sometimes you must travel to Tekek or ABC to set up diving or fishing activities. You will also have to trek around to find dining options, as few of these places have canteens. Yes, you sacrifice a lot, but the peaceful nature of the island is a more idyllic experience when you stay at one of these places.

Best Western Berjaya Tioman Beach Resort. Tioman Island, Pahang Darul Makmur. ☎ **09/419-1000.** Fax 09/419-1718. 380 units. A/C MINIBAR TV TEL. Mar–Oct RM245 (US$98) standard rm; RM340–RM430 (US$136–US$172) chalet; RM500–RM1,200 (US$200–US$480) suite. Nov–Feb RM195 (US$78) standard rm; RM265–RM345 (US$106–US$138) chalet; RM400–RM720 (US$160–US$288) suite. AE, DC, MC, V.

Berjaya Tioman is one of the biggest resorts on the island, and provides all the conveniences you'd want from a five-star Western hotel. For modern comforts and golf, this is the place to be, but be prepared for tourism central. A range of sports opportunities and facilities is offered, including scuba diving, windsurfing, sailing, fishing, snorkeling, canoeing, glass-bottom boat rides, horseback riding, four tennis courts, swimming pools, spa pool, waterslide, children's playground, 18-hole international championship standard golf course with pro shop, jungle treks, slot machines and video games, billiards, and boat trips to nearby islands.

Services include complimentary airport transfers, foreign currency exchange, and laundry services. There are four restaurants and a bar on the premises.

ACCOMMODATIONS IN KAMPUNG GENTING

Sun Beach Resort. Kampung Genting, Pulau Tioman. ☎ **800/888-220.** 70 units. RM30–RM150 (US$12–US$60) double. No credit cards. Located on the beach near the Kampung Genting jetty.

Ten rooms here have air-conditioning, and there's a sports center, restaurant, and gift shop on the premises.

ACCOMMODATIONS IN KAMPUNG PAYA

Paya Beach Resort. Kampung Paya, Pulau Tioman. ☎ **07/799-1432.** 30 units. A/C. RM130 (US$52) double; RM175 (US$70) family. Rates include American breakfast. AE, MC, V.

This little tropical longhouse along the beach has net rooms and hot showers. There's a billiard table and TV room, and diving, snorkeling, and deep-sea fishing are available. Services include airport transfer and ferry transfer from Mersing. Feel free to bargain for lower rates between September and February.

Sri Paya Holiday. Kampung Paya, Pulau Tioman. ☎ **11/716-196** (mobile phone). 28 units. RM30–RM40 (US$12–US$16) standard rm, RM80–RM120 (US$32–US$48) with air-conditioning. No credit cards.

Facilities here include a sports center, and speedboats and bumboats are available for hire.

ACCOMMODATIONS IN ABC

ABC Beach Tioman. ABC Beach, Pulau Tioman, 86800, Mersing. ☎ **11/349-868.** 25 units. RM50 (US$20) family rm; RM25 (US$10) standard double; RM15 (US$6) sea-view chalet. No credit cards. 10-minute walk from ABC Jetty.

Located on a hillside overlooking the water, the landscaped gardens and beautiful beach are as Bali Hai as it gets. The family rooms have a double bed and one extra twin, with a large verandah overlooking the water and an attached bathroom with toilet, basin, and cold shower. There's no air-conditioning in any of the rooms, but family rooms have a ceiling fan. Standard doubles have a double bed, mosquito netting, and a wall fan. There's an attached bathroom with a toilet basin and cold shower. Towels are not provided. The sea-view chalets have two single futon beds, a large verandah, and electricity, but no fan. Communal showers and toilets are in a block nearby. Facilities include a Western restaurant open from 8am to 9pm, a lending library, and safety deposit boxes. Snorkeling gear and speedboats are available for hire, telephone services are available, and traveler's checks can be cashed.

ACCOMMODATIONS IN JUARA

Happy Cafe Juara. Kampong Juara, Pulau Tioman, Mersing, Malaysia. No phone. 5 units. Bargain for very low rates. Traveler's checks accepted.

Rooms have showers, fans, and double beds. It's near the jetty and has a canteen and supermarket.

Juara Bay Resort. Bakar Hill, Kampung Juara, Pulau Tioman. No phone. 15 units. RM50 (US$20) (feel free to bargain). Traveler's checks cashed.

Rooms are air-conditioned, with shower stalls and wooden double beds. There is also a place to eat, the Bougainvillea Restaurant.

Juara Mutiara. RM5–RM40 (US$2–US$16) (you must bargain).

Rooms have showers attached. For RM25 there's snorkeling, fishing, or canoeing.

DINING IN ABC

Nazri's Place. Kampung ABC, Tioman Island, Mersing. ☎ **11/349-534.** Reservations recommended. Breakfast RM5–RM10 (US$2–US$4); lunch RM10 (US$4); dinner RM15 (US$6). No credit cards. WESTERN/MALAY.

Your basic burger and sandwiches joint, this place is on the beach, and decorated with coral in front. During the day it's busy and noisy, but it's worth coming for dinner, when they serve Malay cuisine. The place serves beer.

TIOMAN OUTDOORS

FISHING There are fishing boats you can hire in Tekek for the day, either to troll the waters along the coast or to go deep-sea fishing farther off.

SCUBA DIVING Most of the vacationers here come to scuba dive. The island is very popular for diving, especially for Singaporeans who would otherwise suffer murky waters. There are dive operators at the west coast beaches, and dives cost between RM50 and RM70 (US$20 and US$28). **DiveAsia,** Kampong Salang, Pulau Tioman, Pahang Darul Makmur (☎ **11/716-783**), a 5-minute walk from Kampung Salang Jetty, has classes for all levels of divers, daily dives, night dives, free use of dive suits, and complimentary refreshments. Traveler's checks, American Express, MasterCard, and Visa are accepted. Certification training costs around RM630 (US$252).

SNORKELING   Snorkeling is also a favorite activity, although much of the coral closer to the shore is dead. Either way, the equipment can be rented at the west coast beaches.

TRAIL TREKKING   After you're all waterlogged, you can trek the trail from **Tekek to Juara,** and some of the paths along the west coast. The hike across the island will take around 3 hours. Bring water and don't try it unless you are reasonably fit.

At the southern part of the island are **Bukit Batu Sirau** and **Bukit Simukut,** "The Famous Twin Peaks," and closer to the water near Kampung Mukut are the **Mukut Waterfalls.** There are two smallish pools for taking a dip. Some regular trails exist, but it's inadvisable to venture too far from them because the forest gets dense and it can be tough to find your way back.

6 Pahang: Kuantan, Cherating & Taman Negara National Park

In terms of land mass, Pahang (sort of officially shortened from Pahang Darul Makmur) is the largest state in Malaysia. Up the east coast from Johor, it covers about 35,960 square kilometers of area. Despite its space, there are only one million people living in all of Pahang. Travelers come here for the beautiful beaches, which stretch all the way up the east coast, and for inland jungle forests that promise adventures in trekking, climbing, and river rafting. Much of **Taman Negara,** Malaysia's national forest preserve, is in Pahang, as are the Cameron Highlands and Genting Highlands hill resorts. **Kuantan,** the capital of Pahang, has some attraction, albeit small. For better coastline vacationing, head a little farther north to **Cherating.**

KUANTAN

Kuantan is the capital of Pahang Darul Makmur, and while there is a push for commercial development, you don't really get a feel of being in a big city. If you're staying at the beach at Telok Chempedak, 5 kilometers (3 miles) north of Kuantan, the atmosphere is even more relaxed and laid-back.

GETTING THERE & GETTING AROUND

Domestic flights arrive from other cities around Malaysia at the **Sultan Maj Ahmad Shah Airport** (☎ **09/538-2923**). Bus service is also available from major Malaysian towns. From KL, call ☎ **03/442-1256** for information on the KL-Kuantan Express.

For **local taxis** within Kuantan and to nearby towns, call **Persatuan Pemandu Teksi dan Kereta Sewa Pahang Timur Berhad** (☎ **09/513-4478**).

From Kuantan, **buses** service major cities. For information, call **Transnational** (☎ **09/515-6740**).

ATTRACTIONS

There's not much to see and do in Kuantan, but it's worth your while to stop and see the **Sultan Ahmad Shah Mosque** in the center of town. Time your visit for the evening, when the light filters through the intricate filigree pattern of the walls. It's very beautiful.

The **Infokraft Kuantan,** Jalan Masjid (☎ **09/523-131**), open from 9am to 5pm daily, has local wood, glass, brass, batik, ceramic, and basketry crafts. And if you find yourself in Kuantan on a Saturday night, there is a **pasar malam** (night market) along Jalan Gambut, which is near the main mosque. There you'll find stalls selling local food, clothes, imitation watches, accessories, toys, and leather goods. It's a good place to hone your bargaining skills.

The **State Cultural Centre,** Pahang State Culture Art & Tourism, Jalan Telok Sisek (☎ 09/555-466), has cultural events every Saturday night from 4:30 to 5:30pm. Call ahead for details. As for nightlife, stick to the beach at Telok Chempedak, where you'll find a beachfront promenade with some pubs.

ACCOMMODATIONS

Kuantan is not a very large place, and most who holiday here prefer to stay just a little farther north, in Cherating, which is more established as a resort destination. If staying in Kuantan is important to you, though, the Hotel Grand Continental is a fine, centrally located place. Near the beach at Telok Chempedak, the Hyatt Regency is as romantic and relaxing as any place at Cherating.

Hotel Grand Continental. Jalan Gambut, 25000 Kuantan, Pahang Darul Makmur. ☎ **09/515-8888.** Fax 09/515-9999. 202 units. A/C MINIBAR TV TEL. RM212 (US$84.80) double. AE, DC, JCB, MC, V.

Located in the heart of Kuantan, the hotel is near the central mosque. Grand Continental is a simple three-star hotel, with new and adequate facilities that are somewhat reminiscent of the seventies. The front view of the bridge and river is more pleasant than the view in the rear rooms. Promotional rates can be as low as RM160 (US$64) a night. There's a fitness center, pool, and shops on the premises.

Hyatt Regency Kuantan. Telok Chempedak, 25050 Kuantan, Pahang. ☎ **800/233-1234** from the U.S., or 800/8181 or 09/566-1234 in Malaysia. Fax 09/567-7577. 336 units. A/C MINIBAR TV TEL. RM290 (US$116) no sea view, RM335 (US$134) sea view; RM400 (US$160) no sea-view club, RM495 (US$198) sea-view club; RM650–RM2,000 (US$260–US$800) suite. AE, DC, JCB, MC, V.

The Hyatt Regency is a beach resort on Telok Chempedak, about 10 minutes outside of Kuantan proper. The long stretch of sandy beach is perfect for relaxing and fun, and in the evening the crashing waves are the perfect romantic backdrop. Facilities include two outdoor swimming pools, three lighted tennis courts, two squash courts, table tennis, darts, volleyball, and a water-sports center with windsurfing, sailing, waterskiing, and jet skis. The hotel is near golf, jogging, and jungle hikes.

DINING

There's seafood and local food in Kuantan, but like the other smaller destinations in Malaysia, you'll be hard-pressed to find fine dining outside of the larger hotels. The best evening activities are centered around the beach area at **Telok Chempedak.**

Kampung Restaurant. Hyatt Regency Kuantan, Telok Chempedak. ☎ **09/566-1234,** ext. 7700. Reservations recommended. Entrees RM12–RM40 (US$4.80–US$16); buffet RM40 (US$16). AE, DC, JCB, MC, V. Daily 6am–2am. INTERNATIONAL/MALAY.

From your table, you can feel the breeze blowing in from the sea, and although there's a bit of commotion from people descending upon the buffet, the place still maintains a romantic atmosphere. Go for the local set lunch or the dinner buffet, which sometimes comes with an outstanding seafood barbecue.

Kum Leng Restoran. E-897/899/901 Jalan Bukit Ubi, Kuantan. ☎ **09/513-4446.** Seafood priced according to seasonal availability. Other dishes can be as low as RM5 (US$2) for fried tofu or as high as RM100 (US$40) for shark's fin. Cash only. Daily 10:30am–2:30pm and 5:30–10:30pm.

Kum Leng is probably one of the top restaurants in Kuantan. A bit cramped, it's always doing a good business, but there's rarely a wait. Try the fried chicken with dry

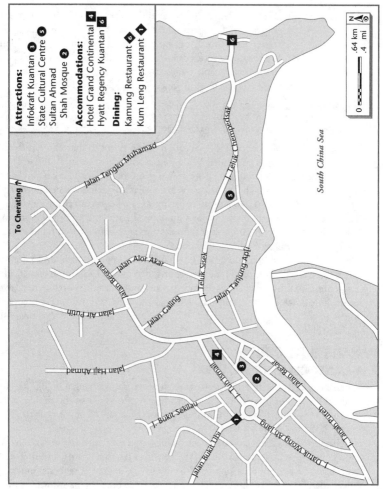

Attractions:
Infokraft Kuantan ❸
State Cultural Centre ❺
Sultan Ahmad
Shah Mosque ❷

Accommodations:
Hotel Grand Continental ❹
Hyatt Regency Kuantan ❻

Dining:
Kamung Restaurant ❻
Kum Leng Restaurant ❶

chili topped with onions and cashew nuts, or the fried chili prawns with shells. They're very fresh and not too spicy.

CHERATING

Cherating is a beach resort only 47 kilometers (28 miles) to the north of Kuantan, and in fact, many travelers skip Kuantan and head straight for Cherating's resorts instead. The site of Asia's first Club Med, it offers opportunities not only for relaxing on the beach and taking in water sports, but also for trolling around the mangroves up the Cherating River in a hired bumboat. You'll also find crafts shops and cultural shows here. A little more than 11 kilometers (6.8 miles) north of Cherating is **Chendor Beach,** which is interesting because you can watch giant sea turtles come to shore to lay their eggs from May to October.

ACCOMMODATIONS

Best Western Ombak Beach Resort. Lot 2466, Mukin Sungai Karang, 26080 Kuantan, Pahang Darul Makmur. ☎ **09/581-9166.** Fax 09/581-9433. 30 units. A/C MINIBAR TV TEL. RM140 (US$56) double. AE, DC, MC, V.

The bad news is this resort only has 30 rooms; the good news is that they're spread out over 1.2 hectares (3 acres) of property, and each has its own terrace and carport. The resort atmosphere is perfect for lying about the beach, swimming in the pool, or enjoying a campfire barbecue. Facilities include an outdoor pool, children's pool, game room, water-sports center, table tennis, and volleyball, and there's a souvenir gift shop on the premises. Try to bargain your room as low as RM90 (US$36).

Holiday Villa Cherating. Lot 1303, Mukin Sungai Karang, 26080 Kuantan, Pahang Darul Makmur. ☎ **09/581-9500.** Fax 09/581-9178. 150 units. A/C MINIBAR TV TEL. RM180 (US$72) double; RM195 (US$78) chalet; RM450 (US$180) suite. AE, DC, JCB, MC, V.

What a resort! This 4-hectare (10-acre) coastline property has three different wings to choose from: The Capital Wing houses modern amenities similar to any international-class hotel, while the Village Wing and the Palace Wing have chalets, longhouses, and istanas. The 13 Village Wing chalets are each decorated in the style of one of the 13 Malay states, and its kampung feel makes it perfect for unwinding. The chalets in both wings range from simple two-bedroom accommodations to a Sarawak longhouse with 10 guest rooms and private balconies to a replica of the Istana Lama Sri Menanti in Negeri Sembilan.

Facilities include two outdoor pools, two outdoor spa pools, a children's wading pool, a game room, three outdoor tennis courts, two indoor badminton courts, a fitness center, a sauna, massage, a beauty parlor, and a water-sports center (with windsurfing, beach surfing, catamaran, sailing, parasailing, scuba diving, jet scooters, canoeing, and boating). Also available are sightseeing tours, island excursions, fishing, and golfing.

PAHANG OUTDOORS
TAMAN NEGARA NATIONAL PARK

Taman Negara is the largest national park in Malaysia, covering 434,300 hectares (1,085,750 acres) of primary rain forest estimated to be as old as 130 million years, and holding within its borders **Gunung Tahan,** Malaysia's highest peak at 2,187 meters (2,392 ft.) above sea level.

Prepare to see lush vegetation and rare orchids, up to 250 bird species, and maybe, if you're lucky, some barking deer, tapir, elephants, tigers, leopards, and rhinos. As for primates, they've got your long-tailed macaques, leaf monkeys, gibbons, and more. Malaysia has taken conservation pretty seriously since the early part of the century, and so Taman Negara is dedicated to preserving this land in as pristine a state as possible, while still allowing humans to appreciate the splendor.

There are outdoor activities for any level of adventurer. Short jungle walks to observe nature are lovely, but then so are the hard-core 9-day treks or climbs up Gunung Tahan. There's also rivers for rafting and swimming, fishing spots, and a couple of caves. For information, call the **Kuala Tahan Office,** Taman Negara Resort, Kuala Tahan, Jerantut, 27000 Pahang (☎ **09/263-500;** fax 09/261-5000).

GETTING THERE　　The entrance to the park is at Kuala Tembeling, which can be reached in 3 hours by road from Kuala Lumpur. You can also hire **taxis** from the Pudu Raya Bus Terminal in Kuala Lumpur, or take a **bus** to Jerantut from the Jalan Tun Razak Bus station in Kuala Lumpur. If you take a bus, you'll have to make the final leg to Kuala Tembeling by local taxi or bus. You can also get there by train from KL and Singapore. Contact the Keretapi Tanah Melayu Bhd. (KMT) (☎ **03/274-9422** in KL) for schedules and fares.

ACCOMMODATIONS

Taman Negara Resort. Kuala Tahan Office, Taman Negara Resort, Kuala Tahan, Jerantut, 27000 Pahang. ☎ **03/245-5585.** 103 units. A/C. RM125 (US$50) standard rm; RM175 (US$70) chalet; RM260 (US$104) chalet suite; RM450–RM550 (US$180–US$220) bungalow. AE, DC, JCB, MC, V.

Taman Negara Resort offers various levels of accommodation (or can rent you the equipment you'll need to rough it at a campsite), and can also provide guided activities. At the low end of the price range are the standard guest house rooms, 16 of which are located in a brick longhouse, and each of which has a private bathtub. The chalet rooms are each in their own small wooden houses and include private shower stalls. The chalet suites, one level up, are also freestanding wooden houses, but are larger and include sitting areas. The bungalow is a two-bedroom house with kitchenette, dining room, living room, and private shower. None of the units has a telephone; however, the bungalow has a television and VCR and both the chalet suite and bungalow have minibars.

KENONG RIBA PARK

Kenong Riba Park is another national park in Pahang, accessible via road and rail from Singapore, Kuala Lumpur, and Kuantan. It's 121 square kilometers small, a pipsqueak compared to Taman Negara, which has more of Malaysia's spectacular wonders and the option of more comfortable accommodations. However, for those reasons, Kenong Riba is perhaps less inundated with tourist traffic, and there's still trekking, climbing, caving, and river activities. Contact **Kuala Lipis District Forest Office,** Government Office Complex, 27200 Kuala Lipis, Pahang (☎ **09/ 312-1273;** fax 09/312-3745), or the **Tourist Office** at KTMB Railway Station, 27200 Kuala Lipis, Pahang (☎ **09/312-3277;** fax 09/312-1117).

PANCHING CAVE

Panching Cave is about 25 kilometers (16 miles) west of Kuantan at the Gua Charah limestone caves. It's a Buddhist sanctuary with a large reclining Buddha inside, and at 11:59am every day, sunlight streams through the hole in the ceiling, illuminating the Buddha. To get there from Kuantan via road, take the Kuantan Gambang towards KL. About 18 kilometers outside of town you'll see a big signboard indicating the park.

GOLF COURSES

There are a few courses in Pahang, some in the highlands and a couple around the Kuantan area.

- **Awana Golf & Country Club,** KM 13, 69000 Genting Highlands, Pahang (☎ **03/211-3025;** fax 03/211-3535)
- **Royal Pahang Golf Club,** Jalan Teluk Chempedak, 25700 Kuantan, Pahang (☎ **09/567-5811;** fax 09/567-1170)
- **Cameron Highlands Golf Club,** 3900 Tanah Rata, Cameron Highlands, Pahang (☎ **05/491-1126**)
- **Lanjut Golden Beach Golf Resort,** Kampong Lanjut, 26800 Kuala Rompin, Pahang (☎ **09/414-5113;** fax 09/414-5112)
- **Selesa Golf Resort,** Bukit Tinggi, 28750 Bentong, Pahang (☎ **09/233-0039;** fax 09/233-0066)

15 The West Coast: Kuala Lumpur, Malacca & the Hill Resorts

In this chapter I've lumped together Kuala Lumpur, Malacca, and the Cameron and Genting Highlands hill resorts. While Malacca is indeed on the coast, Kuala Lumpur and the hill resorts are inland, but are included because they are in the western part of the peninsula. Kuala Lumpur (or just KL), Malaysia's capital city, is located about halfway up the peninsula from Johor Bahru. Genting Highlands hill resort is about 51 kilometers to the northeast of Kuala Lumpur, while Cameron Highlands hill resort is farther away, about a 5-hour drive north from Kuala Lumpur. Malacca is about 4 hours overland travel up the coast from Singapore.

1 Kuala Lumpur

Kuala Lumpur (or KL as it is commonly known) is the number-one point of entry in Malaysia for travelers. The city began as a small mining town at the spot where the Gombak and Klang rivers come together, but by the mid-1980s, Malaysia's economic success had turned the city into a sprawl of concrete and glass high-rises populated by people from all over the world. A bustling and cosmopolitan metropolis filled with beautiful traditional and colonial architecture, it's served as Malaysia's capital city since 1896, and though the seat of government will soon move to nearby Putra Jaya, Kuala Lumpur will remain the business capital of the country.

Kuala Lumpur originated from a small settlement, at which site the Masjid Jame, one of the oldest mosques in KL, now sits. Over time, as the settlement grew, the colonial buildings were built out from this centerpoint. The Merdeka Square, close to the Masjid and bounded by Jalan Sultan Hishamuddin and Jalan Kuching, became the center of the British colonial administration and social life. The areas to the north and east of the colonial administrative area are now built up with modern shopping malls and hotels. Chinatown, another historic district of the city, is just to the southeast of the colonial square. The central street in Chinatown is Jalan Petaling, where Chinese artisans, shops, and food stalls still rule the area, day and night. From the colonial square, if you travel south and southwest, you'll find the Kuala Lumpur train station, the National Mosque (Masjid Negara), and the National Museum (Muzim Negara). Farther west is Lake Gardens, a large park that houses the city's bird park, butterfly park, and other gardens.

Kuala Lumpur

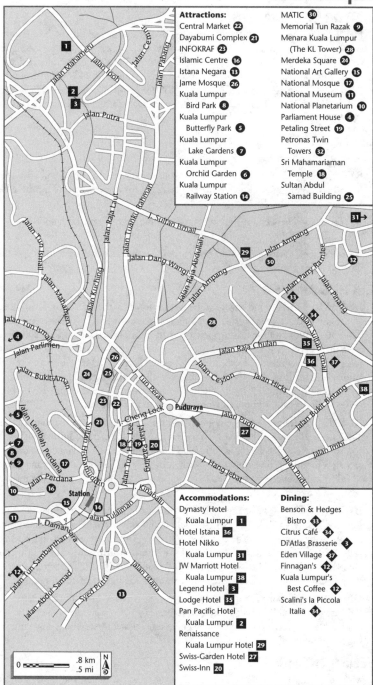

Attractions:

Central Market ㉒
Dayabumi Complex ㉑
INFOKRAF ㉓
Islamic Centre ⑯
Istana Negara ⑬
Jame Mosque ㉖
Kuala Lumpur
  Bird Park ⑧
Kuala Lumpur
  Butterfly Park ⑤
Kuala Lumpur
  Lake Gardens ⑦
Kuala Lumpur
  Orchid Garden ⑥
Kuala Lumpur
  Railway Station ⑭

MATIC ㉚
Memorial Tun Razak ⑨
Menara Kuala Lumpur
  (The KL Tower) ㉘
Merdeka Square ㉔
National Art Gallery ⑮
National Mosque ⑰
National Museum ⑪
National Planetarium ⑩
Parliament House ④
Petaling Street ⑲
Petronas Twin
  Towers ㉜
Sri Mahamariaman
  Temple ⑱
Sultan Abdul
  Samad Building ㉕

Accommodations:

Dynasty Hotel
  Kuala Lumpur ①
Hotel Istana ㊱
Hotel Nikko
  Kuala Lumpur ㉛
JW Marriott Hotel
  Kuala Lumpur ㊳
Legend Hotel ③
Lodge Hotel ㉟
Pan Pacific Hotel
  Kuala Lumpur ②
Renaissance
  Kuala Lumpur Hotel ㉙
Swiss-Garden Hotel ㉗
Swiss-Inn ⑳

Dining:

Benson & Hedges
  Bistro ㉝
Citrus Café ㉞
Di'Atlas Brasserie ③
Eden Village ㊲
Finnagan's ⑫
Kuala Lumpur's
  Best Coffee ⑫
Scalini's la Piccola
  Italia ㉞

VISITOR INFORMATION

In Kuala Lumpur, the **Malaysia Tourism Board** has several offices. The largest is at the MATIC, the Malaysia Tourist Information Complex (see "Seeing the Sights," below), located on 109 Jalan Ampang (☎ **03/254-3929**); another is located at the Kuala Lumpur Railway Station, Jalan Sultan Hishamuddin (☎ **03/274-6063**); a third is at Subang Airport's Terminal 1 (☎ **03/746-5707**); and another is at the Putra World Trade Centre, Level 2, Menara Dato 'Onn, 45 Jalan Tun Ismail (☎ **03/441-1295**).

GETTING THERE

See chapter 12 for specifics on flights, trains, and buses into KL.

BY PLANE   If you arrive at the Subang International Airport it will cost about RM30 (US$12) to take a taxi to the city center. This is the fixed rate for the 24 kilometers (14.4 miles).

BY TRAIN   The Central Railway Station is located on Jalan Hishamuddin, right in the middle of the city.

BY BUS   See "Getting Around," below, for the locations of bus terminals depending on your point of origin.

GETTING AROUND

BY TAXI   Taxis around town can be waved down by the side of the road, or can be caught at taxi stands outside shopping complexes or hotels. The metered fare is RM1.50 (US60¢) for the first kilometer and an additional 10 sen for each 200 meters after that. Between midnight and 6am you'll be charged an extra 50% of the total fare. If you call ahead for a cab, there's an extra charge of RM1. Government regulations have made it compulsory for cabbies to charge the metered fare, but some still try to fix a price, which is invariably higher than what the metered fare would be.

To request a cab pickup, call **Comfort** at ☎ **03/292-6362.**

BY BUS   There are regular city buses and minibuses to take you around the city. The fare is 20 sen for the first kilometer and 5 sen for each additional kilometer. Know, however, that the buses in Kuala Lumpur are not dependable. You can wait at a stop for a long time only to find when the bus arrives that it's hot and packed so full that passengers seem to be hanging out every window. It's not the most relaxing way to get around.

BY RAIL   The **LRT,** or Light Rail Transit, has opened its first phase in Kuala Lumpur. It covers a 12-kilometer (7.4-mile) circuit, with 13 stops between Sultan Ismail and Ampang. The cost is 75 sen between stations, the longest ride costing RM2.95 (US$1.20). Tickets are purchased at LRT stations. Stored value cards can be purchased in increments of RM20 and RM50 (US$8 and US$20). The system operates from 6am to midnight daily, with trains coming around every 5 to 10 minutes.

ON FOOT   Walking is not that easy in KL. The heat and humidity can make walking between attractions pretty uncomfortable. However, sometimes the traffic is so unbearable that you'll get where you're going much faster by strapping on your tennis shoes and hiking it.

SEEING THE SIGHTS

Most of Kuala Lumpur's historic sights are located in the area around **Merdeka Square / Jalan Hishamuddin** area, while many of the gardens, parks, and museums are out at **Lake Gardens.** Taxi fare between the two areas will run you about RM5 (US$2).

Central Market. Jalan Benteng. ☎ **03/274-6542.** Daily 10am–7pm.

The original Central Market, built in 1936, used to be a wet market, but the place is now a cultural center for local artists and craftspeople selling antiques, crafts, and curios. The riverside amphitheater has free cultural performances nightly at 7:45pm. Call the information line (above) for performance schedules. The market is linked to Dayabumi Complex shopping mall (see below) by a bridge over the Sungai (River) Klang.

Dayabumi Complex. Jalan Sultan Hishamuddin. ☎ **03/230-0200.** Daily 9am–9pm.

You can't miss the modern white tower, which was designed to blend in with the surrounding Moorish architecture of the city. The complex is a combination of modern shopping mall, offices, and a General Post Office.

Kuala Lumpur Railway Station. Jalan Sultan Hishamuddin. ☎ **03/274-9422.** Daily 7:30am–10:30pm.

Built in 1910, the KL Railway Station is a beautiful example of Moorish style architecture.

National Museum (Muzim Negara). Jalan Damansara. ☎ **03/282-6255.** Admission RM1 (US40¢). Sat–Thurs 9am–6pm, Fri 9am–noon and 3–6pm.

Located at Lake Gardens, the museum has over 1,000 items of historic, cultural, and traditional significance, including art, weapons, musical instruments, and costumes.

National Art Gallery. Jalan Sultan Hishamuddin (across from the KL Railway Station). ☎ **03/230-0157.** Free admission. Sat–Thurs 10am–6pm, Fri 10am–noon and 3–6pm.

The building that now houses the National Art Gallery was built as the Majestic Hotel in 1932 and has been restored to display contemporary works by Malaysian artists. There are international exhibits as well.

National Mosque (Masjid Negara). Jalan Sultan Hishamuddin (near the KL Railway Station).

Built of a modern design, the most distinguishing features of the mosque are the 73-meter minaret and the umbrella-shaped roof, which is said to symbolize a newly independent Malaysia's aspirations for the future. Could be believable, as the place was built in 1965. There's an underground passage to the mosque from Dayabumi Complex (see above).

Sultan Abdul Samad Building. Jalan Raja.

In 1987 this place was built to hold government administrative offices. The Moorish building looks out on Merdeka Square with its impressive clock tower and copper domes. Today it is the home of Malaysia's Supreme and High Courts.

Merdeka Square. Jalan Raja.

Surrounded by colonial architecture, the square is a large field that was once the site of British social and sporting events. These days, Malaysia holds its spectacular Independence Day celebrations on the field, which is home to the world's tallest flagpole, standing at 100 meters (330 ft.).

National Planetarium. Lake Gardens. ☎ **03/252-1150.** Admission to exhibition hall RM10 (US$4), Space Theatre RM3 (US$1.20), Planterium Show RM6 (US$2.40). Sat–Thurs 10am–7pm, Fri 10am–noon and 2:30–7pm.

The National Planetarium has a Space Hall with touch screen interactive computers and hands-on experiments, a Viewing Gallery with binoculars for a panoramic view of the city, and an Ancient Observatory Park with models of Chinese and Indian astronomy systems. The Space Theatre has two different spacy shows.

Jame Mosque (Masjid Jame). Jalan Tun Terak.

The first settlers landed in Kuala Lumpur at this spot, where the Gombak and Klang rivers meet, and in 1909 a mosque was built here. Styled after an Indian Muslim design, it is one of the oldest mosques in the city.

Petronas Twin Towers. Scheduled to open May 1998. ☎ **03/263-3377** for information.

After 5 years of planning and building, Petronas Twin Towers has been completed. Standing at a whopping 451.9 meters (1,482 ft.) above street level, the towers are the tallest buildings in the world. From the outside, the structures are designed with the kind of geometric patterns common to Islamic architecture, and on levels 41 and 42 the two towers will be linked by a bridge. When they open for business, the towers' 88 floors will hold office buildings, a hotel, and a 30-story retail center.

INFOKRAF. Jalan Sultan Hishamuddin. ☎ **03/293-4929.** Mon–Sat 9am–5pm. Closed Sun.

A popular tourist spot, INFOKRAF is a crafts center that has Malaysian handicrafts and cultural and research exhibits.

Islamic Centre. Jalan Perdana. ☎ **03/274-9333.**

The seat of Islamic learning in Kuala Lumpur, the center has displays of Islamic texts, artifacts, porcelain, and weaponry.

Istana Negara. Jalan Negara.

Closed to the public, this is the official residence of the king. You can peek through the gates at the istana and its lovely grounds.

Menara Kuala Lumpur (The KL Tower). Bukit Nanas. ☎ **03/208-5421.** Admission RM8 (US$3.20). Daily 10am–10pm.

Standing 421 meters (1,389 ft.) tall, this concrete structure is the third tallest tower in the world. At the top, the glass windows are fashioned after the Shah Mosque in Isfahan, Iran.

MATIC (Malaysia Tourist Information Complex). Jalan Ampang. ☎ **03/264-3929.** Daily 9am–6pm.

At MATIC you'll find an exhibit hall, tourist information services for Kuala Lumpur and Malaysia, and other travel-planning services. In the mini-auditorium there's a 10-minute audio visual show at 10am, noon, 2:45pm, and 5pm. On Tuesdays, Thursdays, Saturdays, and Sundays, there are cultural shows at 3:30pm. Shows are RM2 (US80¢) for adults, RM1 (US40¢) for children.

Kuala Lumpur Lake Gardens (Taman Tasik Perdana). Enter via Jalan Parliament. Free admission. Daily 9am–6pm.

Built around an artificial lake, the 91.6-hectare (229-acre) park has plenty of space for jogging and rowing, and has a playground for the kids. It's the most popular park in Kuala Lumpur.

Kuala Lumpur Orchid Garden. Jalan Perdana. ☎ **03/291-6011** for information. Adults RM5 (US$2), children RM2 (US40¢). Daily 9am–6pm.

This garden has a collection of over 800 orchid species from Malaysia, and also contains thousands of international varieties.

Kuala Lumpur Bird Park. Jalan Perdana. ☎ **03/291-6011** for information. Adults RM3 (US$1.20), children RM1 (US40¢). Daily 9am–5pm.

Nestled in beautifully landscaped gardens, the bird park has over 2,000 birds within its 3.2 hectares (8 acres).

Kuala Lumpur Butterfly Park. Jalan Cenderasari. ☎ **03/293-4799.** Adults RM4 (US$1.60), children RM2 (US80¢). Daily 9am–6pm.

Over 6,000 butterflies belonging to 120 species make their home in this park, which has been landscaped with more than 15,000 plants to simulate the butterflies' natural rain forest environment. There are also other small animals and an insect museum.

Memorial Tun Razak. Jalan Perdana. ☎ **03/291-2111.** Free admission. Tues–Thurs and Sat–Sun 9am–6pm, Fri 9am–noon and 3–6pm.

Tun Razak was Malaysia's second prime minister, and this museum is filled with his personal and official memorabilia.

Parliament House. Jalan Parliament. Parliament sessions are not open to the public.

In the Lake Gardens area, the Parliament House is a modern building housing the administrative offices, which were once in the Sultan Abdul Samad Building at Merdeka Square.

Sri Mahamariaman Temple. Jalan Bandar.

A very ornate Hindu temple, this one is the starting places of Kuala Lumpur's Thaipusam Festival (see chapter 2 for info).

Petaling Street.

This is the center of KL's Chinatown district. By day, stroll past hawker stalls, dim sum shops, wet markets, and all kinds of shopping, from pawn shops to coffin makers. At night, from the hawkers' sidewalk cafes, you can watch the street life bustle by.

ACCOMMODATIONS

There are dozens of hotels in Kuala Lumpur, most of them within the city limits. The city's hosting of the Commonwealth Games in September 1998 means that many five-star accommodations have popped up, and with the opening of the new LRT system, hotels to the north of the main colonial core of the city are connected by a short train ride. Other hotels listed in this book are located in the Chinatown area, within walking distance of plenty of shopping attractions and nightlife. Others still are located out in KL's Golden Triangle district, a triangle just south of the Klang River where the business growth has been happening.

Dynasty Hotel Kuala Lumpur. 218 Jalan Ipoh, 51200 Kuala Lumpur. ☎ **03/443-7777.** Fax 03/442-6868. 863 units. A/C MINIBAR TV TEL. RM275–RM295 (US$110–US$118) double; RM390 (US$156) executive/family rm; RM490–RM690 (US$196–US$276) suite. AE, DC, MC, V.

As you step through the entrance you leave behind the noise of Jalan Ipoh and enter into a quiet lobby with lovely marble inlaid floors and elegant wrought-iron details. The rooms in the 27-floor building all have views of the city, and while the size of the rooms varies depending upon the price category, most are of decent size. Deep, warm colors and smooth wood furnishings make these rooms especially comfortable. Facilities include a rooftop pool, a fitness center with gym and spa, and a shopping arcade. They also have a helipad—just in case you were thinking of coming in the high-profile way.

Hotel Istana. 73 Jalan Raja Chulan, 50200 Kuala Lumpur. ☎ **800/883-380** or 03/241-9988. Fax 03/244-0111. 593 units. A/C MINIBAR TV TEL. RM460–RM510 (US$184–US$204) double; RM650–RM850 (US$260–US$340) executive club; RM950 (US$380) suite; RM4,500–RM5,000 (US$1,800–US$2,000) state rm. AE, DC, JCB, MC, V.

Fashioned after a Malay palace, Hotel Istana is rich with Moorish architectural elements. The guest rooms have Malaysian touches like handwoven carpets and upholstery in local fabric designs, capturing the exotic flavor of the culture without sacrificing modern comfort and convenience. The hotel has suffered some complaints from guests about the noise from traffic and local construction work bleeding into the rooms, but they have made efforts to compensate with sound-insulating drapes. Facilities include a large outdoor pool, fitness center with Jacuzzi and sauna, two outdoor tennis courts, a launderette, and a shopping arcade.

Hotel Nikko Kuala Lumpur. 165 Jalan Ampang, 50400 Kuala Lumpur. ☎ **800/NIKKOUS** from the U.S. and Canada, 0800/282502 from the U.K., 800/32292 toll-free in Malaysia, or 03/261-1111. Fax 800/3290 or 03/261-1122. www.hotelnikko.com.my. 484 units. A/C MINIBAR TV TEL. RM410–RM450 (US$164–US$180) double; RM500 (US$200) executive; RM880–RM6,000 (US$352–US$2,400) suite. AE, DC, JCB, MC, V.

The contemporary elegance of Hotel Nikko can be a bit overwhelming. The huge lobby lined with thick gilded columns leads straight back to a *Gone with the Wind*–style staircase descending from the mezzanine level. The rooms are not as austere, but they're not exactly homelike either. They are, however, possibly the largest rooms in Kuala Lumpur. The hotel is most definitely geared for the Japanese corporate traveler, with meticulous decor and service and a level of cleanliness that will make any neat freak swoon. Look elsewhere for a bargain, though. Facilities include an outdoor pool, a fitness center with Jacuzzi and sauna, use of a nearby golf course, and a shopping arcade.

JW Marriott Hotel Kuala Lumpur. 183 Jalan Bukit Bintang, 55100 Kuala Lumpur. ☎ **800/228-9290** from the U.S. and Canada, 02/299-1614 from Sydney, 800/251259 from elsewhere in Australia, 0800/221222 from the U.K., or 03/925-9000. Fax 03/925-7000. 552 units. A/C MINIBAR TV TEL. RM360 (US$144) double, RM460 (US$184) executive double; RM600 (US$240) suite. AE, DC, JCB, MC, V.

Opened in July 1997, the Marriott is one of the newest hotels in town. Modern styling in the guest rooms is sleek, with plush carpeting, light wood furnishings, large desks, and a leather executive chair for great work space. The mix of light and dark tones makes these rooms contemporary and luxurious. The staff is motivated and enthusiastic. Facilities include an outdoor pool; a fitness center with Jacuzzi, sauna and spa; one outdoor tennis court; use of a nearby golf course; and a shopping arcade.

The Legend Hotel. Putra Place, 100 Jalan Putra, 50350 Kuala Lumpur. ☎ **800/637-7200** from the U.S., 1800/655147 from Australia, 0800/252840 from the U.K., or 03/442-9888. Fax 03/443-0700. 60 units. A/C MINIBAR TV TEL. RM340 (US$136) superior double, RM400 (US$160) deluxe double; RM450 (US$180) legend crest; RM620 (US$248) executive suite, RM680 (US$272) family suite, RM8,000 (US$3,200) suite. AE, DC, JCB, MC, V.

Lovely marble in earthy tones creates a luxurious atmosphere in the Legend's public space, which is enhanced with such Chinese touches as carved wood furniture and terracotta warrior statues—now if only you weren't subjected to the nuisance of having to take an elevator up one flight from the ground level to the lobby. Guest rooms are reasonably spacious, and all have views of the city, but ask to face the Twin Towers for the best view. If you just happen to be in town on your honeymoon, they have an Eastern Bridal suite that's to die for: total Chinese / Bali Hai, from the carved wood opium bed and wall screens to the oriental carpets. Facilities include an outdoor pool, fitness center with Jacuzzi and sauna, squash courts, a launderette, and a shopping arcade.

The Lodge Hotel. Jalan Sultan Ismail, 50250 Kuala Lumpur. ☎ **03/242-0122.** Fax 03/241-6819. 50 units. A/C TV (1 rm has no TV) TEL. RM92 (US$36.80) annex (without TV); RM115 (US$46) standard; RM138 (US$55.20) deluxe (all prices inclusive of taxes). AE, MC, V.

The Lodge has a great location in the heart of the city, but it's a bit of the odd little-old-man out among all the upmarket hotels. The rooms are of a good size, however, and though decor is simple and on the 1970s side, it doesn't appear shabby. Views are of either the city or the pool, and, to be honest, the pool is the nicer view.

The Pan Pacific Hotel Kuala Lumpur. Jalan Putra, P.O. Box 11468, 50746 Kuala Lumpur. ☎ **800/327-8585** from the U.S. and Canada, 02/923-37888 from Sydney, 800/625959 from elsewhere in Australia, 800/8555 toll-free within Malaysia, or 03/442-5555. Fax 03/441-7236. 565 units. A/C MINIBAR TV TEL. RM450 (US$180) double; RM560 (US$224) executive club; RM835 (US$334) suite. AE, DC, JCB, MC, V.

One thing you'll love about staying at the Pan Pacific is the view out the glass elevator as you drift up to your floor. The atrium lobby inside is bright and airy, and the rooms are spacious and stately. Facilities include an outdoor pool, a fitness center with Jacuzzi and sauna, and squash and tennis courts.

Renaissance Kuala Lumpur Hotel. Corner of Jalan Sultan Ismail and Jalan Ampang, 50450 Kuala Lumpur. ☎ **800/HOTELS1** from the U.S. and Canada, 02/251-8484 from Sydney, 800/222431 from elsewhere in Australia, 0800/441111 from New Zealand, 0800/181738 from the U.K., 800/7272 toll-free in Malaysia, or 03/262-2233. Fax 03/263-1122. 400 units. A/C MINIBAR TV TEL. RM535 (US$214) double, RM755 (US$302) club double; from RM855 (US$344) suite. AE, DC, JCB, MC, V.

The Renaissance is definitely geared to satisfying the corporate client's needs. The lobby is a huge oval colonnade with a domed ceiling and massive marble columns rising from the sides of a geometric star burst on the floor. You could be walking into a futuristic version of Washington, D.C.'s Capitol building. The guest rooms have an equally "official" feel to them—very bold and impressive. Facilities include an outdoor pool, fitness center with Jacuzzi and sauna, two outdoor tennis courts, a launderette, and a shopping arcade.

Swiss-Garden Hotel. 117 Jalan Pudu, 55100 Kuala Lumpur. ☎ **800/3093** or 03/241-3333. Fax 03/241-5555. www.sgihotels.com.my. 326 units. A/C MINIBAR TV TEL. RM300–RM350 (US$120–US$140) double; RM410–RM550 (US$164–US$220) suite. AE, DC, JCB, MC, V.

Swiss-Garden is conveniently just walking distance from KL's lively Chinatown district, and close to the Puduraya bus station. It's a four-star hotel with touches of luxury you'd find in a more expensive place, making it a pretty good deal if you'd like to pay less but don't want to give up the comfort you want from a vacation. Facilities include an outdoor pool and a fitness center, and the quality of service meets high standards.

Swiss-Inn. 62 Jalan Sultan, 50000 Kuala Lumpur. ☎ **03/232-3333.** Fax 03/201-6699. www.sgihotels.com.my. 110 units. A/C TV TEL. RM130 (US$52) standard; RM145 (US$58) superior; RM160 (US$64) deluxe. AE, DC, JCB, MC, V.

You can't beat the price for comfortable and modern accommodations in Kuala Lumpur. The lobby is small and so are the rooms, but they are tastefully decorated and very clean. Most of the people who stay here are members of tour groups, families, and independent travelers. Its location, near Chinatown and a short cab ride to the other main attractions in the city, makes it additionally attractive. Room service is available from 7am to 10pm only, and VCRs and videos can be rented for a RM4 and RM25 (US$1.60 and US$10) fee, respectively. Guests have access to the Swiss-Garden Hotel's fitness center.

DINING

Kuala Lumpur, like Singapore, is very cosmopolitan. Here you'll not only find delicious and exotic cuisine, but you'll find it served in some pretty trendy settings.

Benson & Hedges Bistro. Ground floor, Life Centre, Jalan Sultan Ismail. ☎ **03/264-4426.**
Reservations not accepted. Entrees RM13.50–RM35 (US$5.40–US$14). AE, DC, MC, V. Daily 7–
10am breakfast, 11am–3pm lunch; Sun–Thurs 6pm–midnight dinner, Fri–Sat 6pm–2am dinner.
TEX MEX/AMERICAN.

The latest in trendy hangouts, this bistro is part coffee bar and part restaurant, decorated in contemporary style, with mood lighting glistening off bronze coffee bean
dispensers. Staff is dressed in black, with casual and hip attitudes to match. Good
entrees are the chicken piccata, roast duck lasagna, or the blackened rack of lamb.
Reservations are not accepted, and on the weekends the wait can be up to an hour
and a half, partly because no one will ever rush you to get you out. In short: Be there
early.

Citrus Café. 19 Jalan Sultan Ismail. ☎ **03/242-5188.** Entrees RM6–RM19 (US$2.40–
US$7.60). AE, DC, MC. Daily 11:30am–1am. ASIAN MIX.

This place has become very popular with the yuppie international set—locals, expatriates, and tourists alike. The theme is Asia, reflected in the decor, music, and cuisine, which ranges from Malay to Thai to Japanese and then more, with some
Western elements thrown in, too. Dishes like the rotisserie chicken and the special
sushi rolls are all served in portions to share at your table.

Di'Atlas Brasserie. The Legend Hotel and Apartments, 100 Jalan Putra. ☎ **03/442-9888.**
Reservations recommended for lunch and dinner, required for high tea. A la carte from RM14
(US$5.60); high tea RM25 (US$10); buffet lunch RM38 (US$15.20); buffet dinner RM40
(US$16). AE, DC, JCB, MC, V. Daily 6:30am–1am. INTERNATIONAL.

Because this place is new, it feels more elegant and modern than many other restaurants in KL. It is also very spacious, with an ambiance that would be suitable for anyone, from businesspeople to families. You can order Asian favorites like *asam laksa*
(rice noodles in a sweet-and-sour sauce made from pineapple, shrimp paste, mint, and
other ingredients, and tasting here just like the genuine stuff you'd get in Penang),
tandoori chicken, or *char kway teow* (fried flat noodles with seafood), and for Western palates there's a creamy lasagna or sizzling tenderloin. The wait staff is extremely
attentive.

Eden Village. 260 Jalan Raja Chulan. ☎ **03/241-4027.** Reservations recommended. Entrees
RM18–RM100 (US$7.20–US$40) and up. AE, MC, V. SEAFOOD.

Uniquely designed inside and out to resemble a Malay house, Eden Village has great
local atmosphere. Waitresses are clad in kebaya, and serve up popular dishes like
braised shark's fin in clay pot with crabmeat and roe and the Kingdom of the Sea, a
half lobster baked with prawns, crab, and cuttlefish. The terrace seating is the best
in the house.

Finnagan's. 6 Jalan Telawi, Bangsar Baru. ☎ **03/284-0187.** Entrees RM15–RM25 (US$6–
US$10). AE, MC. Daily noon–midnight. IRISH.

For a good time in a lively pub atmosphere, Finnagan's is very popular, especially
during the week, when locals come by after work for happy hour and families come
out for a hearty meal. Downstairs is done in traditional Irish pub charm, while the
upstairs resembles a barn loft. The fish-and-chips is very good, as is the fried calamari.
Come hungry.

Scalini's la Piccola Italia. 19 Jalan Sultan Ismail. ☎ **03/245-3211.** Reservations recommended. Entrees RM26–RM50 (US$10.40–US$20). AE, DC, MC, V. Sun–Thurs noon–2:30pm
and 6–10:30pm, Fri noon–2:30pm and 6–11pm, Sat 6–11pm. ITALIAN.

Four chefs from Italy create the dishes that make Scalini's a favorite among KL
locals and expatriates. The roasted sea bass is delicious, as is the beef carpaccio. The

daily specials are excellent and the wine selection is extensive, with labels from California, Australia, New Zealand, France, and, of course, Italy.

SHOPPING

Kuala Lumpur is a truly great place to shop. In recent years, mall after mall has risen from city lots, filled with hundreds of retail outlets selling everything from haute couture to cheap chic, electronic goods, jewelry, and arts and crafts. The major shopping malls are located in the area around **Jalan Bukit Bintang** and **Jalan Sultan Ismail.** There are also a few malls along Jalan Ampang.

A good place for handicrafts is the **Central Market** on Jalan Benteng (☎ 03/ 274-6542). There you'll find local artists and craftspeople selling their wares in the heart of town. Another favorite shopping haunt in KL is Chinatown, along **Petaling Street.** Day and night, it's a great place to wander and bargain for clothing and accessories, as well as cultural treasures from China, India, and Burma.

Pasar malam ("night markets") are very popular evening activities in KL. Whole blocks are taken up with these brightly lit and bustling markets packed with stalls selling everything you can dream of. They are likely to pop up anywhere in the city. Two good bets for catching one: Go to Chinatown, or, on Saturday nights, head for **Jalan Tuanku Abdul Rahman.**

GOLF

Golf is a favorite pastime of vacationers in Malaysia, and around Kuala Lumpur there are a few good courses.

- **Royal Selangor Golf Club,** P.O. Box 11051, 50734 Kuala Lumpur (☎ 03/ 984-8433; fax 03/985-3939)
- **Kelab Golf Perkhidmatan Awam,** Bukit Kiara, off Jalan Damansara, 6000 Kuala Lumpur (☎ 03/757-5310; fax 03/757-7821)
- **Kuala Lumpur Golf & Country Club,** 10 Jalan 1/70D off Jalan Bukit Kiara, 6000 Kuala Lumpur (☎ 03/253-1111; fax 03/253-3393)

KUALA LUMPUR AFTER DARK

There's all kinds of nightlife in KL, from fashionable lounges to sprawling discos to pubs to hang out in. Remember that these places all close by 1am, so don't plan on staying out too late. Generally, you're expected to dress casual for these places, but avoid old jeans and tennis shoes, and leave any very revealing outfits at home.

Bier Keller. Ground floor, Menara Haw Par, Jalan Sultan Ismail. ☎ 03/201-3313. No cover. Daily noon–1am.

Done up like a beer cellar, Bier Keller serves German beers in tankards and traditional German cuisine such as sauerkraut and beer bread. There's a DJ spinning popular music.

Hard Rock Café. Wisma Concorde, Jalan Sultan Ismail (next to Concorde Hotel). ☎ 03/ 244-4152. No cover. Daily 11am–1am.

The Kuala Lumpur version of this international chain has live bands from 10pm onward playing everything from classic rock to the latest chart toppers. The clientele similarly goes from thirsty yuppies to party animal locals and tourists. The bar is shaped like a Fender guitar.

Wall $t. Ground floor, Menara TA One, 22 Jalan P. Ramlee. ☎ 03/446-6666. No cover. Daily noon–1am.

Talk about a funny theme place. Wall $t. is a bar and restaurant designed to appeal to your yuppie side, right down to the TV monitors that flash the drink prices, Wall

Street–style, as they fluctuate according to the "market." Downstairs, the bar entertainment features both a DJ and live bands. Music ranges from light jazz to acid jazz. It's a good place to unwind and chat about the day's news.

Warp Dance Club. Bangunan Life Centre, 1st and 2nd floors, Jalan Sultan Ismail. ☎ 03/262-8163. After 10pm there's a RM25 (US$10) cover charge for the first drink. Daily 9pm–1am.

This two-story club has live performances by Filipino cover bands and DJs spinning R&B, techno, and Top 40 selections. From time to time they'll also stage fashion shows and beauty pageants. It's only been around for a year, but Warp has really caught on with locals and tourists of all ages.

2 Cameron Highlands

Although Cameron Highlands is in Pahang, it is most often accessed via Kuala Lumpur. Located in the hills, Cameron Highlands has a cool climate, which makes it the perfect place for luxury resorts tailored to weekend getaways by Malaysians, Singaporeans, and other international travelers.

The climate is also very conducive to agriculture. After the area's discovery by British surveyor William Cameron in 1885, the major crop here became tea, which is still grown here today. (There's a tea factory you can visit to see how tea leaves are processed.) Today, the area's lovely gardens supply cities from KL to Singapore with vegetables and fruit year-round. As you go up into the highlands, you can see all the farmland on terraces in beautiful patterns along the sides of the hills. Among the local favorites here are the strawberries, which can be eaten fresh or transformed into yummy desserts in the local restaurants. At the many commercial flower nurseries you can see chrysanthemums, fuchsias, and roses growing on the terraces. Rose gardens are prominent here.

Ringlet is the first town you see as you travel up the highlands. It is the main agricultural center. Travel farther up the elevation to Tanah Rata, the major town in the area, and you'll find chalets, cottages, and bungalows. **Brinchang,** at 1,524 meters (5,029 ft.) above sea level, is the highest town in the highlands, surrounding a market square where there are shops, Tudor inns, rose gardens, and a Buddhist temple.

Temperatures in the Cameron Highlands average 70°F (21°C) during the day and 50°F (10°C) at night. There are paths for lovely treks though the countryside and to peaks of surrounding mountains. Two waterfalls, the **Robinson Falls** and **Parit Falls,** have pools at their feet where you can have a swim.

ACCOMMODATIONS

The Cool Point Hotel. 891 Persiaran Dayang Endah, 39000 Tanah Rata, Cameron Highlands, Pahang Darul Makmur. ☎ 05/491-4914. Fax 05/491-4070. 47 units. A/C TV TEL. Off-season RM90 (US$36) superior; RM140 (US$56) deluxe. Peak season RM125 (US$50) superior; RM180 (US$72) deluxe. MC, V.

Cool Point offers clean and basic accommodations. While the modern building has some Tudor-like styling on the outside, the rooms inside are pretty standard. Cool Point also has a restaurant serving local and Western dishes.

Heritage Hotel. Jalan Gereja, Tanah Rata, 39000 Cameron Highlands, Pahang Darul Makmur. ☎ 05/491-3888. Fax 05/491-5666. 170 units. A/C MINIBAR TV TEL. RM210–RM250 (US$84–US$100) double; RM310 (US$124) family rm; RM380 (US$152) junior suite, RM460–RM780 (US$184–US$312) suite. AE, DC, MC, V.

Outside, the Heritage is decorated in a modern Tudor style that's common in Cameron Highlands, and inside it's fully modernized and, except for the paned windows in the rooms—which let onto picturesque views of the surrounding hillsides—

completely devoid of Tudor touches. The rooms are not the most spacious, but are decorated in warm colors to suit the cooler climate. Facilities include a fitness center with sauna and steam, squash and tennis courts, snooker tables, and video games. The hotel can arrange tours and jungle treks, as well as golf.

3 Genting Highlands

Genting Highlands is a hill resort with one main purpose—gambling. While Cameron Highlands has magnificent gardens and quaint towns, Genting is a modern resort complex with little else to do except gamble and take the kiddies to the resort's amusement park. Only 51 kilometers up in the mountains, it's very close to Kuala Lumpur—so close that on very clear days you can see it from the capital city.

GETTING THERE

The resort has its own bus service from Kuala Lumpur. Eighteen buses operate daily from the Pudu Raya bus stand on Jalan Cheng Lock. The cost for one way is RM5 (US$2) for adults and RM3 (US$1.20) for children. The bus lets you off at the foot of the hill, where you take the cable car to the top. The fare for the cable car is included with the bus fare. For bus information, call **Perhentian Puduraya** at ☎ **03/232-6863.**

You can also get there by hiring a taxi. The cost is RM120 (US$48) for the car and an additional RM5 (US$2) per passenger if you are sharing the taxi with another fare—which is often done upon arrangement with the taxi service.

ATTRACTIONS

Gambling, gambling, and more gambling. The resort casino is open 24 hours. Entry is RM200 (US$80) whether you're a guest at the resort or just visiting for the day. By the way, you must be at least 21 years old to enter the casino. Inside it's a gambler's paradise, with all the games you'd care to wager a bet on, including blackjack, roulette, and baccarat. There's also a dinner theater that serves Chinese cuisine while you watch acts by international performers. Shows are usually around RM40 (US$16) for adults and RM30 (US$12) for children, on top of dinner.

For outdoor excitement, the resort has an **outdoor pond** with boats and a **horse ranch** with riding for all levels of experience. For somewhat less excitement (but better photo ops) the **cable care ride** down the mountain from the resort offers aerial views of Malaysian jungle (one-way fare RM3/US$1.20 for adults, RM1.50/US60¢ for children; Sunday to Thursday 8am to 7:30pm and Friday to Saturday 8am to 8:30pm). Additional facilities include a bowling alley and an indoor heated pool.

For children, there's a **kiddie train** around the lake. For older kids, there are facilities for badminton, basketball, table tennis, and more.

The **Awana Golf and Country Club** (☎ **03/211-3025;** fax 03/211-3535) is also located in Genting.

Genting Theme Park. Genting Highlands Resort, Genting Highlands 69000, Pahang Darul Mahmar. ☎ **03/211-1118,** ext. 58240. Free admission to Indoor & Outdoor Theme Park. For attractions, purchase either a ride card for RM10 (US$4) or a one-day unlimited ride pass for RM48 (US$19.20) adults, RM43 (US$17.20) children. Outdoor Theme Park Mon–Fri 10am–6:45pm, Sat–Sun 8am–7:45pm; Indoor Theme Park daily 9am–2am.

The park is huge, covering 100,000 square feet, and is mostly rides, plus many Western fast-food eating outlets, games, and other attractions. The Outdoor Theme Park has four roller coasters, flume rides, and a balloon ride. The Indoor Theme Park has a Space Odyssey roller coaster and a motion simulator. Don't miss the Disco Bumper Cars!

ACCOMMODATIONS

There are four hotels of varying prices within the Genting Highlands Resort Malaysia. Rates vary depending on low season, shoulder season, peak season, and super peak. The calendar changes each year, but basically weekends are peak, as well as the last week in November through the end of December. Super peak times are around Christmas, the calendar New Year, and a week or two in February, with a few other days dotted over the summer.

Genting Hotel. Genting Highlands 69000, Pahang Darul Makmur. ☎ **03/211-1118.** Fax 03/211-1888. 700 units. A/C MINIBAR TV TEL. Sun–Fri RM138 (US$55.20), Sat RM218 (US$87.20). AE, MC, V.

Genting Hotel is a newer property in the resort complex, and is linked directly to the casino. Promotional rates can be as low as RM97 (US$38.80) for weekdays.

Highland Hotel. Genting Highlands 69000, Pahang Darul Makmur. ☎ **03/211-1118.** Fax 03/211-1888. 875 units. A/C MINIBAR TV TEL. Sun–Fri RM138 (US$55.20), Sat RM218 (US$87.20). AE, MC, V.

Highland Hotel is linked directly to the casino. Promotional rates in this hotel are very rare.

Resort Hotel. Genting Highlands 69000, Pahang Darul Makmur. ☎ **03/211-1118.** Fax 03/211-1888. 800 units. A/C MINIBAR TV TEL. Sun–Fri RM9.60 (US$35.85), Sat RM 208 (US$83.20). AE, MC, V.

Resort Hotel is comparable to the Theme Park Hotel, but it's a little newer and the double occupancy rooms all have tow double beds and standing showers only.

Theme Park Hotel. Genting Highlands 69000, Pahang Darul Makmur. ☎ **03/211-1118.** Fax 03/211-1888. 440 units. A/C MINIBAR TV TEL. Sun–Fri RM88 (US$35.20), Sat RM158 (US$63.20). AE, MC, V.

The Theme Park Hotel is a little less expensive than the others, primarily because it's a little older and you must walk outside to reach the casino. Promotional rates during the week can be as low as RM62 (US$24.80) for up to three people in one room.

4 Malacca

While the destinations on the east coast are ideal for resort-style beach getaways, the cities on the west coast are perfect for vacations filled with culture and history—and Malacca is one of the best places to start. The attraction here is the city's cultural heritage, around which a substantial tourist industry has grown. If you're visiting, a little knowledge of this history will help you understand and appreciate all there is to see. I'll be as brief as possible.

Malacca was founded around 1400 by Parameswara, called Iskander Shah in the Malay Annals. After he was chased from Palembang in southern Sumatra by invading Javanese, he set up a kingdom in Singapore (Temasek), and after being overthrown by invaders at Temasek, he ran up the west coast of the Malay peninsula to Malacca, where he settled and established a port city. The site was an ideal midpoint in the east-west trade route and was in a favorable spot to take advantage of the two monsoons that dominated shipping routes. Malacca soon drew the attention of the Chinese, and the city maintained very close relations with the mainland as a trading partner and a political ally. The Javanese were also eager to trade in Malacca, as were Muslim merchants. After Parameswara's death in 1414, his son, Mahkota Iskander Shah, converted to Islam and became the first sultan of Malacca. The word of Islam quickly spread throughout the local population.

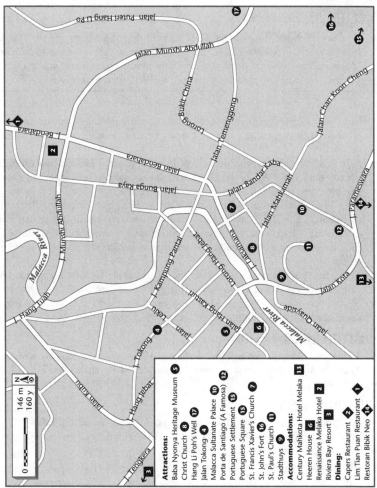

Attractions:
Baba Nyonya Heritage Museum **5**
Christ Church **8**
Hang Li Poh's Well **17**
Jalan Tokong **4**
Malacca Sultanate Palace **10**
Porta de Santiago (A Famosa) **12**
Portuguese Settlement **15**
Portuguese Square **16**
St. Francis Xavier's Church **7**
St. John's Fort **16**
St. Paul's Church **11**
Stadthuys **9**

Accommodations:
Century Mahkota Hotel Melaka **13**
Heeren House **6**
Renaissance Melaka Hotel **2**
Riviera Bay Resort **3**

Dining:
Capers Restaurant **2**
Lim Tian Puan Restaurant **1**
Restoran Bibik Neo **14**

During the 15th century, Malacca was ruled by a succession of wise sultans who expanded the wealth and stability of the economy; built up the administration's coffers; extended the sultanate to the far reaches of the Malay peninsula, Singapore, and parts of northern Sumatra; and thwarted repeated attacks by the Siamese. The success of the empire was drawing international attention.

The Portuguese were one of the powers eyeing the port and formulating plans to dominate the east-west trade route, establish the naval supremacy of Portugal, and promote Christianity in the region. In 1511, they struck, and conquered Malacca in a battle that lasted only a month. It is believed the local Malaccans had become accustomed to the comforts of affluence and turned soft and vulnerable. After it was defeated, the sultanate fled to Johor, where it reestablished the seat of Malay power. Malacca would never again be ruled by a sultan. The Portuguese looted the city and sent all its riches off to Lisbon.

The Portuguese were the first of a chain of ruling foreign powers who would struggle in vain to retain the early economic success of the city. The Portuguese had two major strikes against them: Their Christianity alienated the locals and repelled Muslim traders. The city quickly became nothing more than a sleepy outpost.

In 1641, the Dutch, with the help of Johor, conquered Malacca and controlled the city until 1795. Again, the Dutch were unsuccessful in rebuilding the glory of past prosperity in Malacca, and the city continued to sleep.

In 1795, the Dutch traded Malacca to the British in return for Bencoolen in Sumatra. The Dutch were always far more concerned with Indonesian interests anyway. Malacca became a permanent British settlement in 1811, but by this time had become so poor and alienated that it was impossible to bring it back to life.

The final blow came in 1941, when the city fell under Japanese occupation for 4 years. After World War II, when the British tried to reinstate colonial authority, Malays were vehemently opposed to the idea. Having suffered centuries of foreign domination, they held out for independence, which was granted in 1957.

VISITOR INFORMATION

There is no Malaysia Tourism Board office in Malacca, but they do have a **Malacca Tourism Association** office at 199A Taman Melaka Raya, Bandar Hilir (☎ 06/ 283-1966).

GETTING THERE

BY PLANE   **Pelangi Air** (Malaysia Airways, in Singapore; ☎ 65/336-6777) services the Batu Berendam Airport (☎ 06/351-175) with daily flights from Singapore. The airport is 9 kilometers outside of town.

BY TRAIN   The **KMT** trains service Malacca daily. The train station in Malacca is the Tampin Station (☎ 06/411-034), which is located 38 kilometers north of the city. There is a railway office in Malacca (☎ 06/282-3091) for inquiries.

BY BUS   There are bus routes to Malacca from Singapore as well as destinations in Peninsular Malaysia such as Kuala Lumpur, Butterworth, Johor Bahru, Mersing, and Kuantan. The bus station is located on Jalan Tun Ali.

BY CAR   Outstation taxis can also bring you here from Johor Bahru and Kuala Lumpur. If you care to drive yourself, Malacca is a short distance off the North-South Highway.

GETTING AROUND

BY TAXI   There are no metered taxis within the city. However, you can charter a taxi to bring you from place to place. Costs range from RM4 to RM6 (US$1.60 to US$2.40) for most city destinations. There is a taxi terminal located along Jalan Tun Ali (☎ 06/282-3630).

BY TRISHAW   Trishaws are the mode of transportation for locals. Each trishaw can carry only two passengers. Fares start from RM3 (US$1.20) for the first kilometer and cost RM2 (US80¢) per additional kilometer. You can also charter trishaws for city tours for about RM30 to RM40 (US$12 to US$16) per hour. Make sure you ask and agree on the fares before being taken for a ride.

ON FOOT   Most of the sights are within walking distance.

SEEING THE SIGHTS

Most of the really great historical places are on either side of the Malacca River. Start at Stadthuys (the old town hall) and you'll see most of Malacca pretty quickly.

Stadthuys. Located at the circle intersection of Jalan Quayside, Jalan Laksamana, and Jalan Chan Koon Cheng. ☎ **06/284-1934.** Adults RM2 (US80¢), children under 12 RM1 (US40¢). Daily 9am–6pm.

The Stadthuys Town Hall was built by the Dutch in 1650, and it's now home to the Malacca Historical Museum, which displays costumes and relics from the Dutch and Portuguese periods.

Porta de Santiago (A Famosa). Located on Jalan Kota, at the intersection of Jalan Parameswara.

Once the site of a Portuguese fortress called A Famosa, all that remains today is the entrance gate, which was saved from demolition by Sir Stamford Raffles. When the British East India Company demolished the place, Raffles realized the arch's historical value and saved it. The fort was built in 1512, but the inscription above the arch, "Anno 1607," marks the date when the Dutch overthrew the Portuguese.

Hang Li Poh's Well. Located off Jalan Laksamana Cheng Ho (Jalan Panjang).

Also called "Sultan's Well," Hang Li Poh's Well was built in 1495 to commemorate the marriage of Chinese Princess Hang Li Poh to Sultan Mansor Shah. It is now a wishing well, and they say if you toss a coin in, you'll someday return to Malacca.

St. John's Fort. Located off Lorong Bukit Senjuang. Free admission. Daily 24 hours.

The fort, built by the Dutch in the late 18th century, sits on top of St. John's Hill. Funny how the cannons point inland, huh? At the time, threats to the city came from land. It was named after a Portuguese church to St. John the Baptist, which originally occupied the site. Drive three-quarters of the way up the hill and walk the last 100 meters. You can walk inside for a panoramic view of the south side of Malacca.

St. Paul's Church. Located behind Porta de Santiago.

The church was built by the Portuguese in 1521, but when the Dutch came in, they made it part of A Famosa, converting the altar into a cannon mount. The open tomb inside was once the resting place of St. Francis Xavier, a missionary who spread Catholicism throughout Southeast Asia, and whose remains were later moved to Goa.

Malacca Sultanate Palace. Located on Jalan Kota. ☎ **06/282-0769.** Adults RM2 (US80¢), children RM1 (US40¢). Daily 9am–6pm.

The Malay architecture of this palace is based upon descriptions and drawings found in the Malay Annals. It is a replica of the palace of the Malay Sultanate in the 15th century.

St. Francis Xavier's Church. Located on Jalan Laksamana.

The church was built in 1849 and dedicated to St. Francis Xavier, a Jesuit who brought Catholicism to Malacca and other parts of Southeast Asia.

Christ Church. Located on Jalan Laksamana.

The Dutch built this place in 1753 as a Dutch Reform Church, and its architectural details include such wonders as ceiling beams cut from a single tree and a Last

Supper glazed tile motif above the altar. It was later consecrated as an Anglican church, and mass is still performed today in English, Chinese, and Tamil.

Portuguese Settlement.

Located down Jalan d'Albuquerque off of Jalan Ujon Pasir in the southern part of the city is the Portuguese Settlement, at the center of which is Portuguese Square, an enclave once designated for Portuguese settlers. Some elements of their presence remain in the Lisbon-style architecture. Later, in 1920, the area was a Eurasian neighborhood.

Portuguese Square.

Down Jalan d'Albuquerque is Portuguese Square, an attraction with Portuguese restaurants, handicrafts, souvenirs, and cultural shows. It was built in 1985 in an architectural style reminiscent of Lisbon.

Baba Nyonya Heritage Museum. 48/50 Jalan Tun Ten Cheng Lock. ☎ 06/283-1273. Admission RM7 (US$2.80). Sat–Wed 10am–12:30pm and 2–4:30pm, Thurs 9am–noon.

Called Millionaire's Row, Jalan Tun Ten Cheng Lock is lined with row houses that were built by the Dutch and later bought by wealthy Peranakans. The architectural style reflects the East-meets-West lifestyle of the Peranakans. The Baba Nyonya Heritage Museum sits at nos. 48 and 50 as a museum of Peranakan heritage.

Jalan Tokong.

Not far from Jalan Tun Ten Cheng Lock is Jalan Tokong, called the "Street of Harmony" by the locals because it has three coexisting places of worship: the Kampong Kling Mosque, the Cheng Hoon Teng Temple, and the Sri Poyyatha Vinayar Moorthi Temple.

Ayer Keroh Recreational Forest. Take chartered taxi (RM10/US$4) from the taxi station on Jalan Tun Ali. There is also a Red-Tourist Bus with hourly service from most major hotels in the city (a one-day pass is RM5/US$2).

The 202 hectares (500 acres) of forest that make up Ayer Keroh are home to the **Malacca Crocodile Farm** (☎ 06/232-2349; adults RM2/US80¢, children 6 to 12 RM1/US40¢, children under 6 free; open 9am to 6pm), the **Malacca Butterfly & Reptile Sanctuary** (☎ 06/232-0033; adults RM5/US$2, children 4 to 12 RM3/US$1.20, children under 4 free; open 8:30am to 5:30pm), and the **Malacca Zoo** (☎ 06/232-4053 or 06/232-4054; adults RM3/US$1.20, children 7 to 12 RM1.50/US60¢, children under 7 free; open 9am to 5:30pm). Other attractions include **Mini ASEAN and MINI Malaysia** (☎ 06/231-6087; adults RM5/US$2, children 6 to 12 RM2/US60¢, children under 6 free; open 9am to 5pm), little villages with architecture and exhibits portraying the different cultures around the country and region, as well as many camping and recreation facilities.

ACCOMMODATIONS

Malacca is not very large, and most of the places to stay are well within walking distance of attractions, shopping, and restaurants.

Century Mahkota Hotel Melaka. Jalan Merdeka, 75000 Malacca. ☎ 800/536-7361 from the U.S., or 06/281-2828. Fax 06/281-2323. 617 units. A/C MINIBAR TV TEL. RM300 (US$120) double; RM350–RM1,500 (US$140–US$600) suite. AE, DC, JCB, MC, V.

Located along the waterfront, the hotel is walking distance from sightseeing, historical areas, shopping, and commercial centers. It's a suite hotel that's better for families, and while it's not luxurious, it's more like a holiday apartment. The views are of either the pools, the shopping mall across the street, or the muddy reclaimed seafront. Facilities include two outdoor pools, a fitness center with sauna and massage, tennis and squash courts, mini golf, a game room, a children's playground, access to nearby golf, and a business center. It's across the street from the largest shopping mall in Malacca.

Heeren House. 1 Jalan Tun Tan Cheng Lock, 75200 Malacca. ☎ **06/281-4241.** Fax 06/281-4239. 7 units. A/C TV TEL. Sun–Thurs RM119 (US$47.60) double; RM199 (US$79.60) suite. Fri–Sat RM129 (US$51.60) double; RM219 (US$87.60) suite. No credit cards.

This is the place to stay in Malacca for a taste of the local culture. Started by a local family, the guest house is a renovated 100-year-old building furnished in traditional Peranakan and colonial style and located right in the heart of historical European Malacca. All the bedrooms have views of the Malacca River, and out the front door of the hotel is a winding stretch of old buildings housing antique shops. Just walk out and wander. The rooms on the higher floors are somewhat larger.

Laundry service is available, and there's a cafe and gift shop on the premises.

Renaissance Melaka Hotel. Jalan Bendahara, 75100 Malacca. ☎ **06/284-8888** in Malaysia, or 800/601-1882 from Singapore. Fax 06/284-9269. 316 units. A/C MINIBAR TV TEL. RM250–RM380 (US$100–US$152) superior or deluxe rm; RM400 (US$160) junior suite; RM450–RM480 (US$180–US$192) club rm; RM680–RM3,500 (US$272–US$1,400) suite. AE, JCB, MC, V.

Renaissance is one of the more posh hotels in Malacca, but aside from the pieces of Peranakan porcelain and art in the public areas, not much of Malacca's traditional culture is reflected. The hotel is, however, situated in the heart of the city, making it very convenient for sightseeing even though most of the clientele are business travelers. Facilities include an outdoor pool; a fitness center with massage, sauna, and steam; two indoor squash courts; a tour desk; and a beauty salon. Golf is located nearby.

Riviera Bay Resort. 10km Jalan Tanjung Kling, 76400 Malacca. ☎ **06/315-1111.** Fax 06/315-3333. www.smi-hotels.com.sg. 450 units. A/C MINIBAR TV TEL. RM350–RM450 (US$140–US$180) double; RM500–RM3,000 (US$200–US$1,200) suite. AE, DC, MC, V.

Oh my goodness, this place is so very, very large, but for a resort, they have very modern and polished facilities, unlike the more homegrown kampung-style places along the east coast. It's on the seafront, which makes for water-sports activities, and as far as any other activity is concerned, they've got it. The only thing is, it's way outside the city—about 10 kilometers, or a 20-minute car ride from Malacca proper. But if you'd like to combine the sightseeing with the resort thing, with all the conveniences, this is your place. Facilities include a large outdoor pool; a Jacuzzi; a fitness center with sauna, aerobics, and massage; a children's playground; a putting green; tennis courts; and water-sports facilities. Guests have access to nearby golf.

DINING

In Malacca you'll find the typical mix of authentic Malay and Chinese food, and as the city was the major settling place for the Peranakans in Malaysia, their unique style of food is featured in many of the local restaurants.

Capers Restaurant. Renaissance Melaka Hotel, Jalan Bendahara. ☎ **06/284-8888.** Reservations recommended. Entrees RM34–RM48 (US$13.60–US$19.20). AE, DC, MC, V. Mon–Sat 6:30–10:30pm. CONTINENTAL.

This is the only fine-dining establishment in Malacca at the moment, which means it is quite formal and pricey. Warm lighting and crystal and silver flatware are only a couple of the many details that add to the formal and romantic atmosphere. The signature dishes come from the char grill, like beef medaillon and prawn tempura and the pan-fried salmon fillet with tomato-yam cream sauce on roasted capsicum. Their wine list is large and international, including Portuguese selections, in keeping with the Malacca theme.

Lim Tian Puan Restaurant. 251 Jalan Tun Sri Lanang. ☎ **06/282-2737** or 06/284-6142. Reservations recommended. Entrees RM6–RM28 (US$2.40–US$11.20). AE, MC, V. Daily 10:30am–2:30pm and 5:30–11pm. Closed Chinese New Year. CHINESE/TEOCHEW.

Lim Tian Puan is about as typical Chinese as it gets: a noisy place for family and friends, not big on atmosphere but good on food. The seafood is very fresh, but if it's marked "market price," be sure you ask what the price is before you order. Their recommendations are excellent, like the steamed pomfret Teochew style with tomato, preserved mustard leaf, ginger, and coriander. The chicken and cashew nut is served in a delicious deep-fried ring of yam.

Restoran Bibik Neo. No. 6, Ground floor, Jalan Merdeka, Taman Melaka Raya. ☎ **06/281-7054.** Reservations recommended. Entrees RM5–RM15 (US$2–US$6). AE, DC, MC, V. Daily 11am–3pm and 6–10pm. PERANAKAN.

For a taste of the local cuisine, the traditional Nyonya food here is delicious and very reasonably priced. Ikan assam with eggplant is a tasty mild fish curry that's very rich and tasty. The wait staff serves in traditional Malay dress, and will pass special preparation orders on to the chef, so let them know your preferences.

Penang is unique in Malaysia because, to all intents and purposes, Penang has it all. Tioman Island may have beaches and nature, but it has no shopping or historical sights to speak of. And while Malacca has historical sights and museums, it hasn't a good beach for miles. Similarly, while KL has shopping, nightlife, and attractions, it also has no beach resorts. Penang has all of it: beaches, history, diverse culture, shopping, food. You name it, it has it. If you only have a short time to visit Malaysia but want to take in as wide an experience as you can, Penang is your place.

Penang was first written into the Malaysian history books when Francis Light, an agent of the British East India Company, landed and made a deal with the sultan of Kedah to cede Penang to the British. He landed on what is now the Esplanade in Georgetown, where he set up a trading port that attracted settlers from China, India, and the West. In 1832, Penang was folded into the Straits Settlements, which comprised Singapore and Malacca under the governing power of Penang. It remained a British Crown Colony until 1957, when Malaysia gained independence from British rule.

Today the state of Penang is made up of the island and a small strip of land on the Malaysian mainland. **Georgetown** is the seat of government for the state. Penang island is 285 square kilometers (171 sq. miles) and has a population of a little more than one million people. Surprisingly, the population is mostly Chinese (59%), followed by Malays (32%) and Indians (7%).

1 Visitor Information

There's a **Malaysia Tourism Board** office at Penang International Airport (☎ 04/643-0501). You'll find an additional branch on the third level at KOMTAR on Jalan Penang (☎ 04/261-4461).

2 Getting There

BY PLANE   The international airport lets you fly in directly from other areas of the world or from other cities in Malaysia. **Penang International Airport** (☎ 04/643-0811) is 20 kilometers (12 miles) from the city. At the airport, you can purchase fixed-rate coupons for taxis to take you to your destination. For hotels in Georgetown, the rate is RM15 (US$6), for hotels on the beach it's

RM25 (US$10). There's also the Penang Yellow Bus Company bus no. 83, which will take you to Weld Quay in Georgetown.

BY TRAIN   By rail, the trip from KL to Penang is 6 hours, and you'll be dropped at the Butterworth Railway Station (☎ **04/331-2796**), on Jalan Bagan Dalam (near the ferry terminal) in Butterworth, on the Malaysian mainland. From Butterworth, you'll need take the ferry to the island.

BY BUS   If you take a bus, you'll be let out at the Butterworth bus terminal on Jalan Bangan Balam, just next to the train station. From there, you'll have to take a ferry to Penang Island.

BY FERRY   The ferry to Penang is at Jalan Pantai, near the Butterworth Railway Station (☎ **04/331-5780**). It operates 24 hours and takes 20 minutes from pier to pier. From 6am to midnight ferries leave every 10 minutes. From midnight to 1:20am they run every half hour and from 1:20 to 6am they run every hour. Purchase your passage at the Butterworth ferry terminal for 60 sen (US50¢) for adults and 20 sen (US10¢) for children. Fare is paid only on the trip to Penang. The return trip is free. The ferry lets you off at Pengalan Weld (Weld Quay; ☎ **04/210-2363**).

The ferry will also take cars. Fares range from RM4 to RM8 (US$1.60 to US$3.20), depending on your car's engine capacity. There's an extra charge of 40 sen (US20¢) per passenger.

BY CAR   If you're driving you can cross over the 13.5-kilometer (8-mile) Penang Bridge, the longest bridge in Southeast Asia. All cars are charged RM7 (US$2.80) for the trip to Penang. It's free on the return.

3 Getting Around

BY TAXI   Taxis are abundant, but be warned they do not use meters, so you must agree on the price before you ride. Most trips within the city are between RM3 and RM6 (US$1.20 and US$2.40).

BY BUS   Buses also run all over the island. The most popular route is the Hin Bus Co. (Blue Bus) no. 93, which operates between Pengkalan Weld (Weld Quay) in Georgetown and the beach resorts at Batu Ferringhi.

BY BICYCLE & MOTORCYCLE   Along Batu Ferringhi there are also bicycles and motorcycles for rent to scoot or cycle around the island.

ON FOOT   Around Georgetown, I recommended hoofing it between sights—the close proximity of the major landmarks makes it easy, and the street scenes and small shops in between make it highly rewarding. For beach destinations and sights outside the city proper, it's best to take public transportation.

4 Seeing the Sights

IN GEORGETOWN

Fort Cornwallis. Lebuhraya Light. Admission RM1 (US40¢). Daily 8:30am–7pm.

Fort Cornwallis is built on the site where Capt. Francis Light, founder of Penang, first landed in 1786. The fort was built in 1804 by convict labor. Inside, you'll find a history exhibit and handicraft center. The Penang Tourist Association is across the street.

Cheong Fatt Tze Mansion. Lebuhraya Leith. No phone. Admission RM2 (US80¢). Daily 9am–5pm.

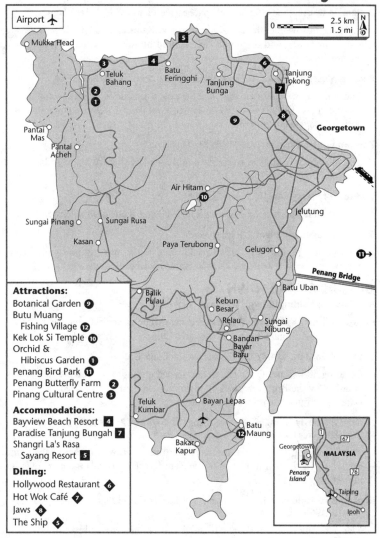

Penang Island

Airport ✈

0 — 2.5 km / 1.5 mi

N

Mukka Head

Teluk Bahang

Batu Feringghi

Tanjung Bunga

Tanjung Tokong

Georgetown

Pantai Mas

Pantai Acheh

Air Hitam

Sungai Pinang

Sungai Rusa

Kasan

Paya Terubong

Gelugor

Jelutung

Penang Bridge

Batu Uban

Balik Pulau

Kebun Besar

Relau

Sungai Nibung

Bandan Bayar Baru

Teluk Kumbar

Bayan Lepas

Batu Maung

Bakar Kapur

Attractions:
Botanical Garden ❾
Butu Muang
  Fishing Village ⓬
Kek Lok Si Temple ❿
Orchid &
  Hibiscus Garden ❶
Penang Bird Park ⓫
Penang Butterfly Farm ❷
Pinang Cultural Centre ❸

Accommodations:
Bayview Beach Resort ▣4
Paradise Tanjung Bungah ▣7
Shangri La's Rasa
  Sayang Resort ▣5

Dining:
Hollywood Restaurant ◆6
Hot Wok Café ◆7
Jaws ◆8
The Ship ◆5

Georgetown

MALAYSIA

Penang Island

Taiping

Ipoh

The 18th- and 19th-century Chinese architecture is stunning in this former home. There are ceremony halls, courtyards, and gardens, and two of the most spectacular features are the tiled roof and spiral staircases.

Khoo Khongsi. Leburaya Cannon. ☎ **04/261-4609.** Free admission. Daily 9am–5pm.

This is one of the most beautiful clan houses in Penang. In 1835, 105 members of the Khoo family from Hokkien province in China built the house for the welfare of their members in Penang. The original house burned down by a mysterious fire on its day of completion. Some say it was because the house was dedicated to Tua Sai Yeah, patron saint of the Khoos, and that it was too ornate for a saint. It was rebuilt to a lesser scale.

P. Ramlee House. Jalan P. Ramlee. No phone. Free admission. Daily 9am–5pm.

In 1926, this wooden house was built for P. Ramlee, a famous Malaysian singer, actor, composer, and director. The restored building is filled with his personal memorabilia.

Penang Museum and Art Gallery. Leburaya Farquahar. ☎ 04/261-3144.

The buildings were built in 1821 and are now a museum of photos, maps, and other historic items. The Art Gallery is a venue for local artists. Outside the buildings is a statue of Capt. Francis Light.

Kapitan Keling Mosque. Jalan Masjid Kapitan Keling.

The mosque was built in the early part of the last century by an Indian Muslim merchant.

Goddess of Mercy Temple. Lebuhraya Pitt.

This Chinese Taoist temple was built in 1900 and is one of the oldest in Penang.

Sri Mariamman Temple. Leburaya Queen.

This Hindu temple was built in 1883 and is the starting point for Penang's Thaipusam Festival, which leads to a temple on Jalan Waterfall.

OUTSIDE GEORGETOWN

Batu Muang Fishing Village. Southeast tip of Penang.

If it's a fishing village you'd like to see, here's a good one. This village is special for its shrine to Admiral Cheng Ho, the early Chinese sea adventurer.

Botanical Garden. ☎ 04/228-6248. Free admission. Daily 7am–7pm.

Covering 30 hectares (70 acres) of landscaped grounds, this botanic garden was established by the British in 1884. The grounds are perfect for a shady walk, and the waterfall in the gardens is very soothing.

Penang Butterfly Farm. Jalan Teluk Bahang. ☎ 04/881-1253. Adults RM5 (US$2), children RM2 (US80¢); free for children under 5. Mon–Fri 9am–5pm, Sat–Sun 9am–6pm.

The Penang Butterfly Farm, located toward the northwest corner of the island, is the largest in the world. On its 0.8-hectare (2-acre) grounds there are over 4,000 butterflies.

Penang Bird Park. Jalan Teluk, Seberang Jaya. ☎ 04/399-1899. Adults RM3 (US$1.20), children RM1 (US40¢). Daily 9am–7pm.

The Bird Park is not on Penang Island, but is on the mainland part of Penang state. The 2-hectare (5-acre) park is home to some 200 bird species from Malaysia and around the world.

5 Accommodations

Where you stay will depend on your reason for coming to Penang. The choice is simple: a beach resort or a city hotel.

The Bayview Beach Resort. Batu Ferringhi Beach, 11100 Penang. ☎ 04/881-2123. Fax 04/881-2140. 366 units. A/C MINIBAR TV TEL. RM290 (US$116) hill-view double, RM350 (US$140) sea-view double; RM500 (US$200) hill-view suite, RM600 (US$240) sea-view suite, RM850–RM3,500 (US$340–US$1,400) other suite. AE, DC, JCB, MC, V.

Located right on Batu Ferringhi Beach, the Bayview is a relaxing resort with all the conveniences you look for in a large international hotel. The feel of the place is

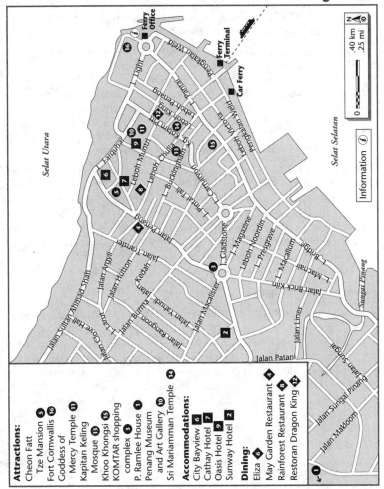

Attractions:
Cheon Fatt
Tze Mansion **5**
Fort Cornwallis **16**
Goddess of
Mercy Temple **11**
Kapitan Keling
Mosque **13**
Khoo Khongsi **15**
KOMTAR shopping
complex **3**
P. Ramlee House **1**
Penang Museum
and Art Gallery **10**
Sri Mariamman Temple

Accommodations:
City Bayview **6**
Cathay Hotel **7**
Oasis Hotel **9**
Sunway Hotel **2**

Dining:
Eliza
May Garden Restaurant **4**
Rainforest Restaurant **8**
Restoran Dragon King **12**

Selat Utara

Selat Selatan

Information *i*

spacious and airy, an ambiance carried over into the rooms—the standard double room, for instance, is quite large. Rooms facing the road have views of the neighboring condominium complex, and can be noisy. Get the sea view so you can take advantage of your balcony. Facilities include an outdoor pool, squash and tennis courts, billiards, table tennis, and a fitness center with Jacuzzi, sauna, and steam. Cycling, parasailing, waterskiing, sailing, windsurfing, canoeing, and boat trips to beachside barbecues and fishing spots are all available.

Cathay Hotel. No. 15 Leith St., 10200, Penang. ☎ **04/262-6271.** Fax 04/263-9300. 37 units. TV. RM51.70 (US$20.70) without air-conditioning, RM69 (US$27.60) with air-conditioning. No credit cards.

Cathay comes highly recommended for its location and price. Within walking distance of the city attractions, it's definitely a budget place, but it has a charming faded elegance. Housed in a traditional Chinese prewar mansion, it has high ceilings, mosaic tile and wood floors, and whitewashed walls. Decorator touches include Chinese lanterns and ceiling fans. You won't find a budget hotel with more style and respectability. The only real faults are that the bathrooms are small and old, and take note that there's no room service or laundry service.

The City Bayview Hotel, Penang. 25–A Farquhar St., 10200 Penang. ☎ **800/8854** or 04/263-3161. Fax 04/263-4124. 176 units. A/C MINIBAR TV TEL. RM180–RM210 (US$72–US$84) double; RM260–RM350 (US$104–US$140) suite. AE, DC, MC, V.

Situated on Farquhar Street, City Bayview has a convenient location for visitors who want to take in the historic and cultural sights of Georgetown. Oriental in style, the decor still has many details revealing that nothing much has changed since the hotel's last renovation in 1975. Still, the rooms are large and have high ceilings, and there's an outdoor pool. Make sure you ask for special package rates.

Oasis Hotel. (Formerly the Tiong Wah Hotel), 23 Love Lane, Penang. ☎ **04/261-6778.** 25 units. RM20, RM25, RM35 (US$8, US$10, US$14). No credit cards.

Oasis Hotel is frequented by Western and Asian travelers who want to save their money for shopping and eating rather than spend it on the big resorts. The owners have been running the place for over 80 years, and have recently upgraded, so it's fresher and less grotty than what you might expect in a budget hotel. It's quiet, too, especially at night when all you may hear is the occasional barking dog. The lower-price categories have communal showers only. There's a laundry room on premises.

Paradise Tanjung Bungah. 505 Jalan Tanjung Bungah, 11200 Penang. ☎ **04/890-8808.** Fax 04/890-8333. 225 units. A/C TV TEL. RM240 (US$96) hill-view double, RM280 (US$112) sea-view double; RM400 (US$160) hill-view suite, RM450 (US$180) sea-view suite. AE, DC, JCB, MC, V.

Singaporeans and folks from all over Malaysia flock to this beach resort to enjoy the sea at the Tanjung Bungah beach. It's a three-star hotel, without as many of the bells and whistles as some of the other beach resorts, but it's quite pleasant, with light wood and tiles. Rooms have French windows looking out on sea views and views of the hill behind the hotel. Rooms are decorated with a tropical feel, which matches the casual and relaxed atmosphere of the entire resort. Facilities include an outdoor pool, fitness center, and video game room. Water-sports equipment rentals are available. Suites have minibars, while other rooms have refrigerators.

✪ **Shangri-La's Rasa Sayang Resort**. Batu Ferrenghi Beach, 11100 Penang. ☎ **04/881-1811.** Fax 04/881-1984. 515 units. RM106 (US$42.40) double, RM149 (US$59.60) deluxe sea-facing double; RM154 (US$61.60) deluxe garden/patio rm; from RM429 (US$171.60) suite. All prices include complimentary American breakfast and buffet dinner for each night of stay, free laundry, free unmotorized water-sports equipment rentals, free local calls, and late checkout. AE, DC, JCB, MC, V.

Of all the beachfront resorts on Penang, Rasa Sayang is the finest. Get a room looking over the pool area, and your private balcony will be facing the picturesque palm-lined beach. The free-form pool is sprawled amidst tropical landscaping and cafe areas, and the rest of the grounds have strolling gardens that are romantically illuminated in the evenings. The hotel is both elegant and relaxed, with Malay-style decor in the public areas and rooms. You'll also appreciate the good seafood restaurants nearby. Facilities include an outdoor pool, fitness center, mini–putting green, and table tennis. Guests have access to nearby tennis courts, sailing, boating, and waterskiing.

Sunway Hotel. 33 New Lane, 10400 Penang. ☎ **04/229-9988.** Fax 04/228-8899. 262 units. A/C MINIBAR TV TEL. RM320 (US$128) double. Ask about promotional rates as low as RM180 (US$72), including American breakfast. AE, DC, MC, V.

The Sunway is centrally located in Georgetown, near the KOMTAR shopping complex and the Penang Museum. Built in 1994, the hotel is warm and elegant, with marble details and a new and modern feel to the open spaces. The rooms are fresh and spacious, and rooms on all sides have views of the city. American breakfast is included with the room rate. Facilities include an outdoor pool and a fitness center with Jacuzzi. The hotel can arrange tennis, squash, and sauna at nearby facilities.

6 Dining

Eliza, The Malay Restaurant. 14th floor, The City Bayview Hotel, 25–A Lebuhraya Farquhar. ☎ **04/263-3161.** Entrees RM8.50–RM14 (US$3.40–US$5.60). AE, DC, MC, V. Daily noon–3pm and 7–11pm. MALAY.

You can get Malay food at all of the local hawker stalls, but they sure don't have the beautiful view of the city and the comfortable ambiance you'll find here. Ask to sit next to the windows, and if you really feel like going local, ask for the tables where you sit on the woven straw mats on the ground. Among the specialties here is the *udang masak lemak,* tiger prawns cooked in coconut milk and ground turmeric and lemongrass. It's rich and slightly spicy.

Hollywood Restaurant. 543 Jalan Tanjung Bungah. ☎ **04/890-7268.** Seafood is sold according to market prices. Entrees RM8–RM10 (US$3.20–US$4). Daily 11am–3pm and 6–11pm. No credit cards. CHINESE/PERANAKAN.

The Hollywood's popularity has dropped off some as people chase the newer, trendier places, but the food here remains fabulous, and fewer people means it's less crowded and there's more delicious food for you. And you can't beat the atmosphere, out in the open and right next to the sea. Go for the steamed king crab. It's eaten for its eggs, which are creamy textured and rich. The seafood spring rolls are also excellent, with crispy skins stuffed with crab.

Hot Wok Café. 125–D Desa Tanjung, Jalan Tanjung. ☎ **04/899-0858.** Reservations recommended for weekends. Entrees RM9–RM15 (US$3.60–US$6). AE, DC, MC, V. Daily 11am–3pm and 6–11pm. PERANAKAN.

This place is very popular with the locals, and no wonder: The food is great and the atmosphere is wonderful. Filled with local touches such as wooden lattice work, wooden lanterns, carved Peranakan cabinets, tapestries, and carved wood panels, the decor will make you want to just sit back, relax, and take in sights you'd only ever see in a Peranakan home. The curry capitan is curry chicken with a thick coconut-based gravy stuffed with potatoes. Their boneless pork ribs are juicy and smothered in a sweet-and-sour sauce.

Jaws. 90 Gurney Dr. ☎ **04/227-6086.** Entrees RM3–RM30 (US$1.20–US$12) (the RM30 item is fish head curry). No credit cards. Daily 11am–9pm. PERANAKAN.

Jaws is set in an old 1940s house, with cracked walls and basic furnishings, but it has the best fish head curry in Penang—*be warned, though:* It's *very* spicy, and not recommended for everyone. Another tasty dish of note is the *joo hoo char:* grated carrots and turnips fried with dried squid. Try everything, as the portions are moderately sized and very inexpensive.

May Garden Restaurant. 70 Jalan Penang. ☎ **04/261-6435.** Reservations recommended. Seafood is priced by kg weight. Entrees from RM8 (US$3.20). AE, DC, MC, V. Daily noon–3pm and 6–10:30pm. CANTONESE.

One of the best Cantonese restaurants in town, it's noisy and not too big on ambiance, but has excellent food. Outstanding dishes include the tofu and broccoli topped with sea snail slices or the fresh steamed live prawns. Don't agree to all the daily specials or you'll be paying a fortune.

Rainforest Restaurant. Leboh Chulia. ☎ **04/261-6778.** Entrees RM4–RM12 (US$1.60–US$4.80). No credit cards. Daily 7:30am–3pm and 7pm–midnight. WESTERN/ASIAN MIX.

Run by a local family, this place is a very casual hangout that's popular with travelers, especially the backpacker set. Done up in a jungle motif, with rattan furniture and plants poking out all over, it's a good place to hit for breakfast. You can get yogurt and muesli, fried noodles, fruit salad, and potato salad, or, later in the day, you can stop in for a beer and look over all the travel information they have on hand, including notes about local rip-offs, great places to visit, and advice from other travelers.

✪ **Restoran Dragon King.** 99 Leboh Bishop. ☎ **04/261-8035.** Entrees RM8–RM20 (US$3.20–US$8). No credit cards. Daily 11am–3pm and 6–10pm. PERANAKAN.

Penang is famous around the world for delicious local Peranakan dishes, and Dragon King is the best place to come to taste the local cuisine at its finest. It was opened 20 years ago by a group of local teachers who wanted to revive the traditional dishes cooked by their mothers. Decor-wise, the place is nothing to shout about—just a coffee shop with tile floors and folding chairs—but all the curries are hand blended to perfection. Try *the perut ikan* (fish maw with long beans in pineapple), the *otak otak,* or the *curry capitan* (curry chicken).

The Ship. 69B Jalan Batu Ferringhi. ☎ **04/881-2142.** Entrees RM12–RM50 (US$4.80–US$20). AE, DC, MC, V. Daily noon–1:30am. WESTERN.

Appropriately named, the Ship is decorated like an old sailing ship, with ships' wheels for tables and international flags hanging from above. A friendly staff in sailor uniforms serves up Western seafood (which is the best selection on the menu) and grilled meat dishes. There's a Chinese menu available, too, with dishes suitable for Western palates.

7 Shopping

The first place that anyone here will recommend you go for shopping is **KOMTAR.** Short for "Kompleks Tun Abdul Razak," it is the largest shopping complex in Penang, a full 65 stories filled with clothing shops, restaurants, and a couple of large department stores. There's a duty-free shop on the 57th floor. On the 58th floor is a tourist information center.

Good shopping finds in Penang are batik, pewter products, locally produced curio items, paintings, antiques, pottery, and jewelry. If you care to walk the streets in search of finds, there are a few streets in Georgetown that are the hub of shopping activity. In the center of the city, the area around Jalan Penang, Leburaya Campbell, Lebuhraya Kapitan Keling, Lebuhraya Chulia, and Lebuhraya Pantai is near the Sri Mariamman Temple, the Penang Museum, the Kapitan Keling Mosque, and other sites of historic interest. Here you'll find everything from local crafts to souvenirs and fashion, and maybe even a bargain or two. Most of these shops are open from 10am to 10pm daily.

Pasar malam, or **night markets,** are a great Penang shopping experience. These outdoor street bazaars provide a taste of local life even if you don't come to buy. Many rotate in a few designated spots, so look in the local paper for the latest locations. Most are open from around 7 to 11pm.

8 Penang After Dark

Clubs in Penang stay open a little later than in the rest of Malaysia, and some even stay open until 3am on the weekends.

20 Leith Street. 11–A Lebuh Leith. ☎ **04/261-6301.** No cover. Sun–Thurs till 2am, Fri–Sat till 3am.

This place is great. Located in an old 1930s house that formerly belonged to local tycoon Tye Kee Yoon, the place has lots of seating areas fitted with traditional antique furniture in the different rooms of the house. Antique lamps and old tiled floors add to the charm. It was opened about 10 years ago, but is still in with Penang's hip crowd. There's billiards, table soccer, darts, and an open-air courtyard for al fresco drinking.

Borsalino. Penang Park Royal, 1 Batu Ferringhi Beach. ☎ **04/881-1133,** ext. 8844. Cover RM15 (US$6). Fri–Sat only, 9pm–2am.

Borsalino is a disco with a long bar. It's modern, with a lot of glass, mirrors, and black and white colors. Pretty popular with the local yuppie crowd and with tourists, most of the clientele are mature—there's not a lot of teenagers here. The DJ spins upbeat dance music with different themes featured from night to night.

Chaser's BBQ & Pub. One Stop Centre, 488D–G–18, Jalan Burma. ☎ **04/227-6488.** No cover. Daily noon–2am.

This is an American-style bar and restaurant where regulars (mostly expatriates) gather. They play American music from rock to pop to country and western, and they'll even play your favorite CD if you bring it along.

Hard Life Café. 363 Lebuh Chulia. ☎ **04/262-1740.** No cover. Daily until 1am.

A reggae pub, this place has the music floating through the air and is decorated with typical Rasta paraphernalia, like knitted hats and Bob Marley T-shirts. Ask for the board games.

Hong Kong Bar. 371 Lebuh Chulia. ☎ **04/261-9796.** No cover. Daily until 11pm.

This bar opened in 1920 and was a regular hangout for military personnel based in Butterworth. It has an extraordinary archive of photos of the servicemen who have patronized the place in all its years, plus a collection of medals, plaques, and buoys from ships. Today it's still frequented by sailors and other military personnel. The place is very laid-back once you get past the glare of the fluorescent lights.

Zulu's Seaside Paradise. Paradise Tanjung Bungah. ☎ **04/890-8808.** No cover. Daily until 2am.

Centering on an African theme, the DJ plays a lot of reggae, African, house, and world music, and the place caters to locals and foreigners alike who come to dance and play billiards and table soccer. They also serve light snacks.

9 Penang Outdoors

It almost goes without saying that **beach activities** are very popular here. If you're staying at one of the beach resorts, you'll have the beach right at your backdoor, but even if you're staying in town you don't have to worry about access to the waves, as all beaches are open to the public. You can take advantage of the "beach boys"—the guys on the beach who rent out water-sports equipment—for any accessories you may need. They're set up in kiosks dotted along the shoreline.

Hiking enthusiasts will appreciate the trails that snake around the interior of the island, taking you through forest reserve and past waterfalls and babbling rivers. The Malaysian Nature Society has catalogued these trails, giving precise instructions on how to find them and where they lead. For more information on the trails, contact the **Malaysia Tourism Board** (☎ 04/643-0501).

Glossary

SELECTED GENERAL TERMS

attap thatch
baba Peranakan man
bukit hill
chi positive energy
five-foot way covered sidewalk in front of shophouses
go-downs warehouses
gopuram the tiered, statued roof of a temple
Haj, Hajja honorary title of Muslims who have made the pilgrimmage to Mecca (M/F)

istana Malay palace
jalan street
kebaya cembroidered Peranakan blouse
keramat sacred grave
kuchu hut
lorong lane
minaret a mosque's tower
nonyas Peranakan ladies
palli mosque
sungai river
tandas toilet

SELECTED MENU TERMS

clay pot rice rice with chicken, sausage, and mushrooms
congee (or moi) porridge with fried fish, salted vegetables, and sometimes boiled egg
Dosai thin Indian pancake
fish head curry fish head simmered in broth of coconut curry, chilies, and seasonings
garoupa grouper (a fish)
halal foods corresponding to Islamic dietary laws
Hokkien mee thick wheat noodles with seafood, meat, and vegetables in a heavy sauce
ikan assam a rich, mild fish curry
laksa lemak Chinese rice flour noodles in a soup of Malay-style spicy coconut cream with chunks of seafood and tofu
mee goreng fried noodles with chili and curry gravy
murtabak thin pancake stuffed with meat, egg, and onions

inside, fried and served with a curry sauce
nasi lemak coconut rice with fried anchovies, peanuts, prawns, egg, and sambal
otak otak toasted mashed fish with coconut milk and chili, wrapped in a banana leaf and grilled over flames
rendang coconut-based curry served over meat
roti john minced mutton and onion in French bread, dipped in egg and fried
sambal spicy chili sauce
sambal belacan condiment of fresh chilies, dried shrimp paste, and lime juice
satay sweet barbecued meat kebabs dipped in chili peanut sauce
Teochew fishball springy ball made from pounded fish with salt and water, served in a noodle soup
vindaloo meat or poultry in a tangy and spicy sauce

Index

See also separate Singapore Accommodations and Restaurant indexes, and the Malaysia index, below.

SINGAPORE

ACCOMMODATIONS

RESTAURANTS

FROMMER'S® COMPLETE TRAVEL GUIDES

*(Comprehensive guides to destinations around the world, with
selections in all price ranges—from deluxe to budget)*

Acapulco, Ixtapa &
   Zihuatenejo
Alaska
Amsterdam
Arizona
Atlanta
Australia
Austria
Bahamas
Barcelona, Madrid &
   Seville
Belgium, Holland &
   Luxembourg
Bermuda
Boston
Budapest & the Best of
   Hungary
California
Canada
Cancún, Cozumel & the
   Yucatán
Cape Cod, Nantucket &
   Martha's Vineyard
Caribbean
Caribbean Cruises & Ports
   of Call
Caribbean Ports of Call
Carolinas & Georgia
Chicago
China
Colorado
Costa Rica
Denver, Boulder &
   Colorado Springs
England

Europe
Florida
France
Germany
Greece
Hawaii
Hong Kong
Honolulu, Waikiki & Oahu
Ireland
Israel
Italy
Jamaica & Barbados
Japan
Las Vegas
London
Los Angeles
Maryland & Delaware
Maui
Mexico
Miami & the Keys
Montana & Wyoming
Montréal & Québec City
Munich & the Bavarian Alps
Nashville & Memphis
Nepal
New England
New Mexico
New Orleans
New York City
Northern New England
Nova Scotia, New
   Brunswick
   & Prince Edward Island
Oregon
Paris

Philadelphia & the Amish
   Country
Portugal
Prague & the Best of the
   Czech Republic
Provence & the Riviera
Puerto Rico
Rome
San Antonio & Austin
San Diego
San Francisco
Santa Fe, Taos &
   Albuquerque
Scandinavia
Scotland
Seattle & Portland
Singapore & Malaysia
South Pacific
Spain
Switzerland
Thailand
Tokyo
Toronto
Tuscany & Umbria
USA
Utah
Vancouver & Victoria
Vienna & the Danube
   Valley
Virgin Islands
Virginia
Walt Disney World &
   Orlando
Washington, D.C.
Washington State

FROMMER'S® DOLLAR-A-DAY GUIDES

(The ultimate guides to comfortable low-cost travel)

Australia from $50 a Day
California from $60 a Day
Caribbean from $60 a Day
Costa Rica & Belize
   from $35 a Day
England from $60 a Day
Europe from $50 a Day
Florida from $50 a Day
Greece from $50 a Day
Hawaii from $60 a Day
India from $40 a Day

Ireland from $50 a Day
Israel from $45 a Day
Italy from $50 a Day
London from $60 a Day
Mexico from $35 a Day
New York from $75 a Day
New Zealand from $50 a Day
Paris from $70 a Day
San Francisco from $60 a Day
Washington, D.C., from
   $60 a Day

FROMMER'S® PORTABLE GUIDES

(Pocket-size guides for travelers who want everything in a nutshell)

Bahamas	Dublin	Puerto Vallarta, Manzanillo
California Wine Country	Las Vegas	& Guadalajara
Charleston & Savannah	London	San Francisco
Chicago	Maine Coast	Venice
	New Orleans	Washington, D.C.

FROMMER'S® NATIONAL PARK GUIDES

(Everything you need for the perfect park vacation)

Grand Canyon	Yosemite & Sequoia/
National Parks of the American West	Kings Canyon
Yellowstone & Grand Teton	Zion & Bryce Canyon

FROMMER'S® IRREVERENT GUIDES

(Wickedly honest guides for sophisticated travelers)

Amsterdam	Manhattan	San Francisco	Walt Disney World
Chicago	New Orleans	Santa Fe	Washington, D.C.
London	Paris		

FROMMER'S® BY NIGHT GUIDES

(The series for those who know that life begins after dark)

Amsterdam	Los Angeles	Miami	Prague
Chicago	Madrid	New Orleans	San Francisco
Las Vegas	& Barcelona	Paris	Washington, D.C.
London	Manhattan		

THE COMPLETE IDIOT'S TRAVEL GUIDES

(The ultimate user-friendly trip planners)

Cruise Vacations	New York City	San Francisco
Las Vegas	Planning Your Trip	Walt Disney World
New Orleans	to Europe	

SPECIAL-INTEREST TITLES

Arthur Fommer's New World of Travel
The Civil War Trust's Official Guide to
  the Civil War Discovery Trail
Frommer's Caribbean Hideaways
Frommer's Complete Hostel Vacation
  Guide to England, Scotland & Wales
Frommer's Europe's Greatest
  Driving Tours
Frommer's Food Lover's Companion
  to France
Frommer's Food Lover's Companion to
  Italy
Israel Past & Present
New York City with Kids
New York Times Weekends

Outside Magazine's Adventure Guide
  to New England
Outside Magazine's Adventure Guide
  to Northern California
Outside Magazine's Adventure Guide
  to the Pacific Northwest
Outside Magazine's Adventure Guide
  to Southern California & Baja
Outside Magazine's Guide to Family Vacations
Places Rated Almanac
Retirement Places Rated
Washington, D.C., with Kids
Wonderful Weekends from New York City
Wonderful Weekends from San Francisco
Wonderful Weekends from Los Angeles